Who Am I Now

To Emma,

Just as I think
this world's unfair,
I meet this girl, who has
pink hair.

She's cheerful, contented,
and never blue.

I realize, one thing's true.
It would be such a blessing,
to have a daughter like you!

Tom ♡

Who Am I Now

As the World Goes
So Go I

Thomas Martens

McCaa Books • Santa Rosa, CA

McCaa Books
1604 Deer Run
Santa Rosa, CA 95405-7535

First published in 2021 by McCaa Books,
an imprint of McCaa Publications.

Library of Congress Control Number: 2021908394
ISBN 978-1-7363451-4-6

Printed in the United States of America
Set in Minion Pro
Book design by Waights Taylor Jr.

www.mccaabooks.com

Dedication

Not only do I dedicate this book to all of the following, but I also gratefully thank them for keeping the honor in our family. To my children, grandchildren and great grandchild; Jay, Abel, Mia, Zachary, Hayleigh, Ashleigh, Kyleigh, Abel Jameson, Sarah, Aaron, Scarlett, Ayla, Christina, Anthony, Michael, and Sofia.

Contents

"As you get older you will understand more and more, that it's not about what you look like or what you own, it's all about the person that you have become."

Author unknown

Preface

Sometimes when we are shaken from our norm, the disruption becomes a driving force for some new action. When a cage is rattled, the bird inside jumps and cries out. Fear has struck and there is no stronger force than fear. If there were no cage, the trapped bird would surely fly away. When I see the world around me becoming unstable, I seem to be called to action before it collapses. I don't want to fly away like the scared bird. My primary response is to stay, examine the whole picture—who, what, why, where, and when. What is actually happening and why? Where is it happening and when did it start, or when will it end? Things have dramatically changed in my world. There are often times I can hardly bear the thought of this place being the future of my children and their children.

As conditions change, it's not difficult to find those things that must be preserved, beginning with the planet itself. One of the techniques I will use in this book is to examine history. By going backwards I hope to get a broad perspective, not only of the cultures and the people who lived before, but of my own history. I don't really want to compose my personal biography, after all, we become who we are because of who we all are, the people who we are close to, and the dictates of our culture. Any biography simply cuts out a small slice of that whole picture. My thoughts and my writings are an attempt to discover who I am at this time. I would also like to find the answers to the whole picture, the current big questions.

I need to ask for tolerance from the reader, since my knowledge of English grammar, sentence structure, etc. will probably be as bad as it gets. I hope you are able to plow through my writing with patience, finding substance in my story, and still see the message. With apologies to all of my English teachers, my publisher, and those accomplished writers who may pick up this book, I will proceed writing as I generally talk.

1

I am Born

I do not remember the moment of my birth or the time I spent in my mother's womb, although medical research has discovered that I did indeed hear the mumbling of different sounds, the muffled voices of family members. I could hear my mother's heartbeat, I could see the brightness and the shades of light through my mother's skin. I have forgotten the incredible moment of intense pressure as I slowly began to move away from this protected environment. I thought I was dying, I became covered in microbes, and then an intense white light appeared, I was amazed at the colors, the beauty of it all. When my mother held me in her arms I felt true love, an honest love that equally traveled in both directions. In so doing the love expanded, encompassing the whole room, affecting everyone who entered.

Before long I began the process of forgetting this exquisite miracle of birth, of beauty, of love. I had passed into a new world, and that world was slowly growing, becoming my own. I was now learning the ways of all humans, I was being conditioned to accept the thoughts and ideas of the culture that I had been born into.

As I continued to age, I was nurtured to see nature as my parents saw it. Fortunately for me, my parents had a pretty accurate take on reality and were very positive people. I was to grow up happy, as an integral piece of the natural world, an adjusted part of my society. For the next few years, I started to learn the English language with all of the verbs, nouns and adjectives, and that's how

I would understand my thoughts, I then began to conceptualize and relate to everyone and everything around me. My intuitive nature was slowly being silenced and overcome by what I learned. In a sense it was being replaced by what I was taught to be right and wrong, beautiful and ugly. Of course all of my perceptions had been influenced by those who developed the English language.

The emotion of absolute joy and the connection of being one with everything that I was born with, became dull and non-existent. I was slowly welcoming my individuality, my ego, as I was supposed to do.

In time I began to build a shell around myself, for protection, a shelter, like a turtle or snail. The material for this shell was made up of many concepts from the stimuli that was pouring in, interpretations of what I saw. Unfortunately some of these interpretations and concepts were not true. And I became destined to carry this shell with me and I continued adding things as I grew older. The ideas that formed my shell were creating a very intricate exclusive covering that became the major part of my personality.

If there is a way that I could go back to the moment of my birth now and look out through those baby eyes I truly believe that I would be blessed with an unfiltered understanding of the true meaning of existence, I would again experience the immeasurable joy as I realized the fabric of this creation. In like fashion, if I could feel and re-live, re-experience the past and the future now at this moment, as if it were all present, the meaning of my life would change. Time would no longer exist. I would be able to understand all time. And knowledge would then probably become all knowledge or total knowledge. I would truly be awakened. Bliss, ecstasy, the words that yogis, gurus, and all spiritual teachers use would make sense to me.

Today I am a homo sapien, I am a son, I am a grandson, I am a father, I am a grandfather, I am a great grandfather, I am an American, I am a 21st century middle of the road average human, living on a planet that is teeming with billions of other life forms. Where I am now is in a time and place that we are told enjoys the best living conditions ever, in the history of mankind. Those of us here and now live healthier and longer than any previous generation. Supposedly, I am someone who is happier and more fortunate than any of my elders.

However, I may be a person who believes in a story that I have been telling myself about who I am. As I look to answer this question I sadly realize that I am not one with nature. I have accepted what my culture dictates and expects of me. I have become a part of the destruction of nature. My mind, my shell, my personality, my concept of reality, tells me that I am in a civilized world and that my way is rational and that I am tolerant of all others. I enjoy free speech, a free press, and a democratic rule. Regardless of all my good fortune, I am not an enlightened soul.

With all the advanced technology of today, it is accepted that we humans now realize all the answers to the serious questions about the world. Through our developments in science and physics and our sophistication in illuminated thinking, it is commonly believed that we are well prepared to face the future and reap the rewards we deserve.

Modern man will reap our just reward, but we may not like it. In reality we have not changed much from the Native American who believed that by dancing in circles around a fire, he could bring on the rain. In respect of the Native American who was absolutely more in tune with nature, he wasn't able to control the weather. On the positive side, his culture had taught him a respect for all living things and a way of life that was mutually beneficial. He didn't speak English.

Most Americans have no clue what it would be like to think in a different language, and don't even realize that language influences thought. The analytical understanding of every single thought, every relationship, is altered by the language in which we think and communicate.

In Japanese there is a word, *ikigai*. It is more than a word. It is a concept that means a reason for being. It refers to having a meaningful direction and purpose for life. In French there is a word to describe the heartbreaking pain you experience when you can't have someone you love. There are literally thousands of such examples. In Africa the word *ubuntu* is an explanation of how you treat others, how you regard yourself in intimate relationships as well as the broad community. To have good *ubuntu* means you use your strength to help others, never taking advantage. The Indian languages are filled with words that describe behavior, *ahimsa* means non-violence toward all living things.

An exclusively English speaking person who grows up without these words has suffered a loss. In Costa Rica the Ticos often call their significant other *media naranja*, which means "the other half of their orange." I'm told by my son who spent periods in the Mideast that Americans can not understand the Koran, because it can not be accurately translated. I can not even imagine how a remote tribesman in Borneo views the world as he thinks through his language, let alone his affected differences through the socio-cultural contexts in which he lives.

My point is this, our understanding of what we witness each day, physically, emotionally and mentally is strongly affected by the words we use, and the tempo of our language. Most American brains communicate with their thoughts, so to speak, in English. We are OK with this, we are like fish who don't know that they are wet. It takes an English speaking person a year just to get some of the Japanese inflections or differences in style and tempo. The gullah language, Jamaican patois, and the many Creole dialects from Trinidad to Belize, all of these create different outlooks on our reality. Basically this understanding should make us all a little humble. Sometimes we are like people who know a little bit about nothing, and act as if we're experts on everything.

When Albert Einstein published his *Theory of Relativity*, science leaped ahead in its understanding of the Universe. This was 1905 and most of us laymen still have little ideas of what he discovered. Working in a cosmological and astrophysical world, he introduced a concept known as spacetime, a unified entity of space and time. The theory transformed theoretical physics and astronomy.

He one-upped Isaac Newton, whose ideas had been solid gold for 200 years.

My time chart shows that I am a person who is an '87% past, 13% future' being. I can recall my past to a degree but cannot physically re-experience any of those 74 years except in some sort of a memory fantasy, and sometimes in my dreams. Yes, I am 'Here and Now.' I am 'Be Here Now'. I am 'One Day at a Time.' In the grand scheme of things, our present actions towards the future are extremely short-sighted. The time we are living in now, and our practices related to the significant changes that are being made exponentially, are far out of synch. It's very easy to become deluded by the now of it all.

In the past I was a joyful infant, an energetic and happy child, a student, a basketball player, a lover, a husband, a diver, a fisherman, a carpenter, an electrician, a gardener, a swimmer, a hiker, and much, much more. But I am still all of this. It is who this time regulated, ecologic member, quantumly complicated being is. What I was is who I am. I assume what matters more is where I'm going. "If everyone has a full circle of human qualities to complete, then progress lies in the direction we haven't been."—Gloria Steinem

I am a complex organism, a gathering of over 37 trillion cells formed into a motor functioning, systemized, thinking entity. I have a personal identity, yet I am an integrated small part of the whole paradigm of existence. I am the same as the other 8 1/2 billion forms of life that I live here with, all striving to exist and procreate. I am like the bacteria or viruses that were here first and that probably created me. The tiniest insect, the largest animal, all of the plants, and fungi, we exist. And the glue that holds us all together is the miracle and beauty of our relationships.

The entirety of this creation, of this planet, solar system, galaxy, universe, is held together and controlled by some sacred form of light energy, an invisible gravity that attracts all mass and pulls us together. We will probably one day collapse into ourselves, it's likely that another death/birth will happen for me as I move along. My physical body will change. My time chart will change, not sure how it will affect my personal identity, but hopefully I will evolve and hang on to the concept of beauty. I have a feeling that eventually my "Be Here Now" state will graduate into a larger frame where I will no longer view a day as today, yesterday or tomorrow. All days will be one.

The present will no longer be that which I am seeing. The organ I now call a brain will be replaced by something that doesn't have so many disconnected parts, connected, but actually working independently of each other. This new brain will function as a whole, possessing the ability to connect to a higher power. I may become something that will create an undivided and connected true understanding of the "Who am I now." Perhaps I will be able to tie the Red shift/Blue shift principle that tells us we are all moving away from each other, with the idea of simple gravity, that draws all mass together.

Most of us live, actually think and function in a small part of our forebrain. The rest of the brain is there but for different reasons we seldom consciously venture outside of the forebrain. Our ego and stress keeps us there. My liver doesn't think. It performs more chemical functions than all laboratories worldwide, but it doesn't think. Like my lungs it is controlled by the brain, the autonomic system. It is told what to do by my brain without my conscious effort or knowledge. It operates with amazing efficiency, as do my kidneys, heart, stomach, bladder, etc., all in different body systems, combining to keep me alive and healthy. All of these systems are controlled by my brain. I know that there is much more to the brain than neuroscience has yet discovered.

I wonder if my brain contains an individual key that will open up the path to enlightenment, probably not. What is consciousness? Do trees have it? Do we really record and retain everything that we have ever seen, heard or felt, probably so. This mass amount of knowledge is all there. All experiences recorded, from the womb until now.

Should I believe that I am what my brain tells me I am? The respected 17th century French philosopher, Rene Descartes, made famous by his statement, "I think, therefore I am," was actually working to find a statement that could not be doubted. Is the inverse of his statement also true, "I am, therefore I think." Well, it's not, because we know that people are alive and have no electrical impulses in their brain. So if I can exist without any knowledge, without any past, present or future, then who am I? If I'm not an individual, would I still be a part of the whole? I would then, only be the whole, I would cease to be a part of the whole.

Philosophy can often bog me down. It is only that, philosophy. Some of the greatest philosophical thinkers in history are constantly being proven wrong by the ever continuing wave of new philosophers. Much of Western psychiatry follows Sigmund Freud's advice, he once attributed much of human subconscious psychological action to repressed sexual issues. I believe he was onto something, but I would like to say to Freud that "Philosophy is to the real world what masturbation is to sex," an individually created fantasy. How far can the mind go to create a reality from thought? Has the conscious mind ever imagined an event with such vivid clarity that it was brought up from the past and re-lived in the present. It's not possible as a biologic entity but it could be done as a spiritual being. It's a little early yet for me to be talking about spiritual beings, although I am inserting the idea here, to be explored later.

Einstein worked to understand and explain the structure of the universe, the physical relationship between the stars and planets, and even galaxies, millions of light years apart. Another genius of modern physics, Werner Heisenberg was soon to discover hidden secrets about the tiny world of the atom. Together he and Einstein have explained how our universe works on a large and small scale. This knowledge should help me in some way, but I'm not sure that it does. Heisenberg claims that the structure of the atom is totally chaotic and unpredictable, an idea that Einstein openly disputed. Einstein believed that everything was in order and could be explained, predicted. His famous statement to Heisenberg was "God does not play dice with the Universe." Yes, even these two geniuses did not agree on things, but their ideas have been the guiding scientific light as we traipse along through our Western twenty-first century life.

There are others who are in charge today, driving this speeding train that I find myself on. In the engine room of this train, which incidentally, no one knows where it's heading, are more physicists, software developers, inventors, scientists, there might even be a few political leaders. There are many chiefs in the engine room trying to combine their ideas and drive this train. Although not even one of them can predict where it's going, One thing is for sure, it's speeding up. It's going so fast that it is now or will soon be, out of control. There is something that is trying to slow it down. That is, we the people, who are in the cars behind the engine room.

The first car is filled with people who are screaming. They are yelling for their lives, afraid of the cow on the tracks. They can see it coming. Today's train no longer has a cowcatcher, like in the days of old. This bullet train will soon smash the poor innocent cow into shreds and there is nothing that will stop it. All of their screaming is for naught. Inside they know it, but their total helplessness at this soon to become, cold hard fact of life, inspires all of the futile responses.

The next car is packed with people, every seat is taken, but no one sees the cow. They are all busy socializing or reading their books, enjoying the ride. A lot of news magazines are open, *U.S. Weekly, The Spectator, Newsweek*, ironically even the *Science News* has found its way into this car. It appears that car number three, as well as car number two must be the premium and business class ticket holders. The seats have more legroom and the passengers have paid more for their tickets. It appears as if the intellectuals and semi intellectuals are in these first two cars. And of course, the elite are here, traveling First Class. It may be a slightly more comfortable ride but it won't make a difference in the long run towards the end of this journey.

I'm somewhere in one of the middle cars with all the other people that are willingly being pulled along the route. The cars at the end of the train are the locked down cars. These people find themselves on a train that they don't want to be on. They have all been herded on. Many never made it on the train, they fought till their death to avoid boarding. Others are in locked rooms, some in chains. They are able to witness the beauty of nature as it flies by their barred windows. They all want to escape into the woods, to run and hide. But I'm afraid that even the woods themselves are on this train. All of nature is in the caboose trying to halt the mad runaway engine. The caboose is our only hope, our last hope.

Today I am living in a most unsettled world, we are in the midst of a health pandemic which is impacting every person in every strata of the social order. No-one is exempt and every one is affected. We have been attacked on a global scale by a new deadly virus. On December 31, 2019 in Wuhan City China an unusually large cluster of pneumonia cases were reported. On January 7, 2020 health officials in China isolated and identified a new type of Coronavirus. Within a few months this new virus called Covid-19 has infected people around the globe.

I lived through other pandemics such as MERS and SARS, both Corona viruses which attacked the respiratory system, but neither of these seemed to be as contagious or as deadly as Covid-19. Most certainly the world did not respond then as it is today. It appears today that science and reason are in a battle with conjecture and instinct to determine public policy. Of course confusion, disagreement and fear have now come to center stage. Everything that most of us cherish has been threatened, our freedom, our social civility and our access to the truth. I have become used to this. It is now almost expected from current news organizations, government officials and the vast number of opinionated social networkers.

2

A Journal

JANUARY 1, 1959

My dad knows Fulgencio Batista, how he knows him I'm not sure. I don't think he's close to him, but I've heard him talk about him as an acquaintance. My dad, mom and I watched the TV news tonight and saw that Fidel Castro has kicked Batista out as President of Cuba and has taken over the country. That's not good news for us because the U.S. doesn't want Fidel in there. He's a communist.

JANUARY 1, 2020

Today I begin my journey. It will be a search, a mission to discover who I am now. I will attempt to blend the timeline from my birth in March of 1946 until December 31 of this year and I hope to find something that will be of relevance. Perhaps I will discover that who I was, is a completely different person than who I am. I have often wondered how much of what I do today becomes the me of tomorrow. I'm jumping on it, and in 365 days from now, I should have some idea.

Although I have never traveled in the Nordic countries, I am familiar with their commonly accepted social code and underlying philosophy for life known as *Janteloven*. It is a wonderful principle that permeates the culture. The idea is that focus should never be placed on individual achievements, rather emphasis should be placed on collective accomplishments. I'm not a recognizable figure who should draw readers in because I'm famous. I'm not a Hollywood actor, a famous entertainer, or an important sports or political figure, My story will be the story of an average guy in any typical year.

JANUARY 3, 2013

Suzanne, Zac and I are about to board our flight back to San Francisco. We've been here in Ecuador for a couple weeks and have seen a lot. It has been my first trip to Ecuador and I especially wanted to bring Zack here. It's sort of like his early graduation gift from high school. He has done such a great job. In June he will be graduating with honors. Suzanne and I are so proud of him. Ecuador is the only country in the world that has given equal rights, equal status to nature. Nature has a say of its own in Ecuadorian law.

We have hooked up with an old friend of mine from my high school, Ron, who has been living here and is acting as our guide through the country. Our adventure began in Quito where Ron has an apartment. For two days we wandered around to see the historical parts of the city. We then rented a car and headed North to a world famous marketplace that has been the crossroads for jungle traders for over a thousand years, Otovalo.

A city of mostly indigenous people who are now selling great art, exquisite wood sculptures, and hiqh quality woven fabric, including world famous Otovalian cashmere. The marketplace comprises 8 city blocks. In all my travels I cannot remember being in a larger market. After Otovalo we proceeded to get lost on some mountain dirt roads and drove around, possibly in circles until the wee hours of the morning.

For our next journey we traveled South through the amazing Andes and made it to Quilotoa, the largest volcano in Ecuador. From there we traveled to Ingapirca, the most famous Inca Ruins in the country. Continuing South we hit Cuenca, one of the larger Ecuadorian cities and home to a lot of retired expatriate Americans.

It is a charming blend of old Spanish architecture and modern design. Cuenca was born in the early 16th century.

After Cuenca we aimed for one of Ron's favorite places, Vilcabamba, staying at an amazing place built by a couple Americans, Meredith and her husband Brian, who had passed away. The area is very special, we decided to stay for a few nights.

We spent the New Year in Vilcabamba and experienced the Ecuadorian custom of burning effigies. Every year a big celebration occurs where the people create an effigy, a symbol of the old year. We had been seeing these dummy-like creations throughout our trip but now understand their significance. At midnight December 31, the effigies are burnt, generally in the street and people gather around to send off the bad and welcome in the good of the coming year. The town plaza in Vilcabamba had a wonderful celebration party with live bands, dancing, and the general happy fun loving atmosphere. Besides effigies burning throughout the town, the local children were setting off fireworks. A memorable cultural experience.

The following day we left Vilcabamba and worked our way through some desert land and then miles of bananas until reaching the Pacific coastline. Up the coast we found a great little beach town, San Clemente that kept us for two nights. From the beach, we watched fishermen pulling nets in the early morning, the seabirds filled the shore and the fishermen were sharing some of their catch with the pelicans and seagulls.. It was something to behold. Nature was getting its just do.

Our nights in San Clemente were spent dining with Eduardo, an Ecuadorian who had spent 20 years as a truck driver in New Jersey, but was now back in San Clemente with his small restaurant. Eduardo had great stories and a deep intelligent basis for his present state.

Yesterday was day 13 of our trip, we left San Clemente in the early morning and drove to a monument and popular Tourist Center on the way back to Quito, La Mitad del Mundo, the Center of the World. The exact spot where the Equator passes through

Ecuador. We arrived too late to visit the Center but we could pose on a painted line, putting one foot in the Northern and one foot in the Southern hemisphere.

We spent a few more hours in Quito at Ron's place reflecting on our trip and packing our bags. It's soon time to head to the Aeropuerto.

JANUARY 3, 2020

Yesterday Trump sent a drone to the airport in Baghdad and killed one of the top Iranian Generals. He claims this guy is responsible for attacks and deaths on our soldiers. My tendency is to believe that Trump doesn't do anything right and that this will have serious consequences, harming us in the end.

Australia is experiencing horrible wildfires now throughout their country. I fear that it will be our time when the heat of summer comes to us. I hope I am wrong about this.

It looks like this virus has its origin in a very large city of China, Wuhan. Over 40 cases were found there and it spread to Hong Kong where there are now 5 reported cases.

JANUARY 9, 2020

The World Health Organization (WHO) came out with its official announcement that China has reported a cluster of pneumonia cases of unknown cause (with no deaths) in Wuhan, China. We know that China is never transparent. Things like this make me so thankful that I'm an American and don't know what it's like to be living under a repressed government.

JANUARY 10, 1995

The Jungle, Barra Colorado, Costa Rica. Today I have started to build the "Jungle Lodge." For the first time in quite a while I am exchanging my life as a filmmaker for that life as a builder. I'll be replacing my camera for some tools and building materials. For the next several months I will be using my construction skills rather than the skills that made me a movie producer.

I have been running around San Jose all week acquiring the things I will need. I'm trying to find the necessary stuff to begin the project. The building knowledge I learned in North Carolina doesn't apply here. I'm searching for familiar ways and means, but it's a different world in Costa Rica.

Tonight I was planning for a fine dinner and a good night's sleep with Joanne before heading out to the Atlantic Coast and the start of the big project, however I just received a call. The truck we have hired is now loaded with materials and will pick me up at 11:30 tonight for the trip to Puerto Viejo.

Joaquin and I are in the truck with the driver. There are two helpers in the back. The 2 ton truck is packed with materials. It's 3:30 AM, the highway from San Jose has now changed to dirt with ditches and potholes. I'm lying on a tiny ledge behind the truck seat. It's hot. I'm tired but so cramped and being bounced around too much to sleep.

It's daylight, or I should say, it's barely dawn. I have switched places with Joaquin to the front seat. We just descended the last mountain, I can see treetops and miles of flat jungle lying ahead.

It is 7:30 AM - Puerto Lindo, beautiful port, ha. No boat is awaiting us here as planned. The truck driver wants to unload everything on the ground but I'm trying to have him wait, so we don't have double work. Eduardo should have the boat here soon.

9 AM - I just hired a botero to bring me to the Delta Lodge so I can find Eduardo.

Wolf, the manager of the Delta Lodge tells me that Eduardo has had car problems and has not made it down from San Jose.

Wolf and I get in a small boat and head to Barra Del Colorado. We're floating down the river now, the damn motor died and won't start. Wolf and I have both been trying to crank it for 20 minutes. I've got blisters between my middle fingers on both hands from pulling the starter rope. It finally starts.

In Barra we found a big lancha to rent. When I arrived with it back in Puerto Lindo, all the materials were on the ground. The two helpers, Joaquin, and I loaded them down a steep bank, into the water and onto our lancha, many board feet of lumber, 150 sacks of concrete, 100 lbs. each. Occasionally a bag would rip, tear open as you struggle it up on your shoulder. Cement gets in your hair, down your back, in your shorts and down your boots. It mixes with water and sweat. The open blisters between my fingers are now hardened patches of concrete.

This heat is more than I can bear. I am so tired, so exhausted. It seems like forever since I slept. The driver and owner of our lancha stopped us before we could load everything. It's too much weight.

We are now again floating down the river, dead in the water. The drive shaft and transmission are dis-assembled, as far as I can tell, it doesn't look good.

It is now 8 PM. We are stuck on a sandbar in the middle of the river with no motor.

It's now 11 PM. We've all been in the water pushing. Small boats have come by and tried pulling us free.

We radioed Eduardo to come with a boat from Delta Lodge, but he is nowhere. It looks like we're going to have to unload the sacks of cement onto the river bank, walking through the water in the dark. It's the only way to lighten the boat and get free of the sandbar. I dread the thought !

NEXT DAY

We finally freed the boat, we offloaded most every sack of cement, working until 2 in the morning, and then reloaded everything onto Eduardo's boat. I slept a few hours at Delta Lodge. It's now 7 AM and we're on our way to Samay Beach. To meet up with Saul, he is supposed to be there with his tractor and cart to move the materials again. - Saul's not here….We're unloading onto the beach. My hands are a mess. My feet are also developing blisters from the boots. Since today is Sunday, Joaquin has mixed a bottle of Coke with some guarro. I've had a few slugs but it doesn't even touch me.

Saul just arrived, he seems to like the guarro.

We have made 15 trips from Samay Beach to Laguna Nueve in the tractor. The trail leads along the sandy beach. It is narrow. There are places where you need to duck, dodging the palm fronds and the sea grape bushes. My hands have been scratched a few more times and I have a couple new cuts. Once a branch tore through my middle fingers, ripping open a cement scab. I have been driving the tractor since Saul is now smashed. He sits on the tractor fender above the wheel. The last two trips I've had to hold him with one hand and steer with the other.

We will need to find another boat to haul over the rest of our materials which are still sitting at Puerto Lindo.

NEXT DAY

We are now lugging the second boat load of materials onto the tractor. It will be a long day. There will be no guaro, Saul must drive. We have two helpers at Samay Beach and Joaquin and myself here at Laguna Nueve to unload and air stack the boards. The tractor trip along the beach is so hot and bumpy. The breathing of all the diesel fumes makes you sick in itself. My arms and back are aching.

The final trip has been made, it's well past dark. Saul has to drive down the beach to his home with a flashlight. He doesn't look so happy. What I wouldn't give for something cold to drink. How I have missed that in these past two days.

NEXT DAY

My feet are as bad as my hands. The new boots do not work at all. I have blisters on four toes and both heels. My tennis shoes are wet but I must wear them. Every chance I get, I try to dry out my poor feet. It is so humid, things don't dry.

Today I built shelves in Juan's house for our food and tools. After sleeping on the floor I decided to put a small addition on Juan's hose for Joaquin and I. We need room and a little privacy. I have a good start on the addition, 8x8, two pieces of plywood, the floor and roof are covered. I am leaving now for the night in Delta

Lodge. Tomorrow I'm flying back to San Jose and Joanne, time off for Semana Santa.

Easter Week, a big celebration in Costa Rica. A have a week off, enough time to heal my cuts. The cut on one finger had become infected and swollen. With Joanne's care I soaked my hand many times. My feet were pretty bad and also swollen. I had cement poisoning from the strong lye in the cement.

TWO DAYS LATER

I'm now healed up and feeling strong again. My feet are in good shape. I have two new pairs of shoes and some river sandals. I finally got clean. Joanne and I, along with her daughter Donya and family are at the beach, a beautiful hotel on the Pacific, in Manuel Antonio, the "Villa Si, Como No," a needed break for me.

LATER THAT WEEK

Back in Laguna Nueve, working to finish up the small room. Joaquin's due to arrive back tomorrow with a truckload of concrete posts and some well pipes. We're digging a new well. This morning I attempted to mark a site for the restaurant. As nearly as I can measure, we cannot meet the required 250 meters distance from the sea. That would put the restaurant into the Lagoon. I've tried to call Karl, but the radio phone won't pick up a line. Even when I walk out onto the beach there is no signal.

I am still looking for Joaquin to show up, now on my third trip to Samay. I received word that he and Karl are at Puerto Lindo, no materials. The truck got stuck in the mud on the road from San Jose.

NEXT DAY

The materials are here, The truck made it. Saul's tractor made it. We're short 22 posts and 2 well pipes.

NEXT DAY

Work, work, work, we're all digging a well, Saul, Joaquin, Juan and I. I think soon I will turn over the digging to Juan and Saul. As the digging gets 3 feet down, using Saul's tractor, we're able to lower one of the *alcantarillas*, (concrete well pipes), down into the hole. I'm now at the proposed site of the restaurant, trying to establish a starting corner. Karl said, "no worries," about the 250 meter line.

There is a law now in Costa Rica which forbids construction less than 250 meters from the ocean's high tide mark. The government conducted a massive survey and set geodesic brass markers, around both the entire coastlines. As best as I can translate, these markers are called mahones, in Spanish.

Karl has brought down a banker and a lawyer and yesterday we all traipsed around the bush trying to find the mahone. An old, very skinny, frail man, a neighbor, came walking through the property and offered to help. He pulled out his machete and within several minutes he located our mahone.

There are times that come into one's life that are meant only for us personally, and on this day I experienced one of those times. Between the 5 of us, I was the only one who spoke English, and I don't believe that even this old neighbor understood the English words on the back of his ragged, hole filled tee shirt. As he stooped down, whipping around his machete, I could make out the words printed in large letters on the back of his dirty shirt. "Tight Butts Drive me Nuts." A shirt obviously given to him by a gringo who passed through at some time in the past.

I attempted to translate the words to the old man, but he just smiled, showing his gums. I failed as a translator, but I had such a moment of laughter that I'll never forget.

JANUARY 21, 2020

The Washington State Department of Health announces the first confirmed case of Covid-19 in the United States in Snohomish County, Washington. The patient traveled from Wuhan City, China.

JANUARY 24, 1995

Laguna Nueve, Costa Rica. We have the well dug and a large bodega built, using palm trees as our posts, 2x6 rafters and a tin roof. It's a simple structure to serve us as a temporary barn/ workshop. We have had another load of materials arrive from San Jose and Joaquin and I have completed setting all the concrete posts that will be the first structure of the Hotel.

According to the plans this will become the hotel's office, laundry and storage. The "Jungle Lodge" will be a number of independent small cabinas. After the larger main structure is built, we will begin to design and build the cabins. The work is difficult, days become hot soon after the sun rises. I've hired Juan and Saul both to help with construction and when we can't use them, they become the maintenance crew and work to make the property suitable.

The site that Karl owns here is beautiful beyond description. To the South the property backs up to the Laguna Nueve, a beautiful undisturbed natural laguna, off of the main River in this Northern Carib region, the Rio Colorado.

At present to get onto the property a small boat is necessary. From the actual laguna a tiny arroyo or stream must be forded for a few hundred meters, and at some point we have been raising the outboard motor and walking the boat.

To the West, the property borders the Atlantic Ocean, and to the North and East lie pristine jungles. The property itself has been cleared and many coconut palms have been cared for over the years. Karl bought this land from Juan and his family, who will continue to live here.

As I said the work is not easy and there have been trying times for me, wondering if I have made the right decision. One afternoon I was sitting on one of the felled coconut trees that we were planning to use for the bodega. I was very hot, sweaty and exhausted, having mixed numerous bags of cement all morning. I had a green coconut in my hand that I was drinking, and a mango in the other hand. I felt despondent when I thought a little deeper of my situation. Had I been doing similar work back in the States, I would be sitting on the tailgate of a pickup, in some hustling residential area with a can of Vienna sausage and an orange soda. I realized, life here is not that bad after all.

JANUARY 30, 2020

The WHO has declared a "public health emergency of international concern" regarding the outbreak of this coronavirus. It's becoming a serious problem and I can only hope that those in charge can stop it before it bursts out like it has in many other countries.

FEBRUARY 1, 1958

As time passed and I moved up in grades I became an altar boy. I ate fish on Fridays. I went to confessions regularly, although I usually just told the priest what I expected he was expecting. I got kicked out of the altar boys for telling a dirty joke in school. Because of my mother, they were to let me back in, "Oh holy night."

As I got a little older, I snatched a bottle of wine out of the church sacristy. My closest and dearest friend Billy Bush and I began our experimentation with alcohol. I remember, oh so well, the very first time that I experienced the joy of drinking.

The guilt of taking wine from the sacristy was a factor to be reckoned with, so Billy and I decided to declare a personal holiday and forget about school. At the Everglades Club in Palm Beach, we knew of a perfect little golf course pump house that would suit the occasion of our civil disobedience. The chosen spot was our private little clubhouse by the pond. We had often snuck into this exclusive golf course and spent hours at our clubhouse, hiding out, making up stories, swimming in the pond, and living suspensefully on the edge. There is some special excitement associated with violating the forbidden borders of the unspoken caste system. Ah yes, the Palm Beach social elite will please forgive me if I label them "responsibly insane."

Parties of passing golfers regularly entertained us. They often searched curiously as to who was creating the noises. Now these golfers had not become residents of Palm Beach and members of one of the most exclusive Country Clubs in the world because they were the people most likely to be fooled by 12 year olds.

Billy and I had a way to lock our pump house door so trespassers could not enter. Being dark inside, the golfers that did approach could never see us. When one or two of them walked to the pump house, we hid in time for our mutual safety. Crouched down in strange positions, wrapped up in each other, we watched their faces as they walked over to the tiny window peering in.

On the morning of the wine adventure, we had excitedly de-boarded the public bus, knowing it was to be a special day at the club. Wrapped in a towel, we had our bottle of sacred wine. Slipping through the bushes, a short dash across the fairway, with precision timing, brought us to our clubhouse, unnoticed. On any other day our pond swimming privileges were very restricted. Today, we were liberated, we became uninhibited, it was to become open swimming groundskeepers be damned.

At our age we were not able to drink much of the wine. To begin with, this holy wine tasted like hell. It was 'gaggingly' sweet. We did drink enough to act more aggressive than normal. On this day, we invented a new sport with the golf course geese. Today these geese were to meet their 'Waterloo.' Today was also to be the very last day that we would ever visit our clubhouse.

Our sport began with catching a goose. We were able to accomplish this when we flanked one, two of us against one of them. I guess we got the oldest weakest one (a matter of natural selection) Billy got the goose and tucked him into his arms. Our plan, to jump off the roof into the pond. Taking the goose deep down under the water was the object. The goose did not take kindly to this game. In the course of our newly invented, wine enhanced action, the biting goose would harm us much more than we would harm him.

With all the geese screaming and our ruckus, we brought on the groundskeeper in short order. Perhaps because we had 'holy wine,' we did not wind up in the Palm Beach police station on that memorable and final day at the club.

Billy and I were to remain best friends during our childhood, getting into much more mischief. Once we climbed up onto the roof of the tallest building in town with a couple large boxes of freshly shredded vegetables, compliments of the fabulous new invention, the Whacko Vegetable Shredder.

Inside the downtown department stores, as salespeople did their respective demonstrations, the chopped up vegetables, (celery, tomatoes, carrots, cabbage, etc.) made their way to Billy's and my turf, the alleyways.

Ah, the alleys, for young kids growing up in the city, those alleys were much like the trails of the rainforest or the creeks of the country woods. There was so much entertainment to be had back there in those overlooked, ignored passageways of garbage. In the alleys we became treasure hunters, we searched the huge bins, excitedly looking for objects of adventure. If nothing else surfaced, we would always drag out the long tube like cardboard rollers that became our swords. Shields were easy to find. We would have sword fights lasting the entire alley block, smashing into the bins, knocking over any small objects in our way, leaping, jumping, and climbing for position. There was no one in the alleys to reprimand us, no one that cared about our reckless behavior. We could become princes or pirates.

On the day that we found the chopped up vegetables, our sword fighting was put on hold. We had discovered the elements for a different adventure, for a new game, veggiefun.

In the hidden alleyways, we battled with our newly found ammunition until we tired of it. The next step seemed like an unspoken understanding between us. There were still boxes remaining and we were just behind the city's tallest building, which fronted the main street of town. It was like the Mount Everest Syndrome. Could it be done? Honestly, we had no idea of the negative side of our actions. A small amount of chopped up veggies flying down on Clematis Street, would be fine. There was something compromising about the beauty of the feat. It was to be more like a sculpture, like a museum installation, like pre-teen art.

How the heavens rained for that brief moment, how much we laughed, and how excited the challenge of escape became. We got away with it.

FEBRUARY 4, 2020

China has announced that it has over 20,000 cases of the coronavirus and over 400 deaths. It appears as if this virus is spreading beyond the borders of mainland China. 200 cases have been reported in 12 different countries.

FEBRUARY 5, 2020

Trump has been acquitted. He was being impeached for abusing his Presidential power and obstructing Congress. Somehow he got himself acquitted. Perhaps I should give him credit for something anyway.

FEBRUARY 8, 2020

It began many years ago here in our country, but it looks as if the insane violent behavior of mass shooting continues to spread around the globe, just like the coronavirus. A Thai soldier went on a shooting/murder spree in Bangkok killing 20 people.

Today Trump fired a Lt. Colonel who testified against him during the impeachment trial. The officer was under oath to speak the truth but Trump fired him for insubordination.

FEBRUARY 11, 1995

San Jose, Costa Rica. I'm back for good in San Jose. I've been here now for a couple days and a lot has transpired with Karl, Joanne and Laguna Nueve. Actually the whole world has turned upside down.

Joanne has been working for Karl for a few years and is basically his number one employee. Karl is German and owns a travel company that brings Germans and Europeans to Costa Rica. When Karl met and hired Joanne, she added Americans and English speaking tourists to his list of clients. This new client base has become even a larger part of the company's business, due to Joanne's abilities.

It appears as if Karl has his fingers in a number of other things and Joanne has been discovering this lately. When I got back to San Jose, for a needed break. Joanne began telling me that she thinks Karl has been laundering money.

Karl, his wife Marie, Joanne and I went out to dinner two nights ago and Marie started in on Karl about Laguna Nueve, saying that he is taking too much money from the business and putting it there. I was shocked. I thought that all the money was allocated for the "Jungle Lodge," and in a separate account. Apparently Karl is funding this as a pet project on a daily basis. That is not the way to build a hotel and I immediately saw a boondoggle happening.

Joanne is afraid of Karl's possible illegal dealings and wants to quit working for him. I'm in exactly the same place. I will not go back again to Laguna Nueve. It's been a love hate relationship. The place is exquisitely beautiful and has so much potential as a unique, remote natural wonder. I bathed every night in the lagoon. I built a crazy fence around our house with driftwood from the beach. I will hold onto so many fabulous wonderful memories in that rainforest.

One Sunday, Juan had left, I was alone and had a serious two hour battle with a terciopello, also known as a fer-de-lance, a highly venomous pit viper. He was mean and would not be scared away. We spotted each other, he was in the unmowed grass, maybe 20 meters from the house. He had his head raised up above the grass when our eyes connected. Neither of us dared to look away. I tried yelling in an effort to scare him away, with no luck. Neither of us altered that plan of attack/defense for quite a while.

For a couple weeks I had been practicing throwing a hatchet that I had brought down, and had been getting pretty good at sticking it into the palm tree. The time had come to see how good I was, and for real this time.

I was able to locate the hatchet and still keep my eyes on Mr. Terciopello. The story does not go as I wished, that I boldly whipped that hatchet at him and cut his head off. I boldly whipped it, but he had no problem dodging my throw. He hardly flinched. I didn't dare take my eyes away.

Of course I had no antivenom medication and I realized that if he got me, there would be no way that I could get our little boat through the arroyo, make the 1/4 mile passage across Laguna Nueve, into the Rio Colorado, etc. etc. I've said it a hundred times and I was about to say it again, "How did I ever get myself into this situation?"

I have no idea how snakes think, and I wonder what kept him in his steadfastness as the clock of destiny ticked away for one of us. Despite my yelling and throwing a few more things in his direction, he was not about to call off this committed hostile combat that we had begun and were now engaged in.

Eventually I came up with my next plan. We had a few stout long sticks of bamboo under the house. I walked backwards, without losing the gaze of my deadly adversary and located one of the poles. Now it was the "me or him" logic that took over.

I got up my courage and charged him, and thankfully I'm here to tell the end of the story. I won the battle. By beating at him an insane number of times with that pole, enough strikes must have landed on his head and knocked his brains out.

Goodbye Laguna Nueve. Goodbye to The Jungle Lodge. I'll never forget you.

FEBRUARY 14, 2020

It looks like the Coronavirus is worse than we thought. China has released the terrible news that over 1700 of their medical workers have contracted the virus. There are reportedly some 67,000 cases now being reported around the world. In the U.S. we now have the 14th case being reported. I hope we can somehow contain it.

FEBRUARY 22, 2020

In the last two days South Korea has reported that it has 220 new cases of Covid. Italy is also becoming infected, it has reported 62 cases. There are now over 2500 deaths worldwide. We are still not as bad as other countries.

FEBRUARY 28, 2020

Stock markets around the world report the largest single-week declines since the 2008 financial crisis. President Trump held a briefing at the White House, and said that there was little chance of the virus causing significant disruption in the United States. Without a doubt, another missed call by our fearless leader. I must warn readers at this stage that I expect my personal opinions and feelings about President Donald Trump will be noticeable, conspicuously flagrant, blatant and outrageous throughout this book. I don't believe I will be able to be purple. That's the way I see it. Trump's actions are definitely shaping my outlook.

FEBRUARY 29, 2020

Today's news....The state of Washington has reported a death from Covid. It has now come to our shore as a killer.

MARCH 4, 2020

Japan has begun a process to quarantine anyone coming to their country from China or South Korea. Australia went a step further and has refused entry to anyone from either of those countries. The virus has begun to snowball throughout the planet. 107 people are reported to have died from it in Italy.

MARCH 6, 2020

Professional sporting events are being affected around the globe. Fans are being stopped from going to the stadiums. Iran is freeing over 50,000 of its prisoners to save them from mass infections. Worldwide we now have over 100,000 reported cases.

MARCH 9, 1951

Today I celebrate my 5th birthday with my family in Kankakee, Illinois. The weather is very cold and I am seeing snow for the first time that I can remember. We have a nanny that lives with us and cares for me and my sister. Her name is Ada, she is Black. This time period is about as far back as my memory will allow me to go.

MARCH 9, 1979

It's my birthday. I'm 33, I made it. I've always considered this year as special. It's the year that Jesus died. He chose 33 to be his final age.

Sunny and I just realized that she's pregnant. We have been together for about a year now and we will soon be having a baby. Holy Cow, I'm going to become a birth father. I've been fathering Abel, but this time the baby will have my genes. I won't be able to love this baby any more than I love my Abel, I know that for a fact.

I better hurry up and finish the log house. Today it's snowing hard and I'm sitting in the little shack with a nice fire going. My mule Shadow is under cover, protecting himself in his stall. Sunny and I will probably get married.

MARCH 9, 2002

Back in NYC, it's been quite some time since I've walked around this place. I've come up here to celebrate my birthday with my friend Judith Adler. We met in Costa Rica on a bus several years ago. Today we plan to spend time with a realtor looking at expensive properties. Judy has a friend from Holland who is quite wealthy and wants to get an apartment here in Manhattan. We'll be looking at places on the upper east side, Central Park West, etc., a far cry from my past experiences of sleeping on the floor, in dumps on the lower East side of the Village.

When I first arrived here in NYC I was wearing a pin on my shirt that read Dump Bush, Judy quickly pointed out that it was politically incorrect. In light of the fact that almost 3,000 people were killed back in September, I immediately pulled off the pin.

In March of 2003 my feelings about Bush had formed. He is an evil man putting his personal desires above respect for human life, above the truth.

On March 19, Bush began the war with Iraq, he launched an attack labeled as Operation Iraqui Freedom. He boldly called this first phase of bombing "Shock and Awe." Our American Forces flew over 1700 missions and in 3 weeks reportedly killed 6,700 civilians. In the 21 days between March 20 and April 9, when Baghdad was seized by Allied forces, 320 civilians were killed each day. His reason for the war was to get rid of an evil dictator that held weapons of mass destruction (WMD's), endangering us and the rest of the world. Saddham Hussein was an evil dictator for sure, but there were no WMD's. And Bush's true purpose was to get Iraq's oil and set up bases in order to gain control over the Mideast. (note) My son Abel was on the front line during this war. He had 18 deployments to Iraq. How could I not hate Bush.

From the perspective of NYC residents and a respect for their condition, I pulled off my pin. They are suffering through the worst deadliest terrorist attack in American history. Until now I have been unaware of how patriotism is offering some sort of solace to the many grieving families here.

Signs of the changes in NYC are everywhere. Judy nor I have any desire to visit the sight of destruction, at the World Trade Center in lower Manhattan. I can definitely feel the pain and anger that permeates the streets. A climate of grief and a desire for revenge exists. This is a far different New York than had existed before 9/11.

MARCH 9, 2020

The WHO declares the outbreak of Covid-19 as a pandemic, the first to be caused by a coronavirus.

Today is my almost 'Big One,' that is, a milestone birthday. I look at next year as being the 'Holy Shit' birthday, 75 will be a rather significant step. I felt as if my 50th birthday was an exceptional one, 49, nah, not so much. I guess it's the same way I feel today, 74, no big deal. I'll just plodge along this year in normal fashion, waiting for next year. By then this Coronavirus will all be in the history books. Hopefully, I will then have a memorable celebration before I have the long wait for the Big 100.

My close friend Brenda is visiting me from Florida and she has made a cake, filled the house with decorations and plans a big Brenda Dinner. Brenda loves cooking and is one of the best at it. She and I have been friends since the mid 70s. We were lovers once but have settled our relationship as best friends. We met in North Carolina and have much in common from those days. As coincidence has it, we both left North Carolina at about the same time, and found ourselves out here in Northern California. She settled in San Francisco and I came further north to Sonoma County.

Brenda arrived in North Carolina as a hippie mother of three, living in a converted bus with her then almost/husband Gary and their three kids. They had been working in the world of State Fairs all over the country. Gary built the games and Brenda was a great 'hawker' calling in customers. After her move to California, her subdued North Carolina style of life was about to change, set into motion again. In San Francisco Brenda began life as a sales person for the Asian yellow pages, she then became a bartender, then Mistress Sadie, a sex phone worker. She eventually began a balloon business with her partner Ronnie. As an artist she designed amazing sculptures out of balloons, made lots of money decorating for businesses and personal events. Brenda created something with long skinny balloons that she called a splash. It's a large group of 2 by 40 inch long balloons slightly twisted and tied together. A splash can be varied in color, it can be hung or even worn on a person's back. Brenda and Ronnie's business became the one to see each year at the SF Pride Parade. SF Balloon Magic didn't have a float, rather, they had hundreds of their friends with splashes on their backs marching and skating along the Parade Route. The balloon industry around the world has picked this up and it is now a common creation in every corner of the globe. "Way to go Brenda."

If, as we jump into a new field, there is a bar of excellence, a new limit to be reached, some such thing as the top of the bar, well I can tell you, because I've seen it over and again, this little girl from the mountain backwoods of West Virginia is the one who strolls in and raises that bar.

Brenda and I have continued our friendship and for 15 years have remained very close. We turned the streets of San Francisco and the woods and rivers of Northern California into our playgrounds, our campgrounds. Four years ago Brenda's mother died and left her a house in Florida. She quit tying balloons, paying outrageous SF rents, and headed south. The change has not been easy for her. Central Florida ain't San Francisco.

MARCH 10, 2002

My visit is over and I will soon be heading to La Guardia. Yesterday was quite a memorable day for my personal history book. Judy and I with the help of Amy, a young, gorgeous South Carolina transplanted real estate agent, toured many upscale, elite Manhattan properties. Of course, 'location, location' translates into the view most properties we visited had: panoramic views of the Manhattan skyline or beautiful vistas of Central Park, the East River, etc. Some of the properties were impeccably furnished, one with a Grand Piano. It was quite the experience as my social status often came into conflict with my imagination. This phenomenon was generally regulated to manageable, by beautiful Amy's strong Southern accent. Somehow when a thing does not seem in place, it draws attention away from an escaped reality.

By early evening we were again in a taxi. This time heading to a popular Jazz club where musicians jammed in improvisation. Amy fired up a joint. I took a couple hits, my thoughts wandered. When my turn to talk came up, I began on the topic of why people are judged by their outward appearances rather than what's inside of them. "What would it be like to be blind," I said, "like Ray Charles or Stevie Wonder?" The taxi came to a halt. We had arrived. We walked in and sat at the bar. By coincidence, a blind Black singer was on stage finishing his set. He approached the bar. "May I sit here?" I was to meet Frank Senior. "How are you doing? I feel great today." he said. "Today's my birthday," he continued, "Yeah, mine too," our connection began.

Frank and I bonded immediately. I told him that I had just been talking about seeing the world as a blind Black musician. I would never be Black, but that night I was to see the world as a blind man. We talked about many different subjects, we laughed, drank and decided to celebrate my final night in NYC together. Judy felt like going home, so Frank and I made our way to more jazz clubs in the Village. I realized how easily Frank navigated with his cane and memory. I closed my eyes, slightly held the back of his arm as he had been doing to me, and let him take over as our evening's guide.

We went to a number of different clubs and Frank led the way. I kept my eyes closed. I had my wish, to experience the people I was coming in contact with, without seeing them physically. We talked with all the bartenders and many of the people at the different bars. At one point Frank asked me what the singer looked like. I had been envisioning a young, pretty blond, but after forcing my eyes to open, I saw an older grey-headed, Black woman. The drummer's appearance also was so unlike the image I expected.

I lost my cell phone yesterday, but I wouldn't trade the experience with Frank for a hundred cell phones. I'm sure that we shall remain friends.

(Note) Frank began a business soon after called New York in the Dark where he repeats our experience and guides people around New York in blindfolds.

MARCH 12, 2020

It is not business as usual anymore for us Americans. We are locked down in our houses, restricted from traveling and required to practice social distancing. Should we venture outside and into a crowd, we must by law adhere to the government guidelines. We are living in such a partisan environment, where everything from our birthing decisions to our death wishes seems to come under dispute. How we connect to this present situation is our choice. We can talk or we can listen. We can tell or be told. We can make noise or be quiet, advise or learn. We're told that "We will get through this together," and that we need to "Keep flattening the curve." We're asked to "Stay safe, work from home," and "Stay safer at 6 feet apart." Of course laws are in place requiring everyone to wear masks to stop the spread. "Stay in place, maintain your space, cover your face." Even the pot sellers are suggesting that we "Stay strong, be calm, and buy cannabis online."

I am not complaining about any of this, I'm taking it in stride as I try and guess how I really feel. I have friends who are telling me that it's all a big conspiracy, convinced as they are that the higher power has begun its move to kill us all or at least to take away our freedom. Some believe that a mysterious evil 'they' created this virus in a lab and released it upon the world. Many of my fellow Americans choose to follow the advice of another political faction that is on the right side of today's very tall barbed wire fence. They have been led to think for a number of reasons that it's all a hoax.

MARCH 13, 2020

President Trump declares a National Emergency, suspending U.S. entry of foreign nationals who have been in China, Iran, and the Schengen Area of Europe in the past 14 days. In late February, when the stock market was beginning to fall over coronavirus fears, President Trump held a briefing at the White House, and said that there was little chance of the virus causing significant disruption in the United States. Without a doubt, another missed call by our fearless leader.

MARCH 14, 2020

Earlier I mentioned that it was a little early to be venturing into spiritual matters, and here I am opening up that 6 panel steel door of politics, the door with hefty locks, and double deadbolts. Some people have all the keys to get through that door, but I don't, that's for sure. Fortunately the door has one of those little peepholes with the tiny magnifying lens. That's how I look through and get my take on everything. Everything is distorted. It looks like all the people I see are from the funny house. When they get close and look back at me their faces balloon out and their bodies shrink to nothing. Rather fitting considering the value of their position. I should say their position as it relates to me. They could be right or left lawmakers or simply the mass of followers that stream in to fight and defend.

What is really exciting is when some group wants in but doesn't have the key to the door. First they'll knock, then they'll begin to beat on the door. Sometimes one of these balloon face people will open the door and try to talk some nonsense into everyone on the other side, but that's generally futile. Then the group leader will bring out the battering ram. All of this will be done with the banner of justice flying high. The foot soldiers are right behind, but all of the unseen ranks are somewhere nearby, it is essential. Usually mob mentality feels secure when it is surrounded by a school of other mob mentalityists. The forebrains in power action.

The other day I drove past a large Tesla plant and I saw many people, worker people, waiting to get into that big door, to work, and return to a semblance of normalcy. And then down the road I passed San Quentin maximum security prison. They also have a big door and I imagined all those people, prisoner people, who wanted to pass through that door. Some people today were wanting to get in while others wanted to get out, and they were both searching for the same thing, freedom. Some were locked in and some were locked out. The government law said that the worker people couldn't get in until the world was safer. The only way that the prisoner people's door would be opened is if the door behind them was locked. There would be no turning back for them. "Here's your freedom buddy, go make the best of it!"

Just before crossing the long bridge approaching San Quentin I passed by the occasional homeless soul, wandering and bobbing across the street, oblivious to my car and most everything else. It was as if he were partially blind. His eyes didn't work like mine. What he was filtering through his eyes did not reach his brain in the same way. He looked rather determined to reach some destination that more than likely wasn't going to change his life much. He was going about it in a twisted sort of way, and I wondered how much he knew about the exquisite miracle of life. I wondered if social networking was part of his biological makeup and if he was affected by our covid-19 world. I wondered where he would sleep tonight and if he would be safe, how many times he would wash his hands today. I wondered about his circadian rhythm. Because of the tyranny of fear that has been oozing out of our digital blue light units, I was aware that he was existing in a high risk group and that he was on a lockdown breach at the moment. I drove on, putting all this into my 'past file.'

Exactly how long does it take until the present becomes the past? Is it five seconds, three minutes, a day? This is important I guess, since the present is all we have, at least that's the most plausible understanding of our position on the timeline. If I could venture ahead into the future it would make my present free of any decisions. Any fork in the road would no longer present a choice that I need to make. Everything in my present would be predestined. In conclusion, knowledge of the future would destroy free will. I don't think that's good.

MARCH 16, 2020

I'm at my good friend Julie's hotel in Palo Alto. We intend to celebrate our birthday together. My birthday was last week but hers is today. News began coming that President Trump was setting guidelines for the public, including limiting gatherings to fewer than 10 people, avoiding discretionary travel, and avoiding eating and drinking at bars, restaurants, and public food courts. Julie's planned flight to Hawaii seems to be in danger. We canceled dinner plans, she rushed to the airport, I headed back north to my home.

It takes over two hours to drive to my house in Sonoma County from Palo Alto. I listened to the car radio and began hearing of the fear that was generating concerning the virus. Not only from the medical experts, but economists worrying about the effects that businesses might bear. Shelter in place orders would soon be coming.

MARCH 19, 2020

The Governor of California, Gavin Newsom, announces the Public Health Officer's "Stay Home Except for Essential Needs" order, requesting all individuals living in California to stay home or at their place of residence, except as needed to maintain the critical infrastructure sectors. Gavin is the former San Francisco mayor, he's hated by Republicans because he's quite liberal and puts his priorities in an order that Republicans think is backwards. I like Gavin a lot. I once did an interview with him that appeared on television in SF.

MARCH 20, 2020

Stay at home orders now apply to over 20% of the population of the United States. It appears that soon everyone in the country will be ordered to stay home. I can choose to be passive or aggressive. I don't have much faith in the government to handle this crisis. Rumors are all over the internet that this is no more than a fantasy, a gross conspiracy. I can choose to believe the Conspiracy Theorists, but why?

THEY

I've got some friends who're scared as shit.

They think that this is really it, Coronavirus, the pandemic are nothing but jokes.

They're not real, it's a government hoax.

People aren't dying, it's just a flu. They're no more sick, than me or you.

Ask yourself, how do you feel, and then you judge if this is real.

Do you personally know of anyone dead? Do you blindly believe what the news has said?

Go to a hospital and then just ask, is there really a reason to wear this mask.

I'm telling you", they say to me. "If you listen to them, you won't be free".

This is step one, locked in your house.

"THEY" are an evil cat, and you're a hopeless mouse.

"THEY've" done all this without firing a shot, and just look now at what "THEY've" got.

Our freedom has gone to walk the street, the markets are changing, as to what we can eat.

The irony is, it started like this, "THEY" made it hard to shit or piss.

I mean, like really, it's rather crass, taking away the right, to wipe our ass.

That's a little much, even for me.

I'm not paranoid, but now I see.

"THEY" are extremely bad, "THEY've" shoved this on our plate.

It's time to act, before it's too late.

Who do we fight, who are "THEY?"

What can we do, what can we say?

Is every government in on this lie. Is what they tell us, what we should buy?

If my friends are correct, the governments are blind, and one day soon these puppets will find, "THEY" are the ones that are in control, the government is simply filling the role.

This all sounds crazy, I don't want to believe it.

But I just might be lazy, I can hardly conceive it.

Is my head in the sand, ignoring what my friends say?

Should I be taking a stand, and fight the "THEY." Do I get out a gun, and never again be happy, and fight everyone who doesn't feel crappy?

If there's ever been a God, who has some say, we need you now, to lighten the way.

God, I really don't know what to do, I try to stay open, and listen to you.

I pray, I meditate, once in a while.

My record of good, you might have on file.

Are you in on this, are you planning the route, are you the "THEY" that they're talking about?

God you know we've fucked up our chance, to make this planet a place we can advance.

We've destroyed the land, the ocean, the air.

We've polluted the world, way beyond repair.

No wonder you want to start brand new, I'd do the same, if I were you.

That's all I'll say, to the God above, the thing that brought us Divine love.

Now there's a chance that you don't really exist, and I better get ready to roll up my fist.

The "THEY" that is here is kinda like the Pope, the religious dude, who preaches for hope.

He wants you to think that everything is in control.

God will handle the bad things, that's his role.

We just gotta have faith that God's really steady, but if he's not even there, then I'm getting ready.

Hey Nelson, hey Gandhi, help me find the "THEY," the invisible power, who's controlling the way.

I wanna revolt, to stage a coup.

I wanna fight, and get rid of you.

Show your face, you dirty scum, what do you think, that I'm a bum.

I'm listening to my friends now, and you're dead meat, there's no Coronavirus, and I'm putting on the heat.

I'm gonna get you, you son of a bitch, I don't care, if you're powerful, and rich.

My name is T Bone, you hear me callin." You better get ready, to start your brawlin.

My temperature's rising, I'll fight to the death, my lungs are filling, I'm losing my breath.

Uh oh, what's happening, I'm down on my knees, I'm feeling weak, I'm beginning to freeze.

It's Covid 19, well mother fuck, wouldn't you know it, just my luck.

So now I'm dead, most everyone else is still there, running around without a care.

Things are re-opened, it slightly changed their life.

To me it doesn't matter, I don't have the strife.

Soon my friends will be dead, just like me.

Then, and only then, they will see.

The truth about "THEY" will come to light.

Clear as day, or dark as night.

Whatever.

I woke up this morning and wrote that silly poem after talking last night for three hours with Judy, another of my ex's. Judy and I were young boyfriend and girlfriend for a few years, beginning in 1964. She's a good woman and a serious Conspiracy Theorist. The Conspiracy Theorists have been at this for a very long time. Most recently, one of the big ones, was that the government planned the 9/11 event. Conspiracy stories date back to the 17th century. During that time period most theories usually involved a vile group of people that were trying to undermine and take control of the established power.

In our talk last night Judy brought up today's dominant theory, this one is the 'Mother' of them all. The 'They' are the super rich. There are a few books out on this subject which I really don't intend to read. Maybe if I woke up one morning and one was sitting on my end table I might read it.

Just because societal power is dominated by the wealthiest of the wealthiest, does not mean that those rich people are Illuminati Satanists, though that is a thing that the conspiracy theorists believe.

Those who like the conspiracy ideas also live in fear of governmental domination, like the days of old. This idea that the existing governments are the bad guys and they are trying to gain stricter control over the masses began with Johannes Guttenburg. He should never have invented his printing press, spreading these opinions at the 'speed of flyers.' Now with the advent of the digital age, social networking platforms make ole Guttenburg's contribution look like a tiny dribble in the 'Sea of Conspiracy.' Manuscripts that made it into the newspapers, or leaflets of scary conspiracy actions, that were passed out in city squares hardly compare to today's methods of information distribution.

A phenomenon, called illusory pattern perception, is what scientists now call the reason that people believe in conspiracy theories. Often people feel threatened and will create a reason for their fear even though in reality it doesn't exist. Then the snowball starts rolling, reading about one conspiracy theory makes people more likely to believe in another one. There have been studies showing that 50% of most Americans believe in at least one conspiracy theory. There is a method of controlling the impulse to believe in or expand on some unproven theory, and that is known as critical thinking.

As horrible as this sounds, the conspiracists might very well have been responsible or at least contributed to the anti-semitism and massacre of millions of Jews during WW2. The theories circulating at that time were that the Jews controlled all the international banking, and thus ran the world of finance. Their goal was world domination. Hitler believed this, and convinced the German people that it was true. Even others like Henry Ford supposedly had half a million copies printed of ideas supporting this theory. The first time I was exposed to conspiracy theories on a grand scale was after John Kennedy was assassinated.

It may be that conspiracy appeals to desperate people. People searching out the essence of any important story as it suddenly jumps out at them. It slaps them in the face and immediately affects their existence. It challenges their intelligence and rears up at them, demanding action, not simple compliance. Without personally being involved in the planning of this action they are offended, knowing that something is wrong. They will not walk a straight line as they are being told, but they will make a sharp turn at the first opportunity, turning to the internet for the deep seated possibility that something is up.

And oh yes, with the internet at their fingertips they will surely find what they are looking for, and then some. Facebook, YouTube have become sanctified troves of video treasures. Like minded citizens with gathered facts backing up any and all conspiracy theories are there, lying in wait for more views, more hits. Conspiracies for sale, take your pick, join the crowd.

The sad part of all this is that all those people searching are only wanting the truth and hoping to spread it around like messianic altruists. They want to help the ignorant. The conspiracy theory situation is much like the strongly divided political parties that have developed in our country, where both sides believe in the veracity of their platform.

Diametric opposition in these beliefs tells me however that one side must be mistaken. My response to this, since neither side will ever back down, and since I gracefully look at my position in time (my age), is to quietly ignore it all. At least that is what I try and do. Why spend such valuable time as I have left in this beautiful world with such conflict. Why look at this anthropogenic position with a mentality of hopelessness. Perhaps there was a time that I would rush to the front line of this battle, hoping to declare victory for my side. But not now, not anymore. "I never allow myself to have an opinion on anything that I don't know the other side's argument better than they do." — Self-made Billionaire Charlie Munger

One of the more popular conspiracy theories of the day states that the Gates Foundation has actually released this virus onto the world with the evil intention of controlling the global population. For me to think that Bill Gates and his wife Melinda, who I know have worked relentlessly to help the poor of the world, are now my staunch enemies, is ridiculous. This conspiracy theory gets worse. It claims that Bill Gates is in cahoots with big pharma and big government and plans to secretly insert microchips into the entire population with the forthcoming Corona Virus inoculations. Apparently there is a viral documentary, *Plandemic*, which explains this theory in detail. It began life on a QAnon Facebook page and was shared by Republican politicians before it was banned on social media sites.

MARCH 24, 1962

My dad has formed a partnership with one of his fishing friends, Peter White, a building contractor. They are planning to build two houses in Riviera Beach, my dad will put up the money. One of the houses is for General Garcia and the other is for General Tabernilla. They were both important members of Fulgencio Batista's former regime in Cuba. Dad told me that Batista is staying at the Breakers Hotel in Palm Beach.

Last night I got out my telescope and tried to see into the rooms at the Breakers. From our house we have a clear view right across Lake Worth.

MARCH 24, 2020

The Dow Jones Industrial Average rose 2,112.98 points to close at 20,704.91, an 11% gain, the largest one-day percentage gain since 1933. The S&P 500 Index rose 209.93 points to 2,447.33, an increase of over 9%. The only explanation that I can see for this is that Wall Street brokers are not in panic. Like all addicted gamblers, they feel that they will win soon.

MARCH 26, 2020

Our lockdown is having profound negative results on our economy, as expected. Initial unemployment insurance claims have risen to over 3.2 million, a tenfold increase from the week prior and the highest level of initial claims in the history of the series (since 1967). According to the press release from the Department of Labor, nearly every state providing comments cited that all this is the impact of the Covid-19 virus.

3

Troubles and More Troubles

The Corona virus has faded out to nothing, it's gone. The lockdown is over, employment is back to normal, the shelter in place orders have been lifted, Trump has resigned, the whole world loves the United States again...April Fools :-) April 1, 2020

APRIL 2, 1964

A police officer carrying a young girl walks past three civil rights demonstrators on the ground next to the Tulsa, Oklahoma, police station. The demonstrators are part of 54 arrested at a Tulsa restaurant. Members of the group, backed by the Congress of Racial Equality, went limp when arrested and forced officers to carry them from the restaurant to the paddy wagon. For me this news is the start of what might become serious political disruption in our country and the beginning of the fight against racism.

Yesterday I was sitting in the Student Union of Palm Beach Junior College as the topic began spreading. Different groups of activists are appalled and want to join the fight. At this time, I don't feel a need to become a part of it. At 18 yrs. old, I'm pretty much a wild teenage fun seeker. I'm not the type to fight any political or social issues that will thwart my present dreams. As I see things, all the future is there for my satisfaction, and protesting is low on my priorities. The world as I look at it today has only one serious problem and that is the Vietnam war. Some of my high school friends have been killed and the draft is threatening to grab me at any moment. For this purpose, to stop this crazy war, I will fight.

APRIL 5, 1970

I just completed an initiation and training course before I board the plane. I'm feeling good about this. I'm excited and feeling confident. Working with me is an acquaintance from high school days, 'Flash.' Many people would not be following me where I intend to go and would not approve of what I will be doing, but 'each to their own,' as the saying goes. This flight shouldn't take very long. I should be back here soon. Hopefully I will be safe and return in one piece. We are gaining altitude and I have a great view of the everglades off in the far distance. I'm expecting this trip to be quite an adventure. I've been planning this for a long time. The plane is rattling a lot. I hope it's just the fact that this is a small plane and nothing more. The pilot is very casual, I'm seated very close to him.

He just reached across me and swung the door of the plane open, I'm now in total disarray. I had been going over things in my mind about the mission, but now I'm totally blown away. Flash yells out over the howling wind, ONE.. I can barely remember my name, let alone any of the training at this point. Somehow I lift my left leg out of the plane and balance it on the wing's strut. TWO, yells Flash. I stand on the strut and grab the wing. By now you must know where this is heading. On THREE I jumped. Flash had hooked up my static line which automatically pulled my main chute open within 15 feet of the plane. I simply stretched my arms and legs out like a spread eagle and before I realized it, I was being tugged upward. My scrambled brain began settling back into its normal thinking patterns. Ah, life is sweet, beautiful. My first skydive is a success.

APRIL 12, 2015

I am now 69 years old, I have had a most fortunate life, raising children, adventuring and living in different countries, learning many skills which have allowed me to become independent. I am in excellent health, I have never had a serious illness and have never been on any medications. There is so much to talk about, so many interesting stories. So much of my life and the lessons that I have learned are worthy of being recorded, at least for those in my family history that will appear or follow me into the future.

One of the most pressing issues of the present day is the fight for racial equality and racial justice. I remember many years ago when the Watts riots broke out in L.A. It was in the late summer of 1965, a Black motorist on parole for robbery, was pulled over for reckless driving. A minor roadside argument broke out, which then escalated into a fight with police. The riots spread quickly and resulted in 34 deaths and over $40 million in property damage. It was the city's worst unrest until the Rodney King riots of 1992.

In Baltimore today a 25-year-old Black man Mr. Freddy Gray was chased and restrained by police on bicycles at the Gilmor Homes. A cellphone video of his arrest shows him being dragged into a police transport van, seemingly limp and screaming in pain. After officers got him to the police station, medics rushed him to the hospital, where he slipped into a coma and died last Sunday. He had suffered a spinal cord injury in police custody. There are presently scattered scenes of chaos here, as demonstrators have smashed a downtown storefront window, threw rocks and bottles and damaged police cruisers. Officers in riot gear broke up skirmishes and made 12 arrests. Saturday's trouble began in the early evening, when a group of protesters, as many as 100 went on a rampage, throwing cans, bottles and trash bins at police officers, and breaking windows in some businesses.

APRIL 15, 2020

The Federal Reserve releases the Beige Book, noting sharp and abrupt contraction of economic activity across all regions of the United States. The hardest-hit industries, because of social distancing measures and mandated closures, were the leisure and hospitality sector and the retail sector (excluding essential goods).

Districts reporting on loan demand said it was high, both from companies accessing credit lines and from households refinancing mortgages. All Districts reported highly uncertain outlooks among business contacts, with most expecting conditions to worsen in the next several months.

APRIL 16, 2020

President Trump announces three-phase 'opening up' guidelines for states and local governments on relaxing social distancing restrictions. The guidelines include recommendations for individuals, businesses, and employers.

APRIL 19, 2015

Baltimore residents have continued protesting Mr. Gray's death for a week now, but Saturday's turnout was among the largest. Asked what has changed since these protests began, the mayor frowned. Surveying the crowd, she said she was glad so many people of different races had turned out, adding, "It shows enough is enough. This is a powder keg right now, New York and Ferguson and all those other places are just preliminary to introduce it to the nation, It could become another Watts. If things don't get taken care of here, the whole nation could be set afire. I don't want that to happen."

APRIL 22, 1964

The World's Fair has opened in New York City. I am hoping to make it up. My friend Billy Burroughs and I have been talking a lot about heading to 'the city.' Experiencing NYC has been something I've wanted to do for a long time. Maybe I will take a break after this semester.

Policemen tangled with demonstrators today at a subway station on the opening day of the New York World's Fair. Youths attempted to stall the train, which was headed from the city to the fairgrounds, as a form of protest on behalf of civil rights for Blacks.

MAY 1, 1964

An unidentified African American demonstrator crouches for protection against blows from a white man in front of a segregated Nashville restaurant.

MAY 5, 1970

Oh my God, there was a horrible shooting at Kent State University yesterday. Four students were killed and nine others injured as the Ohio National Guard responded to student protests and opened fire with rifles. Headlines are calling it the May 4th Kent State Massacre. Students were protesting the Vietnam War and its spilling over into Cambodia. The 300 students had gathered for a peace rally. Never has something like this happened. Today the whole country is in outrage. Students at every major University have responded. Students at high schools as well are staging walkouts. I am sure this is going to be a major turning point in our country's attitude towards the war.

MAY 8, 2020

A lot of banking and government action has been going on for the past two weeks but I won't attempt to relay all of this. I will briefly summarize by saying, loans are being made to help individuals and save businesses. Government stimulus checks are being issued to individuals. The Bureau of Labor Statistics reports that the unemployment rate rose to 14.7 percent. This is the largest one-month decline in employment and the highest unemployment rate in history.

MAY 12, 1964

The racial issues are dominating the news. It seems to me like it will not go away and that finally racism may be seeing it's end, finally. More protesting is happening in different cities of the Northeast. Three or four African Americans were hurt in a series of scuffles between demonstrators and white men and white youths. Civil rights marchers walk through the streets of downtown

Cambridge, Maryland. The National Guard was deployed to keep order after a violent confrontation the night before.

MAY 13, 1964

National Guard troops with upthrust bayonets surround integrationists kneeling in prayer as approximately 100 made a peaceful attempt to challenge the no-demonstration edict of the military commander in Cambridge, Maryland.

MAY 14, 2020

A country that has been engaged in political conflicts during my entire lifetime, a country whose people have been ostracized and have experienced a racial genocide like has never been seen before, has an anniversary today. On this day In 1948, when I was 2 years old, Israel, the birthplace of Judaism and Christianity, became a sovereign nation. This country has weathered so much violence throughout its entire history. The missiles, the bombing, the violence, still continues every day, and yet the people survive it all. They remain strong, united, taking it in stride. America can learn something. We must all be strong during this pandemic like the citizens of Israel are, I'm sure. For those interested, the Bible says that the Israelis are the chosen people, and whatever good news might come from up above will be sent to them first.

MAY 20, 2020

The CDC, Center for Disease Control, announces a Community Mitigation Framework that includes updated guidance for communities, schools, workplaces, and events to mitigate the spread of Covid-19. Major population centers began opening in early May as individual states issued specific guidance, including California, New York, and Illinois.

MAY 25, 2020

In Minneapolis, Minnesota, George Floyd, an unarmed African-American man, was killed mercilessly by 4 white police officers. Violent protests have erupted all over the country.

MAY 28, 2020

The CDC reports that over 100,000 people have died of Covid-19 in the United States.

MAY 29, 1961

My dad and I have been in Maine since the first of May. He and I came here alone and rented a little cottage south of Portland, in the town of Old Orchard Beach. Old Orchard is a quaint little seaside town catering to summer tourists, many from Quebec, and week-enders from Portland. The central drawing card is an amusement complex, built on a long pier extending into the ocean, including an Aquarium at the end.

Some of the Canadian visitors actually go swimming in the ocean. I tried it once, for about 45 seconds, and that was enough. Old Orchard has a boardwalk amusement Park, with rides and attractions. I've got a job working in the games. I was learning to juggle baseballs between customers, but my career was short-lived. Within a few weeks I sprained my knee quite badly while taking the owner's overweight young son down one of the big slides backwards. That has put me into the Saco/Biddeford Hospital.

Before the accident of course, my time in Maine has been precious. It is wonderful for me to spend the summer alone with my father. Every Sunday we have been driving around the state looking for a new site to explore. We visited Cadillac Mountain, where the sun first touches America. There are many beautiful lakes and we've driven to two of them with intentions to see more before the end of our trip. Maine is especially known for its jagged, rocky coastline; and picturesque waterways, as well as its seafood cuisine, especially lobster and clams.

My dad has taught me to love seafood. Generally at the end of our Sunday excursions we would wind up in Booth Bay Harbor sitting on the dock for dinner with a 'lobstah' and a bag of steamed clams. This time is so special for me. I'm looking forward to limping out of this hospital very soon.

MAY 31, 2020

Because of George Floyd's death the nationwide violence continues at a fever pitch. At least 40 American cities have imposed curfews in an attempt to stop the burning, the property destruction and the looting. The National Guard has been called out in 15 states and Washington DC. Our president, as I expected, is no help. The country is in a mess, many in the African-American population and thousands of white supporters of the cause, are on the streets. Again racial discrimination has reared its ugly head and our cities are exploding. The people are demanding equality, justice, and accountability. All the frustration built up with the Covid-19 policies has probably contributed.

Twenty-five years ago this week I remember the Rodney King riots in Los Angeles. Those violent protest riots were triggered by the savage beating of an African-American man by four police officers, three white, and were triggered by the subsequent acquittal of those officers. The riots continued for five days. Similar to what's happening today, the people in L.A. were looting, burning and destroying public and private property. It was a mild reaction compared to what is happening at this very moment. Of course all violent actions are deplorable, and a disgrace to humanity, but there is one message that is boldly being broadcast to anyone who wishes to tune in, "Black Lives Matter." During the past six days these riots have escalated and are spreading throughout our country. I am an observer on the sideline, despite the idea that those who 'stand silent in the face of injustice are complicit.' Tonight I am safe but ashamed of my race.

4

Virus and Protests Continue

JUNE 1, 2020

I didn't turn the news on this morning but I did receive a text from my sister saying that some faction was placing ads in certain magazines offering money to join the riots. She was stunned that even the upscale town of Palm Beach with all of its wealth and snobbery is getting hit with disruption and rioting. The very last thing that the Palm Beach social elite residents would be doing is involving themselves in any sort of riot. Nor would they pay their servants to get out on Royal Palm Way with a protest sign. Why should they? They've got life going pretty much the way they want it.

Of course there is one more extenuating circumstance, being that our President has his winter home there. Any street protest in Palm Beach would be considered by him to be a National security threat. Therefore since protesters involved are not local residents, surely they are being brought in, and I expect that they are being ushered across the bridge to West Palm Beach in short fashion.

This manner of action is terrorism without question. The bigger question, who is responsible? I continue to disregard any talk of a huge covert conspiracy. If indeed the whole violent reaction to George Floyd is being planned and orchestrated by some vile, behind the scenes organization, then they are open terrorists. Their deep reasons for such actions can be a jungle gym for the conspiracy theorists. My hope is that any such organization, if it exists, will be found out and prosecuted by those law enforcement agencies that we trust to protect us. And my stronger hope is that this all comes to an end soon and that justice prevails.

Everyone's thoughts and conversations are filled with issues of racism, police brutality of minorities, and the nationwide violent protests. I can only view the present condition through the eyes of a white, somewhat privileged man. I will never feel the intense emotions that the persecuted Black man has dealt with throughout his life. I can sympathize and try to imagine what physical and psychological damage has been done, but I will never truly know. Empathy, not understanding is the key to my reaction. And for now I am passively reacting. I will not participate in the protest gatherings. However, I don't want to stand silent. I believe my role for now is to write and hopefully record something that might help in some small way. It's what I can now control.

The laws are in the hands of the politicians. Unscrambling this mess and discovering the truth, providing the solutions is the responsibility of our elected leaders. Whether I like it or not this is the law of order as I see it. And now it appears that our entire body of leaders have no real plan. By many others across the sea, our whole country is considered a terrorist group.

Quite obviously for the past several days Covid-19 has moved from the center stage, behind the national and global protesting and rioting. In comparison, if I look at the pandemic today I can no longer hear the cry of emergency. In my county of 503,000 people we have 564 confirmed cases, a little more than 1 out of a thousand people have been infected. In the state of California the figures are closer to 1 in 500. It must be understood that the figures used are subject to misinterpretation since our data gathering and testing is rather rampant.

There was a study done in New York taking 15.000 deaths and breaking them up by demographics. 75% were known to have underlying health issues. But of all 15,000, 96% were 45 or over. Based on this study many people feel that it was not necessary to close down all of the schools and universities in the country? Two sides of the flipped coin, which today is still very much up in the air spinning. It may never land on the ground to show which side of this prevailing argument has won.

In my small town of Healdsburg a population of around 11,000 we have recently constructed a new traffic controlling circle, a round-about. The project lasted well over a year. It ran into all kinds of problems and went way over budget but it is finally completed and now whenever I hop in my car to go just about anywhere, I go through the new round-about. The idea of a round-about or traffic circle is to handle the flow of traffic at a busy junction in a more expedient fashion.

It operates in a simple manner, as you approach the circle you see if other vehicles are in or entering into your section of the circle. If so, yield, if not, go. You successfully merge with the traffic of 4 other roads. They have each come from every opposite direction possible.

This traffic circle is analogous to our present life condition. As we approach a congested spot in our life we may find that someone has been there before us and has built something to help us get through. It may have been difficult to arrive at the solution of the problem, but it has been fixed for us. Often many people are trying to reach this spot at the same time, and get through it as quickly as possible, but they all need to be aware of the other person's presence.

At the new Healdsburg traffic circle there are five roads coming together, five different people with five different personalities from five different perspectives, all at the same spot. If one person doesn't follow the correct approach, a huge accident may occur. Everyone will suddenly be affected, some might become injured, even die. It is without question that they will all be affected.

In order to pass this spot safely, we all must work together, circling around, some in front, others in back. It doesn't matter where we're going, but for that moment we must forget about any aggressive driving habits and work as one. We must maintain the same speeds, follow the driving laws that make it work, and watch out for each other.

We are now at a big traffic circle, we are all in this together, we're at the point when we must all act responsibly. Many others have been here before, and to deal with the present pandemic, we have adopted the plan that those before us developed, staying at home and social distancing. We can look at the 2009 swine flu, or back to the 1918 pandemic. In 1918 the actions taken were similar to what we're doing now, really old-fashioned public health measures. We're actually hiding from the virus by using these same measures, hoping to buy time to a point when a vaccine may be ready.

As for the racial issue, today the entire world is experiencing protests and riots too numerous to mention. Similar to the Watts riot, Harlem riots, Detroit, Chicago, Rodney King riots, there's not a section of our country that hasn't been affected, and it appears as if in the past, we didn't learn enough to fix the problem. We all drove to this point in our lives, we came here of our own free will. Our needs demanded that we now face this human traffic circle.

Have we progressed and learned something from the past? Did the previous riots and subsequent actions change our society in a constructive manner? I honestly don't think so. However, this time in our history may be different. We must slowly approach this circle, proceed with caution and yield to one another as necessary. The Healdsburg traffic circle is working just fine. We all pass through it every day.

JUNE 1, 1988

My daughter Mia, my friend Billy Michaels and his girlfriend Cathy and of course myself have been in Jamaica now for about a week. We have a rented car and have been around the entire island. We took a boat cruise up a river, visited Bob and Rita Marley's home in Kingston, that is now a quaint museum. We drove up the Blue Mtn. region, famous for its excellent coffee, went swimming in the falls at Ocho Rios, and have more or less hit all the tourist hotspots. We're having a great trip.

Billy has a friend here who is helping guide us to some nice off the beaten path spots. Reggae music, my favorite, is everywhere, the car radio, the teenagers' boomboxes , we even hear Bob, Jimmy Cliff, Peter Tosh, Gregory Isaacs and the rest of them coming from the houses as we drive around the island. Many older folks sit on their front porches, smoke ganja and tune in to the reggae music. Music that has now been spread around the world. Thank you Bob Marley.

JUNE 2, 2020

The protests continued last night throughout the country, some peacefully and others violent. This is now the 6th day in a row. Last night New York city had fires and looters. Washington DC called out the National Guard and military helicopters. In Birmingham Alabama rioters tore down a confederate monument. Of course Minneapolis continues to boil as cops and protesters face off. Even smaller cities everywhere are not spared and are experiencing curfews in an attempt to control the rage.

Citizens, normally peaceful, are getting dragged into this battle, often unaware of the real problem, the source of the cause for which they are fighting. The violence bounces back and forth from the protectors to the offenders, from the police to the protesters. It's difficult or impossible to remember Rodney King saying "Why can't we all just get along," when your lighting fires and running away into the dark.

When Martin Luther King accepted the Nobel Peace prize, he said, "Nonviolence is the answer to the crucial political and moral questions of our time, man must overcome oppression and violence without resorting to oppression and violence. Man must evolve for all human conflict a method which rejects revenge, aggression and retaliation." His words go unheeded. At this point there have been thousands of arrests, five deaths and millions of dollars worth of damage.

Of course our politicians continue fighting with each other assigning blame to the opposite party. There is one thing that does appear to me to be true and that is that much of the violence is being triggered by outside organized forces intent on creating fear and chaos. I can only guess that their goal is to tear down our delicate structure of personal freedom, and in essence to destroy the United States.

Since the turn of the century, our country has been the world leader. Our standard of living, our democracy has been the envy of most of the free world. Today I see my section of the world in a state of change. Our country seems to be drifting away into a place of disorder and utter confusion.

We no longer trust our government. Today, as I write, much of the country is experiencing a mild form of anarchy. I do however believe all is not lost, despite the fact that much of our inner structure seems to be built on a "house of cards." I feel that the greatest weapons we have to fight inequality, social injustice, are not stones, bricks or matches, but the things that democracy has given us, the right to have peaceful protest demonstrations, the right to use passive resistance, and mass action. Martin Luther King, Gandhi, Nelson Mandela, these are the leaders whose actions we should be emulating. What is happening today is a disgrace to their honor.

JUNE 3, 1964

I am preparing for my graduation from high school. Tomorrow's the big day. In reality this will be a little disappointing for me. I switched to Palm Beach High from the Catholic school Cardinal Newman last year and it was a mistake. I should have stayed in Cardinal Newman so I could continue playing sports, especially basketball. I've made some new friends while I've been here, but I don't feel as close to them as I did to my other friends from CN. Oh well, live and learn, I guess.

Bob Dylan has just released another new hit "The Times They Are a-Changin" talking about the changes happening in society. Things are changing alright. I have never experienced such a radical time as this. Not only are people on the streets protesting the Vietnam war, but the civil rights issue is coming to everyone's home, on the radio, TV and in family discussions.

There were no Black kids at Cardinal Newman and I only know of one here in Palm Beach High. We definitely live in a segregated society. I hope that all of the Jim Crow laws that legalized segregation will be overturned. President Johnson is supposed to sign a new Civil Rights Bill next month on July 2. The law will forbid discrimination based on race, color, religion, sex, or national origin, and end unfair voter registration. Racial segregation in schools, at the workplace and by facilities that served the general public will be illegal.

JUNE 3, 2020

No signs of the protests fading today, but the majority are peaceful. Perhaps the young firebrands are mellowing. The fight continues in the minds and hearts of us fortunate to be living in America. Our leader still resorts to the violent approach. Yesterday he had his henchmen, his military guards use gas grenades and shoot rubber bullets into peaceful protesters. He was walking to a photo op in front of a church so he could portray himself as "holier than thou," holding up a bible.

I try so hard to resist my natural urge to despise this man. There are many amongst us who don't share my feelings, and personally I don't cherish conflict. Sadly, I often dwell on the America I remember as a child and long to return to that place. I hope to stay on subjects that unite us all, despite our differences.

THEORY OF COMPARATIVE RELATIVITY

I met a man the other day, he looked quite strange, I'd say. His hair was long, he wore a beard. Unlike me, he must be weird. He looked at me, his eyes were kind. I felt as if he knew my mind. He touched my hand, he began to speak. My body shuttered, my legs went weak.

"My son, if only thou could see, from the eye of God, objectively.
It's not for us to hurt our brothers, to compare ourselves with any
others."

"But, you don't look like folks from here. Even your clothes are a
little queer."

"Since our earthly lives are not the same, be careful of becoming
bitter or vain

For deep inside we are all just one, the total creation, you see my
son."

"You mean if I would criticize you, that I will be harming myself
too."

"God's creation is a marvelous story, made of wonder, joy and
glory,

Judging others builds a huge stone wall, preventing you from
seeing it all."

Written sometime in the mid seventies

What we are experiencing today is obviously the result of a
government's failure. This racial inequality, and these types of
confrontations that are occurring almost every day, have existed
since before my childhood. All legal and constitutional means to
deal with racial oppression and inequality have obviously failed.
Economic equality is crucial to racial equality. But at nearly every
stage of their lives, Black Americans have had less than whites.

How is it, that as a nation, we still can not see past the color
of a man's skin. Several years ago the Black quarterback of the
San Francisco 49ers (my team incidentally, ha) Colin Kappernick,
knelt on one knee as the Star Spangled Banner was being played.
He was protesting the cause of racial injustice. The result of his
action terminated his career in football forever. For many he
had disrespected our flag, our country. Well if he was placing his
personal feelings above the respect due to "Old Glory" then so be

it. Those in power in the NFL said there was no place for such action on our playing field.

As ironic as it is, the white police officer who is responsible for today's national upheaval also knelt on one knee, holding it there on a Black man's throat for over 8 minutes. Since he represents justice, that is, the Police Department represents justice, nobody questioned his action, not the bystanders, not his four fellow officers. They watched as George Floyd cried for help, cried for his "mama," and the life drained out of him. Those officers are not our protectors at all, they are the arsonists. They are not the guardians of justice, they are the destroyers.

The search for truth and justice has created the response that we are now witnessing, a response demanding fairness in our policing system, our current system may lead to national suicide. If our government does not provide such a system, the goal must be self-rule and anarchy. This is a critical moment in our history, long overdue. As I have written, we have dealt with these exact issues many times in my life, and very little has changed.

Hundreds of thousands of people continue to gather in the streets each night. Not only in our country but in all of Europe. Paris streets are filled with 20,000 protesters. Despite a ban on public gatherings due to Coronavirus, people are banding in solidarity to reflect on racial injustice and police violence. Four years ago in Paris, a Black man, Adama Traore died in police custody. They are publicly denouncing his unjust death and paying homage to his memory, marching through Paris streets with signs like BLACK LIVES MATTER and WITHOUT JUSTICE, THERE IS NO PEACE. This has been triggered by George Floyd's death, Parisians are protesting in solidarity with the USA.

These actions in other countries make me realize that although America has serious problems, people are hoping that we might once again become the beacon of freedom that we had been for so long. I take solace that our protests here are looked upon as politically and morally correct. It takes my mind away from the violence. I just read that the protests in France extended to the streets of Lyon, Marseille and Lille. Meanwhile, further protests have been planned throughout France this week, in Paris, Strasbourg and Nice. The reaction is now a global issue. Protests are happening in Canada, in London, Germany, Wales, and Italy. Throughout the world most political leaders are involved.

I hope there is a permanent light at the end of this tunnel, a beacon of justice, an eternal flame that will serve as a symbol of an enduring nature, our changed human nature. Joe Biden, the Democratic candidate for presidency in a speech yesterday spoke about what America is and means, he invoked Harriet Tubman and Frederick Douglas as examples of patriots who saw the country emerge from crisis better, fairer, stronger. I can believe this.

I must have faith that Trump's actions are not a government covert plan to invoke martial law. I see these world protests as a natural reaction caused by horrible injustices and we will all survive this sporadic violence. Peace will return to the streets.

I used to think that the opposite of faith is fear, perhaps it is in a sense, but I believe more accurately that certainty better describes faith's opposite.

Being said, there is no certainty as to the outcome of all of this. It follows that everyone, every single living soul, must have faith. My faith is a hope for political, social, industrial and economic change. We must raise the standard of living for all minorities across the globe. We must stop industrial pollution. We must care for those people who need help. As a result the change will affect all races, and every demographic statistic will be affected in a positive manner.

We are all as strong as the weakest link in the chain of our society. Raising up the poorest amongst us is not only our moral responsibility, it is the only way we will survive. I'm currently inspired by the idea "strong ideas, loosely held." As I see it, we must have correct solutions but if necessary in order to implement positive changes, we may need to compromise. So be it.

The Corona virus is still top news as it continues infecting us on a large scale. We very much need to come out of this pandemic as different people. We must understand that disease is caused by an imbalance. In order to heal any sickness and prevent a disruption in the balance of nature, we should not emerge from our lockdown as the same people. We need to come out of this and reconnect to our earth. We need to act with respect to the planet as a whole living entity, we are an integral part of the whole, and have the power to fix this.

We can no longer deplete our natural resources and continue polluting with no regard to the future. This unhealthy planet we now inhabit is without doubt contributing to our condition. We can not build up our immune system when we breathe, drink and eat poison every day. Above all else, as we come out of this lockdown, we need to treat all life with the respect it deserves. Not just human life, but every animal, every flower, every bee, and every butterfly, bird, fox, chicken, cow and pig.

Despite what some think, we are no better, no different than the smallest insect in relation to the inter-connected plan of life here on this planet. Einstein said "If we lose the bees, we have about four more years left on this earth." We should no longer participate in animal cruelty and stand by allowing the heartless, insane management practices that are being used by our factory farms. We must open our eyes and find mercy in our hearts. We should no longer permit giant agriculture to practice chemical farming. It's possible to bring back the smaller family farms that existed when I was a child and a young man.

It is happening. There are progressive thinking people who are succeeding with smaller organic farms, this needs to increase. We need to support these practices whenever we can. If racial equality is not happening around us we need to work and make it happen.

5

Costa Rica

I'm 43 years old and I honestly feel as if I'm still in the prime of my life. I live in Costa Rica, which is a free democratic society. The government is stable, I have a wonderful life here, producing documentaries as a one man producer, shooter, editor, and sales team. For those of you who have not visited this charming country, I should tell you that you better come down now and see it in its glory day.

A few years ago tourism overtook the exportation of bananas and coffee as the number one industry. I am sadly witnessing the change that tourism inevitably brings with it. Most unfortunately tourism doesn't just gently walk on the beaches and through the virgin rainforests and then disappear without a trace. Along with the needed dollars that are brought here, there are some nasty looking strings attached. Cultural changes are slowly happening and will increase existentially. Some of the Costa Ricans want to be like the tourists that they are now serving. They want the large bank account, the nice cars, the beautiful house with five bedrooms and a pool.

I can only say, "be careful what you ask for." The grass is not always greener on the other side of the fence. Beach property that has been in the same family for generations is now up on the market to the highest bidder. The time when sufficient is a feast has disappeared. The exact thing that people come to see is what their actions are taking away. It's a lose lose situation.

There is nothing that I can do or anyone can do to prevent this, other than close the borders. Many more people will come to Costa Rica to experience the joy that nature can bring. Some will want to stay, develop it to their liking, build more hotels or housing projects, put in golf courses, make money. I can recall in Palm Beach county when I was young, experiencing the discovery of Florida by retirees from the North East. I saw a bumper sticker that perfectly describes my feelings, "We don't care how you did it in New York."

The beauty of watching a pair of Scarlet Macaws who mate for life, fly through the air, land in a coconut tree or in an almond grove on the sandy beach is truly beyond description. Most any day I see troops of monkeys making their way through the treetops and toucans and sloths, all living in supportive habitats. If I am working, travelling by river or through canals I see crocodiles, caymans and of course an incredible variety of birdlife, unmatched throughout the world.

When I'm in the larger cities I witness a diversity of people all pooled together without any signs of racial inequality. In the smaller towns and villages throughout the country everyone is operating at a much slower pace than I was used to in the USA. "PURA VIDA" is an expression used by everyone, as a greeting when taxi drivers pass each other, or as a goodbye on parting slogan, used by all Costa Ricans. Costa Rica is truly a paradise. I feel blessed to be here.

JUNE 4, 1989, BEIJING, CHINA

In May this year nearly a million Chinese students and others held mass protests calling for greater democracy and an end to corruption at Tiananmen Square in the center of Beijing. Today Chinese troops with tanks and armored cars stormed Tiananmen Square killing hundreds of protesters when firing into the crowd indiscriminately and arresting thousands of pro democracy protesters some of who are still in jail. Such an inhumane event as the Tiananmen Square massacre could never take place here in our country.

JUNE 4, 2020

Today's news: TRUMP THREATENS TO CALL OUT THE MILITARY.

Yesterday afternoon Trump's former defense secretary, James Mattis sharply criticized the Trump administration's response to the protests. "Donald Trump is the first president in my lifetime who does not try to unite the American people — does not even pretend to try," Mattis told The Atlantic. "Instead he tries to divide us." He further said that Trump has made a mockery of our constitution by using the military to break up a peaceful demonstration. His own Defense Secretary Mark Esper said that active-duty military troops should not be used to quell protests. And General Mark A Milley who's chairman of the Joint Chiefs of Staff reminded commanders that members of the armed forces had sworn an oath to the Constitution which "gives Americans the right to freedom of speech and peaceful assembly."

This afternoon Trump had the military precede him on a walk to a church and spray peaceful protester with tear gas, throw flash bombs and shoot rubber bullets, in violation of the first amendment.

Last night I went to visit Danny, a friend of mine, a very smart man with a memory like you read about. Danny and I sort of embody the phrase "I agree to disagree." During these crazy times when political influences are so dominating in daily life, it's hard to ignore those holding the ruler.

So Danny's got Fox News on his outdoor TV, the right wing station, and he's getting fired up with each story that comes on. I'm sitting there as they tell us that only 10 unarmed Black men were killed by the cops last year. To me the approach of Fox News to this issue is absolutely sinful. Danny starts raving when he sees a protester with the "Black Lives Matter" sign. "What about white lives," he says. Danny just doesn't get it.

I don't openly disagree with Danny since he's my friend and I know I will never be able to change his mind. I think my inaction has to do with our personalities and also with my conviction that most political hardliners as I say, will never, ever, ever change their mind. There is a psychological term, "Integrative Complexity,". It is the ability to develop and hold opposing traits, values, and ideas and then integrate them into larger ones. Danny and I obviously, are not integratively complex.

Sorry Danny, but I need to express this to ease my own conscience. In a few months you will be voting for a man who has no decency, no class, no charm, no coolness, no wit, no warmth, no credibility, no compassion, no wisdom, no subtlety, no sensitivity, no self-awareness, no humility, no honor and no grace.

I honestly believe since our "shelter in place" order I can see more lines coming into Danny's face and a sad angrier look. He and his fellow right wingers are nearly up in arms about the response that has been taken to the Coronavirus outbreak. The attitude being, "It's just another way to take away our freedom."

On top of this health pandemic we must deal with the issue of rioting protesters at their worst. If two opposing sides should ever come together it would involve the ability to move from one extreme to the other as the occasion requires. I see the young Black man who breaks into the store and runs away with a giant flat screen TV, as a person who has lived his entire life in poverty and despair and just got a TV in the only way he imagines that he would ever get it.

The right winger sees a dreadful criminal who should be shot. Conventional tribal wisdom says that the right winger and I should pick either side of every polarity and vehemently fight for it. A complex personality does not imply neutrality, or the average. It does not imply, for instance, being wishy-washy, so that one is never very competitive or very cooperative.

In Danny's mind he feels that his future is doomed, but when the situation turns critical with serious food shortages, as he anticipates, he wants to go out fighting, I can definitely see where Danny is heading, a brilliant man uninformed is not a pretty display.

A big part of the right wingers and actually most Republicans' essential needs, during all this, is to have your weapons loaded and ready. The second amendment in it's worse interpretation. Sometimes Danny is happier than at other times, and those are the times I prefer to be with him. Despite our radical political differences we remain friends. There are times when we arrive at some position at the midpoint between two poles. Danny's a good person. More than likely he'll say the same thing about me.

For the record, I consulted Mapping Police Violence.org, and came up with the following stats. The figures are for 2015, I didn't find any more recent.

- Police killed at least 104 unarmed Black people in 2015, nearly twice each week. Nearly 1 in 3 Black people killed by police in 2015 were identified as unarmed, though the actual number is likely higher due to underreporting.
- 36% of unarmed people killed by police were Black in 2015 despite Black people being only 13% of the U.S. population
- Unarmed Black people were killed at 5x the rate of unarmed whites in 2015
- Only 13 of the 104 cases in 2015 where an unarmed Black person was killed by police resulted in officer(s) being charged with a crime. 4 of these cases have ended in a mistrial or charges against the officer(s) being dropped and 4 cases are still awaiting trial or have a trial underway. Only 4 cases (Matthew Ajibade, Eric Harris, Paterson Brown Jr., and William Chapman) have resulted in convictions of officers involved, with

a fifth case (Walter Scott) resulting in the officer pleading guilty.I will soon be with my other friend Phil, on a sailboat in San Francisco Bay, tacking and jibing. As always heading out under the Golden Gate Bridge to see what we can see. To breathe in the clean cool air and talk about all the things that come up. I am very close to Phil. He's a retired physician who has traveled the world many times over and has stories that could fill this novel. Incidentally Phil will be voting for Biden. So, until tomorrow, Bon Voyage and Pura Vida.

JUNE 5, 2020

Had a wonderful day sailing as usual. San Francisco Bay is always exciting. It is never without wind. The inland areas to the East are always hot, especially in the summer, as a result, the cold ocean air is pulled through the Golden Gate. We often experience gusts up to 30 knots. In addition to strong winds, large tankers are coming in and out of the Richmond refineries and lots of big cargo ships carrying containers are coming and going from the port of Oakland to China. We have noticed obvious changes in the goods coming into Oakland since the lockdown. The ships have often been near empty or half full. They are "high in the water." Yesterday the one ship that we did see, was loaded to capacity.

Sailing in the Bay is not at all like much of my previous years of sailing. In those places of the Caribbean, the winds were mild and I would often be sprawled out on the bow, getting brown and drinking a margarita or guzzling a couple beers. In those days we would always be pulling a fishing line behind us. I do miss that a lot. Phil and I are planning to put out a crab pot next year when the season opens and at my suggestion we do have some fishing gear on board. But honestly, so far the wind has kept us from dropping a line.

Most of our conversation yesterday as we cruised along under full sail, dealt with the unpleasant current events. We related our present condition with the "story" of our lives. Since we are close in age, our pasts were developed in a common culture, a common way of life. Today life's conditions are entirely different from the past that Phil and I grew up in. Our story of hope doesn't fit in so well. Way before Covid-19 and George Floyd appeared, even then, the plight of our planet, the status of our future, appeared rather bleak.

I will be repeating the same message throughout this book. My writing is often streaming thought. With each day, in some way, I begin a new life. Homo Sapiens have stepped way outside of our natural boundaries, tromping on everything in our way. Our assault on the interconnectedness of life has destroyed any semblance of ecological balance. The material items that man has created now outweighs all of the natural biomass of the planet.

Not enough of us realize or care enough about this issue to initiate any change. Worldwide pollution, desertification, global warming, food and water shortages, all lay testimony to this. These are without question the world's most pressing issue. Those of us on the planet who are not starving or struggling every day to survive must assume the responsibility to fix what has been broken. The repair needs to begin on a microbial level. We must re-establish a healthy bond with all life.

We are not separated from the viruses or the bacteria, the fungi or the parasites that float in the air and live within us. We are actually about 10 to 1, bacteria to humans. Today our bodies are filled with antibiotics that are killing and mutating the good bacteria. The effect is, our natural makeup is changing.

The poisoning of our planet began in a most serious way the year that my middle son Abel was born, in 1975. That's when Monsanto succeeded in marketing Roundup, its active ingredient is a chemical called glyphosate, introduced as an herbicide and pest killer. Chemical farming began worldwide, no more tilling necessary.

The medical world was soon to discover associations with Roundup use and cancer increases. Of course Monsanto broke out with their paid medical experts to dispute this finding and, naturally their best paid lawyers began to fight any charges against them. It seems they have laboratory studies where rats were injected with the Roundup chemicals and guess what, no ill effects. But you know what is really happening to those rats? Their DNA is becoming altered. Their babies are being born with many abnormalities and genetic weaknesses. Quite sadly, the third generation of lab rats are even worse.

Roundup is water soluble, meaning that it also floats in the air. We are breathing it in. We eat it in our foods and drink it in our water. It is most certainly making its way from farms to our dinner tables, and from polluted water sources into our drinking water. The fight between so called responsible scientific advancements and deliberate health damaging action rages on.

In 2015, the World Health Organization's cancer agency dealt Monsanto a crippling blow. It determined that glyphosate is "probably carcinogenic to humans." This finding has led to a number of pro Roundup findings that contradict the WHO. The Environmental Protection Agency this month responded to the WHO's decision with pushback. It announced it will not approve such labels for products containing glyphosate, saying it would "Constitute a false and misleading statement."

California's Office of Environmental Health Hazard Assessment called the EPA's decision a mischaracterization of the law, adding that it is "Disrespectful of the scientific process." This fight is so similar to the Republican/Democrat fight. This leads me to assume that all those denying the horrible effects brought on by Roundup are the right wingers and those who would immediately ban Roundup are the left, so called by the right, as a bunch of dumb liberals wanting to stop the "money making machine" and destroy our lovely economy. So many of the agricultural farm workers happen to be illegal Mexican immigrants and God above knows that they are amongst the groups that are being extremely affected.

The Roundup story doesn't stop here, it gets much worse. In 1996 Monsanto created what are called "Roundup Ready Plants."

These are genetically modified plants, organisms, "GMOs" that are resistant to Roundup. Roundup Ready crop seeds have notoriously been referred to as "terminator seeds." This is because the crops produced from Roundup Ready seeds are sterile. Each year, farmers must purchase the most recent strain of seed from Monsanto.

The first to come out of the lab was a soybean. By planting these GMO seeds Roundup can be sprayed by plane over the entire field without killing the soybeans. That means that every single form of life in that field will be killed, not only weeds and all plant life, but every insect, every earthworm, every honey bee and butterfly, etc. Only the mutated genetically modified soybean survives.

Around the globe some of these farms are as large as 30 square miles. Here's the worse part, the soybean is taking in the roundup as it grows, usually before harvest it has been sprayed three times. And then it heads to market winding up in so much of the processed foods that we buy off of the grocery shelves. The majority of these soybeans as well as the GMO corn that was next to be developed by Monsanto goes into our animal feed. The poor inhumanely treated animals who have no way to argue this such as I do. They are fed these poisons, and are consumed by most humans at dinner time along with the other GMO veggies on the plate. It's enough to make you sick.

Sarcasm or irony I'm not sure, but it's the cards that we have dealt ourselves, and if we hope to survive for a few more generations we must change all of this. In addition to corn and soybeans, we now use GMO seeds for cotton (for oil), canola (also a source of oil), squash, papaya, sugar beets, which aren't eaten directly, but refined into sugar. There's also GMO alfalfa, sorghum, and wheat GMO versions of tomatoes, potatoes, and rice have been created and approved by government regulators, but they aren't commercially available, yet.

WHAT'S WITH EMMO

I had a friend named Emmo who was big and strong. Despite his appearances, something was wrong. His skin looked good and his hair was thick. But he always acted like he was a little sick. I could see when he smiled that his teeth were white, but I never told him, his breath wasn't right.

Now Emmo seemed like a really nice guy. He had many rich friends and I often wondered why.

As we got older there was something strange, I was aging, but Emmo didn't change. He never got married, never tried to have a kid. He didn't act like my other friends did.

He became like a person I had never known. We all raised families, but he stayed alone. He seemed to get stronger, and his appearance got better. Then one day he sent me this letter.

"My dear friend Tom, I have a secret to tell, people think I'm perfect, but my life is hell. There's something about me that I've never told. I don't have any parents and I never grow old. I've never had any sisters or brothers. And I don't ever care what happens to others. I have no morals, Please Tom, help me if you can."

"Gee Emmo, you weren't created by God, you were made by man. I'll tell you something Emmo, you're not gonna like, but for the sake of the world, go take a hike."

I wrote that little poem in 1980, 34 years old, living in the mountains of North Carolina, raising Abel and my young daughter Mia. I was a "Back to the Land" type of guy, learning about gardening, raising bees, and I had just finished building my log house. Forty years have passed and my hope that Emmo might take a hike has not happened.

JUNE 6, 1968

Senator Bobby Kennedy died today. He was shot yesterday in a Los Angeles Hotel. shortly after leaving the podium, where he had conducted a press conference. He was exiting through a kitchen hallway, when he was mortally wounded by multiple shots fired from a handgun. Such a horrible tragedy. Bobby Kennedy was a true patriot and may have become our next president. Our country and the world has just suffered a shocking loss. Another heinous act dealt to the already suffering Kennedy family. It is a very sorry day in the history of our country.

JUNE 6, 2020

This morning as I watch the news I'm having a cup of warm lemon water. For the last few years I have followed the same routine, around this time of year I switch from my morning routine of black coffee to the warm lemon water. When the lemon tree outside my front door demands me to pick off the winter crop and make way for the new beautiful little lemon fruit buds that are developing, I cooperate. Nature is forcing me to do the right thing. The internet is filled with information lauding the benefits of drinking warm lemon water in the morning on an empty stomach. Besides the vitamin C and other beneficial minerals, it supposedly protects you from immune system deficiencies. It acts as a detoxifying agent, helps in maintaining the pH balance of the body. The list goes on and on, and I need everything on the list.

The amazing part of this coffee to lemons switch, is that my brain part dealing with habitual behavior doesn't recognize that I've made the switch. I don't miss coffee one bit. I successfully and unconsciously trick my brain by using the same coffee cup, practicing identical sip timing. I could be sitting in a Starbucks and no one would notice that I'm a traitor to the cause. Not even the expert Guatemalan coffee grower would notice my switch has taken place again. There had been a number of times in the past when I had cut off my morning coffee intake and I always noticed without fail, the dull, "where's my caffeine" headache as it crept up about mid afternoon. But this doesn't happen. It's truly a miracle brain tricking psychosomatic marvel.

I absolutely loved watching all of the butterflies this spring as they swarmed the lemon tree and did their pollination work. It seemed to go on forever. Every time I took the time to sit on the deck, the butterfly army was there. I expected that the next day they would be gone, but each day they found some new little flowers. Such an incredible joy. It is truly testimony to the fact that our species are coherently linked together.

This week has brought about a general decrease in Corona virus victims and more and more businesses are beginning to open their doors. People will need to continue social distancing but for sure this will greatly improve the morale of the owners and shoppers as it will lessen the effects of the emotional distancing that has been forced on us. The economy is still in recession but the stock market remains stable. The stock market is such a gambling game. The big time players look ahead about 12 months on average, so I guess they have faith that we will pull through this.

When I first moved to California I was taken with the energy that liberal causes create. Being in close proximity to Berkely of course had its influence. It seems that Berkely is the liberal capital of the universe. I became caught up in the many fights for justice that took place on a weekly basis. My first protest march was for the civil rights of Latino farmworkers. This was being heralded by Caesar Chavez, who in 1994 won the Presidential Medal of Freedom, posthumously. Caesar had been a farm laborer, and worked to create labor unions for all farmworkers.

As our group marched down the route along Market Street in San Francisco we came upon another protesting group, marching towards us, on the opposite side of the street. 'Palestinian Rights' was their cause. As we passed, we smiled and shook hands, gave high fives, and peace signs. It may not have been an unusual circumstance for many Bay Area residents to see such a thing, two different organized protest marches at the same place at the same time. For me it made quite an impression. I realized as I was calling out, "no compra uvas," I could just as well have been shouting for a free Palestine state. At that moment the cause was overshadowed by the principle. It's not quite the same today.

The first step in any effort to promote change is to have a thorough understanding of the problem. Intelligence has been described as the ability to adapt to change. Many of those who took place in the riots this week probably understand the cause for which they were protesting, but have no knowledge of any solution to the problems that have forced these conditions. There are others in the march that could easily have reversed their direction and began marching with those protesting the governmental lockdowns due to the Coronavirus. In many cases it's not the exact cause but rather the principle of injustice that promotes such responses. Some people are made with an ability to identify with the feelings, thoughts, or attitudes of others by means of empathy, a great painting becomes a mirror of the self, and lack of empathy assuredly paints an ugly one.

It is sad to say but the violent looters' ranks were more than likely filled with criminal opportunists, and misguided youth, out to have fun, get some free stuff and prove their manhood. Others in the ranks found these riots a way to quell their smoldering anger. Many people have been sterilized since birth against any empathy or compromise. Those are the impossible ones. They eventually wind up as residents of our prison system.

During these turbulent times everyone needs to remember the words of the amazing Albert Einstein, "Political passions, once they have been fanned into flame, exact their victims." By far, the huge majority of this week's protesters have been non-violent. In unity they find a means to express themselves in ways that matter. And I honestly feel that these protests, this massive resistance against not only police racial injustice but also racial inequalities in general, has succeeded.

This is obviously an issue that people around the world recognize and identify with. Tens of thousands turned out in Australia, Britain, France, Germany and other nations in support of U.S. protests against the death of George Floyd, while denouncing racism in their own countries as well. In Japan, Sweden, even Zimbabwe many came out on their streets in protest. All being in solidarity with those in our country and others who found valid reasons to join the fight.

In Santa Cruz my youngest son Zac is soon to finish his studies. He will graduate from UC Santa Cruz with a degree in neuroscience. I will surely be talking more about him. We are very close and along with Abel and Mia, he and his mom Suzanne are the most important people in my life. Earlier this week the police chief of Santa Cruz went in public down on one knee. His action prompted other officials around the country to do the same. White people like Chief Mills are able to correctly interpret the sign "Black Lives Matter." Many Black people on all levels read that sign now and feel that maybe, finally, their lives do matter.

Action is being made to change the way police are dealing with any minority confrontation. When a Black person is arrested it should be done in the same manner as if the cops were arresting their mother or their daughter. The police academy has given them physical training, and knowledge of weaponry, and the ways to engage in a violent situation. The badge they wear is not a revolver or a rifle. It is a shield and should represent a defensive approach to any and all action.

I can see, I can hope that this time period will define our generation, and equal civil rights for every man, woman and child of all races will emerge from this. I pray that we change now and forever, and in two or three years from now we don't go back to the old ways of racial inequality. We don't see people flooding the streets again. There will probably be a time when I go back to drinking black coffee, but for now I am practicing the better way. And besides, if I do go back to the old way of drinking coffee, It will only affect me.

6

"Good Morning America"

JUNE 7, 2020

Not the best of good in Good Morning, but I assume it's as good as it's gonna get for a while. This is the sad interpretation of how my mornings start. I have just watched the Sunday morning news. I watched and absorbed as the analysis of what is happening in America was discussed and hashed about. People like Attorney General William Barr, former Secretary of State Condoleeza Rice, NYC Mayor Blasio, along with a few other qualified government representatives, talked about current issues. The general message was not revealing.

They all spoke of changes that needed to be made, that we needed to identify and address our differences to prevent such disgraceful rioting. "Policing is the toughest job in the country, but we must change the police use of force policies." At one point Barr was asked about the police force used against the peaceful protesters as Trump walked to his photo op in front of the church. He smirked and said, "Well for one thing, it wasn't a peaceful protest, that's a lie." The reporter responded, "What do you mean, two of our reporters were there Mr. Barr and it was indeed peaceful." He immediately changed the subject. I am positively convinced that Trump is a pathological liar, but it looks like our present "group in charge" blindly play 'follow the leader.' Mayor Blasio did site specific changes that he is initiating in New York, He will be creating a new department designed to listen to the people. The funding will be taken from the police budget. Hopefully others around the country will take similar actions.

Next up, I watched people that are "significantly relative to the present condition," (so deemed by the news channel) from many other countries, weigh in, Angela Merkel from Germany, a government representative from Russia, and Liu Xin who is the voice of China Global television. Her program, an English language program, is broadcast around the world, 30 million listeners a day. There was a Frenchman, a British reporter and a British politician also reporting and educatedly guessing on everything. They all shared the same opinions. Basically they spoke, as I expected they would, as to how and why our country has changed and what America has become in the eyes of the world. Not good news I'm afraid.

All my life, America has been the world's benevolent leader, the champion of democracy and human rights, the most powerful nation, respected by everyone as a protector of liberty and human rights. Our government has never controlled its people through fear and domination, but I'm afraid that is where we are heading if we don't change. November, election day, can not come soon enough for me. Listening to Trump is like listening to a young child trying to explain quantum physics.

In order to remain an optimist I force myself to think intuitively and spiritually, because logical and empirical thought is not the language that I hear from our government. It's tough at times to remain hopeful, and to expect that our future actions will get us out of the social and environmental messes that we have created. But it can be done, I know that we have the answers, and the technology to initiate such change.

I can stop being an evolutionary goof. Just as I quit watching the news today when it was halfway through, I can quit being the person who turned on that TV looking for some hope. I don't want to think that my country, my planet, has a terminal disease. I feel that in order to be a part of the needed change, I must sometimes let go of everything, give up this person that I am, let go of my identity, my belief system and my current behavior. Perhaps I have to let this body die and become something new. By starting fresh I will be able to see the transformation. As Gandhi said. "I will become the change that I wish to see in the world."

JUNE 8, 2020

A huge bright, almost full moon woke me up at 4 o'clock this morning. I tried to cover my face, roll over, stop thinking and go back to sleep. I accomplished the first two but failed on the last two. At 5 o'clock I gave in and I'm now sitting at my desk with my warm lemon water. Some of the thoughts that were infesting my brain as I tried to close it down were: Are Jesus and Santa white? How come Einstein believed in God and Stephen Hawkings didn't? The earth is so grossly over-populated, and the fact that we are on the verge of the biggest holocaust that the human species will ever experience, why are we murdering, wiping out sacred life like never before? Why would someone want to have kids? How does an 18 year old Black man view his future?

First things first. Jesus and Santa can be whatever color I want to imagine them, it's my own fantasy. The second question can never be answered, a belief in God seems to be such a personal and temporal issue, subject to change.

The answer to number three I will never know. Man has been killing each other and other things since he appeared on the planet. Perhaps there was a self serving motive in the beginning, but it is no longer that.

As for the fourth answer, I think it is so natural, so built into the human DNA memory that most people and especially females of child bearing age can not fight the urge to nurture a family, despite what everything else tells them. Children are gifts from God. The irony of this is that nature is stepping in to take care of that dilemma, despite what the young married couple desires. Males have lost 57% of sperm count in all Western countries in the past 40 years. 1 out of every 3 males is now infertile by sperm count in Western nations. Our next generation could experience an extinction level of 95% infertility. Remember the rats of Monsanto. This could really be it folks. We change now or soon the hugs we give each other will be hugs of good bye.

And finally my thoughts on the young Black man. I was in the car yesterday with my neighbor and friend Stuart. He brought the subject up and we, as old white men, tried to imagine how an 18 year old, young, strong, fine specimen of human life, Black, would see his future. Would he see himself as a good faithful married husband and provider for an average family of 3¼ people. Could he imagine himself getting married in a few years and acquiring a good job, one that has hopes for promotions and will lead to a prosperous future? Was his parental upbringing a model for such an adjusted life? Will he be able to get a fair bank loan and purchase a nice house? And of course, will he be a law abiding citizen and never get into trouble with the law, or enter a state or federal prison?

Without going into the grim details, the statistics, I will say with certainty that the odds are against him on every front. And yet so many people, white people that is, ignore these facts and complain about the protests, become angry when they see "Black Lives Matter." Through ignorance and lack of empathy they portray a crippling understanding of the facts and their state of apathetic existence unfortunately, spreads like the virus.

For most white Americans, interactions with the police rarely happen, and often they are treated respectfully, even friendly. I, similar to most of my white friends, can't think of a single person that's behind bars. As a matter of fact I can't think of anyone born into poverty either. I've listened to the story that young Black men tell. It's a story that needs to be heard by everyone. If you listen, you will hear why they wind up in prison. Twenty percent of all Black American males have similar stories to tell. Sadly for them prison is often more than a one time visit. In Oklahoma, the state with the highest overall Black incarceration rate, 1 in 15 Black males ages 18 and older is in prison.

It's no wonder so many young Black males see nothing in their futures that inspire hope.. It's no wonder these young men are now taking to the streets. For them justice comes in different colors. Even inside the prisons, racial tensions often reach boiling points and new chapters are written in the book of racial disparity. For the incarcerated Black man, perceptions of justice have no true standard. It's every man for himself . Moral rightness does not exist. It's not even considered as a possibility. And yet many Republicans, according to Fox News, just don't get it, or a more likely scenario, they just don't care. It makes me sick.

It's now lunchtime in my OK Corral. I think that's what I'll nickname my shelter in place. Everything is definitely Ok for me here. I'm super fortunate. With abounding gratitude to my great friend Julie, I'm able to live on the 'top of the mountain.' Julie owns the house and property where I have been living for the last, what seems like a hundred years. This quadrant (approximately) of my life began when I arrived from Costa Rica and called upon my ex-girlfriend, who I will now call St. Julie.

Because of circumstances Julie was about to leave little Healdsburg heading to Palo Alto, the center of Silicon Valley. She was stepping in to take over the lovely hotel that had been built by her father. It has been quite the journey for Julie, who really knew "not much" about running a Hotel. All that has changed, and she has put her heart into Dinah's Hotel. Over the past several years she has remodeled and initiated many changes. It has been a roaring success, and then came Corona.

My lunch today makes me semi-happy sorta like the semi-good of good morning these days. I'm very happy that I am wrapping my tuna fish in lettuce from my garden. The bummer is that the tuna fish I've decided to eat is probably loaded with mercury. No need to go into the details of that because if you don't know already about the danger of eating the deep water ocean fish then you probably can't or don't read. Which means you won't be reading this. The reason I'm eating this tuna fish today is three fold.

Number one, I really like good ole, once healthy, tuna fish. Number two, I figure that something else will surely take me out before mercury gets a chance. Number three, I think I've built up an immunity to mercury poisoning because when I was a kid I used to get the broken thermometers, I don't remember how they were breaking all the time, but anyway I would take out the mercury and play with it. I didn't eat it but I did everything else a young kid could do with it. Just passing it from hand to hand was amazing. If you have never played with mercury you're really missing something, liquid metal, room temperature liquid metal at that, a true wonder of nature. Mercury poisoning supposedly bestows the following symptoms upon its victims: mood swings, nervousness, muscle twitches, weakness, insomnia, declining cognitive ability, and finally depression. Uh oh, I got all of these.

As I think about this I realize that the tunas that are really loaded with mercury are not the ones that the fishermen have caught. There's no way that a tuna with all those symptoms would not be kicked out of his school. He would then be swimming haphazardly in all his weirdness, and be consumed by the nearest shark. So maybe the one I'm eating now didn't have any mercury in him. He may be the one displayed on the can, the Happy Tuna, dancing on his tail, with a big smile.

JUNE 9, 2020

Lawmakers around the country have begun to consider new policies on policing. It really appears that we are making change, the protests have worked. The general idea is to eliminate some of the work that the police do, and that they often don't even want to do, things like resolving family and school disputes, moving homeless people into shelters and so on. What it actually means, these advocates say, is that police budgets will be reduced and the money will go to funding for education, health care and other social services. Of course Trump is opposed to any logical changes and is saying that the Democrats want to eliminate the police force.

The pandemic is still holding its place as the number two newsworthy item. A new message is coming out that says we should be adjusting our behavior based on where we live. It appears that the virus numbers vary significantly by state. I think we're doing pretty good in California and I see a lot more apparently healthy human activity as I drive through Healdsburg. Last summer we would be having our regular Tuesday night "Music in the Plaza" event. I do miss this and all of the other live music events in our area that have been canceled. On most every day of the week during summer, a nearby town hosts an outdoor free night of live music. I must say On March 16, when all this began, I didn't expect we would still be locked down.

The sun is just now rising up over the mountain range to the east. It is so beautiful here. I've been up for a while, perhaps a little tuna insomnia got me. This is one of my favorite times of day. Since I quit drinking wine and all alcohol, I often sit on the deck (hangover free) and take in the "Golden Hour." All photographers and cinematographers know about the golden hour, it's the period of daytime shortly after sunrise or before sunset, during which daylight is redder and softer than when the sun is higher in the sky. During this time the brightness of the sky matches the brightness of streetlights, signs, car headlights and lit windows. Also, during this period of time there are no sharp shadows because the sun has set or hasn't risen. The golden hour actually only lasts about twenty or thirty minutes. When I was shooting documentaries in Costa Rica I hardly ever missed this opportunity.

Once during the morning golden hour, I was standing up to my knees in the warm ocean water, wanting to capture the shore break, the sandy beach and the beautiful rain forest mountain with all its forest diversity. In many parts of the rainforests of Costa Rica exists the Yliang Yliang tree, (pronounced ee-lahn ee-lahn). The flower of the Yliang Yliang tree, is the main ingredient in the perfume Chanel #5. The perfume scent is not limited to the bottles in department stores, believe me. It permeates the air around the tree and spreads through the forest. On this particular morning

I was literally hundreds of yards away from the nearest Yliang Yliang tree, but the scent was very strong. It was a special moment. I was slowly panning the camera across the scene thinking that there could never be a more beautiful time in my life. And then a pair of Scarlet Macaws flew perfectly framed across my scene. Heaven could not be imagined as a better place than this. Pura Vida Costa Rica.

I just read an article in the *LA Times* that explains perfectly what we're seeing in the protests. It was written by a Black man and honestly, it presents insight that only a Black person can see. "The slimy underbelly of institutional racism is being exposed, it feels like hunting season is open on Blacks. If there was any doubt, President Trump's recent tweets confirm the national zeitgeist as he calls protesters "thugs" and looters, fair game to be shot." The author also ties the Corona virus response into the picture. "But Covid-19 has been slamming the consequences of all that home, as we die at a significantly higher rate than whites, are the first to lose our jobs, and watch helplessly as Republicans try to keep us from voting."

I could possibly scrape the corners of my brain to add something to this article, but it would be inconsequential, since he covers it all. "So, maybe the Black community's main concern right now isn't whether protesters are standing three or six feet apart or whether a few desperate souls steal some T-shirts or even set a police station on fire, but whether their sons, husbands, brothers and fathers will be murdered by cops or wannabe cops just for going on a walk, a jog, a drive. Or whether being Black means sheltering at home for the rest of their lives because the racism virus infecting the country is more deadly than Covid-19."

I would like to tell the author Kareem Abdul-Jabbar, thank you so much. Most of the white people in this world are with you 100%. I had no idea that since you left the NBA, you have become a writer. You have found another gift within yourself that equals your basketball ability. I watched you play and followed you from college and throughout your professional career as you became the NBA's leading all time scorer. Like Caesar Chavez, you have also won the Presidential Medal of Freedom. Well deserved I'm sure. I look forward to continuing to follow you in your new leadership role.

JUNE 10, 2020

Today my son Zac finished the last final of his testing at UCSC. It's official, he will now graduate with a major in neuroscience. I can hardly express how proud I am of him. So much hard work, and he has pulled a 3.5 point average despite the intensity of mostly difficult courses. Today such an accomplishment requires countless hours of work in front of a computer, many all nighters of studying for tests, visits to the school clinic for vision problems, to the counselors for stress related issues.

It has been nearly five years now and the ride has been bumpy for me and I can not even imagine how difficult it has been for Zac. In order to do what it takes, he has given up so much of his freedom, the normal social activities of someone his age had to be put on hold. Those things consequential to a feeling of accomplishment were cast into doubt. He was often unsure if he had even chosen the right field of study. All of his natural impulses were in question as he sat behind the computer and in front of books rather than going to the Lighthouse with his surfboard.

Many, many nights Zac took loneliness and confusion, grief and sorrow to bed with him. I believe Zac's action through all this is termed "above and beyond the call of duty." But now it's over, done.

Until the day I die I will always be grateful to Julie, Uncle Jeff and Aunt Karen for their confidence and support of our boy Zac. And of course to Lauren, Zac's new wonderful girlfriend, I owe the world. However I was created, it was as a relational being. And these relationships speak to me as to what humanity should be. It shows me who we are as humans. When I see Zac, I see a bright future despite the insanity around me, I give thanks from the depths of my soul to whatever gods may be.

Almost 20,000 new cases of Coronavirus were confirmed today, even as states are working toward fully reopening. There were almost 1,000 more deaths, pushing the death toll in the US past 107,000. It is now in question about keeping schools closed this fall, once thought to be a strong but reluctant possibility. It may not be necessary for all communities. The virus still surges overseas. Brazil and Mexico both announced record numbers of Covid-19 deaths, and Pakistan has now announced more cases than China.

Today also showed the world, as Kareem Abdul-Jabbar had written, how Black citizens are treated at voting polls. In Georgia today Black voting precincts were a mess. Black voters were forced to stand in lines for as much as 8 hours to vote in primary elections. Either stand or go home without voting. Excuses were made, problems with the new voting machines, fewer workers because of the lockdowns. Such a scene is despicable and absolutely criminal in my mind. Unfortunately this is the norm for African-Americans. One study of the 2016 election, using smartphone location data, found that voters in Black neighborhoods waited 29% longer on average than voters in white neighborhoods. Michael McDonald, an elections expert at the University of Florida wrote: "I have never seen the scale of election failures happening in Georgia today. This does not bode well for November."

JUNE 11, 2020

Another day, another protest. This is day 17, and serious changes are resulting across the entire nation. In Richmond, Va., protesters ripped down a statue of the explorer and colonizer Christopher Columbus overnight and threw it into a lake. In Boston, a similar statue was beheaded. Across the country, at least 10 monuments to Confederates or other controversial historical figures have been removed, and people have challenged similar monuments in more than 20 cities.

National Football League commissioner, Roger Goodell, said the league had been wrong to discourage political protest by its players. Facing anger from employees, Adidas made a series of concessions, including a pledge that 30 percent of the people it hired would be Black or Latino. The Carolina Panthers removed a statue of the football team's former owner, Jerry Richardson, from outside its stadium in Charlotte, N.C., two years after the NFL fined him for racist comments and sexual harassment.

In Atlanta, two police officers were fired on Wednesday for their role in dragging two students from their car and shooting them with stun guns while they were stuck in traffic during a May 30 protest against police brutality, bringing to four the number of officers fired as a result of the incident.

Throughout our changing country, authors and book publishing employees are speaking publicly about pay disparity in an overwhelmingly white industry. Situations are changing, but they are far from perfect. For example on the flip side of the coin, a group of white counter protesters in New Jersey, appearing in front of a pro-Trump sign, mocked Floyd's death, with one man kneeling on the neck of another who was facedown on the ground. One of the counter protesters was a corrections officer and was quickly suspended.

Of course Trump appears, as always, on this side of the coin. He has renewed his threat to take federal action against local protesters in a late-night tweet on Wednesday, telling government officials in Washington State that they needed to crack down on demonstrators in Seattle. "If you don't take back your city, I will," he said.

George Floyd's brother is having his voice heard, on national media and in front of government panels. "Anybody with a heart," he says, "would know that how his brother was treated was wrong: You don't do that to a human being, you don't even do that to an animal." After delivering his testimony, Mr. Floyd marched to what is now known as Black Lives Matter Plaza, the area near the White House where federal officers last week used chemical spray to clear demonstrators protesting his brother's death.

The pandemic today is also showing two sides. Many businesses and social gathering places are beginning to open up, but it appears as if they are experiencing a spike in new Coronavirus cases. I guess we shall see if business interests wind up on top.

Today as the service began, the New York Stock Exchange went silent for 8 minutes, 46 seconds — the length of time a police officer held his knee on Floyd's neck. It was the longest moment of silence on the stock exchange floor in its 228-year history.

Our two pandemics continue to affect and produce changes around the world. After the lockdowns began to relax, city officials in Milan, Italy have announced that they would modify 22 miles of roads to make more room for pedestrians and bicycles. Milan transport councilor Marco Granelli explained that the city wanted alternatives to car traffic, and to public transit that would allow people to move around while staying apart.

Let's take a big leap from Italy to Brazil. Brazilian President Bolsonaro is threatening to declare martial law as the people are flocking to the streets in solidarity with the protesters in the US, and of course demanding reform in their own country as well. Their President is just as bad as Trump from what I read. He is allowing the destruction of the Amazon at unprecedented rates. So very sad. Biologists are saying that once every 20 minutes we lose another species, and I'm sure that the majority disappear from the world's rainforests.

JUNE 12, 2020

Today I again turned the news on. This is not easy for me since my instincts tell me to ignore it and get on with my happy life. But it appears as if this book has turned me into a chronicler of current events. As such I must keep up, and continue to mention the noteworthy news as I see it unfolding. I'm probably commenting on things with a slant, but despite my extreme feelings about Trump, I'm trying my best to be purple, not red or blue, but a blend of the two colors. What am I not allowing myself to see?

As well as more statues and monuments being taken or torn down everywhere throughout the US, similar actions have likewise spread around the world. Yesterday at home, the Senate, led by a

Republican committee voted behind closed doors to remove the names of Confederate officers from military bases within three years. That includes some of our very large bases. If such a bill is introduced and passed, Trump has promised to veto it. To quote the *New York Times*: "Trump increasingly sounds like a cultural relic, detached from not just the left-leaning protesters in the streets but also the country's political middle and even some Republican allies and his own military leaders."

Sometimes I just can't understand how a human being can be so out of touch, inhumane with absolutely no empathy or sympathy. I keep thinking that maybe he will become so angry inside of himself that he will decide that he can't take it any longer. He must surely know that he has lost any chance of being re-elected, (I pray that this is accurate). And that he will get up one morning and resign. Lo and behold, my wish is not going to come true. He's not going to resign today.

Despite the fact that our country's top military official, Gen. Mark Milley, apologized yesterday for having taken part in that ridiculous Trump photo op at the church. His action signifies the military's position on Trump in general. Meanwhile our bold, cocky, intrepid, brassy, audacious, dauntless, unabashed excuse for a leader is busily planning more rallies.

As for my happy lockdown life, I just came in from outside, playing in my vegetable garden, I've been in the kitchen, sampling the sauerkraut that I'm making, and now I'm heading into the bedroom, to figure out what sweatshirt I will put on for sailing today. I plan to escape the lockdown again and sneak down to San Francisco. In the past few years of sailing Phil and I only decided once that it was not a good day for raising the sails. Today might be the second time, very high winds are in the forecast, we shall see.

Today San Francisco has opened all restaurants for outside dining. If the wind decides for us that we don't sail, we may just scrub down the boat and then make our way to Chestnut Street for a sidewalk dining adventure in a cool neighborhood of the Marina district. Not meaning to offend anyone but I once heard, "*There are only three cities in America, New York, San Francisco and New Orleans, all the rest are just Cleveland."*

JUNE 13, 1964

J.B. Stoner, a segregationist from Atlanta, Georgia, holds a confederate flag as he addresses a large crowd of whites at an old slave market in St. Augustine, Florida, and then leads them on a long march through an African American residential section. The marchers are holding a sign that reads "Kill Civil Rights Bill."

JUNE 13, 2020

The ferocious wind kept us from sailing yesterday, gusts probably hit close to 40 knots. In case a knot doesn't translate, it equals 1.15 mph. A knot is equal to the speed of one nautical mile per hour, now you know. So our early afternoon was spent scrubbing down the boat. We kept in mind as we worked that we just might go out with only our foresail or even under power, but by the time we finished cleaning it was rather late so we canceled and I again headed down to Julie's Hotel in Palo Alto.

Julie and I went for our usual walk down on the Bay, the Wetlands, this completely pristine area is a popular spot for people like us that walk along or jog these trails, some carry binoculars, others have cameras, tripods and zoom lenses. Many have their little kids or dogs. The variety of birds that exist here is rather inspiring. It assures me that all is not lost. Geese and ducks and pelicans and terns and gulls, and of course there are others that I can't name. They are all using these flats. Some are splashing water on themselves, pelicans are finding small fish to eat, everywhere you look is bird action.

I have made a personal goal that when this lockdown is lifted, I will make a list of all the National Parks out here in the West and seriously make the effort to visit as many as possible. I plan on immersing myself in raw nature. In this way I will be able to truly experience the beauty of our world. I need to keep this mentality, and not allow the negative to enter.

So here's some of the negative: There are signs that the coronavirus pandemic is tightening in the U.S. as more than a dozen states see an increase in COVID-19 cases. New virus hotspots are emerging in the South and Southwest, and parts of the South and West Coast are seeing their biggest spikes in cases yet. Some health experts say we could be seeing the impact of opening too early. In Texas, businesses and restaurants, among the first to reopen, could become the first to shut down again. Quoting a Texas Judge: "I want the reopening to be successful. I want the economy to be resilient, but I'm growing increasingly concerned that we may be approaching the precipice-- the precipice of a disaster."

The same reports are coming in from Utah, Arizona, North Carolina, all over the country. "As I've said a zillion times, the virus makes the timelines. We don't make the timelines," said Oregon Governor Kate Brown. Every official is attempting to balance the needs of our economy with practical approaches to the safety of our health and health systems. One bright spot is the report this morning from Governor Cuomo of New York, which at one point was the epicenter of the outbreak. The state now says it has the lowest transmission rate in the country. Governor Cuomo credits the decision to holding off on reopening.

The civil rights protests are continuing around the world. I had a very interesting emotion last night. Julie and I along with Brian, who is the hotel manager, ate dinner at the Poolside restaurant here in the hotel, which has now just reopened. There were many locals sitting at the tables surrounding the pool. A few women were in the water. As we were leaving I passed by a table where a mixed couple was sitting. The man, an African American, looked to be about my age. From a short distance away we looked at each other in the eyes. He smiled and I made some gesture of connection. I felt as if we had both instantly gone over this entire protest, its cause, its purpose and resulting effects. I winked, he smiled a bit bigger and I felt a strong love for Black people. It was not my imagination, I am sure he felt this. A moment that transcends communication as we normally experience it.

I will soon be leaving here and driving to Emeryville in the East Bay, to visit Suzanne. She is a patient and resident of CNS, Centre for Neuro Skills.

7

Suzanne

Suzanne is another close friend, who dramatically changed and directed my life for the past 22 years. Suzanne was born in Lubbock Texas as the oldest daughter in a family of 4, all girls. I will say this with certainty, under different circumstances, she or any of her sisters could easily have made the grade as a professional model. Despite her good looks, Suzanne's aspirations and perhaps the early lifestyle of surviving with an abusive drunk as a father, led her along a different path. She was shy and humble as a child, not exactly the Hollywood/Madison Avenue type. I met Suzanne over 30 years ago, when I first came to California. This was before my life in Costa Rica.

Suzanne is an artist, and a very sensitive, spiritual person. In those days she owned a costume shop that she ran for many years. It was an outlet for her creativity. Her store "Disguise the Limit" was known throughout Sonoma County, and very popular. Customers would drive up from San Francisco. It was unequivocally one of a kind and she had acquired a loyal following over the years. Glenn, Suzanne's boyfriend at the time, was a friend of mine. Glenn was a semi-professional actor. He and a costume shop owner were a natural fit. Suzanne was also a performer with a group of all female dancers. She and Glen would find places to perform within the local community. I fit right in as well, because I was the film guy who had the camera. As mid age fun seekers we shared many good times together.

My life in California at that period lasted for a few years. Because of my divorce, my family had been split up, I was in California with my son Abel. My daughter Mia was in North Carolina with her mom. This had to stop, so I returned to North Carolina to put the kids back together. After 10 years the kids had grown up and were on their own. I found myself heading back to California, I called upon Suzanne. She still had her shop in Santa Rosa.

"How are you and Glenn doing?" "Oh, we have broken up, But I have a new man in my life, his name is Zachary and he's 2 years old." I wound up moving in with Suzanne and Zac was soon to become my son. Suzanne and I never cared about making any official legal documents to validate this relationship and never faced any legal problems because of our rebel attitudes. Suzanne knows I'm Zac's dad, I know it, and Zac knows it. That's all that matters. Since Zac is now 24, we will never face a negative legal situation. My son Abel came to me in almost the exact same way. I took him as a son when he was 3.

Zachary has become the most important focus of my life. I never planned such a thing, but I walked into a world where I again became a father to a young child, a gift that I cherish.

About 4 years ago Suzanne sold her costume shop. Because of online shopping, her business suffered and she got out while she could. After some time off she became a substitute teacher in the local school system, art was her favorite way of reaching the children. One tragic and ill-fated day after school, she was carrying a cardboard box filled with glass to a recycle bin. She tripped and a piece of glass sliced her carotid and sub clavian arteries. She was fortunate to reach the ER in time to save her life. The blood loss resulted in a massive stroke, she lapsed into a coma and after a 6 hour surgery came out alive but as a hemipalegic, paralyzed on the left side of her body. I stayed by her side, sleeping in the hospital for several nights, until she was finally moved from critical care. And I am still by her side.

Things are radically different now because of lockdown. I'm not allowed inside her apartment at the facility but I still drive down to

Emeryville at least once a week, bringing things and just to make some sort of close contact. I'm allowed to talk to her through the semi-opened door for short periods. Her five day a week, seven hours a day therapy has produced a remarkable recovery. The most noticeable deficiency is the loss of her left eye peripheral vision. This leads to a few problems. Confusion with her environment is obvious. Her sense of direction and her balance are off as well. I venture to say that today she is 90% recovered. And we are all extremely grateful to see the old Suzanne back. Initially her doctor kept drilling into me, "She's lucky to be alive." It may be luck, but her recovery might also be due to prayer. So many of her family and friends were in her corner as this long fight was taking place.

In three weeks she will be returning home. I will be taking over as her permanent caregiver. She cannot be left alone. Fortunately I will have help sharing the care that will be required. Sally is waiting in the wings. She's a qualified certified caregiver and will be living in the house with us. There is a possibility that Suzanne will slowly continue improving on a course to self independence. Regardless of her future, I shall never forget, "She's lucky to be alive."

I'm not sure how this radical change is going to affect me. Suzanne and I are not a couple. We are best of friends and she is Zac's mom which unites and bonds us in a very special way, but I do live in my own house in a different town and have my own private life. For now I see this move as the action I must take. It is definitely number one on my priority list and I will do what is necessary.

JUNE 14, 2020

Todays news: Rayshard Brooks, a 27-year-old Black man, was shot and killed by an Atlanta Police Department officer on the evening of June 12, 2020. Brooks had resisted arrest and wrested a taser from one officer as he wrestled on the ground with the two police officers and punched one of them. As he was running away he was shot three times in the back and died later after a surgery.

Senators are working from both sides to prepare a bill concerning changes in the existing "police qualified immunity laws." Seattle has closed down a 6 block area for peaceful gathering of protesters. It doesn't appear to be accomplishing much.

The Rayshard Brooks shooting is so typical of how police mishandle their jobs. Before driving to the Wendy's restaurant, Rayshard had been celebrating his daughter's 8th birthday. While he was getting shot, she was home in her new birthday dress waiting for him to return. I pray that next year on her birthday she will not only recall the senseless tragic murder of her dad, but will see a new, different world, changed from the racial profiling, racial injustice, and racial inequality. I pray that in one year from now she will be living in a world of racial disparity and not one where people of color have given up and are now searching for revenge.

There is no scenario that could be designed in an attempt to justify the shooting of Rayshard. The police knew his identity, they had his car. He was simply a scared decent Black man running away from what he perceived as a hopeless cause. Perhaps he was driving under the influence, although watching the portion of the video of his sobriety test didn't indicate that. He was not innocent, he did resist arrest. He refused to be handcuffed, he fought, and then he ran, perhaps when that cop grabbed his arm he was seeing George Floyd in handcuffs pushed to the ground and then murdered by the police. And then he felt the three bullets rip into his back. He never made it back to his daughter's birthday party.

JUNE 15, 2020

It is so difficult for me to sit in front of the TV and watch the news when I just want to ignore the deplorable current events, the racial reprehensible developments that unfold and are being brought to light each day. I just had to shut it off after seeing Rayshard Brooks' family appear at a live press conference. The pain and despair that they exhibited, lead to tears from every family member. His daughter, his wife, children and cousins all spoke until they couldn't take anymore. They all walked off in unison.

One cousin had to be held back. He was crying and yelling at the press, "they took away my cousin, they killed him." This moment will not leave me for a very long time.

JUNE 16, 1970

I just completed my first real skydiving experience. The previous three had been with a static line. With the connected static line I only had a few seconds of actual freefall before my chute opened, and didn't really experience the thrill of flying through the air. After exiting the plane it takes a couple of seconds just to get "flat and stable." That's when the exhilarating feeling takes over, the feeling of soaring through the air, of "slipping the surly bonds of earth." I was warned when I did the initial training that a phenomenon exists where a person might become so filled with joy that he will refuse to pull, opening his chute. For an extra 5-10 seconds of freefall, he decides to "ride it in." Needless to say that wasn't my case, I flew through the air for the long count of ten, reached into my chest with both hands, and then pulled the ripcord. For those ten seconds, " I joined the tumbling mirth of sun split clouds, high in the sunlit silence, chased the shouting wind along," to quote a WW 2 Canadian Air Force pilot.

John Magee was a young pilot who had flown missions in Europe and once battled with the famous Nazi Pilot, the leading German ace Joachim Muncheberg. Before John Magee's 20th birthday he was killed in a mid-air collision. At the inquiry afterwards a local farmer who witnessed the accident testified that he saw Magee after the collision struggling to push back the canopy of his Spitfire as it descended apparently out of control. Magee succeeded in reversing the canopy and bailing out of the out of control aeroplane, but was at too low an altitude for his parachute to have time to open, and he fell to earth and was killed instantly on impact with the ground.

His poem has been quoted, recorded, made into songs, put on tombstones, It is the official poem of the Royal Canadian Air Force and has to be recited from memory by fourth class cadets at the United States Air Force Academy. In honor of this young man who sent a poem to his mother on September 3, 1941, three months before his death.

HIGH FLIGHT

"Oh! I have slipped the surly bonds of earth, And danced the skies on laughter silvered wings. Sunward I've climbed, and joined the tumbling mirth of sun-split clouds, and done a hundred things, you have not dreamed of. Wheeled and soared and swung, High in the sunlit silence, hovering there, I've chased the shouting wind along, and flung my eager craft through footless halls of air. Up, up the long delirious blue, I've topped the wind-swept heights with easy grace, where never lark or even eagle flew. With silent lifting mind I've trod, the high untrespassed sanctity of space, Put out my hand, and touched the face of God."

JUNE 16, 2020

I haven't watched this mornings' news. I'm planning to ignore negative input today. I'll see how I succeed with this plan. Rereading John Magee's poem gives me a feeling of joy. He "touched the face of God." He did it with a "silent lifting mind," in the "high untrespassed sanctity of space." I can "surround myself with nature." I can "quiet my mind," with meditation, and I can "be a part of the beauty in our natural world, the Face of God," just as John Magee did in 1941.

John Magee was flying into a war when he died. Each day as he woke, he became engaged in a struggle to defend the sane world from the insane. Our problems today seem trite in comparison. He lived when man's inhumanity to man reached an unimaginable level. Genocide, mass exterminations, concentration and death camps, the holocaust, all accepted by the evil Axis. There are very few alive today that had to experience this horror. Through it all John Magee was able to slip the bonds of earth and see God.

Soon I'll be driving off into my war. I need to leave my sheltered in place property and dive into the middle of the masked mass of people that I live with, my neighbors, my town, my community.

I haven't connected with any of them yet today, I didn't turn on the TV, but there are things I must tend to. Life situations, as they often do, are pushing me out of my plane. I'm about to freefall. Today's venture can become total panic or pure joy. I maintain a little control of how I freefall, but in all honesty, the only thing that I really control today or every other day of my life, is my attitude. How I choose to view it. Thank you, John Magee.

JUNE 17, 2020

Today protests are continuing from LA to NYC People are still taking to the streets and demanding change. It appears as if our national government is working in a partisan cooperative way to get bills drawn and passed that will address the issue and provide the changes. Local governments throughout the country are following suit.

An expected spike in corona virus cases is happening as cities nationwide are opening up, business as usual, almost. One of the issues of controversy today is "To wear or not to wear" our masks. As I see it, this is not really something that should be disputed, for now we should wear them. Such firm convictions that masks are useless is simply false, that's not even a hard one. Of course the purpose is to control the spread of the virus. Those that know more than I about this, are the ones guiding us. Yes, we must have correct solutions but if necessary to implement them, we may need to compromise or change what feels good. Personally I hate wearing a mask. I find it difficult to breathe. Even when I was doing construction I would never wear one. But I'm doing it. The rest of the people I come in contact with don't know how healthy I am, ha.

Today, an Air Force sergeant, Steven Carillo, age 32 is being charged with fatally shooting a federal security officer and wounding his partner outside a U.S. courthouse. David Patrick Underwood, 53, was killed and his partner was wounded as they guarded a Federal Building in Oakland while a large demonstration over the police killing of George Floyd was underway nearby. Officials said Carrillo used the protest as cover for the crime and for his escape. Earlier this month Carillo ambushed and killed a California sheriff's deputy and injured four other officers in the community of Ben Lomond outside the beachfront city of Santa Cruz, federal authorities said Tuesday. Apparently Carrillo had ties to the far-right, anti-government "boogaloo" movement. Boogaloo is a libertarian movement that claims to be preparing for a civil war in the United States. These actions are an example of how an advanced civilized society can turn on itself.

I had to call my son Abel after hearing about this. Abel is a Master Sergeant in the Air Force, my inside track to all things military, and a lot of things governmentally. He told me that the killer was not only a sergeant, but also a cop in the Air Force. A cop ambushing another cop basically. One might expect that cops stick together. The "boogaloo" must be one powerful influence. The boogaloo movement, which Steven Carillo's lawyer called a terrorist organization that uses social media to reach out "to vulnerable and possibly susceptible individuals who may be receptive to their messages of hate and destruction."

Carrillo was stationed at Travis Air Force Base northeast of Oakland where he was a leader in an elite military security force and had no record of disciplinary issues. I've been inside that base. I went there to get Abel once, bringing him here for a visit after one of his Iraq tours. Federal authorities say they linked Carillo to the boogaloo movement from social media posts and from phrases he had written in his own blood when he was arrested after killing the deputy. Boogaloo members are easy to spot with their trademark Hawaiian shirts and high-powered rifles and tactical gear. The evidence against Carillo is without question going to convict him. He blatantly admitted his plans on Facebook. How could a 32 year old man be so filled with anger and hate that he would commit such heinous acts. It's common sense that if too much freedom is given to a young child it can be a dangerous thing. I suspect there is but one line of defense, the obvious, insanity.

JUNE 18, 1964

When a group of white and African American integrationists entered a segregated hotel swimming pool in St. Augustine, Florida, a local white racist dove in and cleared them out. The hotel manager James Brock then poured acid into it, shouting, "I'm cleaning the pool!" All were arrested.

JUNE 18, 2020

Big decision by the Supreme Court yesterday has decided that the "Dreamer Children" will be allowed to stay here in the U.S. In 2012 President Obama passed a law that gave children of immigrants brought into the country illegally (through no fault of their own) and have lived, and grown up here have the right to stay. The program is known as DACA, Deferred Action for Childhood Arrivals program, which has allowed nearly 800,000 young people to avoid deportation and remain in the U.S. Trump has tried to overthrow this and deport these people back to Mexico. Yesterday the Court voted against Trump's wishes. That makes three Supreme Court decisions in a row that went against Trump. In January of 2018 after Trump temporarily shut down the DACA program I wrote this poem.

DACA

To change a life with only your word, Destroying a world, emphatically absurd. An unforgiving ruthless power bestowed, Inconceivable at best is told. And those at risk are now forsaken, a child, a family, a future shaken. Dare say the meaning of a crumbled world, that this day can be so cruel. With such a policy that has unfurled, from a man wielding such an evil tool.
How did it begin, who gave you this power? When will it end, what day, what hour? Is there a God who rules from above, with mercy, justice, and infinite love? I question my faith, this can't be true. If only you could see yourself as I see you....To Trump

Another big news story, a book by John Bolton, President Trump's former national security adviser, is being released. Trump's people are asking a judge to immediately halt publication of the book, saying it contains classified information. I may just buy the book. Some of the allegations against Trump are that he pressured China to help him win re-election, praised China's internment of Uighur Muslims, asked if Finland was part of Russia, said some reporters should be "executed," and said it would be "cool" to invade Venezuela. Sounds like our boy in the White House.

The Atlanta cop who shot Rayshard Brooks was charged with felony murder and aggravated assault yesterday. Of course Trump takes the opposite side. He appeared on Fox News defending the cop and blaming Brooks: "You can't resist a police officer, and if you have a disagreement, you have to take it up after the fact." A private video has come up showing the cop kicking Brookes after he had been shot and was on the ground, dying.

Some more news from the *NY Times*: Senate Republicans unveiled a policing overhaul bill yesterday that will compete with a House bill proposed by Democrats. Among the differences, Democrats would allow victims of police brutality to seek damages, while Republicans would not. Philonise Floyd, the brother of George Floyd, urged the United Nations on Wednesday to investigate the police killings of Black people in the United States.

The Good News is, at least for me, I'm going sailing today. As much as I talk about how bad Trump is, hopefully I give equal time to the subject of immersing yourself in nature. We must recognize the beauty and be a part of it as often as we possibly can.

I am sad to say but a connection with nature is not a stroll down Wall Street or Hollywood Boulevard. It's not sitting in front of the TV watching Discovery Channel. You may see interesting, even pretty things, but those examples do not make you a part of the natural wonder of creation. If we hope to change our world as we 'open up,' in my humble opinion we must remember "Who We Are Now." I don't mean recalling who we were, but remembering who we become. We must transition as a member of society in a totally new way, reconnecting with the land, sea and air. And we must recognize and respect and be a beneficial piece of all of it. It really is that simple.

Plans have changed, Phil is not feeling well and decided he better not move too far away from his comfortable bathroom today. He doesn't think it's the virus, and I hope he's right. So my day went as follows. I needed to get Suzanne's car ready for her return home, not that she will be driving it, but it will be ready for our trips around. I'll be her chauffeur. The car needs smogging and registration renewal. The habitual, incurable 'check engine' light is on. Little did I know that this fix would be today's destiny. In my old life as a thriving do anything kinda guy, and when being a mechanic was relatively simple, I would have been on the job with my tools scattered on both fenders. Not today however, my life as a mechanic ceased when the catalytic converter showed up. That was around 1975. I still worked on my old vehicles for a while then came the death of the carburetor. That was in the early 80s. At the same time computers were making their way into cars. Today cars are pretty much computers on wheels, and I am out of the business absolutely, positively.

So the mechanic was able to stick his little gizmo in the porthole and came up with a way to eliminate most of the warning sensors that turn on that stupid 'check engine' light, which was preventing me from going to the smog place. He had a plan, I had to go to the nearest gas station and fill up the tank. That keeps the fume smell at a minimum. When I returned he stuck in the gizmo again. For all that technology sensing there was still a problem. The damn 'catalytic converter.' It wasn't telling the computer that it was doing it's mechanical thing. So the fix is this, I had to get up on the freeway, set the car on cruise control at 60 and head to the next town, Cotati. Then before returning, I had to shut the car off, restart it and get back on the freeway at 60, returning to the shop. That was plan number 2.

This was not the key needed to satisfy the temperamental catalytic converter. Next plan, do the same thing over again only this time on the return trip I needed to drop the car down to lower drive number 2, race it up to 65 then let it drop down to 35, then race it back up to 65, etc. All those drivers that came into my world at this point were not happy with me. I hope that the "Vote Democrat" bumper sticker Suzanne has on her car did not influence a shift in the political arena. Arriving back to the shop, plan number 3 failed. So I pay the guy his $67.50, and we now have plan number 4. By the time I drive back to Healdsburg and the return to his place in Santa Rosa in the morning, the engine should get hot enough to tell the catalytic baby to wake up and go to sleep, meaning not show up on the gizmo. If this plan succeeds then I proceed with plan 5, go to the smog place, Pay that guy his $65, then initiate plan 6. Go to the DMV, pay that lady her $225 and get a valid new registration. I know all this had to be done but if Phil hadn't gotten sick, the sailing plan would have been so much more to my liking.

JUNE 19, 1865

On June 19, 1865, Union troops arrived in Galveston, Texas, with news that the Civil War was over, and that all remaining slaves in Texas were free — an event celebrated to this day as "Juneteenth."

JUNE 19, 1952

In 1952, the U.S. Army Special Forces, the elite unit of fighters known as the Green Berets, was established at Fort Bragg, North Carolina.

JUNE 19, 1964

The U.S. senate passes the civil rights bill. Dr. Martin Luther King, Jr. is in St. Augustine Florida and reacts with great pleasure. This is a great day for me. I've been out of school now for two weeks, I'm finally a high school graduate. My grade point average suffered a lot once I started dating, but oh well, I made it up to C+. I see where Martin Luther King is up in St. Augustine and he is celebrating the Civil Rights Bill being passed. Maybe our city will begin changing. For now West Palm Beach is about as segregated as it can get. All the Black people live on the other side of the railroad track. In Palm Beach it is illegal for Blacks to be walking around after dark without a permit proving that they are servants to the whites in some fashion. Maybe the city parks will get rid of the "Colored" bathrooms and drinking fountains. And maybe the busses will take down the signs, "Colored to the Rear."

JUNE 19, 2020

Sixty eight years ago today the Army Special Forces were established. This is an important date for me and my son Abel. I mentioned earlier that Abel is a Chief Master Sergeant in the Air Force, I didn't mention that he is also an Army Special Forces Green Beret. Today his teams wear black berets. My relationship with Abel is about as close as any father and son can be, given our geographical separation. I'm in California and he's in Florida. We definitely chose different paths to follow.

As Abel was growing from a young man to an adult, he was drawn to the US Military. I spoke earlier about my decision to leave California and take Abel back to North Carolina and unite him with his sister Mia. At that point we all lived together in the log house. My filmmaking career opened up and I pursued the opportunity to work in Costa Rica. I took both children with me. Mia was enrolled in an English speaking high school in San Jose and I got Abel a job as a tourist guide taking people out on horseback rides through the rainforest. He was also responsible for taking care of the horses. Eventually that job ended and I got him a job as first mate on a sailboat. The captain of the boat was a young man 10 years older than Abel. He was a college graduate and had a marked influence on my son.

It wasn't long before Abel called me up to tell me that he wanted to go back to the U.S. and enroll in college. He went back to live with his mom and started classes in the local Junior College. Soon after that I received a call that he was planning on joining the Marines. I then flew back to North Carolina in an attempt to dissuade him. I wasn't able to change his mind but did convince him to switch from the Marines to the Air Force. He became an

Air Force Special Forces Operative, an elite group called Command Control. The Iraq war broke out and off he went. For the next several years I believe he was deployed 18 times to Iraq and Afghanistan. He continued to advance in rank and gained the highest level of Security clearance possible.

We didn't talk much about his missions since they were always secret. I mostly learned from fellow soldiers, and men under his control about what he did. One of his missions in the beginning of the war was to rescue Jessica Lynch, the nurse that had been captured by Saddam Hussein and was being held in a hospital under guard by Saddam's Special Republican Guard.

Abel survived these wars without any physical damage, kicking doors in at three in the morning looking for the 'bad guys,' skydiving in behind enemy lines in order to identify and validate targets for the planes, marching through the rugged mountains looking for Saddam, growing his beard, wearing civilian clothes and giving candy to the village children to learn more about Al Qaeda and the Taliban. Throughout this time I watched the news every night and every morning hoping that I would not hear bad news. Abel was very good at what he did. Not only was he making rank but he was continually in schools for more advanced training. In combat situations Abel often worked with the Army Rangers and before long he was sent to and completed Ranger school. His strength, his dedication, his list of accomplishments, his medals, are testimony to the great man that he is, my son 'the Warrior.'

I once visited Abel when he was stationed at Fort Bragg. I met many of his fellow soldiers and commanders. I can only say that these young men are amongst the most special, dedicated, committed people I have or ever will meet. They make me feel privileged and honored to be an American.

It appears that the government is considering changing the name of Fort Bragg since it is named in honor of a Confederate General. Along the Pacific coast to the northwest of Healdsburg is a small beach town, also named Fort Bragg, the talk of the town is to change their name. To Trump and the right wingers such moves are insanely radical and pure nonsense. To me, it is the proof of a long overdue respect given to all African Americans, "It's the least we can do."

I'm just now back home after dealing with the car issue. At the mechanic shop, the Cat, catalytic converter, light came on again. I repeated the plan to drive a steady 60 mph for a long distance. This time I went beyond Cotati to the next town south, Petaluma. When I got back to the shop, it had worked. The Cat light did not come on. Happily I headed to the Smog Station. I found out that it didn't need to be smogged after all. I just didn't know whether to be happy or sad about this news. So in a semi- state of confusion, I took the $65. saving, and went to the DMV for the registration renewal. I got the little sticker to put on the license plate and the ability to legally drive around for another year. Life in the fast lane, for me, the 60 mph lane, might be over for a while.

Today's news: Millions of people around the country are still marching in protest and some are marching in parades honoring 'Juneteenth.' There is a strong desire and people are pushing to turn this day into a National Holiday. Juneteenth marks the day in 1865 when a group of enslaved people in Galveston, Texas, finally learned that they were free from the institution of slavery. But, woefully, this was almost two and a half years after President Abraham Lincoln signed the Emancipation Proclamation. The Civil War was still going on, and when it ended, Union Maj. Gen. Gordon Granger traveled to Texas and issued an order stating that all enslaved people were free, establishing a new relationship between "former masters and slaves" as "employer and hired labor." As much as Juneteenth represents freedom, it also represents how emancipation was tragically delayed for enslaved people in the deepest reaches of the Confederacy.

Another 1.5 million Americans applied for state unemployment benefits last week, a sign that the coronavirus pandemic was reaching deeper into the economy even as the pace of jobs cuts slowed. Many economists are predicting that as many as 100,000 small businesses have shut their doors permanently since the pandemic escalated in March. The latest data suggests at least 2 percent of small businesses are gone, according to a survey conducted May 9 to 11. The damage has been even higher in the restaurant industry, where 3 percent of restaurant operators have gone out of business, according to the National Restaurant Association.

Fortunately I am not directly affected by either the virus or the economic downturn, yet. Up on my little isolated residence I'm able to maintain, I don't need restaurant food and I don't have an employer to answer to. Of course the 'trickle down' will get to all of us in time. For now the only issue that I deal with is the obvious partisan politicizing as I do venture into society. It starts with masks. Since our society has never dealt with such a thing it is strange and alien to us. Trump doesn't wear one, there you have it.. He's either disguising fear or more than likely he believes it will make him look weak. He also believes the dangers of the virus are exaggerated and his followers are quick to accept his thinking and follow his lead. A team of scientists from Europe and California recently built a computer simulation demonstrating that if 80% of the population wore masks the infection rates would drop by more than 90%. In some people's minds mask wearing may be an unconscious statement that our old lives are gone. There have been too many studies to mention, hundreds and every one of them concludes that masks are effective.

It's such a shame that this prevalent divisiveness has carried over to a health issue that might very well cost tens of thousands of lives. Mask wearers have now become a political and cultural symbol for leftism. Without even realizing it, many people are treating their political belief as more important than their life. Andrew Sullivan of NY Mag.com says, "We are entering the Jonestown phase of the Trump cult this summer. It is not going to be pretty."

JUNE 21, 1964

The Reverend Martin Luther King addresses a crowd estimated at 70,000 at a civil rights rally in Chicago's Soldier Field. King told the rally that congressional approval of civil rights legislation heralds "The dawn of a new hope for the Negro." Three civil rights workers, part of the "Freedom Summer" program, were abducted, killed and buried by KKK members, in an earthen dam in rural Neshoba County.

JUNE 21, 2020

Yesterday Trump held His first rally since the lockdown, in Tulsa Oklahoma, a very Republican state and one in which Trump supporters were expected to show up in huge numbers. But, it was a big disappointment for the Trumpers, only 6,000 were in attendance. The auditorium was only ⅔ filled and the overthrow stage where they expected to see 2,000 had about 20 people. It was difficult to see anyone with a mask. "The president, who had been warned aboard Air Force One that the crowds at the arena were smaller than expected, was stunned, and he yelled at aides backstage while looking at the endless rows of empty blue seats in the upper bowl of the stadium, according to four people familiar with what took place. President Trump and several staff members stood backstage and gazed at the empty Bank of Oklahoma Center in horror," *NY Times.*

John Bolton's book has been released and shows Trump as an incompetent stooge. The effort by Trump's people to halt the release failed in the court system. Bolton is the highest official, National Security Adviser, closest to a president who has ever published such damaging accusations against a standing president. The list of prominent people who have publicly defied President Trump — including onetime allies — keeps growing.

It really does look like Trump's chances for re-election are almost impossible. BUT None of this is an absolute certainty. Past presidential candidates, like George H.W. Bush and Harry Truman, overcame polling deficits bigger than the one Trump currently has against Joe Biden. However sustained weakness is very dangerous for any politician.

JUNE 22, 2020

In the news today the Corona virus seems to be the main area of discussion, surpassing the protest rallies even though they continue without much of a letup. It appears as if almost half of U.S. states are experiencing a rise in the number of Corona cases. Have we let up too soon, is the big question.

JUNE 23, 2020

More deep concern about the new rise in Corona cases. Europe is again looking at the U.S. with more questions. Most European countries have the virus in check while our numbers are jumping. Here in California, Gavin Newsom, our governor, is warning that he might have to reinstate shelter in place orders and close up some of the businesses. The economy is already in the worst shape ever and people will not tolerate it. It's the lesser of two evils, get sick and die from the virus, or go broke and starve to death.

So what is Trump up to? On the news this morning I watched him live as he gave a speech from the 'Border Wall' where they are commemorating the completion of 200 miles of his pet project. When Trump was running for the Presidency he promised his followers that he would build a wall between the U.S. and Mexico and stop the illegal immigrants. He promised that Mexico would pay for it. So here we are almost 4 years later. He has some of it built, thanks to the fact that Republicans control the house and Senate. The border fence begins in Texas, but it's miles inland from the border's edge at the Gulf of Mexico. Elsewhere, fences start and stop with huge gaps in between. This is all pedestrian fencing. Hundreds of miles of fencing is only 'vehicle barrier.' Vehicle barriers are effective at stopping vehicles. These fences alone won't stop people. The "Trump Wall" has been such a boondoggle, a huge waste of money and source of heated arguments between our people. "About three-quarters (74%) of Republicans and Republican-leaning independents have supported this ridiculous border wall, while an even greater share of Democrats expressed opposition from the very beginning (89%)." Younger Americans and Americans with college degrees were more likely to oppose a wall than older Americans and those without college degrees.

Of course the whole idea of the wall is mean spirited, counterproductive and tremendously expensive. It stands as a Trump symbol of undermining the American tradition of welcoming people from around the world. In March 2017, Mexican congressman Braulio Guerra of Querétaro illegally climbed, and partially crossed, an existing 30-foot border fence on American soil dividing San Diego and Tijuana, saying that more walls would be ineffective.

The expression that "you never get a second chance for a first impression," is true. Trump blew his first impression with me. I could never get past his hair. It says so much about the guy underneath it. Why would anyone try, or even want to change himself by doing whatever it is he is doing with his hair? This is the million dollar question. To me it is insecurity, self doubt, uncertainty. It is pompous, egotistical, self absorbed narcissism. If he would stand on his head, his hair would be the foundation for the building he has constructed. The foundation is noticeably weak and any building on a weak foundation is going to crumble.

This morning as I watched Trump giving his speech at an event that was surely another foolish, absurd photo op for his supporters, I stopped hating the man. At least for the moment. Although he damages our country every day, I actually felt sad and heartbroken. I saw a pathetic figurehead constantly repeating himself and struggling for words. I felt truly sorry for him. I'm absolutely assured that the best thing for America would be to remove him immediately, but today I am feeling that he should be sent to a facility where he could be treated. However justice would demand that he deserves at least a few weeks in San Quentin first. I definitely don't want to watch him anymore.

JUNE 26, 1967

The 1967 Buffalo riot was one of 159 race riots that swept cities in the United States during the "Long Hot Summer of 1967." This riot occurred on the East Side of Buffalo, New York, from June 26 to July 1, 1967.

JUNE 26, 2020

Many Latino communities around the states are now calling out against police brutality, echoing similar calls that we have been hearing from the Black communities. The racial inequality issue is still being seen on many fronts and is far from fading away.

Uptick, spike, surge, these are the words of the day. It looks like our re-opening, our relaxation of the restrictions for businesses and public places have caused record days of new coronavirus cases. It's happening all over the country but more so in the Western states and Florida. Yesterday was the second straight day that the U.S. reached a record number of reported cases. Young people and Latinos are making up a growing percentage of new cases.

Joseph Biden, the Democratic nominee has promised to choose a female as his running mate and an interesting candidate has surfaced. Her name is Tammy Duckworth. She is an active senator from Illinois, and a former US Army lieutenant colonel. She lost both of her legs in a rocket-¬propelled-grenade blast in Iraq in 2004. She is quoted by the NY Times: "I can push back against Trump in a way others can't." I feel that the people are ready for such a candidate with an amazing inspirational story. Today people want to feel good about politicians. It's been a long four years.

My friend Julie and I talk every night and she keeps insisting that Michelle Obama will be his VP choice. She wants that to be the case so bad that she keeps predicting it will happen. I can't imagine that Michelle would want to jump back into politics but Julie believes that because Michelle is such a patriot and the fact that she would win so many votes that this is going to happen. I wouldn't bet a penny against a dollar that this will ever happen, but I'm like Julie, I would love the team "Biden and Obama."

Trump announced today that he wants to overturn the Affordable Care Act, Obama Care. It can only be that he is grasping at anything that might inspire his backers to become furious, emotionally charged, to get back on his sinking ship. Again he has acted like an insane person. Why would anyone in their right mind, at this point, attack people's insurance? So many have lost their company insurance during this pandemic, something like 23 million people are at risk to have no coverage. I accidentally saw him again on the morning news and he was calling coronavirus the China Plague.

JUNE 27, 2020

Yesterday I worked to finish my list. I made some adjustments to a ramp I built last week. I scraped the joints of the bricks I had set, leveling the patio. I put together a bathtub chair and installed a grab bar. I changed some lights, put up a towel rack and a new tissue holder. I changed two kitchen chairs to new ones that had arms on them. I brought up a new bed, mattress etc., and assembled it. Then I sat down with Sally and waited for the CNS inspector to show up. Suzanne's house passed the safety inspection.

In two days I will be driving down to Emeryville, more than likely for the final time, to bring Suzanne back to her house. It has been 8 long months since Suzanne has been to her house. Her new life home is soon to begin. It will be a new life for me as well. I will assume the responsibility as her caregiver. I won't be working alone in this job. Workers Compensation Insurance is providing a caregiver of their own choosing to help, 10 hours a day, 5 days a week. Sally, who has been living in Suzanne's house during these months will also continue living at the house and helping with the caregiving. I will share in the joy that Suzanne will feel, to be home at last. The neighbors want to plan a small "Welcome Home" party. Zac will be coming up and I will be putting up some decorations.

And then the settling back, the re-adjustment, the reality of a changed life will commence. Suzanne has never been one to compare herself with others, but now that she is home, she will be forced to compare herself with the prior version of herself. She will no longer drive a car, or take walks alone. This accident has taken away her right to plan her life without an OK from one of us. I anticipate some difficulties ahead but I remain positive. Nothing can really go wrong with a crazy situation in an insane world.

Suzanne takes great pleasure in her yard. She has many varieties of flowers and always gathers seeds from new plants that she finds on walks. As a matter of fact most any walk with Suzanne is a nature walk. She will point out the shrubs and bushes, while I would amble by without taking notice. One thing is certain, I will be putting in a vegetable garden when she comes home. It's never too late. I have terraced my land here and have a wonderful garden. At this moment I am eating on a big raw zucchini. This morning I also ate some spinach and arugula from my garden. Like every other species alive, except us, I am eating it uncooked. My garden provides me with raw live food. Life begets life, I firmly believe that by eating raw food any human will remain much more in balance and sustain good health. I practice this as much as I can. I don't intend to dwell on this subject since this knowledge is available in a million other books.

Many of the different churches send out missionaries to surround the globe and spread the Holy Word. The idea is that every person alive should at least be exposed to the teachings. Even though they don't get great conversion ratings, they still march on. Well, it's the same thing with a good healthy diet. I think that everyone, at least here in America, has been exposed to the truth about food and good health, but the conversion rate sucks. McDonalds and Coke hold the upper hand. I guess they're like the devil. While I'm on the subject, there is one particular fact that interests me. Why are there so many different Christian religions? With so many varieties of Christianity to choose from, how do the faithful pick the right one?

After WW 2 we, American families, grew almost 40% of all the food we ate in our own backyard gardens. Today it's less than 1%. No one bothers, perhaps due to our changed socio-economic conditions. We developed families with two working parents and chemical farming happened. In addition fast food restaurants can now provide relatively cheap meals. It's such a mistake in direction. Of all the rich developed countries of the world, America is the sickest of them all. Since the 1950s even our children, who are supposed to be strong and healthy, have gone from 1.2% to 52% in chronic disease rate. It's unbelievable and one of the primary causes is the food we consume. We go through life with our eyes half opened. As I said before, all the information is right in front of our faces. We must all see it, but so many refuse to follow the right path.

Time now has become very precious, not just to me as a man in his seventies, but to every person at every age alive at this moment. Humankind is now the cataclysmic event happening on the planet. We need to grow our own organic food. We must become healthy again. We have to do things with our eyes wide open, and act, to save our planet. The irony of it all is that making this type of change is not difficult. It's just the opposite. It is so much easier, so much more of a rewarding life than the course that we are on.

JUNE 28, 2020

Another Sunday Face the Nation, it's hard for me to not turn on the news, and see the 'picks of the week.' First up Vice President Pence, facing questions regarding Trump and his denial that the virus is resurging. Other questions: why does the administration discourage mask wearing, why will Trump not acknowledge the slogan, Black Lives Matter? The idiotic responses given by Pence are shameful. Next up a Black Republican senator from South Carolina, Tim Scott. Like Pence he is a deeply religious man, obviously influencing his actions. He wrote a bill concerning police reform which was blocked by the Democrats. He calls it, "race politics at its worst," and claims that Democrats have no desire to actually solve this issue before the election. A big issue with the Democrats is the fact that the bill ignores any accountability by the police, the justified immunity argument. I am not educated enough on the issue to have a real comment on this, but of course I lean towards the Democratic interpretation of what should be written.

Next came Dr. Scott Gottlieb with all the scary facts regarding the escalating coronavirus cases around the world, particularly in the Americas. We are seeing 30 thousand new cases a day. It seems like it's hitting hard in the South and the Southeast. Texas, Arizona, Florida, California, Alabama, North and South Carolina are all experiencing high rates of new cases, Florida has had an increase of 165%. 125,000 people have now died in the U.S. Dr. Gottlieb is predicting big troubles ahead. And stating that we are running out of tools for treatment. We can't shut down businesses again, we can and should mandate a mandatory mask wearing procedure. He claims masking should not be controversial, it's a simple intervention proven to work. Texas and Florida are not mandating mask wearing but he says they will have to.

I know that mask wearing has become such a political issue, some see it as an infringement on their liberty, mostly Trump supporters. The sad thing is that to be effective we all have to do it collectively, or at least most of us. Personally I find it smothering and quite difficult, but I do it when I go out in public. I see the grocery store workers wearing their masks for hours on end. There are people wearing them while they are driving in their cars. My compliments to them, but honestly, I'll just stay home.

An important move that is being studied concerns the reopening of schools and Universities. Everyone is hoping that this will be possible, not only for the sake of students and teachers, but also because it plays an important part in our economy. It seriously affects working parents who rely on the system to watch children while they go to work. And of course the educating of kids probably doesn't work as well without teachers in their faces. None of the experts were able to predict if in fact we will be prepared for reopening.

The issue of racial inequality was brought up again. Martin Luther King Jr. once said, Rioting and protesting are not making front page news, but the subject has not been dropped and I hope we will continue to make positive changes.

Yesterday after a month and a half wait, I received my order in the mail. I thought I had been scammed out of my hundred bucks, but it came, 'made in China" of course. Perhaps it was shipped on a 'slow boat from China' to me which was why the long delay. Anyway it's here now and I am about to go down into the big field and launch my helicopter drone. I haven't been able to figure out how to read the barcode which will allow me to install the app on my phone, thereby having a monitor for the camera. Regardless, I'm going to test out the flying capability of it right now.

Drone Report: Sir, enemy troops spotted 33.25* N, 44*8*E. Actually reporting back to base from the field, there were 5 crashes, and one damaged part. Drone went missing in action for an hour but finally recovered in a huge blackberry patch. Pilot incapable of any simulation of control over said drone, Sir.

I have no idea how I will ever be able to learn about the joysticks, etc. I have two cleared large fields to work with, but once that Launch button is pushed that baby takes off to parts unknown. I can see a little response to my moving those sticks but I'm here to tell you it ain't like riding a bike. I'm glad that I finally recovered it after putting on riot gear and chopping through the briar patch. One of the first crashes was up in a redwood tree. It came to rest on a large branch and I was able retrieve it with a long branch trimming pole. If you happen to be residing in NYC don't even think about getting one of these. It may be good for people in the desert, who own a good pair of binoculars. Learning curve '-200.'

More to report on Trump. One thing about him is he is consistent and continually able to outdo himself. Every day he displays himself as a man without favorable qualities, an opportunist entirely without principle. Just when you think he's done it all, he comes up with one worse. Yesterday he tweeted on a YouTube video showing two of his followers raising their fists and yelling "White Power." If there has ever been a question, Trump just proved his unapologetic racism. He is promoting the spread of white-supremacist propaganda, which is a very serious threat to our nation. We all know the power of the internet, YouTube is designed for the circulation of such content, it has the power to direct its users toward ever more inflammatory material. It is probably the most powerful radicalizing instrument of the 21st century, and Trump dares to display the cathartic rituals of racism that goes on at his rallies.

This action of his should be written in every history book. It is such a descent into what I call 'radical evil.' How is it possible that any civilized society would allow its President to embrace such extreme ideas as "White Power" represents? Someone, perhaps on his staff, had him delete the tweet this afternoon. This just doesn't seem like it could really be happening. Again, it must be an action intended to ignite all his racist followers.

JUNE 29, 1964

The Civil Rights Act of 1964 passed after an 83-day filibuster in the US Senate. The FBI began distributing pictures of three missing civil rights workers, Michael Schwerner, 24, of New York, James Chaney, 21, from Mississippi, and Andrew Goodman, 20, of New York, who disappeared near Philadelphia, Mississippi, on June 21, 1964. There has been rioting in the predominantly Black area of North Philadelphia with no end in sight. Looting was widespread and damage heavy. At least 50 persons were injured including 27 policemen.

JUNE 29, 2020

In two hours I begin the drive to retrieve Suzanne from CNS and bring her back. A huge transition is soon to begin, for both she and me, especially for her, coming home after 8 months of living in a rehab center. Through it all she never lost her positivity. She never replied negatively when I asked her, "How you doin'?" It was always, "I'm good." Now, to keep it going in that direction.

Before leaving I will report the latest. It appears as if the entire world is experiencing new outbreaks of the virus, food markets in Beijing, nightclubs in South Korea, meatpacking plants in England and Germany. These outbreaks are not all the same, The ones here in the U.S. are much worse. Most other high-income countries are dealing with modest numbers of new cases, often an inevitable consequence of reopening, and the countries are responding aggressively. Many are following the advice of public health experts, ordering social distancing, mask-wearing and partial lockdowns and doing their best to track people who came in contact with new patients. The United States is not. Trump and many governors continue to flout scientific advice and send mixed messages about the seriousness of the virus.

Another country that highlights the lessons is Britain. Its prime minister, Boris Johnson, has taken the virus less seriously than most other European leaders but more seriously than Trump. Sure enough, Britain is suffering an outbreak that's worse than in most of Europe but not as bad as in the U.S.

A final point: Trump and Vice President Mike Pence have claimed that the rise in confirmed U.S. cases is largely the result of more tests. That's not true, The U.S., which once trailed Europe in per capita overall deaths, has now endured many more.

I am getting this information from the *New York Times* which is a "No read" for all Trump supporters. That has always been puzzling to me because if anyone looks at the *Times* they will see many articles and editorials that present both sides, right and left, of all the current issues.

After my Drone testing yesterday, I came inside and went into the bathroom, I noticed the rug was wet. On Thursday of last week I had successfully unclogged the sink in the vanity, using the trusted 'snake' method. Or so I thought. What I had actually done was busted a huge hole in the ancient, rusted 'P trap.' Which meant that for the past few days whenever I brushed my teeth or used that sink, the water was being dumped into all those things in the huge straw basket hidden underneath. So my work from mid afternoon till dark meant replacing all those old chrome/copper rusted pipes with their lovely plastic counterparts. I became friends with the plumbing department expert at my local hardware store, he's a nice older man and an obvious 'Trumpy.' We were able to communicate just fine. He didn't believe in masks or the idea that there is a serious virus going around.

I have developed a new "ABC" theory, Assumption, Belief, Conviction. This appears to be the common method that a brain takes as it filters new information. First you make the assumption of fact, then you believe it to be true, finally you are convinced, end of subject, pride takes over, mind closes, growth halts. When a storm comes, or an unimaginable moment of beauty, a higher energy, finds its way into your being, an inspirational switch may be clicked and a change of belief and conviction might take place.

For now I need to get it together for the trip to Emeryville.

JUNE 30, 2020

Got Suzanne home and tucked in yesterday. Not sure when I will get back to routine writing again but for now here's today's basic news:

Trump was briefed on the Russian bounty program months ago. The coronavirus is hitting California hard. And the Supreme Court rules against both abortion restrictions and financial regulation.

8

July

JULY 1, 1946, 1956

The atomic bomb tests continue, the 4th atom bomb explosion occurred, dropped on the Bikini atoll. In 1987, (when I turned 41, I was a guest on a radio program and met a soldier who was forced to watch this explosion from a ship.)

On this day in 1956, when I was 10 years old, Elvis Presley began his career. How well I remember this day, he appeared on the Steve Allen Show. My sister and I watched that night and she was immediately hooked. My sister was 17. Without question Elvis would become one of the most significant cultural icons of the 20th century. He radically reshaped American music and was responsible for introducing rock and roll to the entire world.

I followed Elvis for his entire career. He shook up many religious organizations with his stage appearances. "Elvis the Pelvis" was way too sexy for the religious right. He became an actor, movies were made just for him. He was drafted right around my 12th birthday and served in the army for two years. He was an amazing person. Throughout his career he was extremely generous and kind, known for giving pink Cadillacs away to people around him, even the occasional lucky fan.

JULY 1, 2020

I am now back in my house after staying with Suzanne for the past 3 days. I will be going back to Suzanne's in a few hours. She is "doing good," as she always says, and so am I. The insurance company has sent their caregiver to begin with Suzanne's help. Her name is Cherry, an older woman who seems to be very nice and very caring.

Around the country it appears as if the big news continues to be the spike in the virus. Our Health officials announced more than 48,000 new coronavirus infections yesterday, another daily record and an increase of 80 percent in the past two weeks. Dr. Fauci, who, if I haven't already mentioned, is the nation's top infectious disease expert, warned the Senate yesterday that the number could soon reach 100,000 a day if the country does not act quickly. And I'm sure that will not happen. In the midst of this health crisis, the environment has seen less travel, therefore less air pollution with an obvious beneficial effect. Then enters Trump into the picture..

His administration has just exempted seasonal streams, wetlands, and other waterways from Clean Water Act protections, putting the drinking water for one-third of Americans at risk. It is obviously established that Trump has the worst environmental record of any president in history. He has succeeded in dividing the country on most environmental issues and his actions have always harmed the environment, and nature's ecological balance. He has, and continues to make human life less healthy, less prosperous, less just, and less equal.

It is so scary to imagine what he will do if he loses the election in November and becomes a 'lame duck President.' For those remaining two months of his term he will have nothing to lose and will likely be upset with his "fans" for not electing him again. I could definitely see him doing some Dr. Evil type thing just to prove he can. I think first on his list will be to pardon all his incarcerated buddies, then he will without doubt, make as many executive orders as possible that will have a positive effect on his businesses. He will do anything he can to screw up our country worse than any of us thought possible. I hope I'm wrong about this.

Another sad fact, we have been shown that this crisis continues to disproportionately harm Black, Indigenous, Latin people and all other communities of color. The pandemic has revealed how the communities hardest hit are often the same communities that suffer from high levels of pollution and poor access to healthcare. The fight for environmental justice cannot be separated from the fight for racial justice. The Coronavirus has shown humanity that we need to change our racist, egoistic and exploitive ways against every human and all of nature. If we can connect as the global humanity that we are, life will be transformed into a place of heath, purpose and happiness. I'll say it again, we're here for a reason; a higher purpose and we must remember to think beyond our shell. I hope I'm right with this....

JULY 2, 2020

The coronavirus trends are still not leveling out. The number of new cases continues to surge, unlike in most other affluent countries. And Fourth of July gatherings have the potential to make the bad situation worse. In California Governor Newsom has closed most public beaches again and receives criticism for this action from the Republicans. There is one important bright spot in all the dark figures. The percentage of virus patients who are dying from it has continued to decline. This explains an otherwise confusing contrast. Coronavirus deaths in the U.S. have been falling for most of the last 10 weeks, to about 600 a day recently, down from more than 2,000 in late April.

Of course Trump does not agree with these figures and claims the current numbers are being fabricated by manipulating the cases, claiming that many included in the count are simply people with an elevated temperature. Trump and Pence are both appearing in the spotlight arguing that the continuing decline in deaths proves that the virus is under control. That's not correct, epidemiologists say. But the decline really is good news. The facts are that now medical treatment has improved. Doctors and nurses often diagnose the virus more quickly than they did a few months ago, thanks in part to more widespread testing. They have also had some success treating symptoms with remdesivir and other drugs.

A problem that we are now seeing is that many middle-aged and younger people are acting as if they're invulnerable. Their increased social activity has caused an explosion in cases over the last three weeks, which in turn could lead to a rise in deaths soon.

Another scary development in the news: U.S. officials had briefed Trump as far back as February about Russia's payments of bounties to Taliban linked militants to kill American soldiers. It is now coming up, because Trump has continued his cordial relationship with Putin without addressing this problem. Trump is calling the finding a "hoax," and his national security adviser, Robert C. O'Brien, said the C.I.A. did not brief him orally about the information because there was no "consensus" about it. The response from valid news organizations have said, "It would be unusual, if not unprecedented, for intelligence with grave implications to be withheld from the president on the grounds that it lacked definitive consensus."

There is even a man known who was the go-between in these bounties, Rahmatullah Azizi, a low-level Afghan drug smuggler who became rich after establishing a presence in Russia. He was the one who handed out Russian money to Taliban-linked fighters for targeting U.S. troops, officials say.

JULY 4, 1970

I'm in Byron, Georgia, at the Atlanta Pop Festival. I've been here for four days. Carmine, Michael and I have opened up a watermelon stand. Since I missed Woodstock last year I wasn't going to miss this one, people are still coming in. From the air, cars can be seen all the way to Atlanta. Woodstock was attended by over 600,000, and it looks like this festival is competing to match those numbers. Since the 60s American culture has definitely changed, and in one important way is how our music is often performed. These large outdoor rock festivals are now quite common. Woodstock will probably go down in history as the symbol of this time, and perhaps this Festival will make its mark as well. So much great music, there have been at least 25 bands that have performed since we arrived, including The Allman Brothers, Grand Funk Railroad, John Sebastian, B.B. King, The Chambers Brothers, Poco, Rare Earth, Richie Havens, Bob Seegar, and many others.

I think over thirty musical acts have been scheduled. However it seems like being here is more about the event itself than the music. Most of the people are not exactly your 'Leave it to Beaver' types. There are musicians, hippies, bikers, nudists, Indian gurus, Yoga masters, smack freaks, mud people, whackos, just the general old and young liberal population coming out of the 60s. Everything seems pretty normal for the time. Since we have our watermelon stand, I am privileged and can go backstage. A couple of days ago, after a Yoga session, I went back and sat around with the gurus and Yogi Amrit Desai eating fruit. That was really wonderful to suck up a little peace and quiet for a change (note) By chance, I would run into Yogi Amrit Desai twice again in my life and get my first sampling of the power of a guru. Trust me on this, gurus can make your skin tingle and bones rattle, if you allow it.

The Festival producers have chosen this site away from the city, out in the country of course. We are in farmland, sort of a rolling, slightly hilly location surrounded by pecan orchards. I have just experienced one of the most amazing moments of my life. I was sitting slightly up the rolling hill not too far from the stage, up on top of some scaffolding that had been set up, and was not being utilized. There are half a million people around me, and we are all of like mind. We all have a serious cause. Government politics have polarized our nation. Everyone's choices are now either Black or white. There is no gray matter here. You either accept the Vietnam war and stand by silently as your school friends are getting killed, or you fight the bastards every step of the way, in any way you can. After the Kent State shootings there was no other way. From that point on anything illegal became legal. They, the government, are the bad guys, no questions about it.

That was the feeling tonight as Jimi Hendrix stepped up on stage and began to play to the largest American audience of his career. I was looking down over all the thousands of people sitting on blankets, between the stage and myself. Instead of a Republican or Democrat political party convention, with people in suits holding banners displaying the states of Ohio and Iowa, there were tie-dye flags waving, and giant bananas sticking up, or multi-colored brassieres on sticks. And the people were dressed like natives with feathers, or Tibetans with bells and flowers. Many had no clothes. Pot smoke was drifting in the air like incense in a Buddhist temple. It was everywhere and no cop could possibly stop it. This many people could not all be busted, nor could they all be that wrong.

When Hendrix got on stage people started shooting up fireworks from their blankets. Remember, today is the Fourth of July. At the same time the producers began their huge fireworks display from behind the stage. When their first one went off Jimi jumped and then began to play his famous version of the Star Spangled Banner. There will never be another person who will play it like him, with so much meaning, screaming out from his guitar. The fireworks are exploding everywhere. Everyone is looking at each other in disbelief. We can not believe this feeling, that this moment is really taking place, that everyone here at this moment is a true brother and sister, in a serious revolt statement against our government, a very blatant and loud cry out for immediate radical change.

You can sway around and move but you can't talk, it's too loud, even if there was something to say. People are laughing and crying. Hendrix had to finish the song. It couldn't go on forever. When the song finally ended, the fireworks stopped. People began screaming at the stage and applauding and whistling. Everyone stood up from their blankets, more than half a million people with the most emotion they had probably ever felt in their lives, focused on one thing. "We are brothers and sisters. We want love. We are the flower children." This is what the 60s had done.

Being young in the 60s has been extremely intense for a number of reasons. We all have a country, but it now carries a socio-political condition. It is more like a country lost. We are all old enough to be opinionated and young enough to be idealists. When I look at our government I wonder who really is right. I believe a quote from the great Winston Churchill goes something like this. "When you're 18, if you've got a heart you are a liberal, when you're 38, if you've got a brain you are a conservative." Well most of us here are not yet 38, and we damn sure could not be considered conservative. We have brains, er . . . I must say, they may be a little muddled right now, but I guess we are still liberals anyway, with or without a muddled brain. At some point in the future many of us might become conservatives "of mind," thank you very much Sir Winston.

I guess I will be out of here in a day or two and back to my other life, but I will hold and cherish forever this experience. I now carry a record of comparison. My life has forever been scored by this past week. I have lived in a tribe, and it has deeply imprinted upon me a different culture that I now know exists. I understand the statement by Thomas Wolfe, "I can't go home again." (note) 10 weeks later in London, Jimi Hendrix died.

JULY 5, 2020

Yesterday was a subdued low key celebration in comparison to most previous Independence Day celebrations. For the most part everyone has accepted the new order in which we live and easily sacrificed the excitement of watching local fireworks. The television is there for anyone to watch broadcasts of different government displays. I was with Suzanne last night when Trump came on TV at Mt. Rushmore to give a patriotic speech and partake in a long display of fireworks. He spoke to over 7,000 of his followers, patriotic songs were playing and as the camera panned the crowd, as I expected, there were no masks to be seen. Since 2009 fireworks have been canceled at Mt. Rushmore for fire safety reasons, but Trump fixed that nonsense, and it only cost the taxpayers $600,000.

Suzanne and I are at my house in Healdsburg. We went for a swim in my neighbor Stu's pool this afternoon and soon I will be preparing dinner from the garden. It is such a pleasure to harvest healthy food that you grow yourself. I consider myself very fortunate because most of my life I have been able to feel accomplished in the work I do. This is not the case for many people. If you can make your living by doing something that you really like then you are quite lucky. If you see positive results that benefit humanity at the end of most work days then you are truly blessed.

Once the Industrial Revolution took hold, workplaces for many have become solely a way to finance the other things in life that they enjoy. Since I have been a working adult, I've always felt that people have the right to compromise an unpleasant work situation for more important personal goals, but never at the expense of one's values. It's OK to work in an automobile factory at a boring job for eight hours a day. It's not OK to work in a factory producing silencers for handguns. Was it OK for me to have produced films and videos that brought many tourists to Costa Rica? Is it OK for Century 21 to sell the Costa Rican's land to rich tourists?

There have been very few times in my life when my work forced me to make such decisions, but one instance stands out, I was living in Costa Rica working as a filmmaker and video producer. One morning I was contacted by a man from Canada, he was the owner of a business, 'Phyto Medicinal.' His company was supposedly working to find tropical plants that possess medicinal curative properties. The idea is certainly valid. Thousands of the medicines we use today were originally extracted from rainforest plants. I accepted the job to produce a promotional video. It sounded like I was in for a fun project. Our first shoot was in a large nursery close to San Jose. As usual I began shooting every plant in the place from many different angles. I covered the workers and the different structures that made up their huge operation. All went well, I was accruing lots of raw footage.

Next shoot we rented a helicopter and flew to the closest National Park, Braulio Carillo. I sat next to the pilot, my door had been removed. Most of the park is covered in primary forest. Tree ferns, heliconias, bromeliads, palm trees and poor man's umbrella grow everywhere throughout the park. The latter is easily recognized by its unique oversized leaves. Braulio Carillo has over 600 identified species of trees, over 530 species of birds, and 135 species of mammals inside the park. It was ideal for me to get the great shots of what people expect to see in a rainforest. Again the shoot went well for me, and then the controversial aspect began to appear. Soon I would be weighing my financial interest against my moral convictions.

The next time Mr. Phyto Medicinal (forgot his name) and I met, we filmed him in a beautiful tropical setting as he explained the purpose of his company, quite honorable, principled and ethical. After the interview we drove back to the nursery and he pulled a large sign from the trunk of his car. He strategically placed the Phyto Medicinal sign at one of the entrances and asked me to get out the camera. It was obvious his intention was to show the nursery as belonging to his company.

I realized in the earlier interview, that he had talked a lot about the company's future and the need for investments to reach the potential of all the research. It became aware to me that this could very well and probably in fact was, a well planned scam. I kept thinking that I needed the money so I'll compromise for a while. Within a week my dealings with Phyto Medicinal ended, I lost money, I walked away and prevented going against my morals. Months later I heard that some Canadians had been arrested for fraud and deported from Costa Rica.

JULY 6, 1348

On this day in 1348 the Pope of the time issued a formal decree stating that the Jews were not responsible for a plague known as the Black Death. The Black Death (Bubonic Plague) was the single worst pandemic in the history of the world. Estimates of the death toll vary widely, but is generally believed to have killed between 50 to 125 million people, wiping out half of Europe's population in an exceptionally short period of time. The infection is believed to have originated in China or Inner Asia. It had a fatality rate of around 80%. Recurrences of the plague happened throughout the centuries. Europe's population did not recover to pre-Black Death levels for 200 years.

JULY 6, 1853

1853 National Black convention meets in Rochester NY, ex-slave Frederick Douglass attends

JULY 6, 2020

It looks like in 1348 and 1853 humans were dealing with the same issues we face today. I can assume the pandemic of 1348 was handled as efficiently as possible for the knowledge of the time. This pandemic was caused by a bacteria, not a virus, which in today's world would probably never have spread. The reason for the 200 year recovery time is that the plague kept reappearing. At that time in history there were no no known cures, antibiotics would not be discovered for 600 years.

Today we have been attacked by a virus, antibiotics are useless and our story, as history will tell it, will be similar to the Bubonic Plague. In the meantime we need to learn a lesson, and act to the best of our knowledge. Presently we are six months into this pandemic, the coronavirus has infected more than 11 million people worldwide, killing more than 525,000, A far cry from the numbers of 1348. We have the means to control these numbers if we act responsibly. The "Big If."

The battle we are facing to control this virus, seems to be a serious fight against basic arrogance, the feeling of being too smart, too good for any reasonable advice from qualified advisors. Those who wear masks are displaying badges of cooperation, those who are staying away from crowds, and social distancing are practicing the actions which seem to me to be logical. Those in disagreement with these procedures and not practicing them, are claiming that the medical experts are deliberately lying to us, and the figures that we hear each day are all exaggerated or simply false. The real problem here is that we have politicized this issue because of the extreme division between the 'righties' and 'lefties.' So much so that we are probably endangering everyone. As I mentioned before our country has not been this divided since the Civil War. Partisanship has become a stronger influence than the severity of the virus. Political party affiliation has had a bigger effect on whether people wear a mask or practice social distancing than has the level of the virus outbreaks where they live, so insane. Not even the unjust wrongful wars that I have lived through had caused such divisiveness as I see today. It's very sad and it makes treating this pandemic quite difficult.

Concerning the reference to Frederick Douglas in 1863, most of the conditions of racial inequality that he fought for 150 years ago have not changed much. We only need to look at police misconduct in their biased treatment of Blacks to find indisputable racism. However today there exists another form of blatant racism that doesn't find its way onto the front page. There is a place in Mississippi known as Cancer Alley, or Death Alley. It is an 85 mile stretch of land on the banks of the Mississippi River between Baton Rouge and New Orleans. There are more than 150 petrochemical plants here. Most people living in this region are Black, and, according to the EPA, their risk of getting cancer from air pollution is almost twice the national norm, which brings me to the subject of disposable people. Political self interests as well as racism has created such a revolting term. Going right along with it is the term sacrifice zones. Without disposable people, you can't have sacrifice zones. In our country disposable people, sacrifice zones and racism are one and the same.

The watersheds where we frack the earth to extract gas are considered disposable. Certain neighborhoods in Los Angeles, surrounded by urban oilfields, are considered disposable. Another example is the South Side of Chicago, which for years was a dumping ground of petroleum coke (a fossil fuel byproduct) and where residents are still struggling against pollution related diseases. All of these areas, and the people living in these areas are considered to be of no value. And not surprisingly these areas are 85% Black.

JULY 8, 1975

Preamble to the Free Constitution

All men are born bonded, not free. A state that alters the once natural condition of our species.

True freedom is learned and gained throughout the lifetime, if you be so fortunate. These are the truths which should be held self-evident. All men are not created equal and are not endowed with certain unalienable rights of liberty, freedom and the pursuit of happiness. All men are created different. It is this difference that holds the path to an individual's freedom. We are endowed with this freedom just as similarly as we are endowed with food to sustain life. It is a parallel process of growth energy which truly allows man to live and earn freedom.

When man denies this fact and becomes as a collective substance, a communal particle, he negates the right to freedom, declaring himself equal. Equal to the mass or more correctly to the majority of the masses. Immediately bonding himself to the communal laws, and living on the assumption of true knowledge, he has then assumed his freedom, not gained it or in fact earned it.

To be free is to understand the principle of freedom, to destroy all bonds, eliminate all but personal individual laws. All governments are made for and by fools. The free man does not live under the law.

JULY 8, 2020

I wrote this interpretation of the Preamble to the Constitution 45 years ago. In all those years I haven't changed my outlook. I definitely feel less radical than I was then. However as I read it, I can see how it fits perfectly with those who are objecting about today's policies for handling the epidemic. Sadly I see that as a rebel you have options, "pick your fights." And whichever side of the battle you are fighting for does not necessarily prove you to be correct or faultless. History Implies that the men who fought for liberty from England's tyrannical rule were absolutely correct. At the same time these men were beginning the fight for the inhumane sadistic decimation of the Native Americans.

Today's news: The virus is coming back at us, big time. There is no country in the world where confirmed coronavirus cases are growing as rapidly as they are in Arizona, Florida or South Carolina. The Sun Belt has become the global virus capital. This is attributed to opening up too soon. I can only imagine how the right wingers are reacting to this, forget about the conspiracy theorists. "Bullshit," yells the right winger, "I tried to warn you," says the conspiracy dude. I'm on the sidelines saying, "OK now try and settle down, just relax, and come on don't be so negative, you gotta have faith and hope for the best, everything's gonna be OK." And you know what, I believe what I'm saying, I'm feeding the Lone Wolf.

More news: Mary Trump, the president's niece and the first member of the Trump family to break ranks, is about to release a new book The book describes Donald as a child in an adult's body, whose "sociopath" father psychologically damaged him and who developed anger and distrust as defenses for insecurity. She says that he needs constant reassurances about his actions because he always feels he is wrong. Today Trump is urging for the schools to reopen in the Fall. I must say it's a tough decision and maybe with proper measures it could be the right thing to do.

I haven't seen anything in the news about the racial issues in the last couple of days.

JULY 10, 1979

Today is my new son Abel's 4th birthday. I've taken Abel as my son. It's been almost a year now. He is my wife Sunny's child, and the first child of my life. In a month or two our daughter Mia will be born. I hope to soon be finished building the log house. I feel in one way that my life is just beginning. I just read that China has introduced a one-child policy as part of a birth planning program designed to control the size of the rapidly growing population of the People's Republic of China. Well I'm about to have two kids, eat your heart out China, only kidding…

JULY 10, 2020

Big news, big change in the life condition for Suzanne and I. Last Saturday night I made an attempt to leave Suzanne's house late and come back to my house in Healdsburg. The other person, Sally, who has been living in Suzanne's house for over 8 months now, is supposed to be helping me as a caregiver. She openly complained, saying that she could not sleep if I wasn't there and it's not right, I stayed. The following morning she and I had a talk where she insisted that I should be getting paid by the insurance for the time that I am at the house, which is every hour of the week that the morning caregiver is not on the job, Mon-Friday 8AM to 6PM. She then said I could give her some of the money. She wants it to be under the table.

In essence what she is wanting is for Suzanne's insurance company to see that she needs 24/7 care and to pay for it. Suzanne does need 24/7 care, she can not be left alone. That afternoon I called Suzanne's case worker at CNS. I spoke to Albert, he told me that they were led to believe by me that I was going to be Suzanne's caregiver. That I had made that quite clear to them, that is true, I did say all of that. But Sally is correct also, and I will definitely need to be able to walk away from the responsibility of caring for Suzanne when I want to. I am not ready to give up my life completely. I need to be able to break away, to visit my kids in North Carolina, for example. I will never completely walk away from Suzanne, but for my freedom I need to have that option.

When I spoke with Albert at CNS, at one point I broke down and had to compose myself. Of course I love Suzanne. I owe her the world. She's not my wife, she's my good friend who brought Zachary to me, who gave Zachary to me as a son. Brenda always had reservations about the whole relationship telling me that Suzanne was taking advantage of me and that I was raising her son while she did other things. Brenda admitted that having Zachary took time away from her and I. She complained a lot in the beginning when Zachary moved into my house in Healdsburg, but eventually Brenda gave up and understood that I was never going to give up Zac. Our fun together would include my boy Zac. Many times the three of us were on the road together to one of our regular camping ventures.

Well CNS has responded, tonight they are extending Cherry's hours from 6PM to 8PM and sending another caregiver to stay at the house from 8PM to 8AM. I will adjust my schedule without hurting Suzanne. I also want to be with Suzanne, she will remain on the top of my priority list. My concern is what to do with Sally. We all get along together for the most part, but it will be very difficult for me to be constantly in the house with three women. I may begin to include a lot of day trips for Suzanne and I.

Still the top story of the day is the resurging number of Coronavirus patients. And as the medical experts tell us to stay inside, wear masks, etc. the other side continues with their firm opposition, listening to their favorite radio programs, telling them it's a big fake. "Do you know anyone with the virus, do you know anyone who's died?" These questions can certainly sound as if they should be applied, but, most people shouldn't base reality on what they are personally experiencing, unless they are working in an emergency room or the ICU of a hospital where the virus is now spiking. If similar questions were asked to anyone in Healdsburg, in most cases the answer would be no, I don't know anyone who's got it, therefore it must be a fake. According to this way of thinking then poverty isn't an issue. Racism isn't an issue. Sex trafficking wouldn't be real. Children don't go hungry, and there aren't thousands of kids dying every day from malaria. For some reason it's not very difficult for me to understand the big picture here.

JULY 11, 2020

Not to appear too casual about this situation, since I've never mentioned it, but we have another serious problem in our world, it can be considered the biggest problem of them all, and today's the day that attention should be drawn to it. Today is World Population Day. This day is celebrated in order to raise awareness about the growing global population and the issues associated with it. The issues include gender equality, lack of sex education, right to health, sex-determination of an unborn baby, proper use of contraceptives and many more. The day also highlights the importance of better reproductive health and family planning. UN officials started this celebration in 1987 after the world population grew to 5 billion. The UN thought that something must be done to make people aware of the issues that may arise due to this. So let's think about it for a minute.

Overpopulation is a situation where a population is in the process of depleting non-renewable resources. Under this definition, changes in lifestyle could cause an over populated area to no longer be overpopulated without any reduction in population, now that's a good sign. It basically means that if humans were to change our ways of living, even though we continue our present growth rate, we might just make it. However as I mentioned earlier our male sperm count is declining rapidly.

I slept in Healdsburg last night for the first time in a week or so. The situation now with Suzanne's around the clock caregivers is going to be OK.. She's happy and so am I. I will plan to visit Suzanne every day and spend time with her. CNS keeps reminding me of the seriousness of her brain injury and since I have been spending so much time with her, I definitely see the change that has taken place. It's not easy to pick up on it by talking to her over the phone, but she is definitely functioning on a different level.

Since I'm home now with time on my hands, I think it's a good time to introduce Jay Brown.

9

"Hello, my name's Jay Brown."

I believe that there are times in life when you should exert patience and let things reveal themselves to you. I'm not the kind of guy that goes to a party, meets someone and the first sentence out of my mouth is, "What do you do for a living?" or "How much did that cost?" I really believe that by letting others hold onto their personal lives, you are in a sense giving them some respect and dignity.

I had known about Jay Brown for 47 years. However, I never knew his name, and actually I knew nothing about him. I knew he had been born and that he was a male, and that's about it. Oh yes and I knew his mother and father. Now really that is all I knew about him. However, I did feel a very special connection to this person. I often wondered about what kind of guy he was and if I should try to find him, so I could meet him, and he wouldn't be this mystery person anymore.

I think the first reason I never searched him out was fear. I guess I was afraid of what I would find, and it might not be a good thing. As the years passed that fear was replaced by the second reason I never searched for him. And that was, as I mentioned earlier, that through patience, life will reveal itself to you as it wants to, or as your needs dictate. Now this approach might not seem the most logical to practical thinkers. Common sense explains that in order to learn anything one must make an effort and not simply lie down and wait for information to come to you. But let's look at this subject from a different approach.

Does knowledge stop coming to a Christian nun who chooses a life of solitude in a convent, or for the Buddhist monk who lives his entire life isolated on a secluded mountain top? I would say no, that these two people do not just stagnate, their brains don't rot. Somehow they continue to learn new things. Life tells them things. Life is a living thing, ha. For them a belief in some sort of God as such helps to unscramble the workings of daily existence. With this being said, we return to Jay Brown.

One fine summer day I was sitting around doing nothing, like the monk. I receive a phone call. I am now standing on my deck, feeling pretty good about life in general. I had just returned to my home in California after a month of traveling. Ring...ring.... Ring..."Hello, is this Tom Martens?" "Uh, yes it is." "Is this the Tom Martens who used to live in Florida?" "Uh, yes." "Did you live there in 1963?" "Yes, who is this?" "Hello, my name is Jay Brown. [long pause] I'm your son." Gulp.

This all began when I was a Junior in high school. I was to experience my first true love, Diane. She is such a beautiful person and I fell for her big time. We both entered into our first sexual love affair. And as most high school kids can, we went for it, in both of our parents' houses, in the car, at the drive in theaters. Actually no ground was sacred, our sexuality, our passion, trumped everything else. Speaking of Trump, we once did it on the seawall in front of Mar a Lago. Enough said...So Diane becomes pregnant, and as was the custom for Catholic school girls, as soon as her parents were let in on the news, Diane was rushed off to a Catholic facility for unwed mothers. She had Jay and he was adopted by a Catholic family.

Jay was raised in Florida and had a good family with brothers and sisters. He graduated as a civil engineer from the University of Florida and began a successful business. He has fathered 3 children and just recently became a grandfather, thanks to his daughter Christina, a pediatrician. We are all in touch, his other two boys,

Anthony and Michael have been out here visiting me, I am their new grandfather. I've gone down to Jay's house in Gainesville. Along with his wife Susan, we are now one big united family. Final note, after Jay's adopted father died, he set out to find his birth parents. It was not easy, he hired a private detective. I have a wonderful relationship with Jay, we have many things in common and I know positively that he is not disappointed in who he found, in "who I am now."

JULY 12, 2020

Being back at my house has let me return to the healthy practice of lemon water in the morning on an empty stomach. I just finished watching Face the Nation again. Today the whole episode was dealing with the virus as expected. Here is the latest case count. Cases in the U.S. have soared to more than 68,000 on Friday — and set a single-day record for the seventh time in 11 days. More than 60,000 new coronavirus cases were announced in the U.S. on Saturday. North Carolina, Oregon, Arkansas, Hawaii and Alaska all recorded single-day highs. More than 12.5 million people around the world have been infected with Covid-19, and 3.2 million of them are Americans.

We are experiencing an increased number of cases, just as it happened in the initial stages of this outbreak back in March, 12 states have reached their highest number of infections, and 7 states have reached their highest number of deaths. The states that are seriously being affected are ones that voted for Trump and have Republican governors, go figure. The surgeon general was first up today. He had a mask on this time and is now saying that we should all wear masks. The host of the show played a previous clip where he said absolutely that masks are ineffective and useless. His response was, "Oh yeah. Look, we are all learning about this new disease." Even his buddy Trump was seen in public for the first time wearing a mask and saying, "Masks are good, at the right time and place."

So Jerome Adams, the surgeon general. Predicted the new peak to be in 2 to 3 weeks. Meanwhile Texas and Arizona hospitals are becoming overwhelmed. They are ordering refrigerated trucks to serve as morgues. A CEO of Advent Health, Terry Shaw, was up next. His company manages over 30 hospitals. He said it's not critical that ICU capacities are operating at around 85 to 90%. He also predicts that the peak is a few weeks ahead of us. Scott Gotlieb, MD came on again, saying we're experiencing about 1,000 deaths a day at this time. They all spoke of the testing as being crucial, however the number of daily tests conducted in the U.S. is only 39 percent of the level considered necessary.

Bringing us to the next subject at hand, how is our government handling this? Will Trump be re-elected in 100 days? The three hotspot states weigh in like this: Arizona, dead even, 46% for Trump, 46% for Biden; Texas 46% Trump, 45% Biden; Florida, 48% Trump, 42% Biden. A big concern is what the polling places will look like in November. How bad will the virus affect the turnout? Anyone with a brain realizes that write in ballots will certainly offer a solution to possible problems. Trump is opposed to it.

Finally we turn to the school reopenings and the issue of child care centers. Experts spoke and tried to shed light on this, but it's all conjecture. It looks like it must be attempted and with strict caution, it might work. This is such a serious issue with profound consequences. In my immediate family, it is my daughter Mia who is most affected. She has 4 school age children, my grandchildren, Sarah, Aaron, Scarlett and Ayla.

The sun is now setting, I have Suzanne and her night time caregiver Grace, here at my house. They will be staying the night. The weather has finally cooled off. It hit 102 today.

JULY 13, 2020

Coronavirus still tops all news stories, the condition seems worse now than when we had the initial outbreak. Deaths in the U.S. continued to rise over the weekend, to 1,897 from Friday to Sunday, up from 1,115 during the same three days a week earlier

— an increase of 70 percent. Florida announced more than 15,000 new cases on Sunday, the highest single-day total in any state.

President Trump's advisers undercut the nation's top infectious disease expert, Dr. Anthony Fauci, over the weekend, anonymously providing news outlets with statements he had made early in the outbreak. Like many experts, Fauci initially underplayed the risks, but in recent months he has consistently urged Trump to take the virus more seriously.

A 30-year-old Texas man who attended a "Covid party" died after being infected with the virus. Just before he died, he told his nurse: "I think I made a mistake. I thought this was a hoax, but it's not."

Today a big time investor in Facebook as well as one of Silicon Valley's biggest venture capitalists has come forward with thoughts that have been mimicking mine and I'm sure many others of my age. He is fed up with the way Big Tech is turning out, the hate speeches, the way people are using it for profit without regard to the effects on society, and most importantly how it has been undermining our democracy. It seems like Obama has been urging Biden to get in touch with two of the big shots from Google and LinkedIn, and this guy, Roger McNamee wrote an open letter to Biden.

"The tech industry has been transformed into a poster child for income inequality, toxic masculinity and white privilege. In the era of George Floyd, Silicon Valley's leaders are the last people to provide you with guidance on technology policy. Their companies and their community should instead be targets for reform. Technology can and should be a huge contributor to the American economy, but today its culture and business models produce consistently suboptimal outcomes for society. The best analogies are the chemicals industry prior to the Clean Air Act and the pharmaceuticals industry before the Pure Food and Drug Act. Tech companies are profitable because they are not responsible for the harm they cause."

I hope that Biden has read this and follows the advice of Mr. McNamee. As for reforming those companies such as Facebook, Twitter, Snapchat, etc., good luck on that. Again I state my position, this type of change must be made on a personal level. It's the only way it will work its way up to a platform that is nothing more than a reflection of millions of our personal values. You can't easily, if at all, change who people are, what people want. As long as you hold onto a democracy, you must allow free speech. We are now at a turning point. This is a time like never before in my memory. We now have the perfect opportunity for change. We can come out of this lockdown, we must come out of it, as different people. It is the arrogant feeling of superiority that must change. And you know what, the irony is that the identification with superiority is a blatant expression of ignorance. The ABC theory that I proposed earlier, assumption, belief and conviction can be dropped altogether, replaced with an open mind.

First it's arrogance then it turns to vanity. If you want to know how vanity surfaces, look at Donald's hairdo. People are so sure of themselves and their opinions that their ideas become sacred to them. "As sure as I am alive, there is no coronavirus, there is no climate change or global warming. There is no need to cut automobile emissions or stop coal production, no need to limit oil drilling, unnecessary to stop deforestation or worry about soil degradation." This might all sound ridiculous, but to many, it is the exact platform which they embrace.

Mental illness is actually the inability to recognize or act on the truth, in various degrees. Recognizing the truth and opening that door will lay open the path to right action.. There is never a place that we stand without the door of truth in front of us. It's easily recognized as the most beautiful thing in our life. It's the way it works. We are not alone on this journey. If we believe that to be the case, then we have opened the wrong door at some point for some reason. If we shut that door and climb forward grabbing the 'most beautiful thing' that we see, we will walk toward the joy of our existence. We are opening the door of truth.

In order to reach the top of a mountain, the trail is full of switchbacks. It is not possible to climb straight up, That route is way too steep. As life has shown me, there are always switchbacks. And there is always a handhold to help us up the path. It may be a root in the ground or a protruding rock, or a person, a book, a church, an idea, a vision. I believe we must grab onto that thing, it's the way our lives work. Balanced nature provides.

There will always be someone or something to help us along. And we shouldn't let go of this beautiful thing until the next "most beautiful thing" appears. In that way we are guided to the top where we just might find the purpose for our birth into this world.

If there is another life after we die, then nothing that we have done for ourselves is on that reward chart. It's all about what we have done for others. "From what we get, we can make a living. What we give; however, makes a life." - Arthur Ashe

If we go to a heaven, we go there because we have acted unselfishly. If reincarnation is true, as about half the people in the world believe, and we do return in another life form, our karma will give us our just reward. Hopefully it will be life in a happy situation where we do not suffer and we are able to continue to become one with all of creation, learning the next lesson.

Reopening schools, educating the youth of our world is such an important issue in today's news, as it should be. I love the ideas that are springing forth about organizing outdoor classrooms. It would be difficult in larger urban areas, and I'm far from one who sees the big picture, but I will comment for what it's worth. To lock children indoors, especially younger ones for 8 hours a day is not right. It goes against their natural tendencies, and I dare say that many are negatively affected for life. It won't directly kill them and it may be the lesser of two evils, but the better way for sure is to have them surrounded by nature.

The original Americans had an excellent way of educating their children. By following their parents into the wild, they were taught the skills that would prepare them for their futures. Of course the complexity of today's culture is so unlike the Native

Americans that a comparison is rather like an apple to an orange, but there are ideas that we can adopt. All tribal children realized that they were expected to learn. If they didn't learn, they would be shamed in front of the tribe. Those that learned well were openly praised and honored for their work. The elders taught the children the history and morals of their tribe. At a young age children were all taught to be strong and not display outward emotion. When it was felt that they had learned sufficiently, a ceremony took place, a vision quest. Each child was sent alone into the wilderness. They would stay there without food or sleep until they had a vision. The vision would provide a guardian spirit or a direction for the child's adult life.

True, I can't see many vision quest ceremonies taking place in Central Park, Golden Gate Park or the Boston Common. But I can see outdoor ventures, camping excursions with students to the natural world that is not far from the larger cities. And it makes me happy. I truly hope that this idea of outdoor classrooms becomes a part of the change that comes out of our lockdown.

I once read a book that had been written in the early 1800s, when many different native tribes were still around. The purpose of the book was to get interviews and photographs of the many tribal chiefs before they disappeared forever. Most of the chiefs had similar stories. "The white man came, stole our lands, killed the buffalo, put us on reservations, made treaties, broke them, then put us on smaller reservations." One chief said something that has left its mark in my mind. "When I saw how you white men build your houses, I could not imagine why you would build a house that you can't move." An expression of the distinct change in culture, and a change that defines our unmistakeable break away from a natural order, a split from the ecological balance that the European white man chose. It's time now to get back to the outdoor classrooms.

From the *New York Times:* "Rice University in Houston is building nine big new classrooms this summer, all of them outdoors. Five are open-sided circus tents that the university is buying, and another four are semi-permanent structures that workers are building in an open field near dorms, Kevin Kirby, Rice's vice president for administration, told me. Students and professors will decorate the spaces with murals and video projections. In the fall, the structures will host classes and student activities, while reducing health risks — since the coronavirus spreads less easily outdoors. Kirby describes the construction project as 'a statement to the community.' The statement: 'We're creative. We're resilient. And what we do matters.'"

JULY 14, 2020

Here's some great news for a change. "I do think we've reached a point, a real inflection in American history. And I don't believe it's unlike what Roosevelt was met with." This is Joe Biden talking. It looks like if elected he will be pushing a more ambitious agenda than Obama. "Something's happening here, it really is. The American people are going, 'Whoa, come on, we've got to do something." He adds, "I think we have an opportunity to make some really systemic change."

Biden is calling for police reform, sharp cuts in carbon emissions, a major infrastructure program, universal preschool for 3 and 4 year-olds, a big expansion of Medicare and substantially higher taxes on the rich. Bernie Sanders says the agenda would make Biden "the most progressive president since F.D.R."

We're talking about Joe Biden here, the man who will get elected because people are voting against Trump. Joe Biden doesn't seem like an obvious candidate to be a transformational president. He is not a great public speaker, and he doesn't have a strong ideology. Over his long career, Biden has mostly tried to stay near the center of the Democratic Party, even when that center has moved. But history suggests that transformational presidents usually don't look the part before taking office. I am choosing to believe that Biden will become the transformational president that this country is looking for, that we so desperately need. Things are looking up, now if we could just get the virus in check and begin working on these things, life would be sweet.

I think now is a good time for me to go back in time again to New York City.

1968 NEW YORK WITH WILLIAM BURROUGHS

By now I am used to pot and everyone knows how this drug experimentation keeps leading to bigger things. So I find myself a couple years later in New York City. It is now the summer of 1968. I am standing on the street corner of Greenwich Village with Billy Burroughs, the son of the William Burroughs, famous for his writings like *Naked Lunch*, *Junkie*, etc. Billy and I had become close friends in the process of growing up in Palm Beach. In fact it was Billy who really led me down this road, or should I say guided me. With Billy, it all seemed OK.

One day in our confused boredom we decided to drive to New York together in search of sanity, and as for me, I wanted to try hashish. So, we find ourselves on the corner of Washington Square philosophizing, taking in the action of the Village and looking to score. Billy was looking for everything. He had nothing to lose.

This was a trying time. I had come from a good family who cared for me and loved me without question and Billy had come from the uncaring William Burroughs. I read *Naked Lunch* not that it did anything for me. I could see that William was indeed a brilliant, creative thinker and a gifted author indeed. I enjoyed getting into the flow of his style, but actually, I don't see why his writing is so popular. He is considered by many to be the original beatnik, the visionary, the drug guru, and the man who could break you through to the other side of thinking. I always felt this was the biggest crock of shit.

I met William once, when Billy had been busted in Palm Beach for forging prescriptions. The old man flew over from London to stand by Billy's side, to attend his trial. In all the time I had spent with Billy it was the only time I ever knew the old man to show any interest in his son. It was a big deal for him. Billy had just gotten busted for drugs, a 'chip off the old block.' I think he was just feeding his ego. He showed up on trial day with a top hat and coat tails. I loved Billy and I honestly hated his father. I never got to know him personally Perhaps I spoke 30 sentences with him. But I could see what his influence had done to Billy. Not only that, but also this man had killed Billy's mother, shot her in the head and got away with it. This happened when Billy was a baby. Yet Billy loved him and actually worshiped him, as many others did . . . It is all in his memoirs.

After William had shot Billy's mother, he sent Billy to live with his grandmother who had a home in Palm Beach. The family was wealthy, that's all and well, but by the time I got to know Billy, he had been deprived of a normal childhood. His grandmother was senile and Billy simply manipulated her, while attempting to live up to his old man's reputation.

I think what attracted Billy and I to each other was that we were both so liberal in our thinking, radically liberal. There were not that many 16-year-old kids that could understand where Billy was coming from. He recognized something in me when we first met and hung on. Billy was way out there. In my opinion he had a brilliant mind. It was obviously genetic, after all, his grandfather had invented the adding machine, and he was the Burroughs Corporation. And William Sr. was probably a genius, as much as I hate to admit it.

The guy graduated from Harvard in 1946, dropped out of everything, renounced his family, became a junkie, and lived a most vile form of existence. All the while he was a successful writer, a developer of new style, a free thinker, a cult hero, the man who could survive excess. In my opinion he represented all that was negative and self-destructive. And he also became what was the most important to me, Billy's worthless father. As I said before, because of this, Billy had nothing to lose.

Is it possible to sense my emotions, my bitterness? Well you see, Billy is dead now, he died long before his father. The old man just recently died. Although it should not have been so, he outlived his son by many years. In my mind, William did not only murder his wife, he also murdered Billy. Maybe no one else sees it this way, but maybe no one saw, or knew Billy as I knew him.

Billy and I spent hours upon hours thinking together, talking about those things that young people wonder about. In Palm Beach we did it in plush environments, on the streets of New York it would always be in stressful situations. We were always broke, and once again, living on the edge. Billy played his guitar for tips in a few of the clubs in the West Village. I remember once we picked up some sugar cubes from the diner, wrapped them in tin foil and sold them to some young tourist kids looking for acid. They were preppie types. Real acid would have flipped them out anyway. We never knew from night to night where we would be staying. We were always crashing in some filthy apartment on the lower East Side, waking up with 15 to 20 people crammed together all over the floor.

One morning I woke up in some disgusting place, finding cat shit on me and all over the corner where I had slept. Actually it was all over the apartment, a lot of it was dried up and had probably been there for weeks. I saw the sick, diseased, malnourished cat. In an instant I grabbed it and threw it out the window, 7 stories up. I was not in a right state of mind.

And Greenwich Village at that time meant lots of drugs, and of course, drug busts. That part did not happen to me. As much as Billy and I were alike, there was something that separated us and that made us different. I could not do those drugs. It is not that I did not do any, but I could not do it like Billy. I could not be a junkie. I could not stoop that low, all the way down into the gutter. I had a decent family out there, I had parents that loved and cared for me. I always felt that, but Billy didn't have that, he didn't care.

He knew what the drugs were doing to him because he could likely see it in the mirror as his eyes sunk deeper and deeper into his head. He could see it in his arms where the needle tracks were bruising up and often red, swollen and festering with infections. He felt it in his body as it weakened and he knew it in his brain, when he became incoherent and depressed. I have to stress again that

Billy was smart, real smart. He had a mind that was so insightful it could cut right into the heart of most any subject. He did not have to waste time on figuring things out. Yet here he was, deliberately wasting his life.

Not much time passed before I left Billy alone on the streets of the Village and headed uptown to get my own apartment and a life. I took a job as a busboy in a French restaurant, and rented a small apartment on 86th Street near Columbus Avenue.

Billy would call me up when he really needed somebody. Once he told me he had been awake for 6 days. I got him out of jail twice, both times with the help of Allen Ginsburg and Allen's live-in lover Michael. In case you do not know, Allen was a famous poet, the poet laureate of the times, the spokesman for the intellectual subculture. During this period in the early 60s, Allen became more popular as a writer than William. I got to know Allen. Nobody realizes this, but he copied William. He was one of those who worshiped William Burroughs. There was a slight gap in their ages and the timing was such that Ginsburg hit the 60s running, while William had already been there, done that, and nobody knew it. William did not quit doing it by any means. He was still there, in the midst of the movement, being a junkie, a writer, in a low-key way. At that time William was living in Africa and Europe, while Allen was in the US, being raised up on a hippie pedestal.

I do not mean to take anything away from Allen, he was always nice to me, and he did get Billy out of jail twice. I remember well, looking into his face when we would talk about William, how it would shine up and I could feel his brain turning as he attempted to label the great Burroughs. I also remember the pride he took in helping Billy, the son of his guru. Allen was a very smart man and I guess he was a good man, but I must have hated Allen because he loved William.

Once on my day off, I went downtown to meet Billy. He had hooked up with a very skinny junkie girl and she had a halfway clean place on the West Side where they were staying. That night Timothy Leary was bringing his traveling show to a West

Village club, it might have been the Fillmore, I don't remember. His show was called the LSD (League for Spiritual Discovery). He charged people to listen to him sit around and talk about acid etc. Somehow he knew that William Burroughs' son was in town so after the show, he came over to meet him. Because of his father, Billy had a lot of doors opened to him. I was on the fringe of that and met a few other famous people of the times, like Harold Osley, Bob Dylan and this guy named Monty Rock. What a trip he was.

Well it was on that night that I did my first acid trip. Timothy Leary was my guide, so to speak. He did indeed have 'the power.' There was no way that you could get bummed out and have a weird trip with him around. He controlled it all. Like he was just one small step ahead of you at all times. He was not a big giant step ahead, where you felt intimidated. It was as if you were just about to think what he was just going to say.

Timothy Leary was an intellectual, but in my opinion he became confused over time and his main problem was that he never grew out of the period. I think the acid fried his brain. I have known of many gurus who could not handle the power that they received.

So you have the story, William Burroughs, a brilliant Harvard graduate, Allen Ginsburg, a brilliant poet, Timothy Leary, a brilliant Harvard professor, and oh yes I can not forget about Richard Alpert, who I also met, another Harvard professor. He would quit drugs and turn to eastern philosophy to become Baba Ram Dass. I cannot really call him brilliant. All these men, along with people like Ken Keasey and Jack Kerouac were all condoning and promoting this drug culture.

I would like to comment just a bit more and then finish up with the 60s, that time period which holds so much interest for so many young people. It seems to be a hallowed and revered time period. As I mentioned, it was indeed a time of intensity, of creativity. The great music coming from this period is proof enough. This music will live as long as time. In the 60s I guess I did it all, everything the times had to offer. I went on protest marches against the war, got busted for pot, placed on probation, studied Eastern religions, practiced Yoga, went to rock festivals, studied physical therapy. I even got into business, starting up a computer programming service with a friend. The 60s were indeed confusing, powerful, intense, emotional, and creative. But the reputation that it would earn, in my opinion, is rather a myth.

When my daughter became a teenager she remarked to me that I was so fortunate to have lived in the 60s. "Our generation doesn't have anything like that," she said. I believe that in one way, she is correct. I listened to her music and that of my son's, a few years earlier. If the music is a gauge of creativity, then as I see it, my thoughts are confirmed.

There is so much that has been written about the 60s that I need not go deeper into it. In one respect, I was lucky to have lived it as intensely as I did, and survive. It could easily have gone the other way. I came out of this creative period with relatively little obvious damage, either physically or mentally. I was exposed to plenty and still kept on the safe side. I was not scathed by the horrible war, nor destroyed by drugs. My brain was not harmed. My mind remained open.

JULY 15, 2020

Today is more of the same news. There is now only one high-income country in the world in which the virus is spreading rapidly, and that's us, the United States. Even in Sweden, which has had one of the least successful responses to the virus, the number of new cases has plummeted in the past two weeks. It also appears that our economy is headed for a tumultuous autumn, with the threat of closed schools, struggling businesses, new lockdowns and empty stadiums.

When I recall my time in NYC back in 1968, I ask myself what constitutes, what causes change? I am not the same Tom Martens that wandered around the Village in those years with Billy. He and his father William, Timothy Leary, Allen Ginsburg, Richard

Alpert, have all changed drastically. They are all dead. I'm the only one left to tell that story. And the person telling that story is different from the one who lived it. In this case, the change in me is a modification of my personality, a shift in my thinking, a transformation, a reform in the nature of my being. The content of who I am now, the future course of where I am going is definitely something different from what it was in 1968. In order to feel the emotions of those important life experiences, which I definitely can do, I simply travel back along the timeline.

I'm sure that my 1968 NYC experiences are less influential than some of my contemporaries that were drafted to Vietnam. They were forced to live through the horrible struggles of a war environment. Today I still see many of these individuals displaying their relationship with that part of their past, on their tee shirts, on their caps. In some cases their entire outfit, cap, shirt, pants, pins, even their demeanor, places them, keeps them, 65 years later, back in Vietnam. Their change has been less than mine. Could it be that the intensity of emotion is related to the execution of change, or the lack of it?

As I write this book, I am obviously describing the experiences of my past that are most memorable. I think that whenever an experience is recorded into your memory, an automatic response takes place. The emotion of that time is also recorded. When you call upon that memory, the particular emotion comes up with it and affects your present state. Here's my theory. Although reactions to most emotions are physically visible, the emotion itself is not. You can't pick up anger or hate or love. You can certainly feel it quite intensely, but you can't see it, you can't touch it, dissect it. I am suggesting that emotions are not stored in a particular section of the brain. While the brain triggers emotion and records the sensation of it, emotion itself changes into a body response. At times of heavy emotion, hormones are released and race through the body, triggering galvanic skin response, tightening of muscles, quickening of breath, pupil contraction, rapid heart rate, and other bodily responses, which we then experience as emotion. This explains the physiological reaction to emotions, but not enough in my mind to define love, for example.

I'm going out on a limb here and saying that we are spiritual beings and that the mind is what binds the soul to the body and the brain is simply the vessel of the mind. For the sake of understanding, the words I am using, the concept of an emotion, is a part of our spiritual being and is basically indescribable. There are no words for some things. Our true emotional reactions better describe who we really are, better than any words that come out of our mouths, or thoughtful actions that we perform. Emotions which are not expressed tend to be unresolved and tend to build on an unconscious level.

Our life is like a snowball rolling down the timeline, and it sometimes gets bigger and filled with stronger emotion as it goes. An important point that I am making is that every moment of our life should be filled with positive emotion and every memory that we record should be recorded in an emotion of happiness and joy. So, eat chocolate, love everyone and "be happy, don't worry." Easier said than done.

I talked to my friend Brenda in Florida today and she said she is definitely not ignoring the news of the day, and is ready to fight at any time to save our world. Her feelings about Trump have exceeded way past the demarcation line, the distinct separation safe zone between two combative countries. In this case it's the two different political policies. Brenda does a lot of social networking and she does not hold back when it comes to stating her opinions. I mean we are talking about the former "Mistress Sadie" here. I've never known Brenda to take a timid approach to anything. When I met her she was more or less the leader of all the women in our social world. She will deny that, but I saw it. The North Carolina mountain style of life didn't stop Brenda from being Brenda. She came into this world in 'West by God Virginia,' as she puts it, so the Blue Ridge Mountains were home to her. Where we met in the rural section of Western NC, there was very little social stratification. Most everyone was considered as an equal. Except, that is, for the Black community.

Unfortunately racism existed and it was one of the issues that eventually I found very difficult to deal with. I had lived with this in the South since my birth so it wasn't that surprising and it took a while to affect me. I was experiencing all the good of the Appalachian culture. As they lived, I joined. Sometimes outsiders are not accepted into their world but I came in not wanting to change a thing. Most of the locals are proud and very content with the places where they live. They are very close to nature and that's where I wanted to be. I walked into the woods with a mule and a new chain saw, and I built a log house. I was accepted. Soon Brenda and Gary pulled in with their bus and kids.

I planned to talk more about Brenda but I will come back to this later. I want to now explain about the world I had made for myself as a young adult. We're going for a trip into the natural mountain environment of North Carolina. I wrote this approximately 20 years ago.

10

North Carolina

The Appalachian Mountains are the oldest mountains on the planet, which certainly should count for something. I believe that these old mountains are one of the 'very special places' in the world. Not realizing where I was heading or why I was going there, as a 25 year-old man, it was where fate would deliver me.

In addition to my spiritual life, I began to simultaneously develop a new physical life, a communication with Mother Earth. Along with this step came a more solid attachment to things like nesting, making long-term plans, and lifelong commitments. My girl friend Cathy and I had decided to embark on a new life of our own making. We were ready to leave Florida for a better environment. I had not been in the ocean since Artchie's death. Florida had nothing more to offer me. The area was growing rapidly, and changing for the worse. I was eager to leave.

As a diver in Belize, I had met some people who were farming lobster, raising them in huge tanks. Their operation was on an island in Massachusetts, Martha's Vineyard. Since I was a self-proclaimed expert on lobster, I decided to head there with Cathy. There I would seek employment with my old acquaintances, and we would begin anew.

Along the way we stopped to visit a friend in North Carolina. Upon our arrival, my friend Kenyon, and his wife Denise, brought us on a hike to a most beautiful waterfall, Catawba Falls. Along the trail we picked wild strawberries and listened intently as Kenyon expounded on the surrounding facts of nature. We absorbed his enthusiasm. That evening we met Kenyon's close friend Clyde Hollifield, another Artchie, country style. Clyde is one of the most creative, multi-talented people that I would ever meet. He possesses the quality of respective endearment. Exactly as Timothy Leary, he has a way of leading you without intimidation. Clyde is a teacher and a student at the same time, a rare quality.

Clyde is alive and well as I write this, so I beg his pardon, but he resembles an elf or a hobbit in appearance. He's bald, and short, with a round belly, a scraggly ponytail, and a long gray beard. The first words from his mouth assure you that he is one of the people who have it together.

Clyde has also had a big influence on my life, and I am sure, on the life of everyone that will ever meet him. Because of Kenyon and Denise's warm friendly kindness and because of Clyde's amazing energy, Cathy and I were so taken in, that we would settle, and remain in the mountains of North Carolina for many years.

To me the most impressive products of the North Carolina mountain environment are the many beautiful souls, living peacefully within the hollows and gorges of these mountains. They are in touch with nature. They garden and farm, they hike in the woods, gathering wild flowers and herbs. The beauty of the creeks, waterfalls and lakes are appreciated and respected by them. It is their source of happiness. They are proud to be North Carolinian mountain people. To test the truth of my statement, one needs only to conduct a personal survey. There is no question here, that in today's complex world, the inhabitants of these mountains are far and above, happier, and more well adjusted than most any other group of people I have ever met.

Cathy and I were led to a piece of land next to Kenyon, Homer's land, which we rented for $25 per month. It had a small shack with four rooms, and an outhouse. The parcel consisted of 90 acres, mostly mountainous, with a creek, a waterfall and a piece of bottom land that we would garden. It was to be my first experience with planting anything. Gardening is such a wonderful way to communicate with the earth; and, of course, of relating to all its little insect inhabitants as well, and moles and gophers, and deer. There is much to learn when tending the soil for your food. And it is all fun and valuable information. It should be included in the foundation of every child growing up. My parents and my schooling missed that with me. There is a valuable message in the statement of John Erskine, "I have never had so many good ideas day after day as when I worked in the garden."

I have brought up a key word, 'foundation,' a basic amount of knowledge on which more knowledge can be developed. This is what North Carolina was going to give me in the course of the next ten years. Prior to settling here, of course I had a foundation, after all I was 28 years old. But the foundation I had was lacking many of the basics that I should need to become a complete man. Of the four principles, earth, fire, water and air. I knew only a little about water and nothing about earth, fire, or air. Even my knowledge of water was salt water at that. I was a specialist, not very well rounded, so to speak. As are many people of the developed nations, we have left the simple life, choosing a more complex system with many machines and gadgets. The schools need to teach all the 'gadget operation' courses, there is not enough time to instruct in 'home gardening' or 'hiking awareness.'

There is a popular book in print these days entitled "Conversations with God." One of my friends is attending a group that meets to study this book. As I visited my friend one day he handed me the book and I thumbed through it, I came upon a section about schooling. The idea presented, as my memory has it, is to change the entire school curriculum, teaching courses on 'how to love' and 'how to be happy,' etc. This is a very good suggestion. There is so much valuable information available today and an incredible amount of good books in print, but in my mind, we readers after a while, need to put the books down, and practice that we learn. North Carolina mountain living was to become a nds on' experience for me.

Out of necessity my lifestyle taught me how water comes from the earth and how to catch it and bring it into your house, and what to do with it when you were finished with it. I learned how cars run and how to fix them when they break. I learned what a hammer and nail could do. I learned how to build my own house for my family and myself. I learned how to ride a horse, and raise chickens and goats. I learned how to keep bees and harvest honey. I learned how to milk a cow and make cheese. I learned the principles of electricity, and how one could produce it from a creek or from the wind or from the sun. I learned how to harvest the forest without harming the ecology. I learned to heat our home and cook our meals from the energy of trees. I gathered edible food and medicinal herbs from the forest. I made potions and poultices and salves and tea from nature's own garden.

All of these things, I was not doing alone, I had a friend, a mate, a lover and a wife. Cathy and I married soon after arriving in these mountains. It was so right. For $6,000, we bought a small 12-acre parcel of mountain land with a tiny country shack. The porch was falling apart and the roof often leaked, but in very short order I began to repair these things. While Cathy ground wheat into flour, and corn into meal, and made clothing from cloth, I built fences, out buildings and a barn. In the summer we planted new fruit trees and berry bushes, we put in perennial flowerbeds, plowed our garden with a mule and tilled the soil, gardening, weeding and harvesting together. When fall came we picked fruit from the older existing trees. Our property had apple, peach, persimmon and plum trees. There were many scuppernong grapevines, and of course wild blackberries and strawberries.

Cathy chose to do the canning of our fruits and vegetables. I made wooden drying racks, which we suspended on the porch and over the wood stove. And after summer, when fall came, we began to prepare for the winter ahead. It is such a wonderful feeling to have cupboards filled with your own food and chords of firewood cut, split and stacked, waiting for the cold gray days that would soon approach. And it is such a joyous experience to spend your time in this way, preparing, exerting the energy in such a positive natural manner. There is never time for boredom. There are always chores ahead and plans in the making. We were continually growing, learning, and improving our lives.

Another bonus about living in the country as we did, is that all of our friends had exactly the same lives. A strong bond would form between us. And everyone's timing was the same. We would all be planting in the early Spring and Summer, and gathering different wild foods as they came into bloom. And we would all be harvesting our gardens at the same time. I had never experienced such a phenomena in city life. Such a thing does not exist in cities. I had friends in the city, but they were all doing different things with different jobs and a variety of different social activities. Sure, in the city, friends' paths cross in relative fields of interest, but the closeness that develops in country friendships can rarely be accomplished in the mayhem of city life.

A sad fact is that people seem to become less valuable commodities when their numbers increase, just like inflation, worthless money. Imagine if you were to be offended by someone on the street in New York City. The bad feelings that person would cause you would last for a short while, but soon be gone. And the person that offended you would soon be gone forever from your life. There would easily be someone taking that person's place. Now imagine that the two of you were alone on a deserted island. This incident would have so much more meaning and so much more effect on the course of both of your lives. More than likely, the issue would demand attention. Imagine if the island was a sand mound, only twenty yards wide with only one single palm tree. Ah, but now, parachute in a third person, and the whole dynamics change. The third person's arrival would more than likely diminish the importance of dealing with the second person issue.

As I see it, when "The Big Bang" in human consciousness took place this is what happened. All the personal problems in the world are the result of poor communication. As people became individuals and their minds moved away from each other, problems developed.

Since we all came from the same place, moving back towards our 'center' automatically solves this problem of miscommunication. We would never choose to offend our own self.

There was no better place for me to 'center' myself than in the backwoods mountains of North Carolina. It could easily have been Maine or Vermont or Montana. I am sure that in most rural areas, courtesy, hospitality, and concern for others is commonplace. Humans like all other animals in nature need to have a territorial imperative. They need a certain amount of free reign space in order to maintain proper physical health and sanity and most importantly to survive as a species. The crowding of wild animals into the confines of zoos often brings about, murder, rape, and cannibalism in species that had never before known such actions. And the crowding of man into the confines of the city results in the same such actions.

On the mountain roads where I lived and traveled, residents did not pass by each other obliviously, going about their private and personal business. Making eye contact through the car windshields was common practice. Drivers always acknowledge each other's presence. A hand wave or slight nod of the head was the norm, a practice that I immediately took up. It is such a welcoming, friendly and warm custom.

I must admit that there are times when this practice loses its personal touch and becomes somewhat of a habit. I can remember many times unconsciously waving, nodding my head and whispering "Howdy" to the neighbor's cow as I passed by her in the field. I developed a little 'pinky finger wave' that I could flash out from the steering wheel, if necessary.

The locals in these mountains are never too busy to look after their neighbor's needs. For example, I found that it was impossible to sit on the side of the road, broken down with car trouble, for any considerable length of time. Usually the first person passing by would stop and offer help. They would assist you for hours if need be. It was almost unbelievable for me. "How could they do this," I thought. "Don't they have somewhere to go, something to do?"

Phrases such as 'southern hospitality,' words such as 'patience,' and 'neighborly' took on meaning for me. It was not long before I became one of these people. It is a lifestyle that I wanted, one that I believe, deep inside, everyone wants.

On the other hand, congested freeway driving does not lend itself to waving. On the LA freeway, even my easy to do, 'pinky wave' would probably be considered loony. The priorities are not the same for busy city people. Too many hurried people out there driving too many cars at too fast a speed.

There was an instance when I was still residing in North Carolina and had driven with my family to California on a vacation. We were driving up Interstate 5 from Los Angeles to San Francisco. At that time I had a an older pickup truck with a camper, well equipped with tools, in case of any mechanical emergencies. Somewhere north of LA in the early morning hours, with a very damp fog permeating the air, I noticed a broken down motorist outside his shiny new car. He had nervousness in his manner, confusion and exasperation on his face. I pulled over, stopped in front of him and walked back to offer help. Initially the man was shocked and appeared very skeptical about my motives and me. As it turned out, his problem was simple to solve. He had run out of gas, and it just so happened that I had two gallons of gas in plastic milk jugs in the back of the camper.

I happened to be in possession of this gas because a few days before, I had helped another motorist at a gas station who had accidentally begun to pump gas into his diesel Mercedes. That was in Arizona. I had climbed under his car and unscrewed a drain plug at the rear of the gas tank. We drained the two gallons of gas from his tank, and I put them into my camper.

Well I was able to pour this gas into the car of the broken down motorist. It had a little oil from the diesel fuel tank, but it would not harm his motor. We solved his problem. I felt that we were both fortunate. I was able to help him and he was able to continue on his way. Now then, the gas had been given to me, and I wanted to give it to the gentleman in need. It was a perfect end for this gas that I had been carrying around. However, the man would not accept this as a gift. He insisted on paying me. I remember him saying, "Oh yeah, I know you're a good person and all that, but I'm not taking this for free." It was hilarious. I was trying to be like the North Carolina person that I had become, and he being the Los Angeles person that he had become, would not compromise. Finally I agreed to accept the cost of the gas, which would have been a couple dollars. No way, the poor rich man would not allow me to give him my time for free. He could not accept kindness. He had to pay. I gave in as he stuffed a twenty-dollar bill into my pocket.

In this life it is equally as important to be able to receive as to give, to receive graciously and with respect to the giver. If the man had been able to receive from me he would also be giving to me. I believe there are proper times to refuse an offer. There are wonderful human beings in this world who would give to others even though they cannot afford to be doing so. I have often turned down kind offerings to my family and me, because I knew it was the correct thing to do.

There is another funny twist to this story, I remember keeping that gas in the car for a few days. Leaving Arizona, the price of fuel was continually climbing higher as we approached California. I had been laughing to myself, thinking ironically, that if I waited, these two jugs of gas would become worth a fortune. Thanks to the stranded stranger, the gas wound up fetching ten dollars per gallon.

While living in North Carolina I learned about kindness and the fact that other people's needs should take priority over many of our personal matters. Because of unnecessary haste, most of today's urban societies do not practice this courtesy. What results is an unfortunate snowballing or domino affect of incorrect behavior. By the 'snowball effect,' I mean, that if one family fails to teach their younger members this rule, then all the following generations will suffer without ever knowing what they have lost. As a result many people are born without this basic moral code. They never know about giving to others and they cannot be blamed for their actions.

We are all born with primary instincts, but ethical behavior has to be learned.

What I mean by the 'domino effect' is that if one person falls in the line of kindness, then everyone will fall. For example, assume I have an important meeting that I am driving to. If I stop to assist a stranded motorist, I shall be late for my meeting. Now if the party waiting for me does not consider that my act of kindness to the motorist was necessary, then he will certainly look upon me with unkindness. He has no patience. Perhaps he is scheduled for another meeting soon after our appointment. My delay causes him to be late. Now if he knew that his being late would not be taken unkindly, then he would have had more patience with me and everyone would have been OK. The weakest link in the chain will cause the chain to break, rendering it useless. This is why it is important for all people who live together, be it in a prehistoric cave, or in a complex society such as ours, to work in unselfish co-operation. In order to accomplish this, all members must accept the basic tenets and moral code of the society. The foundation of the society must be strong. It seems like todays progress in science is far ahead of man's ethical behavior

In order for the foundation to be strong, it must be built in the correct manner, with the proper materials. Built with love and unselfishness and made from kindness and generosity. In the construction business, that I was to learn, every step after the foundation is totally dependent on its strength. Unless the basic premise is correct, regardless of the logic, every following conclusion is invalid, and every following action is therefore incorrect. People and their houses are exactly the same. Many are built without a good foundation. On the surface they may appear as beautiful objects, and will survive for many years, but deep inside they are living a tenuous existence. They need to be fixed or else they will surely fall.

North Carolina and its people were fixing the problems with my foundation. Problems I did not realize I had. These problems were never explained to me. The solutions were not spelled out for me nor were they preached to me from a pulpit. They were revealed to me by the inner-actions of the harmonious surrounding nature, and the outer actions of the peaceful old time mountain residents, people like Vilas Hall, Winslow Ledford, and Clyde Hollifield. The truth was not passed on to me by another's words, but rather this true understanding came from within myself. Observing life around me brought it out slowly and methodically. "Do as I do, not as I say." This should be the adage of any honest, knowledgeable teacher or guru. This is one of the Unspoken Truths. North Carolina taught me the correct dos and don'ts of social behavior.

In a sense North Carolina was my divine prison, the mountains were my prison yard, the little shack was my cell. For all the bad things I had done and for all the good things that I deserved, I had been sentenced there by God to serve from ten years to life. I needed to be there. I was put there on the work gang, forced into a life of hard physical labor, toiling to make a living by the sweat of my brow. This is what a prison should be. It shouldn't be hell, but it should be, as the nuns and priests had taught me about purgatory. A confessional should not be a place where you whisper your sins to another human being. It should be a place where you learn to change the force that caused the sin. No one else can cure a spiritual problem but one's self.

11

Continuing Along

Since today's societies demand and need prisons, they should all be divine prisons, places that teach correct social behavior, allowing inmates to grow forward, to become positive creators. They must be transformed from negative holes of depression and abandonment.

If the Catholic religion insists on using confessionals, then they should also have 'good confessionals,' next to the bad ones. This confessional would be a place where the 'happy priest' sits and one could go in and tell him all your good deeds. And if a society has a criminal and civil court where a judge sentences people to pay fines and sends them to jail, then the society should also have a court that issues awards and provides divine prisons. The question is, who should be the judge of such a court. Who has the knowledge, the ability to look into the accused's soul? The power to control the destiny of another's life is an extreme power. If only it could be left in each individual's hands and in the hands of God.

As I write this, I realize that in my childhood I had lived in a divine prison. All of the Caribbean, the Bahamas, Jamaica, Haiti, all of them had been used, more or less, as penal colonies and places where lawless pirates, or buccaneers as they called themselves, lived and ruled. Governor appointments to the Caribbean and Central America were granted as punishment for those who had lost favor with their king and queen. British Honduras was the home of many of the descendants of just such people. But for me this region of the world was a mini heaven. Everywhere I had been exposed to as I developed was perfect for me. Therefore I assume the liberty of calling these places the first divine prisons of my life. Prisons, only because I was sentenced there by the wishes of my parents. Divine, because in so many ways these places are similar to North Carolina.

I was fortunate as a child to have lived in such beautiful places, and I was fortunate as a young adult to again find myself living in God's Country. There are varied reasons that bring people to live in a particular city, region or country of the world. When fate has it that your place of residence is your own choice for reasons other than economics, then by choosing your destination, you have also chosen your destiny. By being able to place economic concerns below other more important priorities, proves that one is living a blessed existence. I mean to say that when one is fortunate enough to have sufficient control over their life's choices, then it is much simpler to take the next step towards balancing that physical lifestyle with a spiritual life.

How is it conceivably possible that in a civilized world, a piece of art work can be bought at a price of twenty million dollars, while simultaneously twenty million people in this same world are starving to death? This is an absolute absurdity, and it is not the result of people that practice a spiritual lifestyle. Not only the guy who bought that piece of artwork, but all of us who have enough food to eat every day, should pay attention to the starving people and help them. The Appalachian culture has bred into their people the desire to help one another. Religion is strong there and there are some church groups that work towards this goal.

To govern such masses of people as are living today is extremely difficult. None of the present systems in our world are working, benefiting the whole that is, democracy means capitalism, which often leads to a class system filled with greed and poverty. Socialism means communism, which destroys individuality, wrecks ambition, turns to inefficiency and leads to corruption. There is an urgent need for a totally new concept, a completely different system. Money represents energy. It is the reward for exerted effort. Yet its distribution is never fair. This is a problem that surpasses most all the other problems in our world today. It is the direct cause for most of a society's social problems.

In the United States we should say to hell with our Supreme Court and to hell with George Washington and Thomas Jefferson and their 'divine Constitution.' Were these slave-owners really qualified? Can we not write a better one? Can we not set up a society where people are not homeless and hungry? Can we not develop a system of law where money does not free the guilty, and the lack of it, force lower class citizens on a spiraling path towards self-destruction? This is exactly what is happening. I do not have the answer to this political dilemma. Perhaps one day by the grace of God, someone will.

JULY 16, 2020

No real change in newsworthy reporting since yesterday. It is still the surging of Coronavirus making headlines. Some analysts refer to this as a big second wave, but actually this is still very much the first wave. It has none of the characteristics of a second wave, nor is there any substantial evidence that the first wave was ever over. What happened was very predictable. Before the first wave was over too many places rushed to reopen which created a dramatic spike in infections. Not only was it predictable, but it was widely predicted. Sadly, the people running a number of US states decided not to listen. They were not unique, many people have fallen into the same trap. But what is less forgivable is that they had the benefit of seeing others fall into the same trap, and yet still blundered in themselves.

The virus and any attempt at control measures is very much still politicized. Americans have always as a rule trusted scientists, not anymore, politics get in the way of that. Since this is the normal behavior, it is absolutely inevitable that in terms of interpreting the impact of Covid-19 people have picked sides, and, evidence be damned, they are sticking to them.

There are only a couple places where racial protesting continues. In Louisville, Ky., protesters went to the streets yesterday demanding justice for Breonna Taylor, a 26-year-old Black woman who was shot and killed at her home by the police.

The hot weather is making news, a serious heat wave has hit the South and the Southwest. Record temperatures as well as the rising coronavirus cases have created a one-two punch for much of that area. . . . Thank you for listening, stay tuned, we'll have more of the same for tomorrow.

So to put a personal look at our present situation I can only repeat myself. It is so obvious and quite sad that understanding and compassion for political opponents is in very short supply right now, and I do not see things changing. Of course everyone is entitled to their opinion, but it is now quite clear that the subject of how to handle the pandemic is not even up for discussion. It seems futile for either side to attempt to change the other. It is unlikely that carefully presented arguments or evidence is likely to dissuade either from their opinion.

Most University philosophy students have heard about John Rawls. Rawls asked us to imagine that we are all in some giant waiting room in the sky, waiting to be born. At this time we don't know if we will be born rich or poor, smart or dumb, handsome or plain, healthy or chronically sick. He postulates that behind this "veil of ignorance," if we were all to sit down and agree how we were going to allocate the fruits of our respective gifts, we would push for as equal a division as possible. We would all be in a compromising position. But then we are born and the equality that we had agreed upon starts to fade away. It seems that the competition which we immediately discover exists, begins to control our behavior. We need to use all of our special gifts and talents to dominate the competitors. Once we begin to win, our primary concern is to keep the things we earn.

And now we create social division, class status. Today this natural way of conduct has polarized our nation. We have, and we have had for some time, a frustrated political underclass who feels they have been marginalized. We have the rich, the poor, the privileged and the abused. I believe it is these circumstances that have caused the divided country that we now live in. Initially I blamed this divisiveness on Trump, but it could have been anyone who jumped in at this time, offering a bold, novel solution. It was pretty much inevitable that a rough and ready newcomer would make a legitimate challenge for high office at some point. He challenged the status quo and promised to get things done his way. And in 2016 it finally happened, and it happened to be Trump. But if Trump had never been born, then it could have been some other strongly opinionated commander in chief. There is nothing particularly unique about Trump the man, what was unique was the circumstances which led to his election. Actually there are some unique traits that Trump possesses, all of them rather dreadful.

His diehard supporters see him as a hero. That's why it doesn't matter what he actually does. He can lie, cheat, abuse, betray his friends and colleagues, slander war veterans and their families, even bargain with a foreign power for his own gain. None of that matters because his followers consider him a star, and feel that he's the hero of forgotten America. Sadly, we now have the pleasure of being surrounded by a number of people just like him: ignorant, selfish, and rude.

At this time within the US, there is roughly about a 60–40 split between those that dislike Trump and those that support him. Outside of the US it is entirely one-way traffic. Pretty much everyone in the entire world loathes him. I read these figures and pray that we are not facing another Trump Term. What he has done to our reputation, our world position, will not be easily repaired.

So, let's continue in this fashion and talk about a true "Trump hater." That would be Brenda. As I mentioned earlier, Brenda has a strong personality and is a leader. By this description, you can assume that she has a positive way with people. She is also very artistic and very attractive. When we met she and Gary were on the outs, Gary was seeing another woman and Brenda was fair game for my advances. We became almost boyfriend/girlfriend and had a wonderful relationship. It's difficult to remember the exact reason for our splitting up, but one thing for sure, it happened in a friendly way and we continued to remain close friends. I do remember that she was pretty close to a guy who had moved from the fair circuit to San Francisco and had started the Asian Yellow Pages. I continued to build log houses for other people in the mountains. And Brenda eventually followed her friend to SF. When my time in North Carolina ended I was off again to Central America.

I put down the construction tools and began my film career in earnest. After several years I had made my way back to California. Brenda and I renewed our close friendship. She had become a city girl but definitely remained 'country' at heart, escaping to the woods with her REI gear whenever possible. She had it all, the best tents, stoves, cots, ovens. Definitely Brenda camped in comfort and style, and I was dragged right into it, as well as many other of her SF friends. Zac was my young child at that time, and he loved camping with Brenda and still does. I remember so vividly the first night Zac experienced true freedom. I had set up a tent for him and another young kid, and when he realized there was no set time for bed, no rules as to where he could wander around, or nobody needed to know when he decided to come back to his tent, he became a free man. We were camping on Jamie's property way north of San Francisco on the way towards Lake Tahoe. Jamie had lots of land and there was no danger for Zac.

A pristine river ran through the property and that's where we would spend our daylight hours. I can still see Zac as he climbed up a huge rock and jumped into the swimming hole, another first. By this time Brenda was in the balloon business and she always brought boxes of light ropes. At night everyone had necklaces, bracelets or leggings of light ropes. Hoops were made and games developed, and of course every night, the tribal fire.

When we went camping we always planned to stay two days but wound up leaving after 4 or 5. Brenda had her way with me. I will never forget the night in hell. It was in the winter and Zac was not with us. It was only Jamie, Brenda and I who remained.

We all had our tents up above, not down at the river. Brenda and I wanted to sleep by the river. Jamie drove us and our gear with the four wheeler down to the river. By this time it was dark. He had some diesel fuel and it spilled into our sleeping bags. When we got to the river the first thing we needed to do was start gathering firewood, the night was getting cold. It continued getting cold and then colder.

We got our fire going and spread out the sleeping bags. It was then that we realized about the diesel fuel. And the night continued to get colder, and the fire continued to burn faster, and all the wood would disappear at warp speed. We had no choice but to wrap ourselves up together in our diesel fuel sleeping bags. Trying to stay warm and fall asleep was not happening. We had to continue getting more little twiggy branch firewood. "How in the hell did I get into this situation?" Walking up top was not an option, it was too far. We continued hitting the Tequila bottle and somehow survived the night in hell. Except for when the fire died down, we stayed wrapped up like one big diesel tortilla trying to conserve our heat. Brenda had accidentally thrown her Reebok sandal into the fire. Daylight finally started to come. Salvation.

And then, there was the other night. Again it was only Brenda and I who remained at the property, even Jamie had left. We were up top with our plush tents. I was falling asleep in a reclinable chair by the fire. Brenda wanted me to stay awake. As was often the routine, she kept saying, "C'mon, don't fall asleep, what can I get you? Open your mouth," and she dumped in another slug from the vodka bottle. Jamie had been working with his toys, using the front loader to dig away part of the hill. He was preparing to make a huge pit for a pig roast that he had planned. So I get up from the chair and stagger away looking for a place to pee, no headlight. Sure enough, over the new cliff I go. I must have been pretty loose thanks to the social lubricants that Brenda had been dumping into me. No serious damage in the fall, over what would become known as Gandhi Falls. I had been given the nickname Gandhi by most of the SF friends I had made. I'm not sure whether I earned that name because of my spiritual inclinations or my short bald appearance. I like to think a little of both.

Another good camping story. We were camping this time on a small mountain lake in a campground even further into the Mountains. Brenda and I were both asleep inside of the tent when she suddenly jumps up and tries to wake me. "Did you hear that?" she said. I rolled over not quite awake. She goes outside the tent to inspect and the next thing I know, she's running back inside, I'm now waking up. She grabs the whiskey bottle from under her cot, rushes back through the door, "God damn bear," she yells. "He ain't eating our food." She was planning to battle that bear by bonking him on the head with her whiskey bottle. By the time I got out the bear was gone, Brenda was alive and she had saved the wonderful stew that she had made that night. Now, in a showdown, who do you think would win, her or Trump?

JULY 17, 1977

I'm waiting to get discharged from the hospital this morning. I spent last night here because of a mean copperhead snake. Yesterday morning I was digging through a pile of scrap wood from my building project when I felt something sting. I thought a bee or a scorpion had got me on my hand. When I looked at it, I saw two little bleeding holes. I then got out a hoe and moved some wood where I had been digging. Coiled up was an adult copperhead. I proceeded to chop him up as my friend Hawk LittleJohn suggested. The belief is that rattlesnakes are not deliberate threats and mercy can be shown to them, but copperheads are mean and aggressive and should not be on or near your property, especially if you have children, which I do.

I called Dr. Denuna asking for his help. He told me to come down to the hospital and he'd meet me in the ER. I told him I didn;t want to stay in the hospital. I know that that is the normal procedure. He said, "Don't worry, just meet me there." When I arrived Dr. Denuna wasn't there. He had sent orders to start an IV and admit me. So last night I was administered the antivenom and had a penicillin shot. An antibiotic dressing is on my hand. It's a little swollen up to my wrist, but it doesn't appear to have any surrounding tissue damage. It could have been a lot worse. I must not have had a lot of poison injected. I think by tomorrow I'll be able to swing a hammer.

JULY 17, 2020

Along with the bad news, yesterday we broke another record for the number of new virus cases, today's news has a bright spot. It appears that some facilities in England have discovered a successful treatment, an intramuscular injection of immune blood antibodies. This company had a jump start on many other research companies. It has been working with the coronavirus since 2018. The doctor who was telling this story on CBS said that unfortunately big pharma and our government as well, is not helping to develop this for approval and release. Of course the reason, economics, no money to be made from them.

Hearing things like this makes it so difficult to keep from descending into a valley of anger and depression. Some things can be expected and in those cases when the bad news hits you, it is a little easier to overcome. So I will hope for the best and move forward. Today's Gallup's polls have shown a gradually rising share of Americans concerned about the environment since the early 2000s. Roughly 60 percent now say that the quality of the environment is poor or only fair, and that it is getting worse, and that the federal government is doing too little to protect it. And more than 70 percent favor tougher restrictions for power plants and vehicle emissions, as well as a push to develop clean-energy alternatives.

The flip side of that coin, a Danish writer, Bjorn Lomborg, has written a book that argues against these ideas. He claims that environmental activists are exaggerating the risks of climate change. The *Washington Post* has this to say about his book. "Skeptical Environmentalist is the most significant work on the environment since the appearance of its polar opposite, Rachel

Carson's Silent Spring, in 1962. It's a magnificent achievement." I shall take this position on the authors' predictions, either way we can't lose.

Bob Marley's family has just redone and released a version of his iconic song "Three Little Birds, Every Little Thing's Gonna Be Alright." The family's idea is to help all the children of today's crazy world. I'm listening to Bob's 15 minute version at this moment thanks to YouTube. And thank you Bob Marley, in the song, you don't tell us what we should do, or how to do it, you simply present your look at things and pass on the beautiful message to us.

I'm back now, I had the speakers turned way up so I could walk away from this computer, into the sun, look out over the mountains and Redwood valley that is my front yard. I am so fortunate, thank you Julie. I moved and swayed to your music Bob. I was back in Jamaica, dancing with my daughter Mia. I realized, you are right Bob, everything's gonna be alright.

And now I'm back again. After the previous paragraph I decided to 'stay away from 'computer' even more. I went to town, met Danny and walked a few miles around the quaint little Healdsburg. Danny was in his usual form, active resistance. He had a mask but it never came out of his pocket the entire walk. I told him it's not right, considering other people's concerns. His solution was to avoid anybody coming our way. We kept crossing the street from one sidewalk to the other. The topics we discussed were, from Danny's viewpoint, the ridiculousness of masks and how the facts point to their ineffectiveness. Also what we can expect in the future, and one Danny bit of data is that in the near future we will not even be allowed to take this walk. His prediction was pretty much implying that these evil plans will manifest themselves within a year from now. Moving out of Gavin Newsom's California is big on his list of things to do. Danny has this big dilemma, his mom, who lives 20 miles north, is in her 90s, and Danny is getting government money to care for her. His visiting schedule always changes. I'm sure he cares for his mom but he hates the fact that she listens to CNN all day and, sorry Danny, but mom is not a Trump lover, quite the opposite. According to Danny, if she were not here, he'd be out of California in a second.

Most of the time as we walk, I keep my mouth shut. I allow Danny to live in the misery that he creates for himself. He asked me how my book was coming and what I'm writing about. I tell him, basically it's my take on things, reiterating that he and I see things differently, and leave it at that.

Responding to my "Whassup?" question. I received a text from my son Abel a while ago, "All kinds of stuff, Florida is the new 'Rome is Burning.' Maybe Danny will head to that Republican governor's state, or possibly Georgia since their Republican governor is fighting against any mandatory mask plans. Although Danny has super respect and admiration for Abel, he can't really believe what Abel believes. He can hardly believe the virus is real. Danny is firm on his convictions and not only does he embrace them as truth, but he preaches it to me. I keep thinking that there are truths that a person can say only after having earned the right to say them. Watching Fox News and listening to right wing radio stations does not qualify.

I gotta say, Danny and I are still friends. He just texted me this: FYI Savage was talking about exactly as you and I were discussing it…I see the light…listen to today's podcast…I will definitely listen.

JULY 18, 2020

Well, I listened to Michael Savage. For an hour I struggled to make sense of what he presented. My biggest challenge was to keep the podcast on for that length of time. I waited for any part that Danny might be referring to and I never heard it. The guy, Savage, speaks from a bad place, dominated by a hateful spirit. He is such an egomaniac, so similar to Trump. At one point he was so incredibly mean and rude to a caller. He continued insulting her, calling her an idiot and finally told her to get medical help because she was insane. The thing is, she was on his side of the fence. I really believe that deeper into Savage's mind is an incredible paranoia that drives him. The sad situation is that so many people identify with the anger and feel justified. If Dr. Michael Savage says it, then he and I are right. They are directed to see life as he sees it. I do not feel comfortable with the anger and can hardly bear to listen to any of it. It must mean that I don't have it inside of me and for that I am fortunate.

Danny is not an ignorant guy with a low IQ, looking for someone to give him answers. He's very smart, yet he can jump on the Savage train and join the savage tribe (with a small 's') I would hope that Danny and all the others would take the time to look out the window of that train. I implore them to see the beautiful things that are still growing. Nature has not resigned. It doesn't look like doomsday to me.

Without any question, we are living in a seriously polarized nation. The battle stage we have created is not on a hillside or in some farmland. We are not firing weapons or charging at each other with bayonets. We are still in many ways homogenized and peacefully blended together. Other than the protesting, where we fight is through our media platforms and in our heads. Danny carried his fight a little further yesterday, to the streets, as he refused to mask up and marched from one side of the street to the other, avoiding the enemy. I think the next time I go with Danny for our exercise it should be on bicycles. Sometimes it might be easier to see who we are not, rather than who we are.

"What we need in the United States is not division. What we need in the United States is not hatred. What we need in the United States is not violence or lawlessness, but is love and wisdom, and compassion towards one another, and a feeling of justice towards those who still suffer within our country, whether they be white or whether they be Black." Bobby Kennedy after hearing MLK was shot on April 4, 1968.

Because of the powerful extreme influences that our virtual world has created, I wonder if it's even possible to hold on to the systemic body of learned behavior passed onto us by our parents. It appears that this crazy contemporary force has stepped in between generations. Many people have lives that are no longer entities of self control. They have become servient riders on the train of technology, realizing where they boarded but unaware of the destination. I feel so thankful and indebted to my parents for the fact that I am not on that train. I truly feel that the dominating force that drives me is a non selfish loving spirit. I'm far from a hero, but I'm happy that I am me.

This may sound strange but I seem to draw a lot of my inspiration from a continual, "I don't know." Along with the lack of conviction comes a comfortable sort of excitement inside that allows me to be satisfied with the search. That search does not concentrate on insight into the future. Regardless of any knowledge that I might somehow telepathically foresee, nothing I do now will change it. Perhaps this coronavirus is just a tip of the iceberg. Perhaps in the future we may look back and say, "Oh how lucky we were when we could walk around in public with masks." Maybe Covid-22 or Covid-23 is not far in front of us, much more contagious and much more deadly. This is not an outrageous presumption.

Again the coronavirus is topping today's news, the spike continues breaking records in many states, no end in sight yet. Trump has pulled off another good one. He sent unmarked federal law enforcement officers driving unmarked vehicles and wearing camouflage to stop the protests in Portland Oregon. Elected officials in Portland have called on the Trump administration to remove these militarized agents from the city. This, following reports of protesters being arbitrarily detained. These actions are "tactics of a government led by a dictator." They have been seizing people from the street in recent days. Savage mentioned this on his program yesterday and he's all for it, agreeing with Trump's move. Portland has continued to see nightly protests for racial justice since the police killing of George Floyd. Perhaps Trump's move can be justified if the troops are only in place to protect Federal property.

Please bear with me but for the record and for anyone who might read this years from now, I can never criticize Trump enough. Hands down he is the worst president not just in my lifetime, but in the history of our country. He destroyed our standing in the world. He inherited a booming economy but wasted it while blaming everyone else. He is corrupt to the point where I fear for the future of the American democracy. He is the first president in my lifetime who openly fuels hatred, denies science, spreads misinformation, and has a history of making filthy remarks about women His entire presidency has been obsessed with undoing all the good things that Obama initiated, and he uses his position to eliminate all of Obama's policies without any valid or intelligent reasoning. Other than that, he is just all around indecent, unprofessional, incompetent, perverted, recklessly deluded, and the first president who is truly a threat to our democratic institutions. By telling this story as I see it I am consciously taking a moral stand. Honestly in my mind Trump and the virus are equally as bad. The good thing being that they will both go away soon, hopefully.

Onto more positive things, I'm about to drive out to the Ocean with Stu. We do this on occasion and generally wind up on our search for the best clam chowder in Bodega Bay. I thought we had it nailed but Stu told me he has heard about a different place. I will be bringing several copies of "Five Days in Bodega Bay." It's a 30 minute documentary I made about the 2017 fire and how Bodega Bay was big in the response to that devastating fire. The Chamber of Commerce wants copies. I was there in an evacuation at that time. I think the doc turned out great, very emotional. I had a local musician help with the sound track, and his work was amazing.

JULY 19, 1982

I just got home from hiking in the woods with Clyde and Hawk. On one occasion we were paused by a small creek branch. On the bank was a patch of yellow root. Earlier in the day Clyde had been complaining about a slight digestive problem. I knew that a tea made from yellow root has beneficial effects on this malady. I asked Hawk if he had noticed the yellow root and if he thought that I should pick some for Clyde. He answered, "Yes, I have seen it, and for this reason I am waiting here. We believe that someone such as

Clyde, who is in tune with his environment, who is one with the Great Spirit, need not ingest the herb to gain its properties. If we wait here peacefully in the presence of this herb, the medicine will go to Clyde."

Of all the things that I have ever learned about medicinal herbs, this was the most valuable lesson. It is possible to help any disordered condition or disease by walking in the woods or swimming in the sea. In order for this to work, you can't be all jammed up filled with stress, you have to be at one with your environment. Your different daily lifestyles have to be in harmony with each other. If you work to damage the environment, nature will not work for you. If you help it, nature will help you.

I also learned from Hawk that one should never take from nature without a prayer of thanks, or without a return offering. Again I witnessed nature's law of giving and receiving. It is OK to pick the herb, but only that which you need, that is what nature wants to give up. The plants, as David had shown me years prior, have lights in them. It is this light which contains the true healing property. The material fibers of the plant contain only a very crude form of that energy.

To believe like Hawk or to live like Clyde, your inner light must shine bright. Then the tiny herb on the forest floor will find your light, and the two will unite. It is exactly as man finding God. The Christians believe that Jesus was the only true Son of God, made in His image. In reality we are all made of the same light, we are all the true Children of God. The Sun of the Great Spirit; without this light to begin it, there would be no consciousness. There would never have been life. It could not have begun.

God made this so simple to understand. Nothing could be more obvious. The light of the sun is responsible for everything on this earth, the oxygen, the water, and the wind. All life on earth would perish in a few seconds without this physical light. Well it is exactly the same in the spiritual world. The spiritual light that ties man to God also ties all nature to man and holds everything together. If that light goes out, there will be no reality, no material world, and no spiritual sanity.

In some earlier civilizations, religion meant worshiping the sun and sacrificing to the Sun God. That certainly makes sense to me. Although it is not totally encompassing, it is closer to the truth than many of today's religions. As a small child, I probably would have taken to this belief much easier than Catholicism.

JULY 19, 2020

Suzanne is with me at my house. We will be spending today here and tomorrow going for her neuro optometrist appointment in Santa Clara. From there onto Palo Alto, staying with Julie. The following morning down to Santa Cruz and spending the day with Zac. Hopefully we will gain some enlightenment from either the physician or Zac. Suzanne's situation could stand some enlightenment. It is not easy to see the change in her and try to adjust.

I have realized in the last two days that she has certain deficiencies now that I must try to fix. The most important is that she is very lethargic, always lying down on the couch rather than sitting up engaging in things. This will only get worse with time. Last week I spoke with her doc from CNS and had him cut back on some pain meds, but I believe more needs to be done. It hurts so much to see her in this condition and when I'm with her I realize that my mood, my energy becomes drained quickly, I can't get the strength to keep pushing her. There is no way I could do this without the 24/7 helpers.

This morning I watched Face the Nation, again. The program began with a tribute to John Lewis, the congressman who died on Friday. He is another true hero of my time. Born in 1940, he began fighting racial injustice when he was 17. He wrote a letter to Martin Luther King Jr. at that time and was asked by MLK to join him. He has not stopped his fight since. In the 1960s he was a leader of the Civil Rights Freedom Riders. He still carries a scar on his forehead from a confrontation in Selma, Alabama, a peaceful march that was violently crushed by police while the protesters were crossing a bridge. He was arrested over 40 times before becoming a congressman. His work continued from the floor of congress. In addition to racial equality he argued for many causes, including gun control, gay rights, health care issues, etc. Even at 80 years old he joined marchers for Black Lives Matter, before losing his battle with pancreatic cancer. John Lewis, a noble humanitarian, a devoted hardworking politician, a selfless, altruistic human being, I stand in awe and immeasurable respect for the life you have lived. It is the life of America. The billy clubs that beat you are hopefully now the new walking sticks of a better life. "Time can turn a scar into a beauty mark."

JULY 20, 2020

Woke up early this morning and as I was cleaning up the kitchen I noticed a little mouse. I now face a dilemma. It's not that I am not willing to kill the little guy for what I determine to be a better cause. I suspect there are many who would only use a humane trap that would capture him or her and then little mousie could be set free back in the wilds, or whatever. Hopefully the "Jain" or whoever it is that buys this type of trap won't judge me and I will do likewise. Now then, normally I would put some peanut butter on a trap and that's that. But I don't have any peanut butter. I thought it'll have to wait, when I remembered something. The last time Brenda was here she was up to her usual activities. She had made some chocolate peanut butter cups and left some of the unused peanut butter in a jar in the laundry room cupboard.

After briefly considering this as an option I am deciding to go for it. Sometimes the little mouse is very gentle and is able to eat the bait without setting off the trap. That might be the case today. Now my dilemma is this, the peanut butter is made with Brenda's special marijuana infused butter. So the mouse will either die or get loaded, not a bad option. God forgive me if I'm doing the wrong thing here.

JULY 21, 1969

We did it. As John Kennedy predicted, man has landed on the moon. Everybody in our country and around the world has been tuned into this historic event. As Neil Armstrong stepped out of the spacecraft onto the moon, he said, "That's one small step for man, a giant leap for mankind." I'm sure these words will live on forever. It feels very special to live in the country that has achieved such a feat, I am proud today to be an American.

JULY 22, 2020

It's been over 50 years since America landed on the moon. I certainly remember that moment. Again I will say that our country was once admired and considered a benevolent leader around the world, "The good old days."

When Suzanne and I were with Zac in Santa Cruz, I called my crew that often help me work, Juan Carlos and his brother Gerardo. I am planning to do more work on cleaning up the property before the expected fires begin in our world. They are both very sick. Juan Carlos hasn't been to the hospital so neither he nor Gerardo are diagnosed, but he told me it is 'muy malo y muy fuerte,' very bad and very strong. They probably have the virus. Within an hour later I received a call from Phil. We had scheduled to go sailing today, but he canceled. His family has also been hit hard with the virus. He has a nephew who is quite the athlete, breaking track records in college, 23 years old. He is in the ICU, complaining to his parents that he can hardly breathe. Phil has decided to stay at home for a while. Other than a casual friend, Eugenia in NYC, I now have people close to me that are infected. It is getting closer to home.

Trump appeared on TV yesterday with a slightly different tune than his usual denial. He admitted that the virus is a threat and that it might get worse before getting better. He also said that wearing masks might be a 'good thing.' He's probably doing this for political reasons but regardless of his intentions there may be a number of his diehard supporters who will listen to him and this will help the fight. People's intentions are not the most important thing, as we're often told. The results of their actions, really, that's what matters. As a leader or an in charge person, your intentions and your actions better be helpful or you should step down and be replaced by someone qualified. Levels of intelligence factor into this as well as moral codes. Ambition should be replaced with honor, personal goals replaced with the collective needs of those being led. Above all else, as a leader, ego and vanity must disappear.

Yesterday more than 1,100 people died of the virus, this is the largest number since late May. There is so much discussion today on how to reopen schools or if that's even a possibility. The issue is a risk either way, keeping the youth away from learning in a classroom is not ideal, but it may be the lesser of two evils. Stay home and study online or go to school and catch the virus. It looks like most states will make their decision based on the numbers of cases in their area. California has decided it will not reopen, at least for now.

The next item of news is the federal troop deployment that Trump is engaged in and planning more of. He's calling it 'Operation Legend.' The 50th continual night of protesting in Portland has triggered the Trump decision. It appears now that he wants the troops sent in to stop a lot of the upsurging violent crime in places like New York, Chicago, Detroit, Baltimore, and Oakland. All of those state state governors are against this tactic saying it exacerbates the problem and promotes more violence. The novelist Graham Greene wrote, "A single feat of daring can alter the whole concept of what is possible." In his work he was referring to an honorable sense of daring, Trump is using the idea in a negative way. Trump is daring alright, he hardly ever thinks things out. Oddly enough it is this trait that makes him appealing to many of his supporters. Their logic is that if you need time to think before acting then you are probably lying and conniving. "Trump just does things, not like all the other crooked politicians." The problem with this logic is that the practice can be extremely harmful when being applied by an ignorant apathetic pathological liar.

The typical Trump supporter seems quite comfortable in allowing him to handle the important stuff. Chaos is often the point. The cruelty is the point. Ignorance is the point. It's a nihilistic, scorched earth mindset that has no tangible goals or purpose. Sadly, in order to combat Trump, those engaged are on the opposite side of a deeply divided political fence. The Democrats and Liberals as well as the Republicans and Conservatives have all retreated to their own corners, and will not compromise on most issues such as this. Nobody wants to meet in the middle. As expected, every state that Trump is threatening to send in his 'Federalies' is governed by a democrat.

As our country continues to polarize with each new day's important political decisions, I cannot help but see the similarities and remember my time spent in Colombia. I will say that Colombia harbors the most extremes of any country I have been in. Their history and present condition will lay truth to my observation. This is a country that has been at war since I was two years old, at war with itself that is. Their civil war lasted for a decade until a military dictatorship was installed in 1953. It took four years to end the terrible period that caused over a hundred thousand deaths. Today that era is simply referred to as "La Violencia." Well guess what, more than half a century later it is still going on. Both extremes, the right-wing paramilitaries and the left-wing guerillas are still at it. Death squads, ambushes, kidnappings, massacres and other horrible atrocities continue to take place. This extreme hopefully will never reach us here in the US, but we must know that it exists.

In Bogota, the country's capital city, you will find Ciudad Tunal, a complex of 30,000 people and the world's largest public housing project to use only solar power to heat its water. That's the good side. While on the south side of the city is Ciudad Bolivar, with two million inhabitants. It is the world's largest squatters' settlement, complete with inadequate water supply, open sewers, etc. We see the makings of this today here in the US in some of our larger cities. Again I say we probably won't reach the extreme of Ciudad Bolivar, at least not in this generation.

A large part of the inner-economy of Bogota depends on their floral agro-business. Just to the west is a rich plateau made fertile over time by deposits from the Rio Bogota. Today that one time food producing region is covered with bubble-like greenhouses, used for the cultivation and exportation of tropical flowers to mostly the USA and Japan. A beautiful eco-friendly business one might think, WRONG. Inside these thousands of greenhouses are chemical troughs and pesticide misters that operate without any government control. The *Río Bogotá*, the nearby tributaries and the below ground aquifers are the recipients of this waste.

Trump took over as our protector in January of 2017. On February 1, 2017 Trump repealed a rule banning the dumping of dentists' office mercury into public water supplies. Five tons of mercury per year are now being discharged into our water supply as a direct result of this repeal. On February 16, 2017 he signed a rule change allowing coal companies to dump toxic waste such as arsenic and mercury into rivers and streams. Are you ready? According to Harvard Law School's Environmental Regulation Rollback Tracker, which is keeping a running tally of the regulatory dismantling program, the Trump administration has so far initiated the reversal of 67 environmental laws. It's hard to make this stuff up. If there is any reason for this we might look at his campaign promise to dismantle American environmental law, which Trump says is stifling economic growth.

Recently it was announced that copper and cobalt mining will begin in the formerly protected federal US lands of Grand Staircase-Escalante National Monument of Utah. The mining is now possible after Donald Trump removed protection from 2.2 million acres of federal land in Utah, the largest elimination of protected areas in US history. It is only a fraction of the protections Trump has removed from federal lands since taking office.

JULY 23, 2020

The coronavirus is so widespread in the U.S. that many schools are unlikely to reopen anytime soon. Already, some large school districts in Atlanta, Houston, Los Angeles, Phoenix, suburban Washington and elsewhere have indicated they will start the school year entirely with remote classes. Yet many parents and children are despondent about enduring online-only learning for the foreseeable future.

Parents who never before considered homeschooling have begun looking into it, especially in combination with a small number of other families, to share the teaching load and let their children interact with others. Some are trying to hire private tutors.

The Trump administration says it will send hundreds of additional federal agents into cities to confront a rise in violence. The plan calls for sending about 200 more agents to Chicago, 200 to Kansas City, Mo., and 35 to Albuquerque. In Portland, Ore., early this morning, federal officers fired tear gas near the city's mayor, Ted Wheeler, who had joined demonstrators outside the federal courthouse. Coughing and scrambling to put on goggles, Wheeler called the officers' tactics an "egregious overreaction."

I may listen to some of Danny's radio stations today to get the right winger's take on all this. There is little doubt in my mind that the Portland protests are being used as a pro-Trump rallying cry.

Changing the subject, jumping to a different time period, I shall travel back to Colombia. An intense portion of my life was lived there, in a rather short period of time. As a young man I set out on an adventure with Mario, and Benjamin, and 'La Cajita de Musica.' For a year and a half I lived in Medellin and traveled through Colombia, let's begin with a positive...

12

Colombia 1972

Most Americans from the United States envision Colombia as a wide open, drug infested mess of a place, with twice as many banditos as good people. Well that is not true. I better qualify my statement. At least it was not true in the early seventies. There were twice as many good people as bad, that's two good, one bad, two good, one bad. No, I am only kidding, Most Colombians are wonderful people. They exhibit a self-pride that is very obvious. They do not see Gringos as someone to use, someone who will become their 'ticket to ride.' In many Latin countries I felt this, Mexico, Honduras, Costa Rica, Ecuador, to name a few.

Leaving Bogota and its narco-floral-economics traveling northwest lies the Choco, a splendid virgin rainforest, the opposite extreme. It is believed to be one the most biologically diverse and natural environments in the world. Only Brazil rivals Colombia for top honors when it comes to a species count, be it animals, plants, birds, reptiles or amphibians. The country has some of the tallest and most rugged mountain ranges in this hemisphere and flat, nearly barren savannas. Because it straddles the equator the temperatures in these mountains are moderate, but its altitude variations bring on the lower temperatures and contribute to its diversity. There is also The Amazon rainforest in the south.

Although the cocaine industry was not in full swing, it was beginning during the early 70s. Virgin jungle land was being cut away to make room for more poppy plantations. On the opposite side, there was a movement underway to turn the barren savanna lands, *"the llanos"* in the east, into what would become an international model for eco-techno combined subsistence.

Gaviotas, a tiny village 200 miles from a paved road was being developed into a future ideal society. Working with native materials, creating building materials from mud, food from jungle nuts and insects, energy sources from windmills and solar panels, Gaviotas was becoming self-sustaining. It drew its ideas and its technical sources from the University students and professors in Bogota, as well as from outside influences. What is referred to as 'third world technology' would soon become reality not only for the indigenous culture inhabitants of Gaviotas and the many engineers, students, adventurers and creative thinkers that would move there, but the rest of the world would soon take notice of this small village.

Simultaneously Arab oil embargoes were creating a global energy crisis and here in the barren mostly uninhabited llanos of Colombia, led by Paolo Lugari, a community was emerging that would not rely on oil products, a community that would soon gain worldwide attention. Gaviotas would build solar panels that worked on rainy days, water pumps that were powered by children's see-saws, hydroponic gardens that would provide abundant food, and most notably forests of new trees that would take root in an otherwise useless soil base. In a few years to come these pine trees would provide Gaviotas with a harvest of resin that is a marketable product. Miraculously the million trees that would eventually be planted would grow and provide new soil and shade to the ground below. A home for new drifting and bird carrying seeds, new species would soon emerge. It would mark the beginning of the world's first man made rain forest. Gaviotas and its citizens exemplify the opposite extreme from those narco-traficantes, and the other extremists involved in rampant political murdering.

At this point I should probably explain what brought me to Colombia. During the later years of the 60s I took an evening job as a doorman in an upscale Palm Beach restaurant, Nando's.

I became a good friend of Mario Escobar, a waiter. Mario told everyone that he was from Spain, but indeed he was as Colombian as Juan Gonzales of coffee fame. Mario had been working in Palm Beach for a number of years and had snatched a cute 'gringa' wife, Mary. She was very nice and cute. Now Mario was cute and nice too, he had some great qualities, very ambitious and hardworking, generous and an overall good guy, but boy did he have a corner on the bullshitting market.

Mario had frugally been hoarding money and finally had enough savings to leave Palm Beach and follow his dream of opening up his own restaurant and nightclub. Many times at Nando's, late in the evenings, when business slowed down, Mario would step outside and we would talk about his dream. He told me what a great country Colombia was and what a cool town Medellin was. He was so fired up about being his own boss and making even more money than he was making here. His enthusiasm was catchy. I would get all fired up also. It was Mario's insistent invitation that had me packing my bags at the first possible moment. His descriptions of Colombia were all true.

I decided to leave the good old US for a while and it wasn't long before I took off for Colombia. When I arrived Mario was in fact turning his dreams into reality.

He had taken on a partner Benjamin, who had also worked as a waiter in Palm Beach, and whom I knew briefly. On the outskirts of Medellin, up on the side of a mountain, they had chosen an excellent location for their club. The site was at one time a lavish private estate with beautiful grounds. It had many rooms and a couple of small guest cottages. Mario and Benjamin were remodeling to accommodate the plan for "La Cajita de Musica," the "Little Music Box." They were both very busy with workers everywhere, opening up rooms, making parking space, redoing the entry drive, etc. Mary was pregnant and most of the time in a tizzy. The club was scheduled to open in three to four weeks.

In very short order, with Benjamin as my social director, I met Dina. Her family had moved to Medellin from Italy when she was a small girl. She was a striking woman who had been an actress for obvious reasons. When I met Dina she had been married, divorced and had a young son. She and her young son were living with her parents, as is often the case in the Latin culture. There exists a very strong Catholic influence in Colombia. This appears to be a carryover of the medieval attitudes that a divorced woman is a second-class citizen. Dina was searching for someone who did not have this attitude. Up to this point all my girlfriends had been single, and of course with no children. The idea of a relationship with Dina fascinated me. I went for her in a big way, she did not dress like most of the other Colombian girls, and she was more like a hippie, which I loved. And as I implied earlier, she was absolutely gorgeous

Dina had a friend who was an artist and adventurer, Gabriel. He was a great guy, also a hippie. He did not really work and had all the time in the world. So the three of us decided to set out for an extended hike so I could see the country. Gabriel would be the guide, since he knew the area. Dina would come along for her charm and beauty, and I would put up the money. Being an ocean person, I decided to go to the coast. I thought we would begin our journey in the northeast Caribbean region and head West across the Panamanian border area and south down towards Choco. We bought tarps for tenting and headed via bus, towards the northeastern coast. The bus ride was an eye opening experience. For that matter, it was so eye opening that it would easily make a blind man see, out of fear. There must be a god in this world that does nothing but keep Colombian bus drivers from hitting each other head on, on curvy mountain roads. Passing on blind curves is award winning driving technique. It is an unbelievably frightening experience that I would not wish on the likes of Friederich Mengele.

Well this Colombian bus ride would throw me back a few hundred years in my spiritual development. I got so scared that I must have dropped fifteen rungs on the ladder of spiritual faith. That was one time I could easily have regressed to my infant years and shit in my pants again. It was worse than my sky diving experiences or my bungee jumping fiasco.

At one of the stops along the narrow dirt roads I succumbed to the country women and kids who were always running up to the bus windows whenever we slowed down. They were trying to sell us all their home cooked goodies, most of which contained meat. I was a vegetarian at this point, but I had nothing to lose now. Hell, it could have been my last meal as I saw it. Besides, I thought, "When in Rome do as the Romans." Here again we have the moderation lesson. A little bit of meat will never kill anybody. So, for the first time in a few years, I bought a couple pork enchiladas and gobbled that meat down, trying not to think about the road ahead.

Surprised as I was, it was not my time to die, the driving didn't kill me, the pork enchiladas didn't kill me, so we made it to our destination, the vacation town of Santa Marta. We did the usual tourist things, saw the sights, and went to a Casino. I had chosen Santa Marta because I knew it was the oldest established city in all of South America, having been settled in 1525. It was also the spot where all Spanish adventurers began their search for El Dorado.

I'm going to leave Colombia for awhile. There is so much more and I will return, but for now, I just picked a big squash from the garden. I'm going to steam it up slightly and have another wonderful meal. This time there will be no pork enchiladas. As I was slicing it up I took a bite, no need to steam it. Yumm.

13

Back to Good Old America

From CNN, labeled as a left leaning news agency, we are hearing some positive news. "Even if a coronavirus vaccine is far off there is reason for hope that a medical solution to the crisis will soon be at hand. Scientists are now developing two types of drugs that show great promise. The first are antivirals that could keep the virus from replicating inside the body. The second class of drugs are mono-clonal antibodies which are lab-created antibodies designed to block the coronavirus' spike proteins from attaching to the cell receptors in our bodies. These treatments that block the infection and even treat the sick could be ready by early 2021. Science will eventually save us."

Okay here's the crazy news. An open letter was published last week by Harper's magazine, signed by 153 prominent writers, academics, and entertainers, ranging from Noam Chomsky to David Brooks, J.K. Rowling to Wynton Marsalis, Margaret Atwood to Bill T. Jones. The letter basically argues for openness to opposing views. The result of this attempt to fix the obvious problem of divisiveness caused nothing but more divisiveness. Thousands of negative responses began appearing immediately heaping ridicule on the letter's signatories for thin-skinned, privilege and, as one person put it, "fear of loss of relevance."

The response to the response, "We're not just a bunch of old white guys sitting around writing this letter," Mr. Williams, who is African-American, said. "It includes plenty of Black thinkers, Muslim thinkers, Jewish thinkers, people who are trans and gay, old and young, right wing and left wing. We believe these are values that are widespread and shared, and we wanted the list to reflect that." From Bertrand Russel, a deceased philosopher, logician, mathematician, historian, writer, social critic, political activist, and Nobel laureate: "The fact that an opinion has been widely held is no evidence whatever that it is not utterly absurd; indeed in view of the silliness of the majority of mankind, a widespread belief is more likely to be foolish than sensible."

In my opinion this proves one thing about us as social human beings. We cannot get along in large groups. It seems to be a trait existing in most of the intelligent species. Dolphins split away from each other after reaching maybe 100. Chimpanzees usually decide to form families of from 3 to 15 members, and never larger than 150. I believe if we could hit a button that would eliminate Alpha males, we might have a better chance of solving this problem.

When I lived in Costa Rica I had a few occasions to visit the Bribri tribes on the Caribbean side. I shot some video of their people and used it on different projects. The Bribri are a small indigenous group of just over 13,000 people. They live in a matriarchal society where the women have dominant power. Bribri are organized into clans. Each clan is made up of extended family, and the clan is determined through the mother/females. Women are the only ones who traditionally can inherit land. Women are also endowed with the right to prep the cacao used in sacred Bribri rituals. I wonder if practicing such a culture would end some of the divisiveness that we are living today in America.

JULY 25, 2012

I am now with Zac in the Yucatan of Mexico. The object is to complete a film I've been working on. We are traveling to some of the southern Maya ruins, we have hired a car and driver. Zac is the shooter and I'm organizing the shoots and finding people to interview. In December of this year we plan to return because that is when the present cycle of the Maya calendar will end. Many interpretations of the Maya calendar have surfaced this year, since a "Great Cycle" of its Long Count component came to an end, inspiring some to believe that the world will end on December 21, 2012. The media hype and hysteria that ensued was later termed the 2012 phenomenon. My research has shown that this prediction is totally false, rather, the educated consensus says that what the ancient Maya believed is, that what will be changing at this time, is a controlling type of energy. The Maya believe that a God governing energy exists to influence all life on the planet. A cycle is ending and will be moving upward.

The Long Count Calendar is an astronomical calendar which is used to track longer periods of time. The Maya called it the "universal cycle." Each such cycle is calculated to be 2,880,000 days long (about 7885 solar years). The ancient Mayans believed that the universe is recreated at the start of each universal cycle. However it is not the end of the world, but a recreated world because of a God given new energy.

Life in the last cycle of the Long Count Calendar has been controlled by a male dominant force, which has caused such a violent, warring world. According to Maya belief we will now be switching to an energy with both male and female influence. If this is true, we might be in luck.

JULY 25, 2020

The United States passed four million known coronavirus cases yesterday. Over the past two weeks, case counts have risen in 37 states. Desperate leaders in Latin America are turning to dubious virus remedies. In Bolivia, the authorities have promoted chlorine dioxide, a bleach used to disinfect swimming pools. People across the U.S. are still waiting days, or even weeks, to get test results. The delays have made the tests relatively useless in stopping the virus's spread. The top five worst known coronavirus outbreaks now are in Oman, Bahrain, Panama, South Africa and the U.S.

Personally I have become much more cautious now that I know a few infected people locally. It has hit close to home and made its mark on me. If I wanted to wander away from 'my shelter,' it wouldn't be possible today anyway. I have re-hired a crew to help with safeguarding against fires. It really is a joke, but the insurance companies have set certain standards which we must conform to if we hope for continuing coverage.

This is actually day two for Billy and his crew. They are at it again, taking out some of the very large fir trees that are close to the house. In the olden days I may have been climbing up those trees, but times change. With age certain limits creep into us. I cringe now as I watch these younger guys at the top of the trees with their chainsaws in action.

Billy's crew has all the equipment, a giant cherry picker, tractors, chippers, big trucks. I think I saw about 6 chainsaws amongst their arsenal. The idea is to get the fire danger away from the house. Good idea, but in honesty I have serious doubts if this will prevent a raging fire from taking the house with it. A few years ago no-one lived with this fear, but now it seems to be just a matter of time before your number is called. Fires came very close last year. It's like the virus, you can't run away. You can hide, hopefully it won't find you.

As for the virus, I've been reading about something called "herd immunity," This idea offers hope for us. Herd immunity, or community immunity, is when a large part of the population of an area is immune to a specific disease. If enough people are resistant to the cause of a disease, such as a virus or bacteria, it has nowhere to go. While not every single individual may be immune, the group as a whole has protection. This is because there are fewer high-risk people overall. The infection rates drop, and the disease peters out. This is probably what causes all flu viruses to disappear.

Herd immunity protects at-risk populations. These include babies and those whose immune systems are weak and can't get resistance on their own. You can develop resistance naturally. When your body is exposed to a virus or bacteria, it makes antibodies to fight off the infection. When you recover, your body keeps these antibodies. Your body will defend against another infection.

Before herd immunity kicks in and the infection rates start to go down, 50% to 67% of the population would need to be resistant. One of today's medical opinions is that the antibodies that normally ward off a second infection from this virus are not acting as expected and some people seem to become infected twice in a row. Hopefully this is not true, I feel it is a little early to make such a statement. I'm not sure that this is positively confirmed. I certainly hope it's not proven to be true.

I haven't given much thought today about the Racial protesting. The idea of 'Out of sight, out of mind,' can certainly be applied here. It's a different story in Portland, where 56 straight nights of protests have been going on, throngs of largely white protesters have raised their fists in the air and chanted, "This is not a riot, it's a revolution." They have thrown water bottles at the federal courthouse, tried to pry off the plywood that protects the entrance and engaged in running battles with police officers through clouds of tear gas. In recent nights, the number of protesters has swollen into the thousands. A sea of white faces in one of the whitest major American cities has cried out for racial justice every night for nearly two months. "There are more Black Lives Matter signs in Portland than Black people."

It appears as if Trump's deployment of Federal troops is having a reverse effect. It is making the situation worse, more violent. The demographic is changing, people from all ages are now hitting the streets. My take on all this may be unpopular and it might be formed because of my age, but I do believe that these protests are no longer protests, but have turned into nothing less than street brawls. Two opponents that actually want to fight are meeting to prove that their side of the story is right. And in my opinion there are better ways to approach this. Trump's an idiot and the citizens of Portland should not try and deal with him on his level.

By doubling the amount of protesters, it is doing things as Trump would do it. Both actions have worsened the situation. Again, it might be a reflection of my age, but I would handle it by backing down, let the Federalies go home, then start again in a peaceful fashion. In North Carolina I learned that the best food is always prepared on low heat, with a slow fire. I will add this, I believe the mayors of those cities experiencing violence are not doing the job.

JULY 26, 2020

Virus spikes, protests, this is the way we must see our world, the way we now live our lives, it's not changing. California, my present home, has leaped ahead with the number of virus cases and deaths. All experts say that the cause is having re-opened too soon. People left their homes, went indoors where the virus spreads much easier. They went shopping indoors, and to visit others looking for needed social contacts. Governor Newsom has reordered shutdowns, business owners, especially the small business owners are worried that this will kill them. It is so difficult to order, to force behavioral changes on 40 million people.

And so many are putting racial protesting as their number one issue, for just reasons. If anyone does not agree that the existing protests are valid and important, then simply open up your history book, starting with page 1917. Look at the protests in the streets of Manhattan. On the same page you'll find riots that year in St. Louis. Next page, 1918, race riot in Chester Pennsylvania (3 Blacks and 2 whites killed). Race riot in Philadelphia (3 whites and 1 Black killed). A few pages ahead and you'll see 3,000 people marching in Washington, DC, 1922. This time, as impossible as it might seem to many, the cause was to end lynching in America. There was actually a bill being proposed to officially stop lynching, with a chance that the bill would not pass. Blacks marched with signs reading "Lynching is the American Principle." and "America, the only spot on earth where a human being may be burned at the stake." On page 1934 you can find people protesting while wearing nooses around their necks, signs reading, "You may be next."

Protests continued, page 1938, a shooting death of a Black man by police in Washington. Racial injustice in Baltimore brought protesters out of their slum, ghetto neighborhoods, marching the streets, pleading for change, 1943. On page 1949 you will read about Paul Robeson, a Black controversial singer, actor, and political force whose singing and oratory skills made him an iconic figure of the 20th Century. One night after his concert at an upstate New York Club, white police beat a Black man to near death, more protests.

Now we enter the period of my lifetime where I was able to witness and remember all of the racism, the blatant civic division. Blacks were separated into their own neighborhoods, their own public bathrooms, they had their own public seating arrangements on all public vehicles. Needless to point out, the Black options were disgusting. It can be found on page 1956 where Rosa Parks refused to go sit in the back of the bus and was arrested in Montgomery Alabama. I well remember all public busses displaying the sign, "Coloreds to the Rear." In all public parks and gathering places I saw Colored restrooms, Colored drinking fountains.

Page 1957, a Federal Court following legal action by the NAACP allowed, actually ordered nine Black students to integrate into Little Rock Arkansas' Central High School. Whites were furious, racial tensions and violence pursued. Page 1958, Black protesters stage a sit-in at Brown's Basement Luncheonette in Oklahoma. And then we open the pages of the 1960s. I enter high school. In Birmingham, Brooklyn, Boston, Baltimore, Memphis, Washington, and all over our country, protests occur often facing violent police confrontation.

When I opened the history book I skipped past so many pages. A comprehensive look at the 60s would fill this book to the end. I won't go in depth here. I feel that the point has been made. For over 100 years the fight for racial equality has been going on and still we have not achieved it. My hope is that we won't have another 100 years of protests, because people refuse to change. Hopefully, our great, great-grandchildren won't have to read about the "Last 200 Years of Protests" in 2120.

Today is the middle of the weekend. I remember when weekends were so special, so different from the rest of the week. School was over for a couple days. Like many families in the good old days, weekends meant a vacation from work, a trip to the lake, the river, or the beach. Backyard barbecues were common. Even the media, the television were special. The only time kids could watch cartoons was on Saturday morning. It was the only time their dads could watch sports on TV. The changes that have taken place, the cultural revolution in our society has rapidly sprung from our developing technology. Our working needs, our values, our current lifestyles have mostly transitioned into what we would have once considered as total chaos, even 20 years ago. Like I said before, this 'speeding train' whips right through the weekend without slowing down, not even a pause or thought of what it's missing. Nostalgia can be a refuge for us older people. The danger now is in lingering too long at the nostalgia station and giving up on hope for the future because of this transformation.

I often see the rest of the world through the windows of the 'speeding train.' There are many windows on that train. We all look out of them searching for a meaning to life. Today's scientists, as well as creating the train, have fitted the train windows with 'time glass.' The windows have a way of distorting what you see in relation to the old understanding of time perception. If we were to walk between the cars of the train we can then see the world, not through a window developed by man, but as it has been created naturally, and that's a good thing.

Well, this is my weekend. I'm choosing one of the train windows showing YouTube. I'm going to put on Bob's "Everything's Gonna Be Alright" again. He's better at lifting up my mood than some of my latest gurus, Sadhguru or Dr. Zach Bush. I've been looking at this monitor here for quite awhile now. I can see the rest of my immediate nearby world through the window behind this monitor, it looks rather inspiring at this moment.

YouTube is not presenting any exclusive on the same natural wonders that Jesus and Mohammed and Siddartha and Moses and all the other great Masters saw, as they contemplated the divine truths and purpose for man's existence. Those views of truth are what I am able to see right out in front of my door. So, goodbye computer, I love you, sort of, in a paradoxical way. Since I'm trying to adhere as much as possible to my 'shelter in place' directive, I'm going outdoors, not to any social gatherings, only to my deck, the sun, the flowers, the trees and all the rest of nature.

I spent the remainder of daylight outside. Before closing tonight, I'd like to talk about today's news. Of course the virus continues to make headlines, still breaking records as for numbers of infections and deaths in many states. The U.S. continues by far to have the largest recurring outbreak in the world, while much of Europe and Asia has flattened the curve. Brazil has the second highest death toll in the world, behind only the U.S. The six cities with the highest coronavirus exposure are all on the Amazon River, according to researchers. Nearly everyone there relies on the river and the boats that travel along it for transportation, food, medicine. Researchers say the boats are behind the spread of the virus.

The region's ability to confront the pandemic has been further weakened under President Jair Bolsonaro, who has publicly mocked it, even though he tested positive himself. He is apparently very much a man like Trump, very egocentric, and with a knack for doing the wrong things. Since he took over, full fledged exploitation of the rainforest has been in practice with no regard for the ecological damage, which sadly affects the entire globe. Since I was a small child I often heard that the Amazon Rainforest is considered to be the "Lungs of the World."

Next bit of news, perhaps equally important to some people, Sports are coming back. (from the NY Times) The M.L.B. and W.N.B.A. returned to play this week after a long hiatus because of the pandemic. Breanna Stewart and the Seattle Storm won the first game of the season against Sabrina Ionescu, and the New York Liberty. The season is dedicated to Breonna Taylor, who died in a police shooting.

There may have been cardboard cutouts in the seats in place of fans, but the return of baseball "was so much better than nothing," our columnist writes. He wasn't alone: Opening day was the most-viewed regular-season game since 2011. The N.B.A. and N.H.L. will restart their seasons next weekend. Our basketball reporter says LeBron James looks as dominant as ever.

Perhaps sports will fill in some of the blank spots in the lives of dedicated fans. I have a strange relationship with sports. It seems that when I get closer to the masses my interest in sports increases. When I was not living in the U.S., I could have cared less about football, basketball or baseball. When the Miami Dolphins had their famous undefeated season in football, I was in Colombia. I had to be reminded that it was happening by my dedicated nephew. When I lived in the rural mountains of North Carolina I never paid any attention, but when I came to the Bay Area of California, I became quite the sports enthusiast. When I was in school I played all the sports, and I'm sure that has had an influence.

I've often thought that such passion for sports is triggered by either some form of boredom, or a personal search for identity, perhaps a little of both. It may be an effort to fill up something that's missing in our lives, or perhaps it is in some way an extension of one's ego. I'm not only a Joe Black, but I'm also a Baltimore Colt. When I go to a game I dress like them, I even wear their players' names on my back. Here comes the good part. And my team's better than your team. That makes me better than you. If my team's a winner, then I'm a winner. The bigger the win column, the larger the fan base, the more seats are sold. This sports fascination exists in most every corner of our world.

14

Take me out to the Ball Game

"Wow, what a game. We won." Yeah, it was quite an experience yesterday, AT&T Park, the Giants Stadium was sold out, the sun was shining, not too hot, a perfect day for baseball, the great American pastime. Before entering the Park I looked around and realized that I was only one of a handful of fans that wasn't wearing a symbolic piece of clothing, testifying to my loyalty for the home boys. What did I know? Eating hot dogs, drinking beer and cheering for victory, that's what it's all about. Actually I don't eat hot dogs and I don't drink beer, and I would have been quite content at the end of the 9th inning to call it a day. What did I know?

You see at the end of the 9th inning, the game was all tied up, nobody had won, more importantly, nobody had lost. So our team, actually a psychological extension of ourselves, had to fight on. Darwin had taught us this simple lesson back in the 1800s, that in order to survive we had to be stronger than everyone else. Survival of the fittest, that's the rule we go by. Nope, can't be satisfied with a tie, that puts everybody equal, can't have that. We gotta be the best. I looked around again and saw 42,000 people, all wanting to dominate and conquer the Miami Marlins.

Co-incidentally 42,000 is about the exact amount of people around the world that starved to death on this day, more than half of those were children. I thought maybe this was Darwin's fault for his teachings, or maybe it was the 17th century economist Adam

Smith who taught us that we best serve our society by looking out for 'number one.'

Something was blurring my thinking here. Why couldn't I just be like everybody else. What happened to the "Be here Now" thinking? Well, "I guess I'm not like everybody else," I thought. I'm not dressed like them, I don't eat or drink like them.

And it really is about more than just "Be Here Now."

It's about the big picture, the present and the future. It's about being part of the whole. The true essence of our being is based on a relationship to the unity of humankind. I realize that I'm bonded to all of the 42,000 people in that stadium, and to all of the other people around our world, even those 42,000 that died yesterday and those 42,000 that will die today. I sadly realized that the cost of one ticket could have fed those that died for a very long time.

It wasn't important that at the bottom of the 11th inning the Giants drove in a run and won the game. We all need to understand that it's just a game. We can no longer think about "winning or losing." It's time to start thinking about another way to live. We need to evolve, and cast away the ideas of Darwin and Adams. It's not my place to argue with all the Giants fans over philosophical points. I need to think like Buckminster Fuller who said, "You never change things by fighting the existing reality. To change something, build a new model that makes the existing model obsolete."

"Come on team, let's go, we can do it!"

So I went out and bought a Tesla.

Tomorrow morning I'm going to spend time with Suzanne. The caregiver is not able to make it, so I am going to fill in. It is a noticeable difference to be with Suzanne for 12 hours, than to be with her for three days around the clock. In the shorter time periods I rarely notice the deficiencies that have resulted from her accident. I see her in a good mood, cognizant and with a directed ambition that makes sense. Time will tell if continued improvements are in her future. I have been told that patients with these type injuries may continue to improve slowly for a couple of years. After that period, not so much. That means there are still 15 months to become better and possibly even self-sufficient.

I believe when life throws something at you that makes no sense, one of the first things you need to do is get out your 'book of priorities,' and put it in the appropriate place. This is far from being easy, but it is an approach to dealing with things you don't understand. Suzanne's accident has been such an occurrence. I talked about this before. For weeks Suzanne's condition, her immediate needs, were number one on my priority list. I stayed by her side. As I said, I slept many nights on a chair in the hospital. It wasn't a choice I had to make. I could not have possibly lived any other way. Now 9 months have passed and I realize that what everyone kept telling me is true. "You need to take care of yourself…"

Not by any sense of the word am I saying that I plan to leave Suzanne or abandon her, but I must look ahead and begin living my life in somewhat the same manner that I was before this crazy accident occurred. I need to begin working, carrying on with the life I had before. My other children I normally visit regularly, they live on the East Coast. I need to get back to them and also to my life as a filmmaker. I can still do these things that I love, but it sometimes means taking trips away from here. I received a call this morning asking me to pick up my camera and help with a regular broadcast, live musical production feed. I agreed. It's up there on my priority list. The good news is that Suzanne would certainly agree with this. She has professional care and is not alone. Basically I'm about to change gears and writing about it is like putting in the clutch.

JULY 27, 2019

Today courts in Michigan are processing criminal sexual assault charges against five Michigan priests, including one who the department is attempting to extradite from India. In the span of less than two days.…The Vatican is showing signs of making progress in its halting attempts to address the clerical sexual abuse scandal that has cast a shadow over the Roman Catholic Church for more than two decades. On Saturday, the Vatican began the defrocking of former cardinal Theodore McCarrick, the former archbishop of Washington, for sexually abusing minors and adult seminarians. McCarrick was expelled from the priesthood just days before leaders of Catholic bishops' conferences around the world meet for an unprecedented summit on sexual abuse. CRAZY...I always thought that priests could be trusted. (note) I was lucky in those days, none of the priests ever made any improper sexual moves towards me or any of the other altar boys that I knew. "I Survived Catholic School."

JULY 27, 2020

It seems that these horrible acts of sinful depravity have been occurring in the Catholic Church since the 1980s. The upper ranks in the priesthood have been aware of the problem all along. They have covered it up until 2019, by transferring guilty priests. Those priests continued with their recognizable psychiatric hideous behavior at their new 'station of the cross.' The children that were targeted were usually from low income families with no father, broken homes. These kids have more shame, less likely to talk.

Studies have concluded that an average of 1.5% of our population are homosexuals. In the priesthood it jumps to 6.5%. So approximately one out of 15 priests are gay. They promise to God and Jesus to take the vow of sexual abstinence when they enter the priesthood. In Religion class at the Catholic school we were asked to make the choice of following a life devoted to our religion (joining the priesthood), or doing other things. I would never have been able to even think about sexual abstinence. I was like so many in my age group, who held sex as the third most important factor ruling our lives. As a young healthy male, if I had food and a roof over my head, sex came next. I honestly believe that's the way our bodies are engineered to keep the species going.

Most of the nuns who taught us said that we must keep our sexual desires in check and to watch out, it's mostly evil. Naturally my teachers, whether they were nuns or priests, were all supposedly abstaining and directing that repressed energy towards God the Good. I always respected that and gave them credit where credit's due. And the vast majority of the so devoted, do indeed deserve such credit. However to those others, it's not all about your intentions, your actions must follow. You can't wake up in the morning, say mass then look into your options as a sexual predator. This is as bad as it gets.

Last night I had a long talk with Abel, I'll say it again, he is one amazing person. He is now on day 24 of abstinence. Not from sex, but from listening to any American news network. He has been directed to continue this for 30 days. He listens to English speaking stations which will affect his view on the truth. The stations are BBC, Al Jazeera, a Chinese one and a Russian one. Abel is presently a teacher for Special Forces, he has them all in his class; Rangers, Seals, Delta Force, the Air Force Special Ops. He not only teaches them but last night he was teaching me. The whole idea of our Special Forces teams being taught by Abel in this position is so encouraging to me. Although our country no longer holds the position as the most powerful, or even the most free, we are so, so lucky to be American citizens. To anyone who disagrees, I can only think that your purpose in life must be different than mine.

Ah, it's Monday morning, another lovely day to be 'sheltered in place,' no earthquakes, no hurricanes, no fires, no virus. Oops I retract that last statement. "Good Morning Covid-19, how are you today?" Maybe Al Jazeera has been talking about you this morning. I wonder what figures are being reported today. No need to wonder, I'll simply find Al Jazeera on my computer and see for myself.

Now then, 30 minutes of Al Jazeera: Floods and raging virus in India, 100 dead, Iraq, protests escalating over lack of government to provide electricity, clean water, 2 protesters killed, a hezbollah fighting group accused of bursting from Lebanon through Israeli border, responding to an Israeli jet killing of a Hezbollah fighter in Syria, Spain seeing serious rising Corona cases, thousands of new daily infections are prompting the government to close all bars, restaurants and public places, Zimbabwe is putting roadblocks everywhere to supposedly stop Corona spreading, but people say it is to contain the protests over government corruption. It is Korean Armistice Day celebrating the end of the war, 67 years ago. Motorcades carrying John Lewis' remains are traveling through Washington DC honoring the hero who was re-elected 16 consecutive terms as 'The Conscious of Congress.' A Memorial service is planned today at Capitol Hill......In order to continue on with this day in some semblance of joy and hope I had to stop Al Jazeera at this point.

Enough about bad priests, bad governments, bad weather, bad people, I'm planning to wander outside, to wonder inside. I'm going to worship the Sun God.

JULY 28, 2020

On my way back to Suzanne's house. I plan on enlarging her very small front deck in order to make it into a place where she can sit with a table. It will be an easy way to give her a new living space. The idea came from Sally and it's a good one. Last night Julie called, her younger sister Milla died and she is very upset. The situation is bad since she hasn't been communicating with her sister for a number of years and was asked not to attend any service. The two daughters of Milla believe Julie is insane and a horrible person. So sad.

JULY 30, 2020

Living within the pandemic has shown me, even more than I realized before, how extremely divided our country is, how opinionated most of us are and what resulting effects come to the forefront. Somewhere I heard that the illusion of knowledge is a much greater danger than ignorance. The illusion of knowledge can be the factor for forming an opinion. When two opposite sides, right wing-left wing, offer diametrically opposed ideas as truth, then one of them must be wrong. Sometimes it doesn't matter what opinion a person holds because whether or not the usefulness of that opinion is important is the question of relevance. Is my opinion as useful as a prominent national politician or a local judge? I wonder if the judgment of the Supreme Court is based on an assessment of true facts or a speculation and assumption that unfolds from collective opinions. My conclusion; I should be writing something worth reading about or I should do something worth writing about. I'm just about to go to Lake Sonoma and play with my friend Mark on his big boat. I will be jumping in the water. This is good, in my opinion.

With many large businesses closing their doors, employees are still on the job, working from their own homes. This has become a practice that could very well extend beyond the lockdown. It could be a permanent change and I think it might be detrimental. It seems to me that getting smart people 'together at the office,' would naturally create new ideas. Two heads are better than one, can't have as an effective think tank online.

15

David

The following experience is an event that has had a strong and permanent influence on my life. Actually this incredible experience occurred during a trip from Colombia back to the States. I had returned to Florida for a short visit, when I received a telephone call from an old friend Valerie.

"I'm so glad I reached you," she said. "I heard that you were back in town and I need to see you. Something amazing is happening. I am babysitting for a family here while the parents are in Europe. The oldest son is going through some sort of transformation. He is leaving his body at night and gaining all this wisdom. You must come over." Valerie knew that I had read a lot about Eastern philosophy.

That evening I went to the house and met David, the 16-year-old child who is the object of this story. David appeared to be very much a normal child of his age group. As I surmised, he was not a child of brilliance, nor one who was out of the ordinary in any manner that was obvious. He had not been interested in spiritual matters, and had no background to prepare him for what was happening, or at least not in this lifetime. Valerie was right, amazing things were happening to David. When I went to the house that evening I certainly did not expect to find what I found, nor did I expect to become a significant part of what was to be.

I prepared dinner for the family that evening and afterwards David, Valerie and I settled into the family den, where David began relating his story to me. For whatever reason, I had brought a small tape recorder with me, which I used to record David's story.

Now in order to make this story easy to relate I am going under the presumption that Eastern wisdom, concerning the nature of life, is totally correct. The basis of which is: every person is born into a body with an independent soul or spirit. This spirit is a part of, and is one with, a larger spirit, which is called God. All animals and every form of life also possess a similar spirit. David will call this spirit a light. So the story begins.

Prior to my arrival David had been leaving his body at night. He had been astrally projecting and going to different levels, different planes of existence. It started on the first night of Valerie's arrival. He was in bed fantasizing about a relationship with Valerie. It appears that Valerie's presence was necessary as it had triggered the event. At the time Valerie was 28 years old and David, as I said, was 16. He told me that he was imagining Valerie was his girlfriend and that he was going to pick her up for a date. He arrived in his Corvette and brought her to the airport where they would fly around in his private plane. As these thoughts were occurring, David said that he suddenly felt as if he was leaving his body. He began traveling to different places, through long tunnels, snowy places, and places of extreme darkness, or as he puts it, "It is not like they are dark, but rather that they are void of light. There is a difference."

And he went to a place which he called 'the library,' and said, "Where there were all these books. And they contained all the knowledge of the world, and you didn't have to read them. You just enter the library and you absorb the knowledge. And there, I met Jimmy Hendrix and Janis Joplin." They had both recently died. "And they were both beautiful people." He continued, "And they did not have a shell around them like most people."

What David was doing was traveling to the different planes that one experiences after death. His descriptions were exactly describing those levels of which I had read. He put it in different words; he did not know any of the accepted terms. We counted the different places that he had traveled to, and there were seven, just as described in the Tibetan Book of the Dead. It had taken him three nights of traveling, each night he went a little further. I interpreted David's library as The Hall of the Akashic Records, where all karma can be found. When I asked David if he thought he could leave his body again and go to these places, he answered, "Why of course."

Within a short period of time Valerie and I noticed that David was lying on the couch with his eyes closed. I assumed that he was again astrally traveling. My assumption was correct, he was traveling to all the levels that he had visited earlier and would even go further, to a point that he referred to as 'the point of no return.' Valerie and I spoke rather softly, waiting to see when David would come back, and what he would have to say.

When David woke up, he looked at me and I immediately knew that he was seeing into my thoughts, into my heart, and into my very soul. It was frightening, never before had I been so naked in someone's eyes. He knew every secret that I had about myself. I tried to turn within, but he was there, I could not take my eyes away from him. It was as if he had a power over me, as if he were a creature from another planet that had walked from his spaceship and hypnotized me with his eyes. Eventually I formed a thought directed toward him. "Is this really happening? David, are you here in my brain, can you read my mind?" I could hear him replying in my thoughts. "Yes I am here, and it is OK, don't be afraid."

I turned toward Valerie. I could telepathically communicate with her as well.

Once before I had a similar telepathic experience, only at that time it was brought on by LSD and it lasted only for two or three sentences. This time with David and Valerie, it would continue for three days. During this time we never left the house. In the beginning I was very, very frightened. Most people will never have to experience this. It is frightening because it is a complete shedding of your conceptual being in an instant. Your entire ego, every false image you have of yourself or that you try to pass off to others is suddenly exposed. Having David inside of my mind made me face up to it all. Up to that moment I had not realized how much of me was a made up character. A large portion of my ego, of my self-image was just someone that I wanted to be, a person that I wanted others to believe that I was.

I did overcome this fear, the embarrassment, and in the days that were to follow, I learned about truth. Without words, one cannot lie. With words one cannot be truthful. There are too many foolish concepts in the way. I will put it like this. When two people come together, there are six different conceptual beings present. On one side there is the person who, at that time, you think you are, there is the true person that you really are, and there is the person that the other one thinks you are. The same scenario is true for the other side. This makes up six different combinations of ways to relate to each other. Without the barriers that words are able to create, there would only be two people communicating the truth through their thoughts.

After the three intense days of being in the house and exploring this new condition, David would return again to the place of a 16- year-old. He told us that this is his place in time, and that is where he needed to be. In the course of those three days I came to understand that everyone is exactly where he or she should be in time. Total knowledge of the future will not change anything for you or for anyone else.

During this period of David's 'awakening,' I asked him many questions about the future. Some things he told me, others were not within my grasp. It was not necessary to voice anything, we remained telepathic, but at times I did revert to talking. There was one fact that was quite surprising to me. I had been raised as a Christian, but as I said earlier, I never believed it. Well what David told me was important. To this day I have yet to find out why. David told me about Jesus, who was the greatest Guru of them all. Jesus was the only one of the great masters who was one with God.

Buddha, Muhammad, all the others had a direct communication line, but according to David, Jesus was indeed the only 'One with God.'

There is one extremely valuable message that I feel I would like to share, about a place that exists beyond telepathy. When I first arrived at David's house, I thought I would have dinner and leave. I had brought with me some camping gear and had planned to go to a favorite beach to sleep out. In my backpack I was carrying a small bottle of oil. At one point when I was searching through my pack, I had picked up the bottle. At that moment I looked over at David and noticed that he was looking at me. I spoke to him in my mind and said, "It is oil of pennyroyal and I use it as a mosquito repellent." In his mind, he replied, "I know you forget that I possess total knowledge, it is not necessary to think the thought." At that instant my whole consciousness expanded, taking a giant quantum leap. Perhaps this is the state that a Zen student reaches when he suddenly understands a difficult Zen koan. It must be the desired state of 'Satori.'

For a split second I believe that I came near the place where David visited, the 'point of no return.' My body began to tingle and soon I could no longer feel any physical sensations. I realized that one does not need to think a thought in order to transfer it to another. Telepathy is for those in the kindergarten of enlightenment. Thought is a very small part of the total knowledge, insignificant at that. We all possess 'total knowledge'. For that brief moment I could feel all of the knowledge. I believe my path to this place was through David. I believe I reached this place by going inside of David's mind. He made the roadway for me, and opened the gate.

God is a creator, God cannot destroy, too much knowledge can destroy, therefore knowledge is revealed as one is ready, and in a position to accept. For the time that I was experiencing this I was given a great amount of knowledge and a great gift that I will always keep, a glimpse of divine truth.

Earlier in this book I mentioned that there are certain things that are my truths, my relationship with David and Valerie is one such thing. It is an experience that is meant only for me. I am happy to finally write about this experience, but it is not worthwhile to write about everything. I would not expect others to believe all of this. Other people will have their own personal experiences.

Valerie married David. I bought them airline tickets so they could fly down and stay with me in Colombia. With Valerie's young baby Tyler, they came, and for a while, lived on Mario's finca, in the mountains of Medellin.

16

My Older Self

So that was my experience with David. It was typical of my life in those days, a 26 year old, who had been influenced and formed as a teenager in such a radical period. The Bible of the day was 'Howl' by Ginsberg. The night before I went over to Valerie's I had gone to a meeting at the local Yoga Center in West Palm Beach to listen to a disciple of a young and upcoming Indian guru, Mahariji Ji. He spoke on the importance of having a guru as a teacher, a Master, and how your guru can take on your negative karma, etc. etc.

I remember sitting cross legged on the floor listening intently, but not buying into it. I thought if I was supposed to be following someone else or some 'thing,' that it would come to me naturally. Even if I had thought to join this new young enlightened guru, I was soon to be heading back to Colombia. I was still too frisky, too spunky, too playful. To sit for extended periods in quiet meditation was not my cup of chamomile. My sense of spontaneity had not yet been crushed by the rigors of making a living. I was not forced to look elsewhere for my meaning of existence. I had no territorial imperative to defend, no house full of belongings to guard. I had wonderful parental instilled values. I had not been genetically assassinated. And then came David.

After the initial experience with David's 'awakening,' I was slowly absorbing all the new information, highlighted by the true telepathic communication, which incidentally became the norm. I realized I had to keep moving forward. The first time I walked out of the house I felt as if I were in slow motion. The cars, the noises of life were so intense, I retreated back to the house. Eventually I returned to my older self. The awe of it faded, but the experience will never disappear. I know of a power that I have and that everyone has, and I still find myself talking in my mind. Sometimes it happens when I'm in a situation where I'm not able to understand a word of what anyone around me is saying. When the banal boring meaning of the blathering makes no sense to me, I remember the power I have.

I also use this power whenever I'm in the presence of babies or animals. It's not a power where I can hear them talking back to me. But I know that on a very important level, they can hear what I am thinking. I am as certain of this as I am of anything. Even more so, because as Gandhi says, there is no God higher than truth, and over time truth prevails over everything. I know my experience with David was real. As with Jay Brown, I have not made an effort to reconnect with David or Valerie, but I still have the future ahead. Perhaps.

Danny just called me and suggested I follow his lead and drive downtown to the Free Food Line. Danny the proud right winger is not shy about accepting a government handout. The non-socialist is receiving a weekly check from the In House Home Services, a medical program and he's the first to get inline for the welfare food program. I'm not judging Danny at all, he has his reasoning, and I accept that. I'm not judging, rather I'm here in my parked car waiting for the workers, mostly young girls, with all those big boxes of free food to open up and begin handing them out to 'We the People.' It's not even with mixed feelings that I am about to accept this. It has definitely not been a regular practice in my life. I have never applied or received food stamps nor have I ever benefited by free government programs. I never felt the need and

I was considerate of those that really needed the help. The world is different today, my life has changed.

Today as I look at my relative condition and present action, I do so without a judgment or conclusion as to motive. I'm just acting on impulse without too much self analysis. There are instances when the only true measure of an action is the consequence. This 'free food' is all new to me. I would assume there are others in this line that are richer and others that are poorer. I'm counting 31 cars in the lines right now, including some very nice newer model cars and trucks. My ride would be way down on the list. I'm talking right near the bottom.

I'm wondering how I will feel when they start putting free food in my car. This should be happening soon. Danny got me here early, I'm like number 10 in the line. The volunteer workers are just finishing the set up now. They erected 8 nice new canopies, keeping the food in the shade. It looks like there's a refrigerated truck as well. Cars are still driving up for this Christmas in August. As I look around I wonder if there are people here that have been going to bed hungry. To some, this is not Christmas at all. I wonder how they happen to be in such nice vehicles compared to my feeble ride. I wonder if Starbucks is represented in one of those tents handing out a free double white chocolate mocha, hold the whip cream. I wonder what life stories the guy next to me has.

There is now a third line of cars, another 20 or so. It's 9:50 I assume we have 10 more minutes of wait time. Another canopy is going up. I'm listening to Lo Cura, one of my favorite groups. They just did Guantanamera. Life is good.

My bladder is like doing bench presses right now. OK Free Food People, it's your move. Ah, the line is moving. I can see Danny ahead, almost at the first canopy. I'm putting on my mask. I think I'll put on my sunglasses too.

OMG, I'm home. My bladder went from bench presses to jumping jacks, but I took care of that and now I'm in amazement at all the stuff. It's said that a picture's worth a thousand words but I'll try and make it in less than a thousand.

Two packages of potato rolls from the local upscale bakery, five big bunches of celery, a bag of rice, a bag of black beans, a bag of raisins, a box of spaghetti, three packages of Lemon Dill Starkist Salmon Creations, a squeeze bottle of strawberry jelly (first time this has entered my abode in quite a while), a large bag of plums, a bag of red apples, a bag of yellow apples, two bags of carrots, six big cucumbers, a can of Premium white chicken, a pound of butter, a sack of potatoes, a can of kidney beans, a can of pears, and a can of tomato sauce, a bag of onions and four boxes of low fat organic milk, a large, frozen family meal size of Fajita Chicken, and one pound of frozen Pork Loin Center Cut Boneless.

Lunch is about to be served. Today's dining will be Wild Caught Lemon Dill Salmon Spread served on two freshly baked Cousteau Bakery Potato Rolls with our own garden grown Heirloom Tomatoes. Normally priced at $15.95, today's special price is Free.

AUGUST 5, 2020

The US is still holding its place as the number one world leader of infected virus cases. Looking on the brighter side, another US drug company has released information that shows its coronavirus vaccine is safe and may be effective. That's three companies with promising vaccine results so far: Moderna, Pfizer and now Novavax. Two other US trials will soon be underway for a possible antibody treatment for Covid-19 patients.

Meanwhile, in the absence of a national testing plan, seven governors have banded together to pursue a deal for 3.5 million coronavirus antigen tests to create a coordinated strategy among their states. The US recorded nearly 1,400 new coronavirus fatalities yesterday, bringing the nationwide death toll to just under 157,000. When asked about the death toll during a recent interview, President Trump replied, "It is what it is."

Congressmen are still battling with each other, trying to agree on the next stimulus bill to bolster our poor economy. The Airline industry struggles to stay open, a few have declared bankruptcy and others are working on safe flying plans.

As for changes in police brutality and injustice, the fight has reached the Federal Court. Tragically, thousands have died at the hands of law enforcement over the years, and the death toll continues to rise. Countless more have suffered from other forms of abuse and misconduct by police. Qualified immunity has served as a shield for these officers, protecting them from accountability.

US Judge Carlton Reeves, a federal judge in Mississippi who wrote a scathing opinion urging the Supreme Court to reconsider qualified immunity, a legal doctrine he and other critics say helps shield police from consequences of wrongdoing.

Another move by Trump is making headlines today. He has ordered the Census Bureau to end its effort to count the number of people living here. Of course the pandemic is hampering the efforts but here's the issue, the census data, which is collected every 10 years, determines the allocation of political representation across the country, as well as federal funding to states and localities. Inaccuracies would skew these figures for the next decade.

The bureau said the recent change was part of an effort to meet the federal deadline, delivering the counts to President Trump by the end of the year. Some critics have called it an effort by the Trump administration to 'sabotage the census to undercount minorities and non-citizens even more than they're undercounted right now, which is substantial.'

Switching gears, Zachary is home, he arrived yesterday to visit his mom and I for a couple days. He has been working steadily at his new job, a guidance counselor for young problem kids. Many of these troubled teens have drug related issues and are put into the facility by the court system or by their parents. None of them are there of their own will. We talked last night about one young kid, 16 years old, autistic, and according to Zac, a genius in the field of chemistry. Zac said he has educated himself to match any knowledge that Zac acquired at the University. This kid's desire is to attend Oxford University, become a chemist, and create new psychedelic drugs. He also hopes to take drugs every day of his life. Zac thinks he may have burst the kid's bubble slightly by telling him that the thrill, the euphoria of psychedelics will eventually wear off.

I can not express how wonderful it is to have Zac as a son and to be with him. His mom shares the feeling. He'll be heading back to SC today with a box of groceries, compliments of the benevolent Healdsburg City Government and the local almsgiving community businesses, and Danny.

Once on a trip together to Hawaii, another gift from Julie, Zac and I were in our First Class seats, joking about starting a new business in Hawaii. Here's my effort.

MAGMATION

Are you pondering your options for infinity? Burial or cremation just 'doesn't get it' for you. Well rest assured, literally, because we have the answer for you. We call it "Death Eternal." With our new service you can become 'Instant Rock' forever.

Magmation works like this. When your time has come to turn in the chips, so to speak. In other words, when that poor old body has given out and no longer works for you, your family members give us a call. We pick up your remains, drive your body up to Kilauea Crater and dump you into the 2,500 degree melting magma. You are then instantly transformed into rock. That's right, good old liquid rock, and here's the good part. At some point you will flow down a lava tube, ooze out and turn into solidified lava rock. You then become part of the island itself.

Or you might form into a new island. In time your island drifts away. Plants and trees grow on you and you rest eternally as a tropical paradise. Yep, ashes or rotting in a box just doesn't compare to our brand new plan.

Magmation is the way of the future. Sign up quickly. Dump one of your family members now and get the second dump for free. Limited offer, call today.

AUGUST 6, 2020

My normal happy casual approach to life was jolted yesterday afternoon as I was sitting on the new deck of Suzanne's, which is almost finished except for the final touches. I received a call from CNS, Suzanne's caregivers. They told me that she was regressing by being at home and they plan on putting her into an Assisted Living Facility. This will kill Suzanne. I was so shocked and devastated. I sat in disbelief until finally composing myself enough to reach out. I called Julie. She is my anchor, my saint and adviser. She was also in shock, but comforted me somewhat by discussing the options. We knew that Suzanne needed to be informed in a way that wouldn't be so shocking or fatal.

I was able to do this by telling Suzanne I had received a call and they were worried about her progress. "You need to start really working hard to show them that you can get better." She had been skipping some of her online sessions, saying she was too tired, I guess all the different therapists have agreed that she is not improving. They can see that her weight gain is out of control, and they don't think that the caregivers are doing much to help her.

After speaking with Julie I called the attorney that we have now hired. He said that of course they can't come, handcuff her and take her away but that this is a serious problem because there are no better people to help her than CNS. He didn't make me feel any better with some surprise good advice. I am in a somewhat better frame of mind this morning, trying to think positive. I will continue to push Suzanne and today when I go over to her house, I will tell her that we need to get her to change her eating habits. One of the therapists told me that the eating problem is a result of the brain injury and is quite common. The change that is proposed by CNS will not take place until the end of this month. I will try and make Suzanne realize how serious this is and perhaps she can improve with the therapists before then. If it doesn't happen then I am not sure I will continue with CNS. I just don't know what will happen, but I don't want Suzanne going to a glorified nursing home. Just yesterday she said, "If I pay you, will you build me a deck on the back of my house? I've always wanted one there." I must stay positive and make things work out for the best.

AUGUST 7, 2020

The idea of the 'Death Sentence,' as I call it, that CNS wants to administer to Suzanne is still very concerning to me but I feel better because I have a plan to fight it. It will mean Suzanne has to really work hard and I hope she realizes this, and is ready and able to react. Today Zac has informed me that he will be coming back home. His work is slow because of an infected counselor and he has the next 6 days off. When he arrives I plan on having a serious meeting with Suzanne. Zac will help to design a weight loss program for her and also encourage a change in her behavior. I will also call to see if her meds can be adjusted. Hopefully this might give her more energy. She is now taking a pain med twice a day, not sure if we can cut this down, but maybe. I am heading over to her house in a couple hours to fill the planter boxes I've made with soil and put up the final rail on the deck.

Yesterday I stayed away and spent the day at Mark's house, in and out of his saltwater swimming pool, and lying on a lounge chair, remembering my past. It was the same scene a week ago, when we all went out in Mark's boat on Lake Sonoma. On the boat I was quiet, listening but hardly engaging myself in social talk with the group. At the pool yesterday I spent a little time reading 'Rolling Stones' magazine. Mark told me that when he was much younger he purchased a lifetime subscription to 'Rolling Stones,' which he now resentfully describes as an extreme left wing magazine.

Danny and his friend Linda were at Mark's also, but I basically stayed at a distance from the three of them, while they had chairs in the shade and talked, drank beer and smoked pot, I was quiet and by myself most of the day. For me, it's not the social gathering that comforts me, but it's the needed break from the present stressful situation with Suzanne.

It is said that our lives are enriched by the differences in our society. This is probably true, but I don't know how my presence yesterday enriched Mark or Danny or Linda. Before we went to the pool I helped Mark on a couple repairs to the boat seats, and when the day was ending I helped him fix the pool cleaning sweeper. So I guess I was physically helpful, enriching in a way. I'm off to Suzanne's now.

17

Artchie

When I returned from Colombia I met and became friends with Artchie, a very special person. Artchie was just discovering the undersea world of snorkeling. He was a strikingly, handsome man, with thick auburn, almost red hair, worn rather short for the times. However at shoulder length it was wavy and flowing. His eyes were blue, smiling and sincere, his mouth, well shaped and sensual. Artchie's most valued and noticeable trait was his positive, creative energy, which everyone felt. It was impossible to be around him without being uplifted by his spirit. The following is his story.

Prior to coming to South Florida, Artchie had been living in New York City, working as a photographer, artist and part time model. He was the creator of a syndicated comic called Artchie Strips. Basically it was a continual running story about his everyday life. It was not animated but composed with photos chronicling his daily life, often in collage form. His work was very 'avant-garde,' perfect for New York, right up there along with Andy Warhol's art.

In New York, Artchie ran with the jet set. He was invited to all the parties and celebrity functions. When I first met him, he had thrown away this high life for a calmer, quieter, family oriented style. He, his wife Tina and their three young boys had moved to the small town of Lake Worth, ten miles southwest of Palm Beach. He was still working on Artchie Strips and also on designing an

233

album cover for the Rolling Stones. It was his second cover for the 'Stones,' Along with Michael Cooper, he had co-designed 'Her 'Satanic's Majesty,' the three dimensional album cover with the Beatles hidden in it, which is now a collector's item.

Soon after meeting Artchie, I arranged a three-day work week at European Health Spa, and had time to get back into the sea. I knew most of the reefs in the area, so Artchie and I became diving partners. We spent many hours spearfishing and setting up tropical aquariums for our houses. It was my 'Colombian' recovery therapy.

One day Artchie came up with the idea of selling our tropical fish to the pet stores and starting our own diving company. Artchie owned an old 1948 Dodge, which became our company car. He had it painted with tropical fish. We couldn't very well use his Volkswagen. It had a beautiful metal flake green paint job, which was OK, the problem with using the VW, was that many marijuana leaves had been designed into the paint job. We bought a rubber inflatable dive boat, called ourselves Atlantis Tropicals and went into business.

Artchie was the real force behind our venture. I had been diving since a young child, but to Artchie this was all new and extremely exciting. In addition to this, as I have mentioned, he was one of the most positive men alive. I eventually gave up the masseur position at European Health Spa in favor of Atlantis Tropicals. I became a full time diver again.

In the beginning of our venture, we moved rather slowly. There are a number of different methods for capturing tropicals. Using plastic nets and setting traps are the techniques we most often employed. We learned many tricks to become more efficient at catching them.

Every day we would be in the ocean by early morning. Our hunting grounds extended from Jupiter in the north to Delray Beach, the furthest south, an area of ocean reefs, covering approximately 60 miles. For the most part, we stayed in shallow water and snorkeled. We would each have a filled bottle, but basically use it only when we had found a fish to catch, switching from snorkel to the regulator sparingly. In this way a bottle would last until noon. The wonder of being on an ocean reef for hours at a time is difficult to explain to one who has never experienced this. There is no place on land where man has the opportunity to interact with such an abundance of living, moving, intelligent, non-human creatures. Unlike most areas on land, on the reef, man is obviously the invading minority.

The summer weather in South Florida is predictable, very similar to the rain forests in which I had lived. The clear sunny mornings gradually change to gray skies and afternoon thundershowers. This pattern would usually force us out of the water by noon. We would carry our day's catch to a large aquarium that we had set up at Artchie's house. Lunch would most often be something we had taken from the sea, perhaps a lobster or red snapper. If nothing better, we could always count on shooting a small barracuda. After lunch, the storms would usually end. We would refill our bottles and be back on the reef until darkness settled in. The reefs in this area had lost a lot of life since my first exposure to them as a small child, but they were still ecologically alive with patches of coral and enough tropical fish to support our small operation.

I should mention now, that today my feelings about this business have completely changed. At the time, it seemed alright to me to be catching these small fish and supporting such a healthy lifestyle for ourselves. This is the life I knew, this is what I had done as a child. Today, over twenty- five years later, I have changed with the times.

For what it's worth, to whoever might listen, it is not right to do this. This is exactly the same as logging out the rainforest or the pristine redwood forests of the Pacific USA. The only thing worse for reefs are the obscene trawling method used by shrimp and scallop fishermen throughout the world. They are the clear-cutters of the sea. Any diver who has seen the bottom of the ocean floor after the trawler nets have come by and scraped, or has been on board those boats, as I have, must carry a permanent tear in his eye.

For Artchie and I to sell these poor little fishies, we needed to safely transport them. The process is to fill plastic bags half full with seawater, half with pure oxygen. After the fish are placed into these oxygen rich bags, they are placed into Styrofoam containers. This maintains a constant temperature, and makes them ready for transporting. We began our business by selling to the local pet stores, but this market was quite limited.

One day after diving, Artchie came up with the idea to load up a hundred fish into the VW, marijuana leaves and all, and drive up to the 'Big Apple.' Within a few days, I found myself back in NY City. We stayed with Artchie's friend in the Village. I sadly recalled my days there with Billy Burroughs.

Walking blindly into the pet shops of Manhattan was our first selling approach. A note for the in-experienced, New York businessmen are unlike any others. The dumbest of them are smarter than the smartest, in most parts of the world. In New York City, it is a simple matter of survival. This I had to learn. I remember how my feelings were hurt by these rude monsters. They were worse than the great white sharks. The fact that we did not know the names of half the fishies did not help much. By the time we called upon the second store we got smarter and had bought a book with all the correct fishie names.

A typical meeting went something like this. We walk into the store and are immediately approached by an aggressive salesperson. We attempt to reach the owner or manager of the store. Our request usually receives an answer such as, "Yeah, well who are you?"

"Well, er, uh, you see, we are Atlantis Tropicals, direct from the Caribbean."

"Yeah, sure you are, what do you really want, are you here to buy somethin' or what?"

"No, really we are, we really are. We even got fish in the car."

"Yeah, sure ya do. Hey Louie get over here, we got a couple a winners here, wanna talk to ya." So the owner comes over. "Whad is this, whad I hear? You'se got fish in da car?"

"Yep, that's right, we got fish in the car." So we go out to the VW and usually there's a few hippies hanging around it admiring the marijuana leaf paint job. We bring in a few baggies with our fish, and we're in. We learned to bring in the French Angels. They are beautiful little Angelfish, black with yellow stripes.

Upon seeing our fishes, Louie says. "Well I'll be a son-of-a-bitch, you'se really got some fish!" The way I see this, is Louie had probably been approached many times by entrepreneuring, over-achieving, young New Yorkers on their way back from a Miami vacation. They would tell Louie that they also owned a tropical fish business, with the hopes of making a little extra cash. Well we actually had the real thing in our hands, little fishes, 1,500 miles away from home. Louie was very impressed with that action.

So he is now won over to our side. He is right there with us, his workers, Vinnie and Sal are there with us also. They are all picking up our little plastic bags, looking at the fish and then looking at us. Artchie and I are looking at each other. We were pretty damn proud of ourselves. By God, we drove all these little fishes all the way up to their front door. Yep, we had impressed these New Yorkers, and that is not an easy thing to do. We had some cute orange and white Clown Fish and some yellow Butterflies, and some Blue Tangs, but they all loved the French Angels best. And to our good fortune, that was one of the easier ones for us to catch.

"All right, OK, you'se guys are for real," says Louie. "How many of these French Angels can ya get us?" Vinnie chips in, "Yo Lou, we been turnin' some Blue-headed Wrasses this week." I looked at Artchie and he's smiling from ear to ear. I could see his brain-wheels shifting into high gear.

When Artchie got going like that, he would talk to you without looking at you. Like he would be staring into outer space. His head would cock just a little to the right. Somehow I always knew that he was in touch with some higher being, some super-intelligence from the Fifth Dimension. It was so impressive, he was so cool, and I remember watching other people unconsciously trying to copy him. No-body could do it. And he would laugh a little, and take you on a roller coaster ride through his thoughts, finally coming down to the point and then at last, making eye contact, with that handsome, happy, smiling face.

Artchie turns away from Louie and whispers to me, "Isn't that the skinny blue one that hangs out on those boulders and eats the urchins in our trap? Yes, I think so." I responded.

So Louie and Artchie take off in heavy negotiations. Why one would think Atlantis Tropicals and Louie's Pet Store were right on the top of the Fortune 500 list. Within a brief period of time, they had worked out details for a working relationship and Lou placed a sizable order for our fish.

"Ya know, I got a cousin Bruce in Brooklyn," Louie says. "He's a bum, but he's got a good business. He wholesales tropical fish, you guys got ta go over and see him." Our next stop was Brooklyn.

Louie was right; Bruce had a good business. He was sending fish all over the country, and he had suppliers like us from all over the world. He was receiving salt-water tropicals from divers in Hawaii, Indonesia, Curacao and Australia. I repeat, this whole business is truly pitiful. Why someone in Boise, Idaho feels that they need a tiny fish from Fiji is beyond my comprehension, but anyway, on with the story. Basically, Bruce agrees to buy anything we can catch. Bruce will even buy the small sand sharks that I would often catch; price, thirty-five bucks apiece plus shipping.

At this point Artchie and I are elated, we have us a good business. All the fish we brought up have been sold. It is now time to celebrate. Next stop, New Jersey. After a few celebration drinks we wind up at Al's Tattoo Parlor. We have decided to get a permanent memory of this day, of our business and of our relationship, a tiny French Angel Fish. We drew a picture of it for "Big Al' and Artchie had the small image tattooed on the outside of his leg, on his lower calf. I decided to put my little French Angel in a spot more hidden. You know where the backside of your two upper thighs butt together, that's where my Angelfish resides, only viewable for a select few.

We were soon on our way back to Florida. Keith Richards from the 'Rolling Stones' had been calling for Artchie. When we arrived, there was a ticket waiting for him and he was off to England to discuss the next album cover. As it turned out, he did not actually work on the album, the Stones only wanted him to be there and party with them. That is the kind of person Artchie was.

While Artchie was gone, I dealt with the problem at hand. We had lost a good number of fish. In one of our large tanks, the water had gone bad. It was always a concern for our operation. It is rather easy to lose the proper Ph balance or the correct salinity and nitrate levels when using large tanks for holding purposes. The tank that went bad was our 500-gallon tank. We lost over 100 fish, which represented a lot of diving time. I changed the water, had the tank up again and was back diving when Artchie returned.

Within a week of Artchie's return, we designed and built a huge metal cage out of steel and wire mesh. Our plan was to eliminate the holding tanks, and keep the fish in the ocean. We would sink the cage on the reef. We purchased a length of heavy chain and a large padlock. One evening, with the help of friends, we drove our huge cage to the ocean. We had decided to sink it at a site approximately 15 miles south of Palm Beach off of a rather quiet beach, Lantana.

Under the cover of darkness, we lifted the cage down the sandy beach and onto our rubber boat. Artchie sat at the stern, driving the outboard. I stayed in the water and hung on to the side of the boat as we drove silently outward toward the reef. With an underwater light, I was able to locate the approximate spot we had chosen to dump the cage. The following morning we positioned it, wrapped the large chain around the cage and reef and secured the padlock. This was to be our new holding tank.

It served our purpose well. Inside of the cage we placed objects where the fish could hide. It was a good environment for them. We would feed them each day, until the time came to jet them off to Brooklyn. On those shipping days, we would load our boat up with pieces of Styrofoam cut to a size that fit through the cage door.

Diving down, we would place one piece at a time inside, until the cage eventually became light enough and floated up to the surface. From the side of the boat we would then scoop out our fish with small nets, and place them into the shipping bags.

Being a successful diver in this business requires knowledge of fish behavior. The ecology of the reef and the ocean in general is quite complex. Every form of life is so intricately inter-related. The more knowledge one acquires, the more fascinating the underwater world becomes. One of the first lessons one learns is that the reef is not the serene and peaceful existence which casual divers observe. On the contrary, it is a hostile and violent way of life, survival of the fittest indeed.

Being underwater in this environment, swimming silently for hours at a time and days on end, I found that my thoughts had slowed down. I was basically working from my instincts. I am certain from my observations of young fish that for the most part, their behavior is also instinctual, passed along through genetics. They obviously learn new things, as they grow older, but are born with a tremendous amount of instinctual knowledge, much different, I dare say, than humans. I suppose that if a method were used to distinguish between learned and instinctive behavior, it might easily be a test based on reaction times, in other words, how quickly one can retrieve the information when prompted to do so through a form of stimulus.

I have witnessed schools of baby fish being born. They know immediately and exactly how to swim against current, how to find protection, when to flee from danger, etc. etc. I have also had the opportunity of swimming with the larger fish, and have definitely been able to sense some form of communication with them. It's not like we could talk and answer verbally or telepathically, but there are times when I was able to have a sort of call and response action. You must believe in some things and when you admit it to yourself, you will see that things begin to happen. Many people experience this on a daily basis with domesticated pets. I've been lucky enough to experience it with wild fish and mammals. In Belize I had pet fish that would come to my house every day. Of course everyone knows of the high intelligence attributed to whales and dolphins. Being classified as mammals, they are separate from fish but acknowledged to be one of the highest forms of intelligence of any animal. A dolphin's brain is larger than a human's.

Being in the water, diving all day on the reef, in the silent underwater world, happened to be the best spot not only for relaxing and slowing down the mind, but also for a type of mind expansion. With Timothy Leary and psychedelic drugs, I had made conscious efforts to expand into more meaningful areas. By practicing techniques of meditation and self-discipline, I had hoped to reach higher levels of consciousness. Yet for me, the secret to reaching those levels had been in front of me all the time, it was something I had lived with all my life. As I mentioned before, on the reef my thoughts were void, my behavior was instinctual. I lived on that reef for hours in the Zen state of no thought. My mind, my consciousness expanded the entire length of the reef. Oftentimes I became one with all life existing here. I was a hunter; at the same time I was the hunted. It was the only way to catch the fish

All day I spent underwater with the natural wonders of the ocean and at night I became more and more interested in the other world, the above water spiritual one, which I had ignored. Many Eastern gurus were making the rounds in the USA, gathering new disciples. For whatever reasons, they were very busy. There were the famous and popular ones, like Maharishi Mahesh Yogi, Maharaja Ji, Muktananda, etc. These Masters had appeared in the 60s and were going great guns by the 70s. I read the books, bought albums, went to meetings and put out full effort to achieve 'Satori,' to become enlightened, to reach 'Nirvana.'

There were many methods to choose from, most very similar, and there were many people on the same path, offering reassurance that this was a correct, valid way to be spending one's time. It was the same mass sanction that was evident to those still in the drug taking culture. "Seek and you shall find." This was the accepted rule.

Artchie and I continued with Atlantis Tropicals into the winter, until one fateful day, diving in 90 feet of water, tragically I would lose my best friend and the world would lose Artchie. It began like any other day. From our boat, I had entered the water first, diving to the bottom and waiting for Artchie to come down. I was busy with my nets, looking up the anchor line and waiting, but I would never see him again. He never made it down the line. In some way, forever unknown to me, Artchie drowned. For three days his body drifted in the sea until washing up on shore. The Artchie that so many people knew and loved was gone forever. Tina, his wife, and their children would suffer an unbelievable loss. And I again had lost my best friend to the sea, the sea that I so loved. I was terribly hurt and confused by this loss. I felt guilty, since I was the more experienced diver, and felt that perhaps I had been negligent. Perhaps I should have waited for him at the surface.

After finding Artchie's body, a sunrise service was held at the beach and Artchie's ashes were thrown into the sea. Articles would be written in a few newspapers about him, and stories would be published in a couple of New York art magazines about the creative young talent who had died in such a tragic, untimely manner.

When Artchie and I were in New York we had set up a small aquarium in the house of Artchie's friend who had put us up during our time there. We left the lady with several of the fish that we had brought with us. During the week of Artchie's death and funeral service, she called me and said that she had made many calls to Artchie's house but was not able to get through. I responded by telling her of Artchie's death. There were several moments of silence and when she came back on the line she told me that on the day that Artchie had drowned, all of the fish in the aquarium died. This was the reason for her call. Artchie's death had a very strong impact on me. I couldn't stay in the area any longer.

18

More August

Last night I was again on my camera, helping to shoot a live Jazz event. Of course the only people in attendance at these Friday night events are the musicians and the tech crew that streams the event. Jessica, the producer, told me it costs a little over $2,000. to put this together.

Today is the 75th Anniversary of the Nagasaki nuclear bombing, three days after the bomb had been dropped on Hiroshima. These 'acts of war' put an end to WW 2 as well as the lives of hundreds of thousands of Japanese civilians. "Let there be no mistake; we shall completely destroy Japan's power to make war," President Harry Truman, who ordered the attacks, declared in his speech hours after the bombing of Hiroshima. "If they do not now accept our terms, they may expect a rain of ruin from the air, the like of which has never been seen on this earth."

Setsuko Thurlow, 88 years old, wrote to President Trump in a letter published Monday in the Daily Hampshire Gazette. "We atomic bomb survivors are greatly disturbed by the continued modernization of nuclear weapons by the United States and other countries, and your stated willingness to use these instruments of genocide. Nuclear weapons are not a necessary evil, they are the ultimate evil. It is unacceptable for any state to possess them."

"There is no question that a dropping of a large nuclear weapon amongst the civilian population is a war crime," Harvard Law School professor Gabriella Blum says. "Under the current laws of war, if you know you are going to impact civilians, you must provide warning, and you must take precautions to avoid harming civilians to the extent possible. There is no doubt none of that was considered, and none of that was seriously weighed in reference to Hiroshima and Nagasaki."

This subject and the morality of the action has been discussed by everyone from the Pope to Obama. Although the law professor I quoted was misleading, because in 1945 the current laws of warfare didn't contain the provisions she states.

Some historians have suggested that the weapons had a two-pronged objective. First, of course, was to bring the war with Japan to a speedy end and spare American lives. It has been suggested that the second objective was to demonstrate the new weapon of mass destruction to the Soviet Union. The end of one war, the start of the next, the 'Cold One.'

There really is nothing more that I could add to this. What can you say, "Well, he threw the first punch, they fired the first shot, we're the good guys..." I have already spoken much about man's inhumanity to man. It exists and we must live with it, unfortunately. This is not heaven on earth. Life is like a garden. Perfect moments can be had, but not preserved. One moment bliss, but tragedy and unhappiness loom around the corner. Our only control seems to be abetted by cautiously treading along the path, staying positive and doing the right things. Our understanding of right, becomes more right, and the path does become easier, or so it appears to me.

Zac is here today with Rocco, Elliot and Chris. They plan to set up guitars outside as soon as the sun lets up a little. I am looking forward to it. They will probably get amps and set up on the lower deck. All of these kids are about the same age as Michelangelo, 23, when he showed the love of a mother for her child. In 1498-1499 he sculpted his first Pieta, perfect by human standards, therefore divine. I know that if you will allow it, despite all else, life can still and ALMOST always be good.

They've been jamming for a couple hours now. The music is soooo sweet and mellow. I'm just about to serve another meal for four. Main serving, thanks to the Free Food People...

AUGUST 10, 2020

Yesterday was a day where I easily forgot about our pandemic. Or I should say that I was able to put it on the back burner. Having Zac and his friends here made the World a different place for me. I have yet to enlighten myself with today's news so I will proceed with a gentle speel about what I think it will be about. In no other high-income country, and in only a few countries have political leaders departed from expert advice as frequently and significantly as the Trump administration. Trump has said the virus was not serious; predicted it would disappear; spent weeks questioning the need for masks; encouraged states to reopen even with large and growing caseloads; and promoted medical disinformation.

In recent days, Trump has continued the theme, offering a torrent of misleading statistics in his public appearances that make the situation sound less dire than it is. Together, the national skepticism toward collective action and the Trump administration's scattered response to the virus have contributed to several specific failures and missed opportunities.

Already, the American death toll is of a different order of magnitude than in most other countries. With only 4 percent of the world's population, the United States has accounted for 22 percent of coronavirus deaths. Canada, a rich country that neighbors the United States, has a per capita death rate about half as large. And these gaps may worsen in coming weeks, given the lag between new cases and deaths.

For many Americans who survive the virus or do not contract it, the future will bring other problems. Many schools will struggle to open. And the normal activities of life, family visits, social gatherings, restaurant meals, sporting events may be more difficult in the United States than in any other affluent country.

But, and this is a rather large BUT, I know that I can weather all this, as I did yesterday sitting on the deck. I will have times affected for certain, just as I have times affected by Suzanne's condition. During these times I will hope to reach inside and remember the feeling of the beauty of life and be able to draw on the emotion of this genuine heartfelt truth. As for everyone else, if we hope to accomplish something big, we need to come together. Trump's actions have helped create this huge partisan divide, with Republican-leaning voters less willing to wear masks or remain socially distant. Some Democratic-leaning voters and less political Americans, in turn, have decided that if everybody is not taking the virus seriously, they will not either. State leaders from both parties have sometimes created so many exceptions about which workplaces can continue operating normally that their stay-at-home orders have had only modest effects.

Just read the news. As expected, more of the same. The Republicans claim their freedom is being taken away. The conspiracy theorists are saying their freedoms are really being taken away and are literally in tears as to what the near future will be bringing. The Democrats are trying to follow the lead of the so called medical and scientific experts. The confusion, the fear, the uncertainty that we are all feeling, however, excludes imagination and individuality, and it reveals how unexpectedly similar our fragile lives and shared humanity really are. Fear, like the thought of dying, makes us feel alone, but the recognition that we are all experiencing a similar anguish should be able to offer some consolation and help us out of our loneliness. In my opinion, groups, small groups, like the boys yesterday playing their guitars, are safe and what we all need. For a better world to emerge after this pandemic, we must all embrace and nourish the feelings of humility and solidarity. Sorry guys, but I'm afraid it ain't gonna happen, at least not for a rather lengthy period of time. The damage that has been done is severe and will not easily be corrected.

I'd like to retreat back to a less complex time period.

1991 COSTA RICA - DENNIS AND LUCRETIA

This story has to do with two lovely people, one an American ex-patriot Dennis and his very pretty Costa Rican wife, Lucretia,

The story begins with me as a Costa Rican resident. Costa Rica has now become my place of permanent residency. I am in my mid 40s, a documentary producer, and working on a historical doc about a particular region in the mid Pacific section of the country, an area popularly known as Manuel Antonio. My plan for the doc is to begin with the discovery of the area by the Europeans and continue through to the present day. I began researching, writing, shooting and gathering stock footage. I was told of a man living there who had accrued a lot of deep-sea fishing footage. I would need to show this as a part of the present day attraction for tourism. This is how I would meet Dennis.

After a phone call I went to Dennis' home in the country outside of the very small town of Londres. We discussed the possibility of my using his footage and worked out a deal. I told Dennis that I would contact him in the future when I came to that part in my editing. A few months later I'm back on the phone, "Hi Dennis, this is Tom, the producer from San Jose, how are you?"

Well poor Dennis was not doing so well. After coming home from a fishing trip, he was shocked to find a note from his dear wife of many years. It was a 'Dear Juan' letter. She had written a brief good-bye and then left him and their snug little farm for parts unknown. Now anyone who has gone through this experience knows how life shattering it can be. Dennis was hurt, shocked and in need of answers and consolation. He had no idea that this was coming. She had blindsided him. Dennis was not ready to talk about video projects at this time.

The opposite feelings were happening in my life. I had just met a wonderful girl and was in the beginning of a loving relationship. I felt for Dennis and began making an effort to help him in his troubled time. I began calling him on a regular basis and trying to give him something else to think about. I listened to him tell me about his unfaithful wife, and how she had been cheating on him for some time. Some of his closer friends had known of this, but not let on. He was venting to me and I had an open ear. I invited him up to San Jose, to visit, and to attend some plays or musical performances. Dennis became my new friend. I wanted to help him. "A friend in need is a friend indeed."

One morning as I was lying in bed with my new love she began revealing more of her past to me. I realized she was familiar with the area that I was covering in my documentary. She even knew the remote area of the farmland outside of Londres. She told me she once lived there with a gringo, Dennis. I began sweating, my knees, even though they were wrapped up somewhere between her thighs, went weak. Everything on my body went limp. "What have I done?" My new love, Lucretia, " How could this be?" I could see the phone over on the desk.

"Don't call Dennis!" I need time to figure this one out. Throughout my life I had found myself in some rather unusual situations, but nothing like this. I didn't want to give up Lucretia. It's him, or me I thought. I had been listening to all this horrible stuff about this terrible woman. All of that wrapped up in this tiny 4'10" frame, with the long black hair, the beautiful Lady Godiva hair that went all the way down to her calves. Once we were coming home from the beach and she took off her wet clothes and covered her whole body in that beautiful long black hair. We had driven for over 50 miles that day, with her long black hair gown. Eventually she dozed off, her head on my shoulder. My sexy little loving beauty, my Costa Rican goddess, my passionate high-energy soul mate, what am I to do?

We decided to hide it from Dennis. That lasted for a week, but soon we bumped into people who knew both Dennis, Lucretia and me. Then came plan two. Lucretia went to spend the night at her mom's house and she would call Dennis from there. It wasn't long before my phone rang. "Hello Dennis, I swear I didn't know she was your wife, you gotta believe me."

"Yes Dennis, I know. How could I do this to you? "

"But I didn't mean to hurt you on top of your other hurt. But I really like her Dennis; I know she's a cheating slut, but I really like her, Dennis." Then came his crying and me feeling like shit and Dennis feeling worse, I'm sure.

"And you know, she's a hopeless alcoholic." He's talking to me, a borderline wino, who had been sending a disproportionate amount of my hard earned money to the Chile vineyards via "Undurraga," "Concha y Toro" and "Gato Negro." Come to think of it, I had noticed a little behavioral change in my love after a couple glasses of the elixir. "Woe is me, what to do."

Needless to say, things would not get any better. Lucretia felt for her ex. Oh yes, he wanted her back, and was relentless. She became confused. After all she was throwing away a man who loved her without reservation and had lived with her for over a decade. They had built a life that many Costa Rican women could only dream of. Dennis also became confused, after all did he really want back a woman who had been lying and cheating. I became confused. Was it worth it to destroy their marriage? Was it only passion and lust that was driving me to her? Maybe she needed to go back to their farm, away from the nightlife of San Jose, and the fast lane movie business that I was offering her. Along with my lifestyle came a lot of and drinking. The Costa Rican film industry is not Hollywood that's for sure, but it was certainly not like her little farm, with their organic gardens and their two little rental cottages. Lucretia was much more suited to life with Dennis, the more quiet, domesticated approach to happiness. With Dennis she used to bake cakes and sell them in the local village. With me she drank beer and wine and passed out in a stupor.

When we finally made up our confused minds, the decision was obvious. The last morning we spent together, I said a final good bye and Lucretia headed to her parents house to think things over. I would soon be handing her this story I wrote and say good bye.

19

Cohosh and Sundew

Near the edge of a large rainforest lived a happy family of Palomas, the youngest of whom was 'Sundew,' Curious and bright was she, and deeply engaged in learning the ways of flight and gliding.

"Shall I stay here in Osawood," Sundew asked herself, "or rather be off to the cultured lands, where I might practice gliding. For it is there where the true teachers reside." As is so often the case with young palomas, uncertainty prevailed.

Nearby lived another paloma known as Cohosh. Somewhat older and more experienced, Cohosh possessed a deeper knowledge of life. He had now become settled and comfortable in the style of Osawood. However he sought a mate with whom to share his time.

One day while flying high in the treetops Cohosh met Sundew. Ahh, but such a fine romance was to begin. Landing in an old Banyan, the couple burst into songs. Whistling and chirping, Cohosh conveyed a brief history of himself. "I have come from the far north, in the Brown Mountains. I have migrated many seasons to several different areas." Sundew sensed much experience in the song of Cohosh. She had migrated only once, and therefore took enjoyment in being with her new friend. Likewise Cohosh was deeply impressed with the brightness and gaiety of Sundew. All that day they flew and played together. In due time their songs became as one.

Atop a high ridge stood a very old Ceiba tree, housing the nest of Sundew and her family. Covering the giant Ceiba's trunk and limbs were beautiful fringed Orchids and bromeliads. Lianas climbed from the forest floor and wrapped themselves tightly around the Ceiba searching for the sunlight. When Sundew returned to her nest that evening she felt quite different, her uncertainty was replaced by a feeling of excitement. "A new friend, interesting and wonderful," she thought.

As Cohosh flew home to his nest, the proud, confident male now sang and danced through the air, like a spring butterfly, bursting from a silky cocoon. Two months passed, Cohosh and Sundew had been together every day. They were beginning to learn each other's ways. Slowly Sundew began questioning herself. "Am I seeing too much of Cohosh? Do I really want such a close friend? Is this a relationship that I want? What of my former life?" Sundew became troubled.

Most unfortunately, with these doubts, with this confusion, a dull barrier came between them. Sundew's song no longer chimed with a heavenly ring, Cohosh's song became flat and blunt. It was a sad time, such a loss. In the paloma's own way, the pair tried to communicate their deeper feelings, yet something had disappeared. They could not solve the problem. It was as if a dark storm moved between them.

One day Sundew left, leaving Cohosh, yearning to return to the security of her former life, but it was not to be. Sundew's plan of returning to the past would not happen, yet she had firmly bid farewell to Cohosh. "Send word to me," Sundew beckoned Cohosh. "I shall think of you," Cohosh replied.

And so they parted. Each had gained, but had also lost. Fond memories would indeed be cherished, but a sadness existed of something gone forever. The next evening Cohosh had a dream. He and Sundew had returned to that warm place where no differences existed. It was the first day that they had met. Time had stopped. There was no future; there was only the moment. Their songs again became as one, and rang throughout the entire forest.

All the wood creatures stopped to take notice. Even the frogs and the fish in the rivers sensed an exhilaration radiating amongst them. All of the rainforest life paused in honor of the two palomas. While Cohosh dreamt, a soft south wind spread throughout Osawood, breathing a newfound freshness. It was a warm damp wind, urging the tropical life to come alive, to boast their mysterious beauty. As the sun rose Cohosh woke to a magnificent unfolding of new life. Sundew was gone, yet he burst into a dynamic song, unlike any that had ever been heard in Osawood. A poet would be hard pressed to capture the meaning of Cohosh's song. A translation would go something like this.

> "For a time I had found a love,
> A love to touch, to hold, to feel.
> But time suggests to wait; not now!
> Such a gift to feel this love in life,
> And greater still, to understand the life in love,
> So long Sundew, my love is with you."
>
> For Lucretia from Tom

AUGUST 11, 2020

Bad News, Good News, No News, Same Ole, Same Ole, Same Ole. It's true that we all have an extent of logic and reasoning within us and it spurs us to act in self interest. The question is which of our three choices should I make today. We have a pandemic, an economy in free-fall, race relations in disarray, health care woes, unemployment and a deeply divided nation. And that's just the start of our long list of troubles. Since just before ending my lovely yesterday, I was engaged in a rather serious talk with my son Abel. He says we should be worried about China. I received a text from Judy, my ex girlfriend, the big time Conspiracy Theorist. She said she has been alone, lonely, crying a lot, and she hopes that I am preparing for what's coming.

In response to Abel, I remember when I was living in Costa Rica and preparing for a move back to the USA. One of my good friends Allen Templeton said, "Why are you doing this, are you crazy?" I know what he meant and always felt a sense of relief that as a Costa Rican resident I had given up my place as a citizen of the world's most powerful and thus most responsible country. It was no longer my place to worry about Russia or China. But now that I'm back here, the question is, do I automatically assume my portion of that responsibility? I can choose to ignore the fact that many other countries have lost faith in the U.S. and are now pledging their allegiance to the country which they feel will better serve their needs. Somehow, I'm watching my country fade and split apart over this lying, cheating, scummy, scamming, lawless grifter and his crew who are now infesting the White House.

I realize that the 'all powerful nations' eventually die and pass over the empirical baton. The Romans, the Greeks, the British, the Spanish, Chinese, even the Portuguese once held the dominant position as world leader, and they all faded away as we are about to do. The death of our dynasty will not be the end of us, I am assured of this. Our place and our purpose in the world will change. Perhaps I will exist without purpose, as that truly really indeed at times feels to me what this reality is about. When our country makes it through the present fog, hopefully we will start to see the sun again

In response to Judy, I am reminded of the lesson that David taught me so many years ago. "Too much knowledge will destroy, and God cannot destroy." In other words, whatever Judy is basing her present outlook and conclusions on, are not valid, and if she truly believes in such a negative future, the value of accomplishing something or participating in something today should become even more important knowing that we may not have a tomorrow. Beethoven is two hundred and fifty years old this year. His music is as meaningful today as when it was first conceived.

My next option, Good News. For the last few days I have been pushing Suzanne toward more daily walking. She is on board and has been making better times each try with her 'around the block' walk. Why does she even go for walks? She always ends up in the same house she left. Well, it's not about the destination, it's about the act itself. Sometimes we must see life in this way. It's OK to be happy even if Dr. Fauci, Bill Gates and Donald Trump are all in cahoots with Big Pharma to kill us all. We can still walk around the block.

And for my final option of the day I can choose, No News . . .

AUGUST 8, 2020

I discovered last night that the 'Sun is bad.' I began to realize that my day of lying in the lounge chair last week at Mark's pool has damaged my poor skin. In the good old days I would have noticed nothing more than a tropical tan, but 'yowzer,' I got more than that. I have little bumps and what looks like mini sores sprinkled all over my chest. I now know why so many people cover themselves up with big hats and umbrellas. Next time I see one of those people in the big straw hat, they won't look silly to me. My world has changed. Sure, in 5 billion years the Earth will be consumed by the Sun and almost certainly no further trace of the human race will ever be found, but from then until now I need to prepare a battle plan to protect my ancient damaged skin from the devastating rays of my malevolent pseudo-friend.

It must be the dwindling ozone layer. Our defense system has weakened since my youth, when I would go without a shirt for months at a time. I was one with the solar system. I lived in a world where everything matters because everything is connected and interacts with everything else in good ways that are impossible to imagine today. No shirts, no masks, the rule of the day, in my transitory past. The earlier memories of my life experiences apparently ignites in me a flame that is hard to put out. I often hope for my old world to materialize out of the present shambles.

AUGUST 9, 1974

Nixon resigned today. The first time in the history of our country a President has resigned. He had no choice, he would have been impeached without a doubt. The proceedings have been going on now for 2 years. Watergate finally got him. So many of his people have already been found guilty and are in prison. Justice has almost come, he should be locked up like the rest of them. It's hard to imagine what's going through his head. I wonder if he feels that his actions were justified, crime for the greater cause, his re-election. I'm glad that I've chosen a life away from politics. I can read about this, but I don't feel close to it.

AUGUST 15, 2020

A week away from writing and I haven't really thought about much to be scribbled into these pages. Interestingly, one of the most influential philosophers coming from our distant past was Socrates. He didn't believe in scribbling down his ideas, his philosophies. He thought that personal dialogue was the better way. We only know about his ideas because his students, especially Plato, wrote about him. I can probably conclude that he would be against modern politics, so called scientists, and modern universities. Many people loved Socrates, especially the youth who had not yet been set firmly in their ways, and who would listen to his words and fight against society's injustices. Plato wrote that Socrates believed truth can only be part of a process that is made among men and women as a by-product of their confrontation, free from biases and prejudices.

We definitely are engaged in a lot of confrontations today, free from biases and prejudices, absolutely not. There have been a small number of people who have changed their minds about our socio political condition and have passed under the fence of political division, that is, away from Trump. Many minds still remain closed, many faces are still masked or unmasked depending upon political persuasion. it seems to be just a matter of numbers now as to the future results of our upcoming election.

And for the present news, well Biden has picked a Black woman to be his VP running mate. Kamala Harris, a senator from California will be on the ticket. She is the daughter of a Jamaican-born father and an Indian-born mother, very light skinned, and I do believe that the almost non-racist whites accept this type of Black easier. This is difficult for me to say and quite controversial. I honestly hope I'm wrong on this, but I think that if Obama had the distinct features of a 100% African Black male, he would have had a much more difficult time winning at the polls.

Several months ago I read in an online diversified media platform, www.thesun.co.uk, about a young Russian child prodigy. Born in 1996, Boris Kipriyanovich, who goes by the name Boriska which means "little Boris." He is considered a child genius. His mother is a doctor, and she knew he was special as soon as he held his head up without any support just two weeks after being born.

She claims he started speaking a few months later and by the age of one and a half was able to read, draw and paint. While Boriska was going to kindergarten at the age of just two, his teachers couldn't help but notice his incredible writing and language talents along with his astonishing memory skills. The boy has repeatedly claimed that he was previously a martian pilot who traveled to Earth.

Boriska's mother and father claim they didn't teach their son anything about space as a child but say he would often sit and talk about Mars, the planetary systems and alien civilizations. They say his fascination with space soon became his number one interest, and it wasn't long before he started claiming to have been born on Mars.

Researchers have described him as an extremely shy young man with above-average intelligence. His outstanding knowledge of the solar system has confounded experts around the world, including scientists. Boriska is now 21. He claims he's from Mars, and that he has been sent to Earth to save humans from an apocalyptic nuclear war. By the way, the Sun says more people have died of the flu than coronavirus for 7 weeks in a row. And there you have it for today's writing.

20

Chen Tai Li

AUGUST 16, 1973

After the months spent on the sea in Belize I would return to my other life, that of a typical US citizen. I needed to work into the economic chain. I needed money to rent an apartment, buy a car, get furniture and clothes, go to restaurants and movies, and do all the other things that make up the 'circle of life.' The circle I have now chosen that appears to have no end or no beginning.

I am planning to watch the cycle of the seasons, of the moon, of civilizations, women's cycles. I will watch as people die, others will be born. Leaves will grow from the trees, then fall from them. Land on the dirt and fertilize it. The Tree grows bigger and bigger, then it too eventually dies, falls to the ground, and fertilizes it. There is no end. Only beginnings. I was beginning, something. Within a very short time I was averse to this routine, combating my newly found boring ways. I looked for the way out of all this, the answer. I found Chen Tai Li.

Chen Tai Li was a name that Richard had taken himself. As nearly as I could tell, he was an American who had lived abroad for many years. I cannot remember the details but through some connection, I was invited to a small gathering where Chen Tai Li was speaking. The man was rather small in stature but had an extremely powerful manner, making him appear much larger than his size. He did not have a loving, happy face that many of the gurus possessed, rather it was an intelligent, serious face, with the most deep penetrating eyes I have ever seen. When he looked at you, whether it was to tell or ask something, he almost looked as if he were going to cry, as if the knowledge he held was almost too heavy to bear. What a powerful man he was.

Artchie had the same power but whereas Artchie used it in the physical world, Chen Tai Li directed this energy toward the spiritual world. I do not know from where he came, but at this time in his sojourn, he was in the process of impressing many 'seekers' and gaining a number of followers in Palm Beach. There are many older wealthy people in this world, 'seekers' who are much like Shirley MacLaine. Their money enables them to explore the world at will, but their findings rarely offer them the answers that they seek. They are destined to seek, seek, and seek.

Chen Tai Li was in Palm Beach, being sponsored by one such wealthy woman. In his first talk, which I attended, he spoke about many of the interesting rituals in the Tibetan religious world. If what he said was true, he had lived in the Tibetan Lamasery and had studied and become a Lama. I had no reason at the time to question his honesty, so I believed him. I realize now that Tibet has always been such a closed country, and that it would have been impossible for an American to become a member of a Tibetan Lamasery.

He talked about bringing one's desires into reality. In Tibet the practice was called 'raising tulpas.' He talked about 'astral projection.' He planned at his next session to instruct on how one could see auras, those energy fields that surround our bodies. By seeing auras, which are bands of many different colors, one can tell much about a person's health, spiritual being, etc. Today there is a photographic technique known as Krillian Photography that can actually record these fields of energy. It's a spiritual bargain, yesirree only $25 a shot.

I try to be serious but sometimes I cannot help but jest about the paths toward a spiritual world. Honestly, it is such a struggle for many people, myself included for many years, when in reality, as

I now know, the spiritual answers that we seek are about the most simple explanations that could possibly exist for anything. All the gurus are telling us, and all the revered Holy Masters throughout the ages have told us this. First, know yourself and then all the answers will come.

Chen Tai Li's talk was very interesting. I wanted to hear more. I joined the ranks of those that were to become his flock. This was not a run of the mill group, as one might find at the local corner church. We had automatic writers, self-proclaimed witches, healers, astrologers, mediums, and myself. At the end of the second meeting, Chen Tai Li approached me in private asking if I had ever come close to death or if I had ever had a serious brain injury. I responded, "Yep, I sure had that, that's for sure."

Without any of the occult credentials of the others, I guess I had just qualified. He then asked me if I would work closely with him and help him. He wanted me to become his acolyte. Since my time was somewhat freer than many people my age, I became involved in his world. He was a house guest in the wealthy widow's home, but he would usually begin his day by coming to my apartment, and we would soon be off on some adventure. He was conducting private lessons for some parties interested in the many different occult sciences. He was helping an elderly couple to change their restaurant from a successful bar-be-cue establishment over to a Chinese restaurant, at his suggestion. He was searching for the 'powerful energy rock,' which had been traced from all over the world and was presently believed to be in the Miami area. And he was fighting off all the non-believers who were getting wind of his presence.

Oh yes, and one of his most important missions was working together with another sponsor in an attempt to bring a well-known psychic healer, Tony Agupulgo, from the Philippines to the United States. I was not impressed with many of the other things, but the psychic healing really interested me. This was one of my fields, curing people's bodies. At one of our regular weekly meetings, an 8-mm. film was shown by one of the members of our regular group. The woman had gone to the Philippines, searched out this man in a remote village and attended one of his surgery sessions. She had taken the film with her own small camera. I knew her and I believed that the film was authentic. It showed Tony doing a number of operations without any surgical instruments, antiseptics, or anesthesia. I could hardly believe my eyes as I watched these films.

Tony would pass his hands over the skin of the patient, and the skin would open. There would be very little bleeding if any, and he would perform the procedure. I watched the film of him performing an appendectomy, and removing colonic tumors from two different patients and doing a hemorrhoidectomy on another. He also did something with sinuses on a patient, but I could not tell what it was. In all, the film was approximately 25 minutes. After the surgeries, the skin would close as he rubbed his hands over the openings, and there would be no scar visible.

With finances from one of our group members, Tony was being flown into New York. Apparently the efforts to bring this man into the United States were vehemently opposed by a group of physicians. Chen Tai Li was quite disturbed one morning and told me that Tony was finally here in New York but that he had been arrested and was being charged with practicing medicine without a license. He was offered deportation or a trial that would lead to prison.

One day Chen Tai Li and I left Palm Beach for a drive to Miami in search of the 'Rock.' I never really quite got the full meaning of this, but I went along for the ride. Again, it was a female leading this adventure. After the woman picked us up, I sat in the back and observed the emotions surrounding this search. The lady convinced Chen Tai Li that the rock that we were searching had power beyond any imagination. She knew that if he came close to it that he would feel the vibrations and be able to lead them to its location.

The scenario unfolds in Coral Gables. We are driving around in this up-scale section of Miami and Chen Tai Li is casually holding his hand out the window of the lady's new Lincoln. He is silent for a long time and then suddenly says, "Here, turn to the left." We proceed a few blocks when he again directs another turn. This goes on for a while until at last he says, "Stop here, this is the place."

Now I was quite disappointed, but we did not find the Rock that day, and the ending of this venture is far from dramatic. But there is one incredible point to note. I do not know how Chen Tai did this, but whoever lived inside that house knew something about the Rock. Or at least that is what the woman told us after going into the house. At Chen Tai's direction, the lady had walked up and knocked on the door, entered, and stayed inside for approximately a half an hour. The occupants of the house were also 'seekers.' Our patron this day was so excited when she returned to her car. The 'Rock' was not inside the Coral Gables' house, but her search was given a new jolt, that was enough for her. She was still able to seek, seek, and seek.

That afternoon we went for lunch in Miami Beach. After our meal we walked along the sidewalk and came upon a large group of people gathered around one man. It was Cassius Clay, Muhammad Ali. He was training in Miami for an upcoming fight. I assume he had just walked out onto the street. What followed was very funny. He walked up to a small Cuban man and started expounding in his braggart fashion, "Why I'm going to beat the man to a pulp." As he was saying this he threw several air punches directed at the little man's face, falling just inches short of his nose. The little Cuban was terrified. He turned to the crowd and asked in Spanish, "Que dice? Que dice? What did he say? What did he say?"

As Muhammad Ali was shouting on, "Why, I sting like a butterfly and float like a bee!" The Cuban had shrunk back and I noticed Chen Tai Li trying to catch Ali's eye, but Muhammad never looked at him. As I mentioned before, Chen Tai had piercing eyes, they were an unusual color of blue gray and could strike deep into one's being. It would have been interesting to see if Muhammad Ali would have noted something unusual, had their eyes met.

When we left, Chen Tai Li told me that Muhammad would win this upcoming fight but would soon lose, which turned out to be an accurate prediction.

There is a big difference between religious groups and spiritual seekers. People in many of the major religious groups assume that they possess the one and only truth. They believe that everyone who does not believe as they do is wrong. This attitude is dangerous; it often breeds fanaticism. There are many right wing violent Christians, and many murdering terrorist Moslems, attesting to this fact. Those believers go beyond the laws of government and society to further their own objectives. Ironically, it is all done in the name of good.

Unlike most conventional religious groups, in the world of 'spiritual seekers' there are many casual visitors, who drift in and out like the tide. There are other seekers who are obsessed with the search, who approach the subject with a passion that becomes all consuming. Most of these seekers are functioning, contributing members of society. They might be just as radical as the fanatics in the religious groups, but since they do not claim an exclusive hold on truth, they are not as likely to violate another's rights. From my observation of most truth seekers, I found that contrary to the definition of a seeker, many are extremely opinionated and quite closed-minded.

Now let me talk about the particular group of 'spiritual seekers' that was following Chen Tai Li. There was no one here that would blow up airplanes or bomb abortion clinics. But there were astrologers who knew without question, that the complex planet configurations are controlling everyone's total behavior. And there was a Tarot card reader who proclaimed the power to foresee the future of anyone willing or daring, as I felt, to pick the cards. Most of the people in our group were friendly, good people, but very defensive about their spiritual opinions. As much as I am able to remember about that time, I dare say that I was not the norm.

As a younger person, I did not accept the Christian doctrines, and now as a man in my late 20s, was not buying the occult sciences, or at least not to the degree in which others seemed to believe. I read and watched and listened, but could not firmly believe. I had not yet learned who I was.

It was not that I did not try or was not a seeker, indeed I was. Since my first exposure to this broad wealth of knowledge, I hungered for more. The somewhat hidden sciences of the occult were very interesting. The desire to try out the ways of the mystics and the challenge of achieving the mind state of the Yogi held up a fascinating goal for me that I strove for. All of this semi-secret knowledge blended in easily with eastern philosophy, which I had been leaning towards. Even in the craziness of Colombia, I had brought down a copy of the 'I Ching' and would often consult the book. To believe these teachings, allows one the hope that it is possible to go to heaven without dying. That is a lovely concept.

Heaven is all good, all beautiful, all truth. Dr. Edward Teller, the brilliant physicist and the dearly beloved father of our hydrogen bomb sums up Western ideology, "On earth, the good is controlled by the politicians, the beauty is the responsibility of the artists, and the truth is the business of scientists." In our small group, we all individually, wanted good, beauty, and truth. It seemed that perhaps Dr. Teller was correct; it seems very difficult to achieve all of this.

I remember reading about Alfred Russell Wallace. This man was one of the greatest minds of the 19th century. He was a naturalist, an explorer, a scientist, and a philosopher, all rolled up into one. His buddies were Charles Darwin, Henry Bates and Richard Spruce, all of whom were important contributors to our present sense of "fitting in." That is, fitting in with the rest of nature's creations. Darwin termed it the "Evolution of Species." They all lived in jungles for many years and studied the 'how's and why's' of it all. Yet Alfred Wallace was different, he wound up with a passionate quest, communicating with the dead. Now I shall call that an open mind, and leave it at that.

On one occasion, I was with Chen Tai while he was giving a private lesson to a wealthy, obviously bored couple. He was instructing them in 'astral projection.' We were all gathered in their indoor swimming pool area. Chen Tai and I were sitting on a bench facing the couple, who were relaxed on a couch. I had read much on the subject of astral projection, including Lobsang Rampa's "The Third Eye," where he devoted much time and provided a lot of information on this Tibetan art. To astrally project did not interest me in the slightest. Chen Tai had been speaking on the subject for more than an hour, offering techniques to relax your body and reach this state of wakeful dreaming. I was rather bored myself as he began to explain how your spirit inside would begin to bounce up your spinal column toward the top of your head. "It will be like a rubber ball, bouncing towards your highest chakra."

As he was saying this, I felt it happening to me. It had never happened while I was sitting in Hatha Yoga's lotus position, or diving quietly on the reefs. But something strange was happening now. I had spent many hours in meditation, so it was not too difficult for me to become silent, to turn inward, and explore this strange feeling. I was not imagining this. I did not even want this to happen. The couple that was paying the money wanted this, they were supposed to be doing it, not me.

The more Chen Tai spoke, describing the method, the deeper I dove into my consciousness; I was doing exactly what he was describing. The next thing I knew, I was out of my head, at the top of the screened-in enclosure, which encircled all of the patio area. I was looking down on the four of us, sitting facing each other. I could see my body, but I was not inside of it. I could hear Chen Tai talking about the silver cord, and I noticed the couple staring at my body. Chen Tai turned toward my body and smiled. He began snapping his fingers in front of my face and I woke up, back in my body. For a brief moment I felt very weak. I knew what had happened. I was surprised, and especially fatigued by the brief experience. There would be times in the future when I would attempt to do this again, but would never succeed.

At one of Chen Tai's weekly scheduled lectures, a middle aged Christian woman showed up with a few young people. They had come from her Christian halfway home to debunk Chen Tai and expose him as a false prophet. Every fourth sentence that they spoke was "Praise the Lord." There was a true battle that evening, between the Christians and the devil, as they viewed Chen Tai Li. I spoke to the woman after the meeting and she pleaded with me to get away from this false prophet and come to her home and see what real religion meant, what truth was. The next day when Chen Tai arrived at my apartment, I asked him to come with me, that I wanted to bring him someplace for a change. He was indeed surprised when we walked into her home. The battle of words ensued. I was very impressed with the amount of Bible knowledge that Chen Tai had.

The way I saw it, Chen Tai won the battle. I would not believe that he was a false prophet and an evil man. I began to understand that in order to follow someone's teaching, you need not believe everything that is put before you, but rather take those things that apply. In that way I would slowly begin to lose some of my skepticism. No teacher has to be perfect; no religion has to have all the answers. In this way of thinking, every human, every form of life becomes a valid teacher. Again I was learning the lesson of moderation.

My last notable experience with Chen Tai Li was during the trip that we took together up into the middle of Florida in order to attend a Faith Healer's Revival. I believe it was the first time either of us had seen the traditional service. This particular Revival took place in a large tent in the remote countryside. We watched intently as the sick and lame of the congregation walked up the dirt aisle to the front of the crowd and the preacher placed his hands on their heads. The preacher screamed out, beckoning Jesus to come and heal this person. Through his prayers, the prayers of the congregation, and the faith of those to be healed, it was all working. It appeared that everyone one was healed by the healer. He was batting 1,000. The people here got what they paid for. I could imagine all those young people in the halfway house delightedly shouting, "Praise the Lord."

It was soon after this time that some of Chen Tai's followers began splitting away from the group, claiming that he was drawing his power from the "Dark Side." One early morning, in urgency, an ex-member came to my apartment. "Are you still with Chen Tai Li?" she asked. I nodded. She replied, "Then you must immediately, for your own safety, return any items he has given you. Take these candles and place them around your bed. For three nights you must light these candles and sleep within their light." I actually lit them one night. It made me feel silly. I thought, "What in the hell have I gotten myself into now?"

It was not long after this experience that I bowed out of Chen Tai's fold. I watched him as he turned more and more towards becoming a healer of his own proclamation. It was way too much for me to accept. Some years later, I noticed a feature story in one of the tabloids at the supermarket checkout counter. There on the front page was a picture of Chen Tai Li. I recognized him immediately, although he had a different name. The story was about the Tibetan Chakpori Lamasery Healing Center located somewhere in Texas. The article focused on a physician with an incurable skin disease. The disease was so disfiguring that the physician had been forced to work as a government employee, not able to face the public. But after the Healing Center got hold of him, he was cured, opened a private practice, and lived happily ever after.

21

Finishing August

At this time of year huge herds of wildebeest, zebras and gazelles have left the Serengeti and Tanzania, and are now heading into Kenya's Masai Mara, where green pastures await them. I'm seeing these herds in my mind. I have never been to this yearly migration but thanks to Discovery Channel, and discussing it with Phil, I've envisioned the enormous herds on their march to survival. It must truly be a sight to behold. There are millions of animals in these herds.

Now then, if we can possibly imagine a herd of humans 160 times bigger, all infected with Covid-19, and mixed in randomly with everyone else, then we are on the way to conceiving our situation and we must realize the need for a solution to this problem. But that's only the scene in the good ole USA. We have only 4% of the world's population.

So, imagining that the enormous herd of Americans have already had Covid, then hopefully they are now antibody rich, immune citizens, they become the keys to stopping the hungry virus. Because with fewer hosts to infect, Covid will peter out or at least it will make its way through a community much more slowly.

This is all great news incidentally because In the early days of the crisis, scientists estimated that perhaps 70% of the population would need to be immune in this way to be free from large outbreaks.

But over the past few weeks, more than a dozen scientists have expressed their opinions that herd immunity probably lies from 45 percent to 50 percent.

This brings up our next move, our next plan of attack, 47.5% of us can get rid of the masks and begin sneezing at each other, or we can get a vaccination as soon as it arrives. I don't like either option. Might I consider myself socially responsible if I hide in the 52.5% that does neither? Since my polio vaccinations in the mid 1950s, I have not been injected or infused with science's inoculating approach at alleviating the virus of the day. I will have this choice to make soon, because Russia has already released a Covid vaccine and we'll surely be next. I expect this will become a hotly debated topic. What will Trump do?

One thing that he is doing lately is to mess with the Post Office. He's doing everything he can to make sure that mail in ballots for the election will not be a possibility. It seems that he and his Republican co-conspirators object to mail-in voting because it blows up their most effective and successful voter suppression schemes, generally the higher the turnout the worse Republicans do.

Among some of his claims, Trump has said ballots would be stolen out of mailboxes, despite very little evidence of such fraud over the past 20 years. Trump has also said universal access to mail-in voting would boost Democrats and prevent Republicans from winning future elections.. One of his more radical claims, without any evidence is that foreign countries would print and send in millions of mail-in ballots. "IT WILL BE THE SCANDAL OF OUR TIMES!" he tweeted.

AUGUST 18, 2020

It's hot ! We must now accept the hot weather as normal, even though our bodies have not made any adjustments. Such a change, adjusting to our globally warmed world, will probably take a few thousand generations, if ever. I doubt that when the humans began migrating away from the equator, winding up in the frigid poles, that their physiology went through some radical switch. Those cold weather tribes just put on more furs. Life takes its time switching from gills to lungs and back. It's 125 degrees in parts of the Middle East this week, that makes the 106 in Healdsburg look quite acceptable.

I am now sitting in the air conditioning of my house after going through quite an abrupt routine jolt a few hours ago. Just as I finished my work this morning and got back to my landing pad, my phone started blaring with a security alert. There is a wildfire close by and I was directed by the Sonoma County Sheriff's Department to get ready to evacuate. 'Here we go again.' The light outside is so strange, the sun is a red ball filtering through the huge cloud of smoke. It feels like a solar eclipse is about to happen.

For the past three hours I have been getting the motor home ready and packing my bags, sorting out what is important in my life. I have been choosing what I will need to move forward should the fire head this direction, and burn up whatever possessions I leave behind. I've been through this routine before.. It has been a yearly event for the past four years. I have evacuated twice. The first time on Oct. 11, 2017. The fire came over the mountains from the northeast. It was a Thursday night when the radio warned that should the wind switch, Healdsburg would be in danger. I decided not to take any chances, I packed up my Toyota Chinook and headed to the ocean, Bodega Bay.

I stayed in Bodega Bay on the beaches and at the Marina. The fire burned for several days in Napa and Sonoma County, taking at least 40 lives and destroying over 6,000 residences and businesses, although the fire never hit Healdsburg. When I first arrived I went to a gas station and met Patrick O'Gorman, a volunteer fireman who lost everything except what he now had in the back of his pickup. He was telling me his story and began crying. With his permission I got my camera and began taping his experience. I would continue doing this for the next five days.

Over 200,000 acres in three counties were burned and an estimated 90,000 people were evacuated. Many sought shelter and fled west to the safety of the ocean. Three basic relief shelters were set up in Bodega Bay and I documented the efforts and eventually edited a one hour doc titled, "Five Days in Bodega Bay." It's a very touching sentimental video. Several months later, I had the premier screening at the Bodega Bay Fire Station. There were a lot of tears in the audience.

Last year around the same time in October, another fire came roaring through Santa Rosa. I was at that time in the hospital with Suzanne. Her accident occurred on Oct. 21. Our area of Healdsburg was ordered to evacuate, but I was sleeping on a recliner chair in Santa Rosa Memorial every night. Suzanne was in a coma. Again Healdsburg was saved, or I should say barely affected. Some houses in the outer valleys were burned, including my friend Pamela's family home.

This fire activity is a new phenomenon brought on by rising temperatures, caused by global warming, which right wingers, including our brilliant leader, call a hoax. If we might continue living on this planet, we must immediately turn all global efforts towards solving this problem. It may be too late. To coordinate every government in every country to work together is what it will take.

AUGUST 23, 2020

For the past five days I have been dealing with the wildfires in our area. It has set the canyons and hills very near my house into an uncontrollable inferno. The afternoon of the 18th I realized that my motor home was not reliable so I left the house after loading a different vehicle with family photos, titles, some DVDs of past movies I have made, a couple external hard drives and some flash drives. "I can live without everything else." I left for safety to Suzanne's house, 15 miles away. That evening I thought of all the things I left behind. "I wish I could go back.'

Early the following morning I was driving back, hoping to get some more things. I discovered a roadblock was set up, but I found a different route in. I then filled up Suzanne's car with what

I considered the next most important things in my life. I got that car away from my house and into town, parking at a grocery store parking lot. I now had only Zac's old car, a Jeep, and my pickup truck left at the house.

Next Day, same story, I wished I could get some tools and my pickup out of there. With help from Suzanne's caregiver, and Suzanne's car, I repeated the routine, got in and filled up the pickup with tools. Starting with what I felt were essential hand tools, skill saw, jig saw , drills, planers, sanders were loaded up. I then topped that with my table saw, chop saw, three chain saws, a weed whacker, more wrenches, socket sets, I then muscled up on top my air compressor and the two long air lines, with two pneumatic air guns, and my best drill press. Filling all empty gaps with more smaller tools, I drove back to Suzanne's. I left Suzanne's car parked in the middle of Safeway parking lot. I covered the whole bed of my pickup with a blanket and tied it down with ropes. It's now in the safety of Suzanne's driveway.

Next day, overnight more thoughts on things I'd left behind. I still had Zac's Jeep at the house. After seeing that the fire had not reached my area I was back again, snuck around the roadblock. This time it was my computer, keyboard and monitor, suitcases filled with more clothes, and artwork, masks from Costa Rica, so many pieces of Mayan sculptures and works that I had thought I would live without. I parked the Jeep in a different Healdsburg grocery store lot and Suzanne's car is now shuffled back to her house.

For the next couple of days I repeated the same procedure. Each morning waking up early, since I don't really sleep that well, I get back to Healdsburg, up to the house, and try to get an idea of what's ahead. The only vehicle remaining is the motor home and if I survive this fire intact that Winnebago carburetor and motor if necessary will be completely rebuilt. I've been quite disappointed that I have not kept it in top shape.

AUGUST 23, 2020

I am now at Julie's Hotel in Palo Alto along with Suzanne and my Toyota 4-Runner. It is packed with the chosen, most essential belongings of both of our lives. Those things that fit in the back. We left Suzanne's house yesterday afternoon, evacuation warnings are now in effect at her house.

I had been sleeping at Suzanne's for the past few days since my evacuation from Healdsburg. Two days ago I was loaded up and parked at the top of Mill Creek Road watching the large plumes of smoke rising from just behind a neighbor's house, less than a mile away. Fire trucks were barreling westward past me, getting to the edge of the fire, 2 1/2 miles away. They have now considered this to be a top priority. Large 'Bombers" have been flying in dropping retardant along that line. There are over 600 wildfires basically uncontrolled, roaring across California, burning millions of acres, being battled by 15,000 firefighters.

A lady turned on our road and stopped to talk. She works for KRON TV and wound up doing a live interview with me. I could only say what I profess in this book, " we know very little, but should stay positive." Some friends almost immediately began texting me saying it was very inspirational, ha.

There's not much to do here at the hotel. However I'm not near the frontline of any fire and it definitely feels different, better. I hadn't realized that I was living with the stress of the situation, engulfed within the energy field of the location I was in. I realized that this is similar to listening to one of your favorite musical groups on the radio, or being present at the live performance, really no comparison.

I'm now watching the news channels to monitor what my future life and relationship to Healdsburg will be. One of Zac's closest friends who he grew up with, will no longer have a place on Mill Creek Road. A beautiful home, Sam Henderson's parents' home, on a large tract of land with nature trails, four wheelers, and beautiful wooded areas, is all gone, ashes remain.

A related news story, more crazy weather, and for the first time in history back to back hurricanes are heading towards the Louisiana Coast. In approximately a week these two storms will probably hit within two days of each other. Two hurricanes have never appeared in the Gulf of Mexico at the same time. According to records going back to at least 1900, the last time two tropical storms were in the Gulf together was in 1959. The last time two storms made landfall in the United States within 24 hours of each other was in 1933. Global Warming is doing a great job of making one forget about the pandemic.

This is the time of the year for the Political Party Conventions. They are happening to inspire everyone as they officially nominate their candidates, that is Biden/Harris and Trump/Pence. The Democrats finished Saturday, lots of speeches from not only both candidates but many other key figures affiliated with and representing the Democrat Party. Tomorrow the Republicans have at it. This year the events, which extend for 4 nights each, are of course virtual with no huge filled conference halls.

AUGUST 24, 2020

Biden spoke on the final night of their scaled back affair and has been given an A+ by most reviewers. Trump must have been impressed because he tweeted that it was a prerecorded speech, since he obviously felt it was too good for Biden to have done it live. I plan to watch the RNC Convention tonight if I can. Sometimes I just can't sit through too much of the deranged madness that the Republicans represent. It honestly makes my heart ache and brings up sorrow and anguish, even bitterness. I don't like that part of me. Trump plans to speak every night of their event, typical of him.

This morning's weather is not severe as was predicted, no thunder or lightning, very little wind. Should it continue without change we have escaped what might have been a very serious surge of the fires. Suzanne and I are in our room at the Hotel. Yesterday we drove to a nearby preserved area, Shoreline Park. It's a beautiful 700-acre park with a saltwater lake, rolling grassy hills, and bay trails. We walked a little up the trail with Suzanne's cane and our masks. From 1968 until 1983 this land was a San Francisco landfill. It has gone from a dump to an incredible site for shorebirds, egrets, gulls and pelicans. We watched flocks of sandpipers and ducks flutter down to their special spots. It's a nice way to relax and forget the turmoil of each day's confused direction.

From Shoreline Suzanne suggested we go to a spot that we might be able to take off our shoes and walk barefoot. I thought I knew the perfect spot. I headed to a large athletic field owned by Stanford. It looked like what we wanted until my barefoot took its first step. I should have guessed. Silicon Valley grass is made of plastic. We put our feet in the small patch of sand between the cement and fake grass and laughed as we grounded to Mother Earth. Grounding, also called 'Earthing,' is a therapeutic technique that involves doing activities that ground or electrically reconnect you to the earth.

I was exposed to the principle of Earthing years ago. The theory has not had a lot of scientific research and would be dismissed by most, but I love the idea. Every animal and plant species on the planet is grounded to the earth except humans. That is, every advanced life form.

We humans have created a lifestyle that prevents us from a direct connection to the earth. We wear leather, plastic or rubber shoes. We live in houses above the ground with some insulating barrier between us and the earth. When we move, we travel on top of the ground and only our rubber tires contact the ground

Since the invention of electricity abnormal vibrations have entered the natural world. In large doses these waves, known as EMFs, electromagnetic frequencies, are harmful. EMFs are emitted from electric power lines, telephones, TVs, etc. There have been studies showing cancer rates increase near large overhead power lines with huge transformers.

The basis of the Grounding theory is that as the EMFs enter our bodies, they pass through, but leave some sort of negative charge, unless we are grounded, where they will then pass through us with no reaction. Supposedly even if you do build up negative charges, by contacting good old Mother Earth, the charges will then be freed to ground. Thirty minutes a day, is the rule.

When I decided that this might be true, I was younger and doing a lot of editing, sometimes 10 straight hours in front of the computer. I found an old piece of copper sheeting, cut out a 12" diameter circle. I then soldered a no. 10 copper wire to it, drilled a hole through the wall and connected it to a grounding rod outside. I can sit in front of the computer with a barefoot on the plate and zingo, the EMFs can't get me.

There happen to be a few scientists that have studied and researched the theory and claim the following: Grounding affects the living matrix, which is the central connector between living cells. Electrical conductivity exists within this matrix that functions as an immune system defense, similar to antioxidants. They believe that through grounding, the natural defenses of the body can be restored.

That theory is similar to the concept of acupuncture, the ancient medical practice developed by the Chinese. Acupuncture was considered nonsense by most Western countries. However, in the 1950s it was slowly introduced, it has now become widely accepted in the Western World and found to be effective. The principle suggests that an invisible energy, Chi, flows through the body and if it gets blocked, health problems soon develop.

Everybody who is a gardener in this country already has a solid connecting relationship to the earth but they don't necessarily have a language to express that. They have a sympathetic relationship to the land and what grows on it. So, believe in grounding, believe in acupuncture, or not. But these are the types of science that although not proven, may be true and we all have these possibilities to build on.

Perhaps in a better future we will all be sitting on some beach, digging in the dirt, planting gardens, walking barefoot and hugging trees as part of our normal routines.

AUGUST 26, 2020

Back from Julie's Hotel and her gracious gift of escape that she gave us, especially me. We arrived back here yesterday afternoon, that evening at 11:30 Stu called, saying that the fire had grown to a position very close to our houses. He had spoken to a firefighter who told him that a big effort was being made to bulldoze trees and create a firebreak on the ridge, just at our neighbor's house.

I slept a few hours after that and lied in bed waiting for the sun to rise. I was then back to Healdsburg, the roadblocks had been moved, but fortunately, after showing an ID, the sheriff deputies allowed me up Mill Creek Road to check on my property. Track bulldozers had been driving on Mill Creek Lane leaving tracks in the asphalt. A large field just below my house had been totally scraped of the wild grass, obviously as a small firebreak. I drove up the neighbor's steep driveway to see if I could see the crews making the large firebreaks. At the top, there were a few firetrucks, an emergency vehicle was coming up just behind me. I didn't see where they were working, but I realized that I might be obstructing things so I left and headed back to town. I had a coffee and I'm now back at Suzanne's. The news says that this fire is 30% contained.

I will now forget the fire for a while, as I take Suzanne for a walk.

Last night we watched the Republicans as they boasted of all their accomplishments of the past 3 ½ years. It actually sounded rather impressive. I imagine some of the party members who are undecided might have been swayed to recommit their allegiance to the Grand Ole Party. The one important fact however is that their message was often untrue and misleading. A fisherman was quoted claiming that the Obama-Biden Administration had ordered thousands of square miles of ocean off-limits to commercial fishermen. This is true but the rest of the story is that by this action of extending the Pacific Remote Islands Marine National Monument, they were protecting an endangered area, and allowing for the regeneration of the sea life.

Donald's son Eric claimed that Biden wants to defund the police, when in fact the opposite is true. He doesn't want to defund them, he's been quoted as saying he thinks they need more help and more assistance.

Tomorrow night the Convention finishes up with Donald and another speech.

AUGUST 31, 2020

Today is Mia's birthday, also my sister's, 40 years separate them. Of course, I've been on the phone with them both. My preference would be to share this day in a more personal situation, where we would be together, hugging and laughing. I must accept this long distance relationship for now. It saddens me not to be with my family, but I take comfort in knowing that I'm here to help Suzanne and that I do have a few caring friends.

22

September

So Trump gave his speech, riled up and provoked all his followers I'm sure. It was the longest nomination acceptance speech in history, breaking the record he had set in 2016. Adolph Hitler once spoke for 8 hours straight. When Hitler decided to expand his domain he went first to Austria. He didn't roll in with tanks, and take it by force, he was elected. When Hitler spoke, he promised that a vote for him would end unemployment and provide help for all the families. Austria was in horrible shape at the time. They elected Hitler by a 98% vote. Austria was then annexed to Germany.

There were no jobs in Austria, farmers and businesses were declaring bankruptcy daily, but after the election German officials were put in office and conditions improved immediately. Education and businesses were becoming nationalized. Then the war started and horror followed.

I am not suggesting that Trump will follow suit, although his method of reaching people is quite similar. He appeals to his followers' emotions. Sadly, much of his following are people filled with anger, not good. Last month Trump wanted to get Greenland by a fair trade, giving Puerto Rico to Denmark in the deal. I suspect he looks at it like a prosperous real estate deal. The Danes thought it was a big joke but Trump was serious. He had no clue that Greenland belongs to the 57,000 people that live there. Believe it or not, I don't make this stuff up.

I honestly believe even with Trump at the helm we are still the greatest country in the world. I pray that we will make it through his term, and that our democracy will survive. Because you know what, after America, there's no place to go.

I once read, "As idiotic as optimism sometimes seems, it has a weird habit of paying off." It's been very difficult surviving the challenges of the past week, but I have made it through and I'm now almost settled back into my unburned house. The fire is contained, the air is bad but it doesn't bother me. It has been a roller coaster ride. One day I thought the fire would not come over the ridge, and the next day, it looked to be spreading towards me. Each day that I made it up to the house I would load up my vehicle with new important belongings. I now have a new word, 'importanter.' Today I finally finished the last of the unpacking back at my house, and hanging up all of my clothes.

I slept at my house last night for the first time since the evacuation. Somehow I lost my phone and had to get a new one today. Those phone places got it down as far as closing the sale. When I first went in, the guy wanted to sell me the newest iPhone. "No, no, I want the smaller one, the cheapest you have, just like my last one."

Well, of course, that phone no longer exists. Next option is this one, "But not to worry, I can get you a 20% discount." This is like buying a new car, which incidentally, I have never done. It's even easier for these phone people than the car salesmen, because they are already collecting money from you every month. It's nothing for them to simply throw in a few hundred dollars on the back of your bill, making it look like the only important financial concern to you is how much you have to pay today.

As the young salesman is realizing he has an easy mark sitting in front of him, I'm trying to figure out what sort of inspiration had encouraged all of the assorted mishmash of tattoos that adorned his arms, hands and fingers. At this moment I am more concerned with trying to put together some sort of connection for the rose, the panther, and what looked like Chinese writing. I am in an obscure place, fascinated by the smiling lady with a hairdo from the 1930s, when he comes on with explaining that, my plan needs to be addressed.

You see inside your iPhone lives two brothers, Sim and Gig. You can see Sim and dig him out of your phone with a paperclip. He's powerful and smart, he holds a lot of information that helps you. I used to think he was responsible for keeping track of all my contacts, my photos, videos, etc. but apparently Gig does this. Gig's invisible and somehow lives in your phone and the clouds at the same time. He's remarkable because even though I lost my old phone and my old Sim. My old Gig can come out of the clouds, with all that pertinent information, now referred to as 'data', and resurrect into the phone that I'm about to buy. The salesman is telling me that I better buy some more Gigs to help me with my new Sim Plan. I had to shift my thinking away from his tattoo presentations in order to say no.

My final bill for the day was only $39. Happily, I walked out of the store. I got even with them. I didn't buy their $40 case or their $40 plastic cover which would protect the face from all the impending scratches. He could have gotten me a 15% discount on those. He wasn't selling me on that one. He didn't know who he was dealing with. I learned a long time ago that if you don't ask the right questions, you get the wrong answers. I think I wound up paying about $350 for this stupid, amazingly incredible, phone, clock, calculator, camera, GPS device, music playing, web browsing, emailing, calendar, compass, flashlight, amongst all the other things I'm forgetting.

Now if I just don't lose it. Oh yeah, the phone people are not only the sellers and bankers for their product, they are also the insurance company. I think I bought the insurance, ha ha.

There's one good thing about dying, when you get to the Pearly Gates, St. Peter is there and he has a box with your name on it.

Everything you've ever lost in your life is in that box, and that would include my old cell phone.

After all that, I get home and discover that every one of my neighbors have lost their water. Our creek has dried up, meaning the water table below has petered out also. Pretty obvious that the fire trucks sucked it dry. I still have water coming into the house but I'm not sure if my holding tank is getting filled. I may be down to my last several gallons, my last shower, my final cup of coffee and toilet flush. Woe is me, tomorrow's job.

SEPTEMBER 5, 2020

Another sudden unexpected occurrence, another time of sadness. My neighbor and very close friend died last night. I've spoken of my friend Stu, it was Susan his wife of 50 years, Susan has gone away. It happened so quickly. During this evacuation I had a lot of time to be with Susan. Every day when I returned to check on the house, Stu and I would drive up together. In the afternoons Susan and I would be in lounge chairs at their hotel pool. On the final day of the evacuation Susie and I took a long walk along a trail. With our masks in place whenever we approached someone, we walked probably 3 or 4 miles. I was wearing flip flops and I still have the little band aid on my toe where I rubbed a blister.

We talked about the current life and about our past. I told her how I saw her and I on the time life chart that I explained earlier in this book. We reminisced about all the wonderful experiences we have been through and what possibilities our future holds. We talked about life after death. The next day Susie began having severe pains in her abdomen and went to the ER. It was a problem with her intestines and she was off to a hospital in San Francisco for an emergency surgery. Three days later she's dead.

Susie was a very special and unique person As a young very attractive woman she left Florida for a greater adventure. Florida couldn't hold her. She came to California and began working for the rock band Commander Cody in a managerial position. She eventually met Stu who was crazy about her. They soon married, and have never left each other until now.

Because of Susan and her brother Billy, I first came to live here in California. It was sometime after I had separated from Sunshine and I was on a vacation adventure trip with Abel. I knew that an old high school friend, Billy was in Northern California visiting his sister. He invited me to come to Healdsburg to see them. I wound up staying.

I began using my construction experience to help Stu modify, repair, and remodel all of his properties, extending from the Bay Area to Lake Tahoe. He provided me with a beautiful house to live in, I now had my first hot tub. While Abel and I lived in this great house, Susie sort of adopted Abel and became like his missing mother. She took him shopping, she attended all his functions at school. We became one big family, and it has never ended.

In those days, money grew on trees for Stu and Sue. They not only had many properties but Stu was to become interested in classic cars while I was here. At one point he had 4 Ferraris and a few Jaguar XKEs. I was paid more than I had ever made in North Carolina and started saving in a box at the bank. Stu was also buying gold and burying it on his property. I remember once digging up a few hundred thousand gold Krugerrands, so he could get one of his Ferraris.

Life was one big party. Basically with youth, good health and that kind of money, you can go anywhere, and do anything you want. Music, sports, outdoor activities, it's all yours, in first class, for the taking. I'm talking front row seats at the 'Who' concerts, sky boxes at the World Series, the coolest wooden speedboat on Lake Tahoe. Stu and Sue were living the life and I was right there with them.

However, life does have a way of taking turns and things change. Abel and I were living in the amazing house that Stu provided us. It was the next property from Stu and Sue, separated by several acres of woods and a pond. It even had its own guest house with a pool table and a couple of pinball machines, and Stu's wine collection. In typical Stu fashion he had told me to help myself when I wanted wine.

One night I had our neighbor Julie over for dinner, and when I broke out the wine she was shocked. "What's the occasion?" That bottle was worth $200. I was accustomed to drinking Carlo Rossi wine from the jug. And incidentally, years later Stu sold this house to the granddaughter of Carlo Rossi.

Abel and I were pretty much settled in California, Abel was in Healdsburg Junior High. We were living the high life, but one thing was wrong. I missed my daughter terribly and I wanted my kids to be together. One night Stu, Sue, Julie, who was now my girlfriend, and I, were celebrating my birthday at a French restaurant. I got a little drunk and broke down crying. It was time to go. Abel and I headed back to North Carolina. I began the next phase of my life, but have now returned to California, living in Julie's house, right below me, down the hill is Stu.

As I write this, I am now experiencing a difficult part of being my age. Susie just became another one on the list of so many of my life friends who have 'passed on.' And I hope that expression holds true. Most of the time I am certain of eternal life, but what if I'm wrong? For me now, it's all about Stu and their two kids Willie and Robbie. I hope I can help.

SEPTEMBER 6, 2020

Yesterday morning I didn't know whether to call Stu or leave him alone. He called me, and I went down. I found he and Willie engaged in paper work at the dining room table, a necessary evil business of the death. Stu was showing his grief. I have never seen him like this, he has always been one of the most calm, collected and strong people I know. It is so sad. Stu suggested I talk to Willie about the situation. He couldn't talk about it. I told Stu I loved him and that I will always be by his side.

Since early last week, I have had a sailing trip planned with Phil, so I left for San Francisco, stopping first at Suzanne's house. Caregiver/housemate Sally was in rare form and began some of her usual bullshit. She kept me for ½ an hour, raving on about how the other caregivers were probably stealing Suzanne's food and generally doing all the wrong things. Sally always has Suzanne's best interest in mind and her good traits in this regard outweigh the bad ones by 99%. I do my best to see through the times when we disagree. With this finally settled, I made it to the Marina where Phil was waiting.

As I crossed the Golden Gate Bridge I saw a huge group marching together, some had balloons and many seemed to be wearing similar colors. I soon saw a sign that said, SAVE BELARUS. Presently a revolution is taking place in this small Eastern European Country. The woman from Belarus who had been leading the revolution was kidnapped yesterday. The protests against the ruthless dictator and his oppressive government are not passing through the Bay Area unrecognized.

Phil and I were soon in the Bay raising the sails. It had been several weeks since our last time on the water, thanks to Covid and the fires. The day was warmer than usual. We both had short sleeve shirts and didn't wear our jackets. As always, there was strong wind in the Bay. Just as life comes at us with persistence, the wind in SF Bay is always there.

You can't change the course of the wind, but you can adjust the set of your sails. If you don't do that, you will be adrift without any control, and your life will idle away. This I know. You must set the sails in the way that brings you to your desired destination. It is possible to learn to sail on your own but most sailors have been taught and helped along the way, learning to set their sails most efficiently. It has always fascinated me that even if the wind is blowing due north you can head south. Again, just like life, if you are aiming against the course, you must veer in one direction and then come back. Due south is not possible against a due north wind. As I have mentioned earlier, the trail up a steep mountain always has its switchbacks.

Phil and I have a mutual love for being on the water. I am so grateful for our friendship. It is his boat, and his initiative that makes this available to me. Not only are we sailing in an amazing piece of the world, but our stories that we share during this time, give me, and I'm sure Phil also, the reassurance that we understand the most important values of life. And that we are living the right way. Thank you Phil, thank you Sally, thank you Susie, and thank you Stu.

Today's weather forecast predicts an even hotter day than yesterday, a high of 108 for Healdsburg. I'm going to get Suzanne and go somewhere more hospitable.

SEPTEMBER 7, 2020

Healdsburg broke a record yesterday, 111 degrees. It was unbearable to be in that heat. For the first part of the day Suzanne and I were at Goat Rock Beach. I tried to push her to get ready and be at the ocean before the rest of California arrived, that was not easy and it was probably 11 AM before we arrived. As I expected, cars were being turned away as we drove down to the parking lot. We did have one card to play, so I continued down the winding road, into the full lot until reaching the turn around spot, and there we played our card, we had a handicap permit and there was our vacant spot.

We unloaded our food bag and beach towels and with Suzanne's cane we slowly walked through the sand, closer to the ocean and the cool breeze. I left Suzanne on the towels and came back for the large shade canopy I had brought. After loading it on my shoulder and lugging it to our spot, I knew we would be set for the day, cool ocean breeze in the shade.

I opened the heavy contraption to find out that it was only the aluminum frame without the top covering. I made a trip back to the car and brought Suzanne a pair of cotton pants to cover her legs, and I found an umbrella in the trunk, and some duct tape. I drove her cane into the sand and duct taped the umbrella to it. It was enough shade to cover her face and a slight bit more. She lasted another couple of hours under our crude tabernacle of sun ray thwarting.

In spite of it, she began squirming, becoming restless. I told her to close her eyes, quit jabbering and listen to the waves. "Travel back in your timeline to a wonderful place that you have experienced in the past." I was envisioning the beach that Herb and I had lived on when we dove lobsters. Every night the waves put me to sleep. Suzanne said she would think about her time in Bali when she stayed in a thatched hut on the beach.

Sorry Goat Rock, it's not that we don't like you, but the condition was that we were jammed in with a few thousand people from Sacramento. We were still pretty hot and uncomfortable. Under our jerry rigged spot, we needed a little psychological embellishment. Both Suzanne and I do have our magical time charts that we can relive, so why not. We spent the next hour dreaming and going back to those special moments of the past. And then, back to Suzanne's house.

23

Lobsters and Costa Rica

On the Pacific coast of Costa Rica the lobsters, for some unknown reason, will not enter traps. There have been numerous attempts by many fishing companies, all unsuccessful. One cold winter, my best friend Herb and I decided to set out for Costa Rica, and try our own hand at trapping. We would experiment with a number of different trap designs and various baits.

Cathy and I packed our bags and drove to Florida. In Palm Beach we joined up with Herb and his girlfriend Gwen. To equip ourselves for the venture, we purchased a small aluminum boat, a rubber boat, some outboard motors, diving gear and various other supplies. We prepared Herb's truck for the long trip. By putting a camper shell on the truck we were able to pack all the gear in the back, load the boats on top and we were soon heading for Mexico. From the US-Mexican border in Brownsville Texas, we expected a two weeks drive through Mexico, Guatemala, El Salvador, Honduras, and Nicaragua until arriving in Costa Rica. The Pan American highway, as we were informed, was in excellent shape. For the most part, this was true.

The border crossings were not always smooth. Since we were very heavily loaded with gear and supplies, many of the border guards took advantage of this. They demanded extra pay for their troubles. In Mexico this practice is called *mordido*, I don't know if it's taken from the word morder to bite, or morir, to die. Whichever the root of the word, it is a negative practice, one that most Americans in the USA never experienced. The mordido/bribe shakedown would occur not only in border crossings, but every time a cop or military man could stop you. At first the mordido was amusing. The officers only asked for ten or twenty dollars and could be talked down at that. But soon I looked upon this practice as a disgusting symbol of man's corruption. We were forced to pay ten separate mordidos. Many of the smaller village policia would see us coming. It was easy for them, since we had the boats on top.

As soon as these bad cops spotted us, they would rush into the street and wave us down, claiming that we had committed some infraccion. By the time we reached southern Mexico, we were running right past them, speeding by as they waved and yelled at us to stop. Our bravery in this matter was furthered along by the fact that they had no vehicles and could not chase after us.

To be out of Mexico was a great relief. Guatemala was a welcomed sight. It was a joy entering into this less arid, lush environment without being targeted for the mordido. One of our planned stops in Guatemala was the famous Lake Atitlan, one of the world's most beautiful mountain lakes. Surrounded by three conical volcanoes, Atitlan is simply breathtaking. Our loaded down truck was barely able to make it up some of the roads approaching the Lake. When we had finally made it to the ridge that surrounds this lake, we headed down a very steep dirt road. Although quite challenging, it was a most rewarding trip. The beaches of Atitlan are all clean and unpolluted. The water appears pure, virtually like a blue crystal.

According to geologists, the lake was formed following a gigantic eruption millions of years ago, so huge in fact that it destroyed all plant and animal life in Guatemala. The impact would have been felt all the way to Costa Rica and the ashes were probably spread as far as Florida in the USA.

On the lake are small fishing boats and along the shore, groups of Indian women and their children. Attired in their hand woven dress, their textiles are outstanding for the colors and variety of designs, which distinguish one town from the other. Colors vary from deep navy blues to scarlet reds. The variety of colors and the floral, zigzag patterns are unique. The women's blouses are made of three pieces of cloth woven on a back strap loom. All the families appear dignified and extremely happy. Laughter fills the air, echoing from the mountains as the children splash in the water and frolic along the shore's edge. The mothers are often busy, washing clothes in the lake.

Guatemala's population is 60% indigenous Indian, all true to their culture, obviously holding on and loyal to traditions from the past. Men and women alike wear long beautiful black braided hair. Many of the women are carrying their wares on the tops of their heads, and their babies in slings. This region in the Guatemalan highlands is a stunning, most beautiful area.

The following day as we were leaving we were forced to unload half our supplies at the bottom of one of the steeper grades. Our truck did not have enough power to make it up this sharp incline. By reducing the load, our truck was able climb to the top. Once arriving on a level stretch, we unloaded more of our gear and returned empty to pick up the load we had left at the bottom. Fortunately there were enough of us to stay with the loads and guard them. By making two trips we eventually made our way up the steeper stretches of that road and left Lake Atitlan.

Crossing into El Salvador, we were faced with another problem. In order to get a little bit of money from us, the border guards insisted that we either unload all of our gear from the truck for a thorough inspection, or hire an army sergeant and drive him from the northern to the southern border. Supposedly, this was their assurance that we would not sell any of our possessions along the route. If we were to sell things, the government would lose the import duties.

Well, as it turned out, our new friend, the sergeant, was asking us to sell him practically everything we owned. He seemed to be genuine and harmless in his desire to buy our stuff, but I could see a trap and we continuously refused to sell him anything. At the very end of the trip he even begged us for our rear view mirror.

With the sergeant as our guest, we passed through El Salvador without incident. Although it is the most densely populated of all Central American countries, it is also one of the tiniest in land size.

One of my strong memories was having lunch in a small seaside restaurant. The afternoon was typical, a cool ocean breeze and high clouds against a deep blue sky. We were seated on the edge of a mountain, on the edge of the continent in fact, overlooking the Pacific, and had just ordered a few seafood dishes when two young boys with snorkeling gear, came trudging up the steep cliff carrying gunny sacks.

Of course they immediately zeroed in on us, the tourists. They plopped their big heavy sacks at our feet and began to dump out their catch, *ostras*, big, fat delicious oysters. For a few pennies each, we began gobbling down their wares. At this point, I did something that I hadn't done for 18 months, I ordered a beer. It was the breaking of an alcohol fast that I had started back in North Carolina for a couple of reasons. There was no better time to have quit that nonsense. The beer tasted so fine. However I must say that I didn't like the feeling of the alcohol afterwards.

Without going into further details at this time, I will say that a driving trip through Central America can be quite a pleasant adventure. Indeed it is never without some hassles, but generally worth the trouble, considering all the wonderful sites. Driving only in the daytime along with other sensible precautions should be practiced.

Along our trip the absolute worst stretch of the road was in northern Costa Rica, in the province of Guanacaste. We hit potholes that burst our tires and damaged the front end of Herb's truck. But eventually we made it to our destination, the Pacific port town of Puntarenas, where our friends lived, Rosita and Theo.

Puntarenas is the second largest city in Costa Rica outside of the Central Valley where the capital San Jose and the larger cities of Heredia and Cartago lie. Puntarenas is the only seaport on the pacific coast, and is important for shipping and fishing. The city has been built on a rather long and very narrow spit of land with an estuary on the west and the large Nicoya Bay to the east. At Rosita and Theo's house the land is barely as wide as a soccer field. An electric railroad splits the town, running along the shore and heading up the mountains to San Jose.

Puntarenas has a character all of its own, with four bars on every corner, and the dirty, open market as the center of town. With its smelly fishing industry, and its oppressive heat, the town is in a class by itself. Costa Rica was soon to become discovered by the world as a tourist destination, but Puntarenas would be left alone. The prostitute bars would remain for the fishermen, and the local drunks would continue to live on the streets picking up food from the garbage, sleeping side by side with the hundreds of buzzards that pick up old fish carcasses from the water.

The estuary wreaks with raw sewerage and oftentimes the mosquitoes and *perujas* control the atmosphere, yet there is something about this place that I really like. Everyone is awake and outside early in the morning, it's difficult to sleep late with the ever-present heat. Bicycles are going by, school kids are in their uniforms heading to school. It's like a very mini-New York with its bustling activity. By ten o'clock the pavement is too hot to walk on. People are stripped down to the bare minimum of clothing, and life goes on somewhat like a Costa Rican Steinbeck novel.

Rosita and Theo are transplanted Americans, who were at the time eking out a simple living in their newly chosen world. Theo had built a fishing boat and would motor out to sea every morning to set baited long lines. Rosita baked cakes and each day pedaled her wares from her bicycle. Their small home became our base as we searched out the most likely spot to begin our diving operation.

We soon met Jose Sanchez, who owned a beautiful stretch of beach land across the Bay. His property, eighty acres planted in coconut trees, was his primary source of living. Jose had a 35-foot boat with a large storage hold. Twice a week he would come from across the Gulf of Nicoya, into Puntarenas to sell his coconuts. In Costa Rica the green immature coconuts are known as *pipas*. The coconut water inside is very sweet and tasty and a popular drink for all Costa Ricans.

Because of Herb's charm, Jose agreed to let us use his house on the coconut farm and begin our lobster fishing from there. He would be able to transport our catch back into Puntarenas and sell them for us at the huge seafood supplier Tunamar. He also offered to bring us ice back on his return trips. In order to keep our lobster catch fresh we needed ice, since the beach had no electricity, nor refrigeration.

It was on this remote beach property that we set up our diving and trapping venture. Our living quarters were simple. We had a four-room house with a wood fire cooking set up in the kitchen. Actually, as simple as it was, we had it better than most rural families, since we had brought along a double burner propane stove as well. There existed a shallow well on the farm that provided us with brackish water. The well water was fresh enough to bathe with and for washing our dishes. For drinking water and cooking, we used pipas exclusively. We always kept a stalk of them in the kitchen with the machete on hand for opening.

In Puntarenas we met Richard, an old fisherman/carpenter from the Caribbean side. He had the hammer and saw, and offered to build our traps for us. We bought the necessary wood, gave him the plans for our designs and left on Jose's next trip back to the coconut farm. The trip across the Gulf took four hours and was planned according to the tide. A very small river ran behind the farm and Jose always arrived in and departed from this river at high tide. The river would only become deep enough at that time.

After arriving at the farm, we soon set out to explore the sea around us. We dove all along the immediate coastline, searching out good lobster spots and looking for the likely areas to place traps.

Our sixteen-foot aluminum boat would serve us well for a while. However the motor we had brought along was only 1½ horsepower and did not allow us to cover a wide range in a day's time. We found that the lobsters were plentiful and we were catching a fair amount in our day's diving. There was no coral along this coast, only piles of rocks that we dove on. On a good day I would dive up thirty to forty. Along with Herb's catch, we did OK. We always carried along the small spear guns that we had brought down. With the guns, we did not miss many of the lobster that we came upon.

I had two slight diving accidents during this venture. The first occurred as I was chasing a small school of snappers, planning to shoot one for dinner. I had followed them very close to the shore and got caught in a sleeper wave, one of those unusually large waves that roll in without warning. The large wave picked me up and sent me crashing and tumbling into the rocks. The power of these huge waves tosses a person around like a little peanut. I have learned from a number of these experiences, all you can do is try to stay flat in a spread eagle position and protect your head. When the surge lets up, you try and swim off the rocks into deeper water. I received many cuts and bruises from that episode. Scraping barnacles cut like a razor, I gained a few new scars.

The next incident could have been more serious. Herb and I were on top of the water, swimming along with snorkels, when I spotted a large rock with five or six lobster beneath it. I swam to Herb, who was a little ahead of me, motioning him to come back.

The rock had two holes where the lobsters could escape. The plan was for Herb to cover one side and I would cover the other. In that way we would get them all. I went down first, stuck my head under the rock and reached out to grab the largest one. Just as I did I heard a familiar sounding chink. It was Herb's gun. He had shot at the same lobster and his spear hit my hand. It tore into my cloth glove and ripped through my skin, piercing a second hole in the glove and sticking in the sand. The spear had torn through the web of flesh between my last two fingers. It was paining me and blood was gushing out, but the worst thing is that my hand was stuck in the glove, which was stuck on the bottom, which had me stuck down there with it. We were free diving in about 15 feet of water, and I had no air.

All turned out well. I was able to tear the spear from my hand, jerk my hand loose off the glove and make it to the surface, but if that spear had hit two inches in, more towards the center of my hand, I would have been in big trouble. Herb almost got me that time, but there was another time when he saved me.

On this occasion we were coming back out to the beach on Jose's boat. Since the tide was high that day at 7AM, we had to depart from the Puntarenas dock at 3 in the morning. The four of us had come into town, Herb, Gwen, Cathy and I. We decided that rather than sleep for a few hours at Theo and Rosita's, we should bring our sleeping bags to the dock and wait there for Jose.

When Jose arrived we were all fast asleep on the dock. We woke up only halfway, long enough to set our bags up on top of the boat's wheelhouse and lie back down, four abreast. Jose started out through the back estuary and all was calm. We began falling back asleep. It was soon after we had cleared the Puntarenas coast that the wind picked up. The sea became choppy and continued to get worse. We were rolling around up top like four marbles. We banged on the roof but Jose couldn't hear us.

Herb and I were on the outsides hanging on for dear life. All four of us had our elbows locked. We were being thrown from side to side. Had Herb or I dropped over the side, we would not have come to land for many miles. The wind was blowing fiercely and we had little to grip to. By some miracle Herb was able to crawl over the side, through a small porthole and into the wheelhouse without falling. He alerted Jose immediately to our dangerous situation, and we were all saved from Davey Jones' Locker.

Perhaps I could be a sport diver again some day, but I don't think I shall ever set out to sea as a sailor. I have been in some bad seas, and those rough ocean experiences have worn me down. There was once a time when I was on a ship with a large crane. Once we were in a severe thunderstorm and lightning kept striking the crane every two or three minutes. It was a dark night and difficult to see, but I would say that the waves were easily 25 feet. The ship had little control to begin with and when the lightning would strike, it felt like she was going to snap apart. Even our captain was shivering with fear and seasick also. The gods spared us all on that horrible night.

On a more positive note, I can recall a beautiful nighttime ocean experience off of our coconut beach. It is these times that balance out the bad ones. Herb and I had just come in from a good day of diving and were cleaning the lobsters, planning to put them into the coolers. The ice was very low and we had nearly 100 lobster tails that needed to be iced down. Jose was scheduled to pull in with more ice from Puntarenas. He came with bad news, electricity had been down in Puntarenas for two days and there was no ice to be had. Our lobsters would go bad.

In order to save them we had only one choice available. Not far away was a small island with a residence, a generator, and a freezer. If we could make it there, then perhaps we could freeze the lobster. The problem was that it was one of those pitch-black nights, with no moon or stars. If we took our boat out, we would not be able to see beyond a flashlight beam and more importantly, no other vessel would see us. It was a risky move.

The girls begged us not to go, but Herb and I decided it was worth the risk. We launched the boat from the beach as we had always done, only this time we were launching at night. What happened next was quite amazing.

On that night there must have been an incredible amount of phosphorus in the ocean water. Our motor prop churned up the sea and the phosphorus lit up our entire 12-foot boat. We were brightly glowing and made our trip to the island in a bubble of light. It was a beautiful experience. Herb and I were so shocked at the brightness of the light; we could not even speak to each other. We just shook our heads in surprise. The guard at the island residence accommodated us, taking our lobsters to the freezer.

Herb and I dove every day for lobster as the girls explored our new home. They hiked inward, away from the coconut beach, and became familiar with the land around us. After a couple weeks we went back to Puntarenas. We did more grocery shopping and looked up Richard, in order to pick up our traps. The lobster traps used in Costa Rica all have a top entrance. Our idea was to try the entry on the sides. We had different sizes built and kept a record of different baits, thinking we might discover the correct combination to lure the lobsters. As events turned out, nothing we tried would work.

We checked them most every day before diving, until one week when a big storm blew in. We were out of the water for several days, and upon our return to the water, our buoys were gone, and the traps had been blown away. This discouraged us from any further attempts with the traps. We continued to dive for a few more months, but began to feel as if we were fishing out the area. Had our motor been bigger we could have covered more area and continued longer but it was obvious that it was now time to quit diving.

Winter had passed in the states, but we weren't quite ready to go back. We had a back up plan should the lobster diving not work and that was to go into watermelon farming. We had brought two large bags of watermelon seeds with us, and 50 lbs. of a super concentrated fish emulsion fertilizer, which should be sufficient for one large crop of melons.

Approximately 10 miles inland from the beach was a small village, Paquera. The walk from our beach was somewhat of a challenge. The locals had a trail, but sections were rather muddy and swampy. We were at the end of the dry season so now the trail was at its best. Cathy and Gwen knew the route since they had been to Paquera on a number of occasions. We all set out one day in order to meet with some local farmers and try to find a parcel of land with a small house to rent where we might be able to put in our crop.

The Nicoya Peninsula is rich in wildlife, like most parts of Costa Rica. On the hike into Paquera we spotted toucans, monkeys and many iguanas, so many in fact, that Herb decided one day he should get a rifle and do a little hunting for some new food. Like many other times in my life we were living on this beach and basically existing on a seafood diet. As in Belize, we ate lobster, every type of fish, oysters, clams, periwinkles, and seagull eggs, hearts of palm, and lots of coconut. Herb was able to get a 22-caliber rifle and we did hunt iguanas in the month that followed.

One funny thing happened to me while I was on this beach. Included in the equipment that I had carried down from the states was a small bag of medical supplies. I had gathered a rather thorough kit including antiseptics, burn salves, plaster casting material and all types of syringes and sutures for dealing with cuts and lacerations. I had learned much about taking care of emergencies in the Marion hospital. One day a nearby neighbor was injured and I offered help. I mistakenly referred to myself as a *medico*, meaning to say that I was a medical technician. Well medico in Spanish also means doctor, and I had unintentionally led him to believe that I was a doctor.

There was soon a steady stream of patients coming to our small house. The whole village of Paquera had heard of the gringo doctor living on the beach. When we would come in from our day of diving I often had a waiting list. Most of the problems were bacterial infections, there were people with cuts and viruses, babies with diarrhea. I could handle most of this, but when the women wanted me to examine them for female problems, I knew it was time to take down my shingle. I learned about the word medico and tried to stem the tide by telling the people I was not a doctor and it was not right that I was doing this. To them I was better than nothing, but for me this responsibility was quite dangerous and very risky. I was glad to be able to help some of them, but I was also glad when we left that beach.

When we first walked into Paquera, our reputation had preceded us. It was easy to locate a farmer who would lease us the land that we desired for our watermelons. We were offered a large enough piece of good land but it was difficult to find any living quarters that would work for the four of us. We probably could have searched further but Cathy and Gwen were a little antsy and were feeling a need to move away from this isolation.

During the Easter holidays, Jose, along with his wife and children came out to the beach and camped. They were extremely gentle and accommodating people like most Costa Ricans. They insisted on sleeping in the tents while we continued on in the house. One evening we made some popcorn for them. They were amazed, for they didn't realize that popcorn could be made on the stove. They had only seen popcorn come from one of the machines that we see in the theaters. Since our friend Rosita in Puntarenas was making her living selling cakes, Cathy and Gwen decided that they would like to go into Puntarenas, make some small bags of popcorn, and sell them on the street. They soon had their wish and became vendors of these little doves of corn, *palomitas de maiz*, as Costa Ricans called them.

We left Nicoya Peninsula and the coconut beach and made a short trip up the mountain to San Jose to find the corn. For the next month we lived in Puntarenas at Theo and Rosita's. The girls began their venture. They were an instant success. The novelty of their product and the fact that they were good looking gringas helped immensely. In Costa Rica at that time it was the custom to serve a small appetizer with each beer that was served at a bar. These appetizers are called bocas. The palomitas were perfect for this and somewhat of a palomita route was set up for the local bars. It was fun for the girls and since our needs were minimal, they were actually covering our daily expenses.

At the furthermost southern point of Puntarenas, where the estuary meets the Bay, there is a small breeze. There were many nights at Rosita's house when the heat would keep me up. I would sometimes make my way to this southern tip of Puntarenas, set my hammock up in an almond tree and find sleep. As the sun rose, I would slip down, wander to the market, have a coffee and an open fired, smoke flavored plate of eggs, rice and beans with lots of hot peppers to kick off the day of sweating. I always felt the chiles would kill some of the bacteria that I was most certainly ingesting.

Since it was now the girls who were working, we boys became a bit bored. One day Herb and I went to the docks and met the

Puntarenas version of a harbormaster. Since we still had our diving gear, we offered our services as bottom cleaners for the large Tuna boats. We were soon back in the water scraping barnacles from the hulls and cleaning sea strainers for the boat owners. Some of the fishing vessels were foreign owned and many fished the waters off the coast of Chile. The captains were all complaining about the lack of tuna compared to the old days. To our surprise they paid us well. By law, we were only allowed to be in the water for four hours a day, and for a diver down, one tender must be on board watching and holding lines. It worked fine, we could get in an eight-hour day between us, and our pay was $100. for the day, which was an excellent wage for Costa Rica.

The work was difficult, the water was dirty and the surge was strong. You were constantly fighting to stay in place, and one hour of diving was all you could take at a stretch. It was not the type of work that either Herb or myself wanted as a career. Within a month the girls had their fill of the palomita business. We were soon saying good-bye to Theo and Rosita and leaving Puntarenas for a final exploration trip to other areas of Costa Rica.

MORE OF COSTA RICA

We explored the mountains of the Central Valley, driving up to the volcanoes Irazu and Poas. We then headed east to the Caribbean coast, visiting Limon, and the small villages of Cuahita and Puerto Viejo. The residents along this coast are strongly influenced by the Afro-Caribe culture, this region of Costa Rica reminds me much of Belize. The locals are descended from those who had come here at the turn of the century. Many were Jamaicans hired to build the railroad that runs from Limon to San Jose. Everyone speaks the familiar patois version of English, which is common throughout the Caribbean. I did hear a different accent more like an elegant Jamaican style. The coastline here is absolutely exquisite, other than some banana, coconut and cacao (chocolate) farms, the land is unspoiled by any development.

We didn't stay long in Limon, but drove south on a dirt road to the Talamanca region and the village of Cuahita. There were only a few lodging facilities available; they rented for five or six dollars per night. Along this stretch of the coast there were very few paved roads or well constructed bridges, horses grazed on the grassy paths between the houses. The residents here were independent farmers and fishermen.

In Puerto Viejo, a town owned diesel generator cranked up at dusk and ran for five or six hours. It provided lights and a lot of noise for those close enough. The logging trucks were digging their way south towards Panama, turning the foot trails into roads that would eventually fill up with people, houses, farms and resorts for tourists. The coming of the roads was inevitable, economical progress, development, it's always a sad sight.

Today these people have been shoved unwittingly into our exploding twenty-first century. The grassy paths and trails are now dusty streets. The economy is now based on tourism. While we were there on this, my first trip to the area, a law was being passed prohibiting any building or development within 150 yards from the high tide mark of the sea. The area south of Cuahita was declared a National Park and the region south of Puerto Viejo was made into a wildlife refuge. This is a valiant effort by the Costa Rican government to preserve what remains of the wonderful culture and unique lifestyle of this area.

In Cuahita we snorkeled in what would soon become the Cuahita National Park. It is an underwater coral garden, and for me was a welcomed sight, much more beautiful than the rocks we had been diving on in the Pacific. I was told that the coral was not growing anymore. Apparently the fertilizers and toxins from the banana industry further inland were washing down the rivers out into the sea and onto these beaches. These chemicals were poisoning and smothering the reef. I noticed a number of blue plastic bags under the water clinging onto the coral. These bags are used to cover the banana stalks during the growing process.

Further along our journey, in Puerto Viejo, we took a long hike southward along the shoreline. This area is absolutely pristine. On the hike we spotted many beautiful parrots and other bird life, we saw troops of monkeys playing and eating in the trees. At one point we came upon a family of three toed sloths, a mother with her young, she was nursing a small baby. I had seen a number of sloths in Costa Rica but this family was living in a very young coconut tree, only about two meters tall. We were able to observe this family at close up range. It was indeed a joy and I found it difficult to leave this spot.

The next small town before Panama is Punto Mono. In the past an earthquake had its way in Punto Mono, adding land in some spots, In other spots exposing much of the coral above the water.

Our last sightseeing excursion in Costa Rica before selling the truck and flying back to the states was our trip north, up to the tiny village of Tortuguerro. The only method of traveling north past the town of Moin is by boat. A regular scheduled service up to Tortuguerro leaves once a day. We made a reservation from the port city of Limon. Similar to Puntarenas on the Pacific, Limon is the sole Costa Rican port on the Caribbean side. It is too large of a city for my tastes, and one of my least favorite places to be in this country.

We stayed overnight in Limon, went to the market in the morning and were soon off on our boat ride to Tortuguerro. This trip is supposed to take about six hours, but our boat blew its motor. We waited a long time for the next boat to come and tow us. That boat blew its motor also, but we finally made it to our destination by the next day.

Tortuguerro had only one tiny hotel for accommodating visitors. It was on the beach and the modest rooms were much more comfortable than the boat benches that had served us the night before. For our meals, we arranged ahead at one of the local's houses. These Tortuguerro mothers would cook you a meal if you contacted them early enough. It was usually fish or chicken in the evening and eggs in the morning. Of course rice and beans, always. We had a pleasant stay in Tortuguerro, wandering around the beaches. I found so many of my favorite seeds, the 'ojo de bueys,' that my pockets could not take any more. Although we were a little early for the annual nesting, the undeveloped beaches here in Tortuguerro are one of the few remaining sites for the nesting of three different turtle species, the hawksbills, the giant leatherbacks and the green turtles.

We were able to stay occupied for a few days, hiking along the beaches and into the jungles. This area is much wetter than most parts of Costa Rica, this is true rain forest country. We were soon planning a trip to the furthest northern village of Barra del Colorado, very near the Nicaraguan border. The morning of our planned departure, everything was canceled. The war in Nicaragua was in full force and a very serious border intrusion and confrontation with the Sandanistan Army had occurred. A Costa Rican government official had been shot while in his boat on the Rio San Juan. The Rio San Juan is the border between the two countries. Barra del Colorado had become off limits for travelers.

We were slightly hesitant about the long boat trip back to Moin, but this time the motor functioned well and we made it without a problem. The Caribbean side of Costa Rica with its black and white sand beaches, and all of the tropical, lush vegetation is very different than the dry pacific side where we had been. I knew that one day I would be returning here to spend more time.

24

Back to the Present

So it's now almost noon here in Healdsburg the temperature is 97 and rising. I have not yet fired up the AC. Suzanne and I have been watching the news. Yesterday over 50 new fires started around California. This time conditions will be much worse. The extreme heat is seriously working against anyone fighting them, and now the winds are blowing, as much as 40, 50 miles an hour. A large group of 150 campers were evacuated out of a Sierra National Park by military helicopters. The fire was so big and spreading so rapidly that these campers were surrounded with no way out. California will soon become uninhabitable, if something doesn't change. Insurance companies will no longer offer home policies, people will no longer accept the idea of getting evacuated. Living in much of California is like living in a war zone, and it will become worse. Sadly the enemy is Nature.

In Colorado they expect a huge cold front to blast in. Their temperature will go from 95 today to 30 tomorrow and maybe a few inches of snow. I can't decide whether to look for some explanation to this insane condition in the Bible under Armageddon, or in my science book under Global Warming. Of course I'm still of the belief that global warming and climate change are responsible.

I just walked outside to the garden and picked the remaining ripe tomatoes. My garden hasn't been watered since the fire began.

Due to the water scarcity here, the poor plants will have no more allotment. I am watering the lemon and lime trees, but gardening is done for this year.

SEPTEMBER 9, 2020

The night before last Stu woke me up, his headlights in my driveway. He had the news that we were being evacuated again. He had to drive up and warn me because my new phone had dropped out of my shallow shorts pocket and was on the seat of Suzanne's car, after our day of escape to Goat Rock.

By midnight I had my car repacked, this time with a far less amount of what I deemed, "possessions I could not live without." Again I drove to Suzanne's house for safety. Same routine, in the morning around 6:30 AM, I was back up at Healdsburg. I called Stu, who had returned to the Hotel. We both had no real reason to sneak back to our property this time. I had no intention to try and save the other vehicles in my driveway which I had brought back. And I was OK if my tools and other things burned to oblivion. By noon the mandatory evac was downgraded to an evac warning.

I spent the last two nights at my house, my car remains packed. I am trying not to be a living example of the story about the boy who cried wolf. I don't want to believe that the evacs are unnecessary. This morning at 8:30 it was dark outside, the sky was a pumpkin colored orange and visibility was minimal. I had never experienced such a site. I felt like a dinosaur when the big one hit the Yucatan, or someone living in a nuclear winter. I worry about what could possibly come next.

Most other world news has lost its importance for me. There are many critical events taking place, more riots, political rallies, more books being released by former Trump government employees. It's all more of the same. Those being abused by police brutality, those participating in protests, those attending Trump or Biden rallies, all have their own just reasons for whatever actions they take. To me now, it almost seems frivolous, how sad is that. I expect that if I am not re-evacuated again I will soon be reading my weekly Newsweek magazine. I have three weeks of catching up.

SEPTEMBER 10, 2020

Another orange sky with smoke. It's difficult to create a daily plan in such an environment. I will handle my responsibilities today, and then what? I will be at Suzanne's at noon to receive a phone call from a local physician. This is a virtual doctor's appointment. We are setting up a local physician for her care. Then I plan to go with Suzanne shopping, to get her essential things from Costco, paper products, laundry soap.

I have been watching the morning news. President Trump admitted to Watergate journalist Bob Woodward months ago that he knew the coronavirus was deadly and intentionally downplayed its threat to avoid panic. Woodward just released his book. More than 190,000 people have died from COVID-19 in the U.S. Avoiding panic is an absolutely irresponsible excuse for Trump's actions. Any study or manuals written regarding such a condition, state that under no circumstance should the truth be hidden from the public. Not only did Trump lie, but he suggested a path that was very harmful and deadly to our population.

How this will affect the upcoming election is now the topic with the news analysts. My opinion is that it will have no effect. I repeat, his backers will never change their minds. It's all about the emotion of anger, or for the smaller percentage, it's the idea that his policies on the economy and isolationism are best for them. The election is moving closer, I believe when the winner is declared I will finish this book.

I'm about to change the subject now and bring you back to Colombia, to meet a man worse than Trump.

25

Pablo Escobar

The next character on the list, last but not least, the one and only, believe it or not, the true Colombian bad man, the man who would become one of the biggest drug lords of our time, the head of the Medellin Cartel, Pablo Escobar. Now this man was 100% pure solid trash, a murdering maniac, and a true psychopath. And the worst thing of it all, you would never know it to meet him. He appeared to be a gentle, loving and caring man.

I never really got to know Pablo. I met him only a few times, twice when he came to the club and the other time when I went to his house with my friend Mario who was a distant relative of Pablo. This was when the club was just opening and I was about to return to the States for the band. I don't know why Mario brought me to Pablo's house, I believe he may have been borrowing money from him. Pablo's house was grand, typical of wealthy Colombians. It had a gated wall with a small guardhouse. This was to keep out the common thieves, the *ladrones*. Inside the gate were beautiful grounds with tended gardens, and a sprawling white-stucco house with a red barrel tile roof. All upper class families have houses with covered front porches. The porch is where meetings and business is conducted with those of the lower class. Poor people are never allowed to enter into the house of a wealthy Colombian.

On the day we were to visit Pablo, Mario and I were graciously accepted into his house. The house was huge, built in a Colonial design. Upon entering and passing through a small entryway, long halls turned to both the right and left. I noticed a number of large ceramic pots filled with flowers sitting on the floor, along the hallways. The floors were all covered in large terracotta tiles. Sculptures and statues were lit up in tiny alcoves built into the walls. Directly in front of us were double wooden doors, ornately carved, with large black strap hinges. The doors were open, leading into a courtyard.

We were directed through by one of Pablo's servants and led across the patio to a small open dining area. It was covered with a sloped roof, but had only two walls with the open sides facing the courtyard. It also had a tile floor, smaller ceramics, decorated with many hand painted designs. There was a large Zebra skin rug towards the back wall. This wall was mostly made of windows looking out to more flower gardens. In the middle of the room, sat a beautiful antique dining table of very dark wood. It had been fastened together with pegs. It must have been hundreds of years old. The other wall had an arched doorway leading into the kitchen.

Mario and I sat down at the table, which was set with brightly colored plates and cups. Soon, a female servant came from the kitchen with coffee, a plate of cheese and fresh baked bread. In Colombia, cheese is commonly served for breakfast, perhaps a carry over from old European customs. The tipico Colombian cheese is a simple type of white cheddar, slightly salty, also very tasty. Colombian coffee is excellent, it is served very strong. We helped ourselves. It was not long before Pablo was to join us.

Pablo was carefully dressed in black, which rather emphasized his gold watch and ring. His hair was wavy and worn just below his ears. He had a candid air about him and seemed to be a good, honest man. After customary greetings, he and Mario began talking business matters. I rose from the table and wandered out into the courtyard towards the swimming pool. I remember that day very well, the sun was shining brilliantly, the clouds were high in the sky and the weather was cool.

Medellin is somewhere near 5,000 feet in altitude, with ideal year round climate. It was a perfect day and the house design brought the sunlight inside. I was feeling that it was very beautiful in this house, such a shame that Pablo was not content with what he had.

Later Pablo took us through the house into a large room that served him as a den/library. From a business desk he withdrew a large box containing many emeralds of various sizes. I was quite impressed with the collection. I don't know a thing about jewels, but I do know that Colombia has the finest emeralds in the world. The business between Pablo and Mario was soon over. I thanked Pablo for his hospitality and we left.

On the drive back to the club Mario told me that Pablo wanted to give him a glass tube of emeralds for me to bring to the States. Of course the tube would be inserted in my butt until clearing Miami customs. On my behalf Mario refused.

After that day, Pablo never entered into my world again, like Fabio or Primo would, but I always knew that he was there, not so far away. This seemingly polite and dignified man with the little mustache and white Nike sneakers had presented me a temptation to make money with emeralds. This was money that we needed desperately. As I look back on this time, I realize that I was young and so very dumb at times. I had done many stupid things, however I had a family that loved me. Pablo's temptation was never strong enough.

I could never have imagined that Pablo would one day become such a horrendous human being, that in fact he was already horrendous and I didn't see it. This chubby man with the bold appearance was a car thief and a hired gun. Within five years he would start his Cartel, smuggling tons and tons of cocaine into the USA, killing and kidnapping hundreds of people. He would become the world's richest criminal, hiring an army of 2,000 to protect him. He would buy politicians. He would strike deals with the CIA. He would run for political office and become a senator's standby.

Assassinations, murders and torturing were his means. Power, fame and the love of the Colombian people were his goals. He saw himself as a political hero, taking money from the gringos and giving it to the Colombian people, which he did. He built schools and housing projects for the poor. His love of soccer prompted him to build many fields and even install lights for nighttime playing.

Growing up as he did in a time of uncontrolled violence produced this man with such a strange attitude. He would have his enemies hung upside down and burned to death while he walked in the poor neighborhoods handing out soccer balls, hugging the street kids and receiving accolades from the adults.

His drug business became so large and he became so infamous that the USA had to stop him. For some time President Nixon had wanted his extradition so he could be charged with drug crimes, but Pablo had either bought off every politician up to the president or terrified them with death threats to them and their families. In that way he was able to prevent extradition. He had even murdered one presidential candidate who boasted to capture Pablo and allow him to be brought to the USA courts.

Pablo and some of his associates became known as The Extraditables. Car bombing was another of his methods to force his will. Pablo eventually agreed to give up and go to a prison, a prison that he designed and built for himself. Those were the terms he set for his surrender. However, after surrendering, he soon tired of his own prison, escaped, and became the most hunted man on the planet.

Although he continued running his drug trade while in prison, the government was able to make some progress in stopping him. They raided some of his cocaine labs, intercepted some of his planes and began confiscating some of his many properties. The Cali Cartel, Pablo's rivals in the drug trade were making strides while Pablo was in prison. He came out, back on the street with a vengeance, assassinations and murders increased.

When he bombed an international airline, killing over 100 people, the pressure from the USA was too much. The Colombian government gave in. Special agents and tactical forces were sent to Bogota and the hunt began. Pablo became the world's most wanted criminal. Spy planes, and a crack team of American special forces were on the hunt. They came close many times but he always seemed to know they were coming and escape just in time. It was his use of cell phones that finally brought him down. A USA tracking plane and a team of Colombians with sophisticated listening gear on the ground pinpointed him to a Medellin neighborhood and he was spotted looking out of a window. It was never a question of capturing him. Pablo was a marked man and he would not be taken alive.

I remember seeing pictures of him after he had been caught and shot. There were many soldiers picking up his dead body, holding it up for a picture, like a hunter with a trophy deer. To this day Pablo's gravesite is a popular attraction. Many visitors come and pay respect to the image of a man they view as Colombia's Robin Hood.

In all my life, this is the closest I ever came to such a bad man.

26

Twin Towers

Today is the anniversary of the attack on the Twin Towers It has been 19 years since passenger jets hijacked by terrorists slammed into the World Trade Center and the Pentagon and crashed into a field in Shanksville, Pa. Nearly 3,000 lives were lost, some 2,700 of them in New York, in the deadliest attack in the country's history, a blow to America's psyche.

Very sad that such a situation occurred, displaying man's 'inhumanity to man.' Innocent men, women and children all killed out of revenge for equal atrocities committed to the terrorists' home lands. Will such things ever end, or is man destined to live forever in this state?

Last night I had an incredible thought or dream, I really can't say what it was. If it was a thought, it was inspired, but if I dreamt it, then it was one of the most memorable ones I have ever had. It felt so real when I woke up. This enlightened experience had to do with reincarnation. I had been reborn, but not as some new individual, but reborn into my own body as the same person, a newborn baby, little Tommy, with all the knowledge I had acquired in this life. I saw my mother and father in the delivery room. My mom was 28, my dad was 31. I saw them, and I realized that I was now going to be able to relive my whole life over and not have to suffer as I learned right from wrong.

As my dream continued, I was reliving many of my young child experiences, I was helping in our kitchen, licking the bowl as my mom made a cake, I was in a swimming pool in Kankakee, Illinois playing with a large group of Black kids. I had remembered that time and my action as being inappropriate in Illinois in 1953.

In this new life I realized that everything in my world, and everyone else's world, would change as I made different decisions. I then realized that everyone else in the world were more like actors, that were only here for me. This is my world to go around again and make things better, and I thought that's the way it should be. But then I thought about past history and all the other people who lived before 1946.

At this moment, I was sitting on the floor of my kindergarten classroom. I was so filled with joy. And then a giant Matrix began to form, and everyone else's life was fitting in to this complex puzzle, everyone who had ever lived. And they were not actors. Perhaps they were all in a stage of being reborn into their previous lives, and all the new changes worked in unity. I understood that the world was going to improve as each person died.

As many scientists suggest, life only exists on this planet. If that is true, then why would there be an infinite amount of galaxies and why would the extreme size of space be needed. It may be a sign, a symbol for us who have life, a tiny look at the complexity of the Matrix. The beginning of an understanding of God.

"Whether it is to be utopia or oblivion will be a touch-and-go, race right up to the final moment," a quote by Buckminster Fuller. He must have said this many years ago since he died in 1983. This inventor, designer, architect, poet, educator, engineer, philosopher, environmentalist, and, above all, humanitarian was indeed a genius of my time. He denied it and said, "Geniuses are just people who had good mothers." But he had indeed predicted the future of our world today.

Perhaps at the time of his quote he was referring to overpopulation, it wasn't until the late 80s when global warming became a serious issue, and the internet had not become viable to the general public until the early 1990s. I make this statement because social media has put the world into a very dangerous situation. Beginning with today's youth who are seriously endangered, and extending to everyone who now uses these platforms such as Facebook, Twitter, Snapchat, etc.

The population of the entire world is being used, manipulated and molded for one reason, financial incentives. None of the social media platforms began with this intent, but this is now what they have become. Not only are we being told what to buy, we are being trained how to think, and what to accept as 'the truth.' I once saw a sign at a protest march saying, "Don't believe the truth."

We are now not only the consumer, but the product itself. We are being sold. Once we start to select through our phone or our computer, we become part of the computer algorithms, and its job of data processing and what is referred to as automatic reasoning. These supercomputers are able to perform frequency analysis, and we become targets. These computers are smart, much smarter than you or I. And their ability to attack us with success is based on our use of their platform.

Most citizens of the world are victims and don't realize it. A most serious result is that we are now divided into 'think alike' groups, those groups that appeal to our intellectual vanity are the ones we choose to communicate with. They become 'our friends.' The opposers are threats, they become our subconscious enemies.

Never before in the history of humankind has something appeared that is even close to social media in reaching people and selling them on products or ideas. We have acquired all this technology and it is being used for so many of the wrong reasons. As for negative results, I will present an easy short term prediction and I hope I am a hundred percent wrong: Civil War.

One solution is to immediately stop our youth, our children from becoming addicted to their phones. So many figures, easily available, show the health damages as kids rely on social media for their sense of reality. Teen suicides, mental health problems have risen over 100 percent in the last few years. Our old way of life where children would meet each other and hang out with them in person is such a better way. To address the problem must be a responsibility of those who have created this virtual reality. The CEO's of all the social media platforms must recognize this problem and somehow devise a way to fix it.

"If humanity does not opt for integrity we are through completely. It is absolutely touch and go. Each one of us could make the difference." Buckminster Fuller

SEPTEMBER 13, 2020

V for Victory, that's what appears to be today's message. Just finished watching Face the Nation and the relevant topics were the Voting issues and the Vaccine. Yesterday in a rally, Trump accused the Democrats of rigging the votes and causing fraudulent results in states that elected Democrat governors and senators. His lies are so harmful to the trust we have in our electoral system. He is tearing down the fabric of our democracy. He's doing the work for his buddy Putin and the Russians, whether he realizes it or not. No president in this nation's history has done more to undermine the confidence of Americans in their voting systems than Donald Trump, even though just about everyone involved in those systems, Republicans and Democrats, insist he is flat-out wrong.

The experts weighed in on this issue and explained that our voting system is as secure as it could possibly be. The process is complex to be sure, involving mechanical voting machines, scanners, the Post Office, drop boxes, signature verifications, hackers, etc. Some of the safety practices are elementary, of course, but if our confidence in the voting system is being shaken by the claims of the president, elementary descriptions of how the system works seem to be the solution. This information is available to anyone who wants to do the research.

As for the progress on vaccine development, it is as expected, number one priority for our medical labs here and around the world. Some advances are being made, but stumbling blocks have appeared. No-one in my generation has been through such a crisis as we are experiencing today. Perhaps I should say no American citizen. My grandparents lived during the Spanish flu pandemic of 1918. At the time it was the deadliest in world history, it infected an estimated 500 million people worldwide, about one-third of the planet's population, and killed an estimated 20 to 50 million people. And it seems that the people all wore masks without objecting. That epidemic came in two periods, months apart. The second wave was much more deadly than the first. The first wave had resembled typical flu epidemics; those most at risk were the sick and elderly, while younger, healthier people recovered easily. October 1918 was the month with the highest fatality rate of the whole pandemic. In the United States, 292,000 deaths were reported between September-December 1918.

The people at that time experienced what we are going through now and recovered, returning to normal life, as before. This should give us all hope and eliminate despair. Rumors are flying, thanks to guess what, social media, that we are doomed, that this is only the tip of the iceberg and humanity will soon perish. This is it, the Armageddon has come. Armageddon is God's war against Satan and his demons, and the wicked on earth. He destroys the wicked and places Satan in a spiritual abyss or confinement where he is unable to have any influence over righteous mankind. I'm not a Bible reader so I don't know what it predicts as the outcome, but I think it implies that life on earth is done with. Goodbye lovely earth, goodbye galaxies and infinite space, goodbye the non Christians throughout the planet. Hello Heaven, it's nice to meet you God. I got a few questions for ya, do I need to set up an appointment? I know you must be super busy, but one quick one, does life exist anywhere else?

Today I will be picking up Suzanne and again heading down to Julie and her Hotel. Thank you again Saint Julia, you are for sure gonna rise up with all the Good People. Suzanne and I will be guests tonight at a special event, a 'pop up dinner.' I am looking forward to this. Julie has been praising the man Lanai, who along with his talented crew, are bringing this from Hawaii to Palo Alto.

Not only will we be experiencing an amazing multi course dinner, but I can hardly wait to meet Lanai, who Julie says is one of the most amazing people on the planet. After spending the night, we will drive back to the mortuary in Santa Rosa to pay our respects to Susie, actually to Stu, Willie and Robbie.

SEPTEMBER 15, 2020

Starting a new week this morning, The weekend was atypical. Suzanne and I had a great visit with Julie and we met Lanai and crew. His presentation of the 6 course meal was actually more impressive to me than the food. He explained each dish before it was brought out and explained its history. It was an interesting culinary class on Hawaii, and its food variety. The meal began with Ahi Poke, and a glass of Riesling wine accompaniment. Next came Shrimp Lupia, then Ginger Noodles. As each separate dish was brought out, the cook, a young Hawaiian, came to the mic and explained how the dish was created. The second wine was served and discussed by another crew member, a Hawaiian sommelier. It was a Pinot Noir from Handley Cellars, Julie's family winery. The dish served was then Mochiko Chicken Katsu. Finally came Braised Short Rib Kalbi served with pickled vegetables and Kim Chi. A white bubbly wine Venetto, was poured with the dessert, Pineapple Bibingka, a sweet cake made with rice flour, pineapple and coconut milk, served with toasted coconut and Hapia sauce (coconut custard).

So there it is, Lanai's creation, quite an event and a pretty cool way to spend the early afternoon, dining by Julie's beautiful pool. Julie, Suzanne and I sat together at two tables, socially distanced, our masks became chin guards and then sat on the tables when the waiters began their food dancing. We were part of 40 other people, living the good life of the rich and famous.

Next stop was the drive back to Santa Rosa and the funeral home to see Stu, Willie and Robbie. Susie's body was lying in the casket. As I walked in, Stu was sitting with a friend. I mentioned to him that I never really care to go up to the casket, it's just not my thing. But Stu said, "Oh, go on up Tom, pay your respects." I did and of course the body was a sad replica of what Susie really looked like. I had planned to sit in meditation, to pray and talk with Susie's spirit, but I couldn't concentrate, let alone pray with any part of my deeper self.

We came home, I dropped Suzanne at her house and went to a scheduled meeting for some possible work. I wound up with three jobs, building a 25x10 foot loft and two bathroom remodels, tile work. These will be the first real jobs I've taken on in quite a while.

Yesterday both Trump and Biden were out on the campaign trail. Biden is concerned as usual with the Big Four, that is the pandemic, climate change, the economy and racial disparity. Trump held an indoor rally, most of the attendees were unmasked. As Biden was expressing empathy and concern for the victims of the West Coast fires, Trump was blaming it all on lack of forest management. Biden cited the issue as global warming and drought. Trump said "Science doesn't know." Not only does he feel as if he should do the thinking for all of us, by withholding the truth, but I guess he wants to think for the scientists also.

Another example of Trump apathy, a federal appeals court ruled upholding a Trump administration policy that could lead to the deportation of about 400,000 immigrants who originally came to the U.S. in emergency circumstances, like earthquakes or civil wars. Trump just can't imagine that the luck of the draw could have gone against him in 1946 and his name could have been Jose Arguello, and he might have been born in Guadalajara, Mexico.

JOSE AND RAUL

I'll tell you a story about two little boys. Jose and Raul, they didn't have any toys. Their parents worked hard, but couldn't get ahead, until one day when their father said, "I love you my boys, but I'm going away. There's a land up north where I can get better pay. I'll send your mom money, and you'll have more to eat. You'll have better clothes and shoes for your feet."

Poppi walked out the door with tears on his cheeks, He knew he'd be walking for several more weeks. He arrived at the border and made it across. Not without thinking of the family he'd lost. He found work in the fields, on very large farms. It was a strain on his body and it weakened his arms.

His will kept him going, he never lost sight. He took a job in a restaurant and worked through the night. Once a month on Sunday he would go to the phone, and call to his family, who waited at home. "Did you get the money I sent in a letter? How are my boys? Are your lives a lot better?"

"Poppi we have more clothes now, and more food too. But our life is not better, 'cause we don't have you."

"I'm so sorry my boys, but I'm working to arrange a different type of law that will bring about change. We'll be together soon. I can feel this, I can tell. The people here know it will help them as well. Today I marched so people will see, that all we want is just to be free. The U.S. needs me for the work that I do, but I want to come back and be there with you. When this reform takes place, there will be more peace in the land, and then my boys we can be a family again."

I wrote this after attending a march and rally in February 1999.

In two more days, I will be mounting up the cameras at Paul Mahder's Gallery, preparing to shoot the next Jazz band that Jessica has lined up. Since I began helping with these events I have instituted a change. We are going from two cameras to four, and it's making the production much better. It has been a true pleasure being at these performances, the bands have all been excellent.

This pandemic has stopped Jessica from producing her Annual Jazz Festival. The big week for this Festival always came at the end of May and the first week of June, covering two weekends with the highlighters. During the week, events took place every night, with great performers but not the international stars that she booked on the weekends. Well that has all been canceled this year and Jess is putting on these live broadcast events for her diehard fans and jazz lovers. For 21 years, since the first Festival, I have been the official videographer, working with Jessica to record and archive these events. It has been a long haul and I have certainly learned a lot about Jazz in this time.

The Festival is only part of the work that Jessica does. Throughout the year she brings musicians to play in Healdsburg, She has had a number of different venues, bars, restaurants, the Healdsburg Plaza, and even private residences on occasion. She has also put together a Jazz Education program for the local schools which takes place in a week's time, with many different musicians, many from the Bay Area. I have taped all of it. My job with the Festival also included a lot of editing, producing some documentaries about different musicians that were generally a part of the Festival and had died. Their music lives on.

The first was a trumpet player, Lester Bowie. He died the year the Festival began and was only 58 at the time of his death. Lester was a close friend of Jessica's and prompted the work on this doc. Don Moye came to Healdsburg with boxes of footage accrued from performances worldwide. Don was the drummer in Chicago Art Ensemble, the last group that Lester played with. With Don's help we chose clips and completed the doc. That film was shown as an event during one of the Festivals.

The second was Kahlil Shaheed, another trumpet player who served as one of the Bay Area's most prominent jazz music educators and performed for several years with the drummer Buddy Miles. He had also performed briefly with Jimi Hendrix. Kahlil was a big part of the Jazz Education program and also came up here to help with Jessica's Black History month program. He died in Oakland. A wonderful man and a friend. He was 63.

On the Tenth Anniversary, I put together a doc with clips of the previous events. It was shown at each venue before the music, during those weekends of the Tenth Annual Healdsburg Jazz Festival. Throughout the year I was always doing some projects for Jessica as promotion or as a requirement in applying for grants.

Jessica and I have developed a working relationship and most of the time it goes along smoothly.

But we've definitely had our moments, when I was ready to give it up. She wouldn't like my edit choices and I'd be insulted, or tech glitches would happen and she'd be angry. We always vented and then came together in the end. Many people have been hired by the Festival, faced similar issues, and quit. Besides Jessica, of course, I'm the only person who has been with the Festival since the beginning.

At the beginning of this year when I was so occupied with Suzanne, Jessica called and said she needed me to put together a short video for some grant. Those jobs require a lot of work, finding the footage, going over all of it, making the first cut, etc. I had been seriously considering quitting for the past two years and that did it. I told Jessica I could no longer work for the Festival and I officially resigned. She and I had both discussed quitting on a number of occasions. For Jessica it was dealing with the Board that had been created to help run things, raise money, and all the other things that boards do. For many years it has been difficult for Jess to give up control. In August Jessica also announced her retirement and these Friday night events will be her last hoorah.

When she started these events, she found a Production Company to produce the live feed. It is actually the first time in 20 years that I was not the Video Production for Healdsburg Jazz. A little over a month ago Jess called and asked if I wanted to come anyway. She was happy with how things were going and thought that maybe I would enjoy being there for the live performances. She was right. After this Friday night's show, there will only be one more event for Jessica and myself. On September 26, Charles Lloyd, Zakir Hussein and Julian Lage, an amazing trio of musicians, will be performing together for the first time. This event will surely be streamed around the world. Charles Lloyd is a very close friend of Jessica's. His accomplishments as a musician are too numerous to mention. It was he who brought Jessica into the world of jazz, after hearing his famous album, "Forest Flower."

Julian Lage has appeared many times at the Festival and for other functions. Jessica began the relationship with Julian when he was 12 years old, the same year he performed at the Grammys. I have been taping his performances, a child prodigy, since that time and have watched him grow into one of the top Jazz guitarists in the world. It could not be a more fitting way for Jessica Felix to bow out.

It was 1999, when I first arrived back in California. That was the year that Jessica decided to put on a Festival. What she created is accepted as one of the most prestigious small Jazz Festivals in the nation. She has brought many of the top jazz musicians in the world to our small little town. And now for Jessica, 21 years later, it is coming to an end. The thoughts are that the Festival will continue without her, but I honestly have my doubts how long it will last without the Jazz Maven at the helm.

SEPTEMBER 20, 2020

The Supreme Court Justice Ruth Bader Ginsburg has died and the Republicans are jumping quickly to appoint someone to take her place. Looks like the Democrats have no way to stop this from happening. This means a strong conservative will be joining the bench. Good-bye to any sensible health care plans for the poor or even average income people. Good-bye to Roe vs. Wade and women's right to choose. Voting rights, civil rights, environmental protection, all issues that will be directly affected. Rather historical, but this will be the third judge appointed by one president and of all people, it's Trump. Looks like the evil man has won a big victory in getting his wishes and affecting the future of all Americans, too bad.

In the very beginning of my writings, I mentioned I wanted to present a 'purple view' on political issues, not a red or blue slant. That certainly didn't happen, I wasn't able to hold in my feelings. Politics is quite similar to religion, in the sense of a person's defense of a position. When or if you form an opinion, you then become obliged to justify two contradictory propositions. In respect of the truth it is often the case that only one position can be correct. There either is a God or there's not. However grey matter exists in many complex issues, even in the statement, "If you're not part of the solution, then you become part of the problem" That statement is not true.

It's impossible to be an atheist and think, well maybe there is a God. What happens when an unstoppable force meets an immovable object? Nothing will happen, because no such scenario can exist. There is either an unstoppable force or an immovable object. There can't be both. It's impossible to vote for a percentage of Biden and a percentage of Trump. No grey matter here. On November 3rd, our vote will be either right or wrong. And that's the way it is. Voters will be considering only the two extremes. There is no continuum of intermediate possibilities Mistakes will be made, many of them. There will be regrets, anger, happiness and sadness. This overwhelming example of free will, of democracy, will come into play. Hopefully the correct result will muddle forward, amidst the hundreds of millions of Americans who vehemently disagree on very crucial issues.

It really is amazing to me that everyone knows whoever is appointed to be the new judge will vote on issues in a way that reflects their personal views. Any judge on any court, should be judging each case based on the law and our constitution, that is not the way it works. It is such a dismal and disgusting reality, and everyone accepts it. I can't find one news station that even brings this point up.

One of Trump's picks is a young female law professor at Notre Dame. It is a given that when Roe vs. Wade comes before her, she will vote for 'right to life.' She is a strict Catholic and believes abortion under any circumstance is sinful. She will blatantly mix her religion with her responsibility as an impartial judge.

It was just on June 30th, less than three months ago when the Supreme Court judged a case and ruled against restricting abortion laws, the vote was 7-2. Well the religious anti-abortion proponents will never stop their fight. There are existing similar suits filed up to the Supreme Court, and soon the judges will be called on again to interpret the law and decide. They will again vote according to their personal beliefs and Roe vs. Wade will more than likely be overturned. There will be countless numbers of unwanted children born and many of them will never have a chance in life.

It seems logical that women should have the right to choose an abortion, or to agree with the bumper sticker saying, "If you don't like abortion, then don't have one." This is a sensible approach.

On the other hand, if abortion had been legal in 1964, Jay Brown, my son, and all his kids and his grandchildren would not be here.

Regardless of any argument concerning this idea, it is an accepted fact, and there have been a number of different studies done suggesting that 18 years after Roe vs. Wade was decided, the huge drop in crime happened because of this new abortion law. The conclusion is that the kids who would normally be committing these crimes are not here.

Since the early 1990s, crime rates in the U.S. have fallen by about half. A paper from the National Bureau of Economic Research finds that legalized abortion following the Supreme Court's landmark decision accounts for 45% of the decline in crime rates over these past three decades.

The paper's authors, Stanford University economist John Donahue and University of Chicago economist Steve Levitt take new data and run nearly the same model they used in their influential, and controversial 2001 analysis published in the Quarterly Journal of Economics, where they first suggested an association between abortion and crime.

In the 2001 paper, they found that legalized abortion appeared to account for up to half of the drop in rates of violent crime and property crime to that point. They also predicted crime would fall an additional 20% over the next two decades. Levitt featured the research in the 2005 bestseller Freakonomics. Of course his book has become quite controversial.

For every argument there is a counter argument, to be sure. If this particular subject has an effect on you, then I guess it is your option to pick a side, and then determine if you want to act on your decision. Compared to the environmental concerns, the abortion laws are extremely difficult to argue. I know how I feel, but I could not expect anyone else to follow me. I'm not about to stand in protest with a sign, yelling at the other person who has their sign, differing from mine.

We are a collective group of animals trying to get along and survive in a safe, happy world. In my world at this time, this is not my fight. Who I am now certainly respects those who are fighting for their freedom, their principles and morals, in order to defend or change the existing law. And you know what, even though I'm not joining the fight, I hope my side wins.

My previous life is directly connected to this issue, because when my high school girlfriend was pregnant with Jay we were seriously hoping the pregnancy would go away. As I said earlier we would have been in line at the abortion clinic.

SEPTEMBER 21, 1965

Upon entering high school there is something that I learned very quickly. Most everyone that is in a Catholic school wants to get out of it. For Catholic school kids, the public school is a looming, beckoning pool of liberal freedom. There are no uniforms to wear and the public schools are always so much bigger than the dinky parochial schools. They allow lunches off campus; the list goes on and on. Wow, did I jump at the chance to get out of Cardinal Newman. In retrospect, that move turned out to be one of the biggest mistakes I ever made.

Palm Beach High School was to become my Alma Mater. Not only did I get my wish to be in a larger, more liberal school, but I also got everything else that went along with it. I was ineligible for any school sports participation. I did not think that would matter. I had girls, the current, undaunted focus of my life. Prior to entering Palm Beach High, I had no clue that there were lower class people in the world that could sit next to me and come into my life, just like that. I knew these people were out there, and that I could see them and that I could walk by them, but I did not realize that there were so many of them.

Now Cardinal Newman was not a snooty upscale prep school, but it certainly did not house the type of people that the public schools had. It took a while for this fact to dawn on me. I could see it in later years. I hope I am not prejudiced to social standings, or a class structure advocate, but I had been protected from some rather sleazy characters. It is interesting to think about the differences that would have occurred in me, had I not spent many formidable years in St. Ann's, St. Catherine's and Cardinal Newman. I don't know whether to call private schools blessed protectorates or sheltered realities, however my heart knows, I should have stayed in Cardinal Newman, Sister Mary Richards and all.

Having been a jock in school, I had not really spent much time learning how to dance or listening to the grooviest bands. I think maybe that is why I became kind of a 'one on one' type, always wanting a girlfriend of my own. I would go from serious relationship to serious relationship, unlike this guy Frank Donnely. In baseball, Frank would not have been able to strike out a peanut leaguer, or in football for example, lover boy Frank wouldn't have lasted 2 seconds in a game of 'toss up and tackle', but boy did he have the girls. I would see him out at the parties and all the social dances with a different girl each night. He could really dance well, and the girls were hanging all over him.

There was a part of me that wanted to be just like Frank. I guess I was afraid to be out there on my own. At this stage of my life I needed a girlfriend at all times. Obviously, I was not so self-assured.

I then entered into a junior college, furthering my education. Girls were put on the back burner and psychedelic drugs consumed my head.

From the very first moment that I had heard about pot, I knew that I would try it. In the early 60s there was not much availability for pot or any psychedelic drugs in Southern Florida. I had met a fellow college student from Fort Lauderdale who had spent time with the surfers in Southern California, and had a Mexican connection. Next thing you know I was buying a key. I did not realize that a key was a kilo. I had never even seen a picture of the stuff. Why, he could have sold me sugar cane, and I would have paid the asking price, $90.

So, we meet at night, halfway between Palm Beach and Fort Lauderdale. I have my checkbook in hand, trying to act cool. We are parked on Ocean Avenue. I get in his car and he says, "You want to try the stuff?" I didn't smoke cigarettes and I honestly did not know how to smoke anything, so I watched him as he sort of cupped his hands around this joint and took a hit. I imitated him, cupping my hands. What a trip that was. I proceeded to get stoned, despite myself, and then began a rather stupid, uncontrollable giggle.

I thought I was buying a small bit of pot, enough to perhaps fill up a matchbox. Then I saw the grocery bag stuffed with all the weed. I must say I was somewhat dumbfounded at that moment. When I attempted to pay him with my check, he thought I was nuts. Meanwhile, I am still giggling from the joint, trying to keep a straight face and convince him that it is a good check and to let me go to a restaurant and try to cash it. My first lesson in the underworld, one is not supposed to buy drugs with a check.

Here we are doing something illegal, probably the first time such a transaction had ever taken place on this spot (there would be many similar events in the years to come). We were sort of like on the forefront of the movement. My marijuana connection was rather nervous by this time and did not want to drive back to Lauderdale with the stuff. He had no choice but to be a little accommodating, although he was quite bummed out. Somehow I got a local restaurant to cash my check, traded for the grocery bag full of pot and began what was to be the long drive back home.

I stopped in Boynton Beach, walked down to the sea's edge to pee. It seemed as if I was standing there peeing for hours. I remember thinking, "wow, pot really screws up your kidneys." For those who have never smoked pot, it does not screw up your kidneys. It is your time perception that plays tricks on you. There are many things that pot does to you, none of it is that bad, as far as I can tell.

I was not a typical drug dealer by any means. My bust happened because one of my fellow students in the Junior College knew that I had pot. I had made him somewhat of a friend, Peter DiDonato from New York. He kept asking me to get him some and I did. He turned me onto one of his people, and I got this guy a key, er twice. I guess that move did make me a typical drug dealer, but I never got bigger than that. His people was an FBI agent. Without going into all the slimy details, my parents got me the best lawyer and I received a 5 year probation sentence. I was charged under the 'Youthful Offenders Act,' and supposedly the offense was removed from my record after my probation period. Incidentally I was a good probation criminal, my probation officer really liked me and I got off after just two years.

SEPTEMBER 22, 2020

I'm sure I'm not exaggerating when I say that today's news seems like a lesson on Panic Control. The Public Health officials are all worried because it appears as if the Fall surge in Coronavirus cases that was predicted is upon us. The number of new daily confirmed cases in the U.S. has jumped more than 15 percent in the past 10 days. It is the sharpest increase since the late spring, and it has arrived just before the official start of autumn, which is today. We have just passed the 200,000 deaths mark and that grim milestone helps to scare everyone, except Trump that is. He claims that without his wonderful efforts, the number would be 2 million. He now wants to slow down testing. Actually he has never hidden his ambivalence about testing.

In June, when he told an arena of supporters in Tulsa, Oklahoma, that he had instructed his people to slow the testing down, please, the disclosure prompted one of the more dire news cycles of the pandemic. The president said repeatedly that he wanted the United States to reduce its testing. But in the weeks that followed, testing increased.

Testing, regardless, is a mess. None of the results are stored in any national bank of records where it can be accessed and used to treat the virus as you would stop a spreading fire. If one state is lowering the cases but has no idea or control over what is happening in the state next to it, they will certainly be in danger. Without a competent leader setting up a national co-ordinated effort, it really won't work. It's like trying to keep a swimming pool clean by setting up one corner as the official peeing section. The pee will spread, the virus will spread and the fires will spread. Bringing up the next point, climate change, global warming.

Nature is unleashing it's negative power upon us in an unprecedented way. Natural disasters are everywhere, record breaking fires in the West, burning millions of acres, destroying entire communities, killing countless people, turning the West into a hellscape, not to even mention the wildlife disasters. On the East Coast and in the Gulf area, states are being continually battered by tropical storms and hurricanes in numbers that have never been seen. The storms are powerful, moving slower and carrying more water. The extensive coastal flooding has affected Texas, Florida, Alabama, Louisiana, Georgia, South and North Carolina. And the flooding often extends up to 25 miles inland. Those on the sea's edge are experiencing rising water, in some cases surging 10' above normal. People have lost their homes, businesses, and are forced to live without power for unknown amounts of time.

There have been so many storms that the U.S. National Hurricane Center has had to turn to the Greek alphabet to put names on the storms. The seasonal average numbers are 12 tropical storms, six hurricanes and 3 major hurricanes. We've already doubled those numbers and the season extends to November 30.

The political issues are sharing the negative airwaves as parties fight. Democrats are desperate in the attempt to stop Trump's ability to put in another Supreme Court judge. Democrats are screaming hypocrisy to deaf ears. The Republicans stopped Obama from appointing a judge near the end of his term, claiming the next president should have that right. The prize of a lifetime appointed judge is too big to worry about being called a hypocrite. The Republican senators will gladly accept a hypocrite label from people they don't care about anyway.

As I was driving my old pickup truck to the dump today I thought of a good test to validate a stance in a contested case. I will call it the "what if, then what" test.

Democrat: Masks are absolutely helpful in controlling the virus, we need to wear them whenever we are in the public. What if you're wrong then what? Well, a lot of people will be somewhat uncomfortable for long periods of time.

Republican: Masks are useless and do nothing to stop the spread of coronavirus, we shouldn't be wearing them. What if you're wrong then what? 100,000 people will lose their lives needlessly and millions will contract the disease.

Democrat: Global warming is caused by human interference with our environment, we can make changes and reverse the situation. What if you're wrong then what? We will have laws regulating CO2 emissions, laws protecting rivers, waterways and the oceans from industrial pollution. We will eventually have ways to produce all of human's energy needs from the sun, rivers, and wind. We will save our beautiful lands and National Parks and protect our oceans from disastrous oil spills, etc. We will create thousands of new jobs. We will have laws which regulate pollution from cars and trucks and at some point will all be driving electric vehicles. We will wind up with clean air, but, it will still get hotter.

Republican: Global warming is a natural cycle and has nothing to do with human's actions on the planet, we don't need to change our ways at all. What if you're wrong then what? The planet will continue to get hotter, droughts will become worse. Many parts of the planet, even entire continents will become uninhabitable. People will not be able to grow food, mass starvations will become commonplace. Everyone in Africa will attempt to migrate to

Europe. All of our southern states will become too hot to live in and people will make efforts to move northward into large cities that will not be able to handle the influx. All people from Central American countries and Mexico will be heading across our border in an attempt to survive. This same scenario will happen in Asia and China. The planet itself will eventually be unable to support human life and we die.

This test can be used to look at every important major difference between our two parties, health care, abortion, immigration racial inequality, gun control, taxes, etc. In many cases it helps to see which course of action is the better one. In other cases, no.

Democrat: We need to reduce military spending and use that money for social causes......What if you're wrong then what? We eliminate the homeless population, more people come out of poverty, facilities are built to help with mental problems and drug addiction. China or North Korea decides we are weak enough to attack. We all wind up on work gangs and in concentration camps.

Republicans: I told you so, you leftist commie. Oh well, I better come up with another test, the what if, then what test is not the panacea I was hoping for.

SEPTEMBER 25, 2020

Washington is honoring RGB (Ruth Ginsburg) by services and laying her casket in repose at the White House. This is the first female and the first Jewish person that has been given that honor. That seems rather strange, another barrier broken. So often we find religious and sexist practices that have been occurring without even realizing it.

Actually it wasn't until 1981 that the first female Supreme Court Justice was sworn in, that was Sandra Day O'Connor. As coincidence has it, it was on September 25. She was a Republican, sworn in by Ronald Reagan, and served for 25 years.

Because of the political fight now occurring, it seems that the entire issue of lifetime appointments, and even the power of the court itself is now coming under scrutiny. Many are coming to realize that the whole idea of relegating such extreme power to a Supreme Court, composed of non-elected judges, might be a serious mistake, more to come on this, I'm sure.

Another pertinent event occurred on this day back in 1789, the Bill of Rights was created. As could be expected, it was met with all kinds of political disagreement. Some feeling that the Constitution should never be changed or altered. The Bill of Rights was actually the first ten amendments to the Constitution. So much of these amendments, these new laws are forefront issues today. Famous amendments include the First Amendment: "Congress shall make no law respecting an establishment of religion, or prohibiting the free exercise thereof; or abridging the freedom of speech, or of the press; or the right of the people peaceably to assemble, and to petition the Government for a redress of grievances."

We can see today how religious beliefs deeply affect the abortion issue, and how politicized the rights to assemble and even free speech, freedom of the press are being affected. Armed vigilantes are appearing at the peaceful protests with the intentions of stopping the protesters. It is happening right now in Lexington Kentucky.

Months ago a Black lady, Breonna Taylor, was shot in her own apartment in Lexington and yesterday the court decided not to file any murder charges against the officers involved. Police investigators Brett Hankison, Myles Cosgrove and Jonathan Mattingly fired their weapons during the botched operation in which police shot and killed Taylor.

Hankison was charged with three counts of wanton endangerment, the court announced Wednesday. No charges were filed against the other officers whose use of force was justified because Taylor's boyfriend, Kenneth Walker, shot first, according to Attorney General Daniel Cameron, who spoke after the grand jury reported its findings.

"Let's be clear," State Rep. Charles Booker said in a media briefing. "Justice failed us today. It failed us in the way it has been failing us for generations ... a woman, a Black woman was killed in her home by the agency paid to protect and serve her. That is wrong. There is no justifying that."

Today it's Taylor's killing that is the key issue in protests over racial inequity in America, particularly how law enforcement has treated Black Americans. Yesterday, in the moments following the indictment, anger and disbelief was expressed by protesters in Louisville and Lexington as well as others on social media. Protests are again happening across the nation.

The Second Amendment, "A well regulated militia being necessary to the security of a free state, the right of the people to keep and bear arms shall not be infringed," is always invoked in arguments about gun control. I saw the issue come up on this morning's news by a reporter at a Trump rally and for me it was scary. It reminded me so much of a time in my past when I went to a KKK rally.

I did this in North Carolina. It was impulsive. I was working on a film for another producer, living on location in my converted school bus. One evening I was driving in the countryside and passed an armed guy in military fatigues on the side of the road. He was trying to wave people into a large field. I saw many people and then the sign, KKK Rally Here Tonight. I passed by, continuing to my friend's house for my shower. I thought if they're still there when I return, I'm going to stop and see for myself.

They were there, and the guy was still on the road. I drove in, backed my pickup in a space where I could see the stage. I lowered my tailgate and sat down, listening to the hateful, disgusting speakers as they took turns. Some actually pulled out their pistol and fired into the air. It was so ridiculous I remember thinking in a way it was funny and couldn't be for real. When a young teenage boy got on stage raising his fist and yelling, "White Power," I had enough. I slowly got back in the cab of my truck and drove away.

Our next headline news issue of the day. Coronavirus is not letting up. It's common to say that viruses don't care about political parties. And it's true that no matter the outcome of the election, we'll probably still be dealing with rampant misinformation and a Congress and country as divided as they have ever been. But it's also reasonable to expect some changes in the coronavirus's prospects under a Democratic administration.

Joe Biden is already building a team of advisers to deal with the pandemic if he is elected, and he has vowed to do most of the things that Trump refuses to. For example, he will encourage states to implement mask mandates, coordinate testing at the national level, and rejoin the World Health Organization.

He could also restore integrity to the nation's scientific institutions. I think if Biden wins, we can hope to see the F.D.A. and C.D.C. exert scientific consensus again, and from there, I think, a more sensible, coordinated federal response will take shape.

Let's try and lighten up. I am preparing, with my limited tech capabilities, to set up this computer so I can put everything appearing on this small monitor over to my giant TV screen. Tomorrow night is the big Charles Lloyd, Julian Lage, Zakir Hussein event. Jessica has hired a different team to be the producers and I won't be there due to Covid restrictions. Zack and Laura are coming up tonight, we will have the streaming event on the big screen, if I can get this working. I'm on my way to buy a 20 inch HDMI cable, first step.

Tonight, it's taping my friend Mark's band. They have a 3 hour gig outdoors by the Russian River. Should be fun.

SEPTEMBER 27, 2020

The weather has turned hot and windy this weekend. The firefighters down in LA are in trouble. So far no new fires have started up here. My outlook is just a matter of time. I'm not sure if I'm being negative or a realist, I guess both. It's crazy to have to live with this fear looming over you. That statement is relative to what I have established as my norm. That will change in time just as living with Coronavirus restrictions could. There are some people, including my friend Tim, who believe that today's Coronavirus lifestyle will never change.

Tim is a musician, a sound engineer, video producer, computer repair expert and finally, a for real tech nerd. I called him the other day for advice in getting my large TV set up to watch the big Jazz event. Again, he was able to explain the steps and I succeeded. When we finished talking I said, "OK Tim, hope to see you soon, when all this Covid stuff let's up." He replied. "You don't want to hear what I've got to say about that." He was right, I didn't want to hear him.

The concert with Charles Lloyd, Zakir and Julian happened last night at 7 PM. I was so ready for it. Zac and Suzanne and Zac's good friend Rocco were here waiting. Rocco and Zac had been playing music together down at Stu's poolside deck yesterday for a good part of the afternoon. Sarah, Rocco's girlfriend sat in with her violin for a short time. It was so sweet. Suzanne and I listened with great pride. At 6:30 we came up to the house and as things turned out the server for the concert crashed. I assume the bandwidth couldn't handle the volume. The good news is that this morning the link is working and as soon as Suzanne wakes up I will be playing the taped version. It won't be live, but that's OK.

Onto this morning's news. Trump has nominated Amy Coney Barrett as the pick for the new Supreme Court Justice. We've barely had time to mourn Ruth Bader Ginsburg who fearlessly stood so strong and so long for everyone's equal protection under the law. During her last breaths, she once again tried to block those who will steal power. Trump's pick, Amy Barrett symbolizes everything she fought against. The Sierra Club released it's opinion. "Today is difficult to stomach -- our world just became even more dangerous knowing the progress and protections we fought hard for can be re-decided as Republicans continue hijacking courts. A 6-3 extremist Supreme Court will weigh the Affordable Care Act as more than 200,000 have died from COVID, decisions on climate laws and EPA's authority while the sky is on fire, the final say in any contested election, and so much more at stake."

Our lives are much like a balance beam scale. We are the fulcrum, the two plates on either side of us can be filled with whatever we choose. Let's say the right side are negative things and the left are positive. These things are our ideas, thoughts, and actions. When one side gets more things, the scale tips, that side goes down. In order to stay in balance the other plate needs some things. Assuming we are filling up the right side with negative stuff and keeping it that way, I can see that the rod or the pole, the fulcrum, that holds these plates will begin to bend in that direction.

Since in this analogy we are the pole, we are now leaning to the right. The more negative thoughts or actions we have, the farther we lean. It becomes much harder to see any of the positive things on the other side. We wake up in the morning, call our friend and start talking all about the bad news. They reassure us and add some more bad news. It is so important to fill up the positive side of our scale and make our lives bend in that direction.

Considering that, I will find something today to balance this bit of news. A brain-eating amoeba was found in the water supply in eight Texas cities, leading to a disaster declaration. Tim should get on the phone and call Judy to hash this one over. Or maybe they could rent a billboard with a big I TOLD YOU SO on it.

It won't matter if Trump eliminates the Affordable Care Act, rules against Roe v. Wade, cuts Social Security, and Medicare, and continues destroying nature, since the brain eating amoeba will soon be eating all our brains, except that is for the Evil Power Boys. They will have the only pure water to drink. I don't understand why they released that amoeba in Texas first. That's a red state.

While I am waiting to watch the concert I can talk more about the idiot Trump. His latest thing is continually raving that the election is going to be rigged and the only way he will lose is through fraud. There is absolutely no doubt that unless it is an extremely lopsided Biden victory we can prepare for some serious trouble. This such a thing has never before happened in our country. Even the best scenario is that no matter the outcome of the election, we'll probably still be dealing with rampant misinformation and a Congress and country as divided as they have ever been.

It's also reasonable to expect some changes in the Coronavirus's prospects under a Democratic administration. Joe Biden is already building a team of advisers to deal with the pandemic if he is elected, he has vowed to do most of the things that Trump refuses to.

Dr. Carl Bergstrom, a government advisor is an infectious disease expert who's been thinking about the relationship between biology and social systems. He agrees that if Biden is elected that a more sensible, coordinated federal response will take shape.

Just finished watching the concert, quite a show by three Masters. Makes me proud to have been a part of all that for so many years.

27

Computers

I began my computer business in late 1966. It started off quite successfully. We had clients from all over the country, including the Dept. of the Army, Navy, many Universities and a number of big name industrial companies. Carmen Butarro, my partner was in his mid 40s, I was half that age. Carmen, a hot-tempered Italian, with a great head for creating things, but not much discipline for follow through, had moved to South Florida from Los Angeles where he had been a professor at UCLA. We had become close friends since our personalities seemed to compliment each other. I was a good listener and Carmen had quite an adventurous background. He was younger in spirit than his age dictated. He loved sharing his experiences and found a welcoming ear in my inquisitive mind.

At the time we met, Carmen was employed as a salesman for an office supply company. He was traveling to different businesses and pushing Olivetti-Underwood computers. At this stage of development the computers were basically advanced desktop calculators, simple character generators, no advanced graphics, and they were not at all user friendly. In order to boot up any programs, one had to type in long commands. There was very little software available. The lack of software made his product difficult to sell. Carmen discovered that many of the people he called on had small computers and were spending many hours developing programs for their own needs.

What our company did basically, was to set up an exchange house where people could donate programs that they had developed, become a member of CPX Corporation, (Computer Program Exchange) and receive free catalogs. For a small fee they could order programs from the catalogue that suited their particular business needs. We would then send them the commands for their computer format. Simply put, the business began as another 'Carmen idea.' I then put up the money for a sample mailing to known computer owners and the response was amazing. We asked for three programs or $50 to become a member.

Companies began sending not just three, but many programs they had developed, along with letters of gratitude that we were out there. From our first random mailing, we received hundreds of programs and many $50 checks. Money began rolling in and I accepted the challenge of putting this thing together. My wild experimenting with Billy Burroughs and that style of life ended.

The money came in, but it was all on paper. I never really did get the cash in my hands. I bought an older style Porsche, but other than that I would never see any of the real dough. We were doing more mailings, finding the best mailing lists, trying to find the few computer experts that were out there, to interpolate commands and check out the programs as they came in. We were printing up catalogs and trying to guess where to go next. Our business did not last long. We grew too quickly. In an upscale part of West Palm Beach we had rented very impressive office spaces. We even bought an offset printing press to produce our catalogs. Our business consisted of selling software suited for engineering firms, medical research facilities, etc.

Then one day Carmen met a sharp businessman on the beach who was starting up a marketing research company. We merged his company with ours and soon he would steal our business from under our noses. The most important thing I learned from the whole experience came one day in a meeting with H. Jefferson Mills.

H. Jefferson Mills was one of the heads of IBM. At that time, IBM was the leader of the computer industry with hardly any competition. They had real computers, with mainframes that ran on tubes and took up half a block. One of their larger executive offices was in Palm Beach. Our interest with IBM was as a possible investor to buy stock from us, so we could have more operating capital. That would allow us to purchase our own computers to sell along with the software.

The meeting with IBM took place around a big walnut conference table on the 5th floor of their office building on swanky Royal Palm Way in Palm Beach. We had already been to two or three meetings and it looked certain that IBM would invest in us. At this final meeting, IBM's lawyer, their accountant, a marketing executive, and a couple of different department heads were all present. Besides Carmen and I, we had our lawyer, our new partner Michael, our secretary Linda, and the middleman, an investment broker who had put us together with Mills. This man was going to make $10,000 right off the top, big money in those days.

Everyone at the meeting was sitting around trying to hammer out the final details. There were all kinds of papers and folders spread out on the table, money phase-outs, time projections, record books, letters of intent, and general information on our business. I was trying to keep my mouth shut, since I was, by far, the most inexperienced and unqualified to be doing this type of thing. In reality, I could not believe that I was sitting there, way out of my league and almost ready to get a couple hundred thousand dollars given to us. This was a large amount of money. I mean, like I was very impressed with myself, barely 20 years old with all these older sharp business execs. and the deal was almost secure. I was relying on Carmen to bring it home.

Suddenly one of their people stopped reading his notes, turned to Carmen and said, "Mr. Butarro, now if we do agree to this proposal you know that we shall need a firm commitment from you and a solid contract regarding your responsibility here. You will need to promise us unequivocally that your full time will be devoted to this business for the next several years."

Now the concept of a several year commitment to Carmen was more than he could possibly handle. They might as well have told him that he was going to be sentenced to life in prison without any possible chance of parole. I knew Carmen quite well, and with this pending deal, he was seeing the money that would come in, and he was envisioning the beaches of Fiji with native women, rum and coconut drinks.

Like I said, Carmen was a hot-tempered Italian. He had a big artery that came from the middle of his bushy eyebrows and headed straight up to his bald head. And when he would get mad this artery would start to bulge out. I saw it coming. He looked back at the guy and started to stutter and cough a little. The next thing you know he was grabbing up all our papers and folders out from in front of everyone. The investment man's jaw dropped to the table and his eyes almost came out of their sockets. He had just lost his ten grand. Carmen was mumbling, "We don't need this. This is bullshit, we don't need this." So, that was that.

After everyone's shock was absorbed a little and Carmen cooled down somewhat, we all knew the deal was over. Out of professional courtesy no one just came out and said, "Good-bye, it's been nice knowing you." Instead the second in charge under Mills began speaking and said something like, "Well we can probably negotiate on this and we shall take this under advisement and blah, blah, blah."

Then H. Jefferson spoke up and said something that I will never forget. It was a simple message, but I got a lot out of it. With a firm and assertive style he spoke, "You know, we get people in here every day looking for investment capital, and most of their ideas are good ideas, most of them would make us money. But you know what, we don't buy ideas, we buy the people that came up with the idea. We don't want your business, we want you."

CPX never survived this failed meeting. Michael, our relatively new partner, knew then that Carmen would not make it, and he started scamming to start his own company and ditch us. One morning Michael came in the office with great news, he had found another investor, Hewlett Packard. He packed all our programs onto microfiche to make the deal and headed to San Francisco. We never saw Michael again nor any of the programs he had taken.

I just walked away from the business. The last thing I knew about Carmen was that he was on his way to Houston with an old footlocker filled with tattoos. While rummaging through an old house being demolished, he came upon a collection of a tattoo artist's samples. They were from the 1800s. I saw them and, to his credit, they were unique. Carmen knew that he could sell them to Shell Oil Company and they could transfer them onto drinking glasses, which could be given out as promotional items with gas fill ups. Thanks to Carmen I learned that the line between genius and insanity runs very thin. It is a good thing that I never let my probation officer invest in our company. He wanted to.

SEPTEMBER 28, 2020

Barely conceivable, unimaginable, unthinkable, the fires are back. Less than 24 hours after I was writing that the fear of fires was not uppermost in my thoughts, it is back. I did say yesterday that it's just a matter of time, not realizing the time would be a mere 12 hours. Last night after returning Suzanne to her house, I received a call from Zac's girlfriend Lauren. She was at her mom's house in Eastern Santa Rosa. They needed my help and my pickup truck to save some of Lauren's sister's paintings. At 10:30 I started over and only made it about ¾ of the way before Lauren called back and said they needed to evacuate immediately. This morning large scale evacuations are taking place from Eastern Santa Rosa and further north and east towards Calistoga and St. Helena. At this point over 11,000 acres have burned., and 50,000 people have been evacuated.

The smoke is horrible, preventing any air support in the fight. The only good thing is that the wind has quieted down since last night, but those firefighters have an immense challenge trying to control this huge unpredictable fire. I've been receiving calls from Suzanne's health and care giving centers checking on her condition. Her house and mine are safe for the time being. As closely as I can tell, Suzanne's house is 4 or 5 miles from the areas of evacuation, mine is probably 10 miles away.

The thing I have learned about fires is that they don't burn everywhere equally at the same time. Even where they rage, they still miss patches of vulnerability, just by chance. In other words, if horrible things are happening all around you, you can remain unscathed, this is a message of hope. Viruses enter some people without adversely affecting them.

It's somewhat absurd how disproportionately powerful geographical positions are in exerting pertinent influences. Neither Trump nor any of his evil party members, McConnell, Graham, Barr, etc. can hardly ring the bell at my check in desk right now. All of their devious plans are taking place many miles away. Today they cannot affect me. Besides, I'm as susceptible to confirmation bias as anyone else. That is the tendency to look for ideas that confirm what we already believe, and I don't have to search very much to find this type of information.

SEPTEMBER 29, 2020

Throughout the world, polarity has created prejudice, discrimination, demonization, and even war. Tonight is the first debate between Trump and Biden. It will be entertaining, but as far as a factor for people's votes, I don't think so... It will be nothing more than confirmation bias in action. I suspect there are very few undecided voters who have not already chosen sides. I've seen polls that show from 7.6% to 13% are in the group of undecided. To me even the lower number seems larger than it really is. I'm sure that tonight's debate will be like so many other political campaigns and concentrate on the faults of the opponent. When Trump defeated Hillary, so many votes were cast simply to deny Hillary the Presidency.

Tonight's topics as chosen by the network are: the candidates' records, the Supreme Court, the Coronavirus, the economy, race and violence in cities, and the integrity of the election. Each of these issues have a direct influence on most everyone's life. The one most important consideration that must prevail with the candidates as they discuss the issues is the truth and nothing but the truth. Can we expect this, will we get it?

More news: The fires in California, which include huge ones up north of us in Butte and Shasta Counties are all raging ahead with no containment. The fire closest to us has now burned 36,000 acres, and hundreds of structures have been destroyed. I'm not sure if Lauren's parents' house is still there. The Coronavirus is acting just like the fires, numbers are spiking in many states. The race for a vaccine is continuing and just as politicized as ever. Russia has begun inoculating its citizens with an improperly tested vaccine, and Trump wants to do the same here. He has now found a new doctor to be his spokesman and Dr. Fauci no longer speaks on behalf of our government.

Influenza pandemics have occurred regularly every 30 to 40 years since the 16th century. Societies have dealt with terrible pandemics almost since there's been human beings, so history is on the side of resilience and coming back. It is so terribly difficult to keep this in mind. When I'm not worried about Suzanne, or thinking about these things, I attempt to occupy my thoughts with temporary distractions.

One of my heroes, actually a modern figure during my lifetime is Nelson Mandela. He was a South African lawyer who spent the majority of his life fighting for his people. After being arrested in 1962, for fighting against apartheid, he received a life sentence and during the prime years of his life, he was locked away and served 27 years in varied South African prisons.

In 1990 the world became a better place, people began paying attention to this terrible injustice. Amid growing domestic and international pressure, and with fears of a racial civil war, then President of South Africa released him. I can only imagine the experience he must have had during the time of his incarceration. Somewhere I read that during his time in prison, he recited this poem every day. I have it memorized.

"Out of the night that covers me, black as the pit from pole to pole, I thank whatever gods may be, for my unconquerable soul. In the fell clutch of circumstance, I have not winced nor cried aloud. Under the bludgeonings of chance, my head is bloody but unbowed. Beyond this place of wrath and tears, looms but the horror of the shade. And yet the menace of the years, finds and shall find me, unafraid. It matters not how straight the gate, how charged with punishment the scroll. I am the master of my fate, I am the captain of my soul."

I need to remember this time, this man, and this poem. By comparison, my life is not so bad right now. Most importantly, still, "I am the master of my fate, and I am the captain of my soul."

28

Colombia

SEPTEMBER 1972

Just to the west of Santa Marta is a small town called El Rodadero. It has an aquarium, which is one of my favorite things. The aquarium is not on the scale of Miami Sea Aquarium or the Marine World of San Diego. It is much smaller of course, and in my opinion it is better. It is like the public Zoo of Belize. They both blend into the surrounding environment. They are both built where they belong, directly on the sea, and directly in the jungle. No fancy visitor centers, theme cafeterias, or entertainment stadiums, and the construction didn't require a thousand concrete trucks or millions of dollars. They are not ostentatious displays of huge business ventures, built for the almost rich, by the richer. The places look like something you or I could build ourselves if we had the dream. This is exactly the thing that I love about underdeveloped, non-industrialized nations, the third world. "Praise the Third World, and Pass the Rice and Beans."

The El Rodadero Aquarium is nothing more than a system of rock walls extending out from a sea wall into the shallow sea. There are many small square pools with different species of marine life. There are much larger rectangular pools with the big fish, and there are shark pools and sawfish pools, manta ray pools, and pools filled with eels. You can walk all around these tanks with no rules governing your behavior. You could jump into one of them if you liked. This is the way all life should be, freedom to walk about the planet without all the laws and rules that man has found necessary to invent. It's a shame that we have to force other people not to throw their garbage onto our front steps? I don't know whom I'm quoting, but I remember hearing some place, "Laws are made for and by fools, the wise man living under the law becomes unhappy, the fool living outside the law becomes unhappy." I rest my case, your honor.

I left the aquarium feeling very happy. I was luckier than most of the visitors to that aquarium. I had seen all of those fish swimming out free in their natural environment. Not only had I seen them, but I had also been fortunate enough to live with them, spending hours under water watching them. Unfortunately I even shot a lot of them with my spear gun, sorry about that. Moderation, moderation, that's the answer.

Even further to the west of El Rodadero is a tiny little fishing village. It lies over the mountain, requiring another life threatening bus ride. I shall stop saying this all the time, but just for the record, it is an understood given fact that every time we were to get into a bus, I was scared shitless and we all should have died at any given curve. I would like to give my wholehearted thanks to every holy force in the universe that we finally made it to where we would begin our hiking.

I cannot remember the name of this little village. It was situated in a cove, on a beautiful pristine bay similar to ones I most often discovered on the Pacific side. The mountains dumped right down into the sea. The land was dry at this time of year, covered with brown scrub grass and cacti. I was dying to see what it looked like under the sea. Neither Dina nor Gabriel were very good swimmers, so we had only brought one set of fins and a mask.

To my disappointment, the underwater life was not at all exciting. I did not see any incredible sights nor find any neat treasures. One thing I remember vividly was the amount of sea urchins. There were millions of them out there, more than I had ever seen anywhere. There were lots of cactus plants on the bottom, decomposing. Some were floating on the surface as well. It was not a very choice diving spot. I saw a couple lobsters but there was no way I could grab them out of their holes, with all the sea urchins. I had been stuck by sea urchins many times and I did not want to add to my record.

The very first time I got stuck by a sea urchin was in the Bahamas, in Nassau. I came out of the water with about five of the spines in my heel. I had stepped on one getting up over a wall. A young Bahamian boy noticed me grimacing and came to my aid. "You go to pee on it, mon," he said. Turns out that this is true advice. I did not believe the kid, I thought he was pulling a trick on me, so I went to an older man who was standing near the dock. I asked his advice and he said, "You go to urinate on it, mon." The curing action is a chemical pH balancing that takes place between the urine and the poison. It works to a degree for most stings that one would get from the sea. However a bottle of ammonia works better.

While I was snorkeling that afternoon in the small Colombian village, Gabriel and Dina were making friends with a couple of other foreign travelers and two Colombians. One of the Colombian fellows was traveling and the other lived in this village. The local offered to let us all stay in his house and make beds on the floor. That evening we drank cervezas and had a good time. When we woke up the next morning one of our new friends, the traveling Colombian was gone. He had helped himself to as much of our stuff as he could carry. I still had my money and my camera, but he had taken my backpack and some of my clothes, nothing serious. We had just paid our dues.

This is precisely what I do not like about third world countries. Since my belief is that people are 'as moral as they can afford to be,' in a third world you are going to be ripped off quite often. I expected to run into the thief again one day, wearing my blue jeans and the orange tee shirt with the mirrors on it. It was not to be.

After leaving this small village, Dina, Gabriel and I worked our way westward, slowly exploring this rather populated section of the coast. We passed through the larger port cities of Barranquilla and Cartagena, each night staying in small cheap hotels. I learned a great trick for blasting what I call 'room mosquitoes.' For my procedure to work, the room has to have white walls. That is so one can see the little black mosquito bodies. Rule #1: Make sure your room has white walls. Rule #2: Have a wet towel ready, preferably the size of a dishtowel, a wet tee shirt will work. Rule #3: Get a room with a pretty good overhead light.

Now go to sleep (ha-ha). When you hear the little suckers start buzzing around, jump up quickly and turn on the light. Have the towel in hand and get ready to fire it at the walls. There will usually be two or three of the varmints flying around. You can zap them pretty easily by throwing the towel in their general direction. Throw it hard, it will spread out some as it's flung through the air but you don't want it to be too spread out. You will see some of the smarter mosquitoes sitting on the walls; get them next. Don't worry about waking up the next room; throw the towel as hard as you can.

Then, if the windows have curtains, shake them with your off hand and keep the towel ready in your good hand. There will usually be a lot of them hiding in the curtains. Get em all. Don't give up until you've checked every possible hiding place. Tear the room apart if you have to. Don't spare any women or children. Don't take any survivors. Kill em all. Destroy! Kill! It's them or you! Got the idea? Now go back to sleep and hope that their reinforcements don't show up too soon.

After we passed Cartagena, we got off the lovely bus system and began our hike. Our plan was to hike along the ocean for approximately 30 or 40 days. Our goal was to reach the Panamanian border, 350 kilometers away. I bought a burro that I named Jake. He would be carrying a lot of our supplies. There were other small villages along the way. We could get more food as we went. Basically we ate rice and beans, and vegetables as we could get them. Dina did most of the meal preparations. She was good at it. We kept blocks of raw sugar for making drinks. In Colombia, these sugar blocks are called *panella*. We also gave Jake *panella* to eat.

Our trails were a geographical puzzle as it turned out. Hills, mountains, farmland, marshland, jungles and oftentimes the beaches became our highway. We came upon farmers and ranchers and small little gatherings of ten or twelve families living close to each other. In these small communities there was usually a shack serving as a central meeting place. It would be used for a number of things, a church, a celebration hall, and a place for the doctor to set up his clinic when he came.

The countryside was beautiful, we were walking along the edge of the Cordillera Mountain range. The people we met were all very friendly. They were quite excited to see us. Most of them had never seen a tourist passing through. We came upon a slightly larger village called Arbolettes. Just as we passed through Arbolettes, our trail led us along the beach. It was very hot and humid this day. I decided to jump into the ocean for a swim. After the swim I realized that I had lost my blue jean shorts.

There was a trick that I always used to hide my money. With a razor I would cut the string under the belt loops of my pants, opening up a pocket that exists there. In these shorts, I had rolled up four hundred-dollar bills and slid them into this opening. Fortunately, I had not put all my money there. We retraced our steps and searched for the shorts for hours. They apparently had been lost to the sea. A shame, in Arbolettes 400 dollars was a small fortune.

From Arbolettes we hiked along for two weeks with perfect weather. The trails led inland at times and then back again to the ocean. None of the beaches in this part of Colombia have ever been altered by man in any way. They are exactly as the first Spanish explorer had found them, filled with driftwood. The coastline is not like the Caribbean that I was familiar with. The coastline here is more exposed to strong winds, and so the beaches are not as inviting as those in the Caribbean. The beach sand does not extend for hundreds of meters up to a nice green lawn and blue swimming pool. You do not have the urge to run out onto the sand and lay down a happy little beach blanket.

For the most part, our hiking here was difficult. The amount of driftwood was staggering, huge piles often blocked the entire beach down to the shoreline, which was constantly being battered by huge breaking waves. The surf was always rough and the sea white-capped. Our latitude was 10 degrees north of the equator, and as such, the sand would become quite hot on sunny days. Actually, the beaches were much friendlier from a distance. The climate in this part of Colombia is hot and humid.

One of the things I always do when walking along beaches is to search for two small seeds. One is called the ojo de venada or deer's eye, and the other is corazon del mar, or sea heart. The ojo de venados, sometimes called ojo de bueys' or ox eyes, are found throughout the world on most tropical beaches. They are hardwood seeds resembling a buckeye in size, although each one is unique in its coloration. They are somewhat flat with a black band running around them. Some have a little yellow color above the band and resemble miniature cheeseburgers.

It is said that ojo de bueys will bring good fortune to those who find them. They were once used as trading objects, like the cowry shells in the South Pacific. I have seen buttons and earrings made from them. It is possible to sand them, making them shine like ebony. I often carry ojo de bueys in my pocket. They will shine more as you carry them around. The seed comes from a vine, which grows in the rainforest, often near water, or close to a river. To me, these seeds are precious jewels. I once inlaid a small gold coin into one. The beaches in this part of Colombia are filled with them.

For many years I never knew where the Corazon del mars came from. One day, not so long ago, I discovered its origin. It was on an uninhabited rainforest island, 300 miles off the coast of Costa Rica, a rather famous island, Isla de Coco. This island, which is in a direct line with The Easter Islands and the Galapagos, supposedly hides billions of dollars worth of Pirate treasure. During my visit to this special island I found the tree bearing the corazon del mar seeds.

I was climbing up a small mountain hand over foot, lugging camera gear through a muddy trail. Supposedly, Isla de Coco is the wettest island in the world. Reaching the top of a very steep climb, I paused to rest. From this vantage point I could see much of the Island and beautiful Chatham Bay where our ship was anchored. The sun was shining brilliantly, I could see a waterfall gushing into the sea. I felt so fortunate to be in this place. It was one of those wonderful moments that we experience in life. I was setting up a shot and looked down at my feet, there was the corazon del mar. It had dropped from a tree that I was standing beneath. At that very moment a white dove flew directly overhead and began fluttering, hovering above like a helicopter. In Costa Rica this dove is known as the Paloma del Paz, the Dove of Peace. It was quite a memorable moment for me.

Both of my favorite beach seeds work their way to the rivers, get washed out of the mouths and into the sea. They float around the sea for miles, drifting along for months. Eventually they float up to the beach becoming part of the driftwood. It has to be my imagination, but it seems when I find one, there are always more very close to it. On this journey, on the beach of Colombia, I could not collect many seeds. I looked at them all, and made note that maybe one day I would return here.

Our normal hiking routine would be from early morning until 4 or 5 o'clock in the afternoon. Since we were near the equator, daylight and darkness were of equal lengths. We probably hiked 8 or 9 hours a day, allowing ample time to set up camp and collect firewood before nightfall. Gabriel and I would do those chores and Dina would tend to Jake and the food supplies, keeping the food bags tied up in trees away from any animals. Most of the time we stretched our tarp and plastic between two trees making a lean-to tent.

In good weather Dina and I would sleep alone, but oftentimes it would be all three of us huddled under the tarp. Dina and Gabriel began having personality conflicts. They would often argue about minor points. She refused to sleep next to him, so I would always sleep in the middle.

When we hiked through the marshes we had to stretch hammocks in the trees and sleep above ground. I remember spots where there were thousands and thousands of land crabs everywhere. As we walked through these areas, it would be like a rippling crab field. Wherever we were, the crabs near us would be underneath the mud, hiding in their holes. Ten meters ahead of us they would all be standing very close to their holes, waiting for us to approach. Twenty meters ahead they would still be wandering about in the mud. A million crab eyes would be staring at us at any given time.

As we took a step, those crabs closest to us would dart down into their holes. The next platoon beyond them would be walking toward their holes. Behind us, they would be coming back out of their holes. There were small ones and big ones, and blue ones and red ones. Everything was happening in unison as we hiked on. From an aerial view it must have looked like a precision marching band of crabs. We were like their band directors making them do "the Wave."

One evening we were about to set camp in a small clearing above the ocean. We were in cattle land. A young cowboy came out to meet us as we were beginning to put up our lean-to. He and his family were the owners of this land and much of the surrounding land as well. They had a small house made from sticks with a palm-thatched roof. His land was quite beautiful, we had stopped because of the view. Our chosen site was on a little plateau, a small cliff separated us from the beach below. The young man was so interested in who we were and where we had come from. He stayed with us late into the evening, sitting around our campfire. He gave us many vegetables and would not accept pay. He wanted to sell me the land that we were on. When I calculated the price from pesos to dollars, it was only $600. It was a large piece of land, perhaps ten or twenty acres. He would build me a house like his for another

$600. I thought about it seriously, but realized if I were to buy this, I would stop here. At the very least, be slowed down from knowing what lies down the trail. As things were, all of the land was ours already, as long as we didn't abuse it.

When we left the next morning he came again to say good-bye and offer us milk. That was a treat for us. I insisted that he accept a tee shirt from my bag, one with English writing on it, which was very popular for Colombians. He accepted the shirt in a shy manner and quietly handed me a small item from the pocket of his ragged shorts, it was a corazon del mar. The corazon is shaped like a heart, slightly larger than the ojo de buey.

As I mentioned it is an extremely hard wood. Somehow he had hollowed the seed out from the top. At the apex of the heart was a little cork he had made to fit. On the side was glued a piece of sharkskin. Inside the corazon were small wax matches, typical in Colombia at the time. The sharkskin was used to strike the matches. I kept this gift as one of my most treasured pieces from that journey. In later years I passed that corazon on to someone else whom I knew would cherish it as I had.

Some of our days, the hiking was very strenuous, going up and down mountains in the hot and often humid environment. During those days, we would walk for hours without speaking, preserving our energy. When the trail would take us from inland back to the sea, we were always relieved, because of the ocean breezes. At one campsite, I looked back along the coast toward the direction from where we had come. That day's hiking had been all inland. It was the first time we had been back to the sea since breaking camp early in the morning. Perhaps we had been hiking for ten hard hours. When I looked back down the coastline, I recognized the point of land where we had our previous night's camp. I felt accomplished. It was a good feeling. I knew that I was experiencing the same emotions that many of my forefathers must have experienced, those that had lived before cars and boats and trains, before the industrial revolution.

Our burro Jake was something else. He had a personality like a mule. Most of the time he would hike right along with us, but other times he would become intentionally paralyzed. Nothing we could do would get him to move. I would jerk on his rope, and then try to talk to him very sweetly like one would talk to a pet dog, first in Spanish, then in English. I'd jerk on him again, try the Caribbean slang on him. Ole Jake was really a trip. We all loved him. He would make us laugh so much. Sometimes in the middle of the night he would start his hee-hawing or whatever you call it, waking us all up. He would do this for about ten minutes and then go back to sleep. One of the worst experiences with Jake was when he got stuck in the mud.

Dina, Gabriel and I had made it OK over a stretch of soft muddy ground, but Jake was too heavy and sunk down to his chest. We got the pack and supplies off him and hoped that he would be light enough to get free, but it wasn't so. Each time he struggled, he sunk deeper in. The mud was almost like quicksand. Nothing we tried would free him. For three hours we worked, to no avail.

Finally a local farmer came along and graciously helped us. He freed Jake, accomplishing this by digging down into the mud, actually getting his whole body under it to the point where he reached Jake's feet. He then stretched one of Jake's feet forward and as Jake moved it back to normal, he would inch slightly ahead. Little by little, a foot at a time, an inch at a time, Jake came out. We owed this man a lot. Jake owed him his life.

Not keeping a diary, I never knew what day it was or in accuracy, how many days we had been hiking. I believe it was some time after the third week when we reached the furthest most point heading west on our trail. We had a beautiful campsite. Had we been able to see across the Bay, we would have been looking directly at Panama. The winds had died off and the sea was calm, we all went swimming in the warm ocean. Prior to this afternoon, it was always me, swimming alone. Dina and Gabriel would swim in the rivers but never in the ocean. That evening they appeared to bury the hatchet and work out their conflict. We had a wonderful stew that Dina prepared with yucca and chicken (actually it was a rooster). She called it Sancocho, which is one of Colombia's national dishes. Things were turning around for us all. The mood was better and our route turned due south. However, very soon we were to encounter one serious problem.

The problem was with Jake, and it was to alter our plans. He had developed a large sore on his back from the pack. Our attempts to cure it with sulfur powder had not worked and we could no longer travel with Jake. I thought about shooting him like they did in the Old West (only kidding). At this point we were one day's hike from a rather large village, Turbo. We took the pack from Jake's back, doubling our loads and strenuously made it to Turbo. It was to be our first night in a long time of sleeping in a room, a dry room with a real roof.

Turbo is situated directly on the sea in a very marshy area, the houses are all built up on stilts with elevated wooden walkways connecting everything. The place is not very sanitary. It has no sewer system. Everyone there seemed to be happy and content however. There were docks with many small motorboats. I remember seeing all these large green duffel bags sitting on the docks and being loaded. In later years I met someone who told me that Turbo is a major port for shipping out marijuana. It was probably true.

After a good night's sleep we went to the dock to see what other options we had for reaching civilization. There were many boteros, men with long dugout boats, who were transporting supplies and people in and out of Turbo. I worked a deal trading Jake for passage for the three of us to a larger city, Quibdo. Giving away most of our camping supplies we boarded a long narrow dugout. The boat was probably ten meters long. At the bow was a small covered hold. One of our passengers, an older woman, had a burlap bag with three small pigs, which she threw into the hold. Then came a big pile of coconuts, then came mangoes, and then we sat, with about six other passengers. There was no extra room in the boat, to be sure.

Instead of heading down river, we left the dock and turned backwards. I discovered that we were heading back to the river's mouth, the boca, and would be going out to sea. This idea did not please me, I know how turbulent river mouths can be. Even making it safely through the boca, I wasn't overjoyed about our travel plans. We had to cross the Bay and enter into Rio Atrato, the larger river that is the route to Quibdo. As I had feared the boca was rough.

The motor would not hold us against the force of the huge crashing waves. The boteros had a system that worked well. Two of them were needed to get through. They each had a very long pole made from a small tree trunk. Standing in the front of the boat, the lead man would stick his pole into the sandy bottom as the wave approached. The back man used his pole to keep the boat from drifting sideways. It is most important to keep your bow into the wave, if you slip to the side the wave will crash over you, you will be swamped and sink in an instant.

As the waves crashed into our bow, the men would walk up the poles with their hands. Our boat would rise and the men would reach right to the top of the stick. As we descended the backside of the wave the back man would push us forward and the front man would reach out with his pole for the next position. We gained a little ground until the next wave came. It was a frightening experience; our lives were truly hanging on the skill of these two men. The pigs were squealing in the hold, Dina was sobbing her heart out.

The boteros were quite proficient; we made it out to the ocean, started the motor and began our ride across the Bay. We immediately came to a narrow channel between two giant rock piles. The water was very rough there as well. This was affectionately referred to as the tiburon pass. Tiburon is Spanish for shark. I know for a fact that bocas are often filled with sharks. I had always heard that they gather at the bocas to feed on freshwater fish. I knew a little bit about shark behavior and I didn't believe the story, until one time when I was flying low over a dangerous boca in Panama.

Being above them on the small plane I saw clearly 40 or 50 sharks, directly in the waves. They weren't there for the surfing.

Our next surprise on this boat trip came late in the afternoon. We were informed that the trip across the bay would take longer than one day and that we would be sleeping on a tiny island. It was nice to get off the boat and out of the sun. It was good to stretch and walk around. We had been so jammed into this boat with no room to wiggle. We were three people who hadn't stopped walking for over four weeks.

Now the unpleasant parts were, number one; we had no sleeping gear and number two; the island should have been named Mosquito Rock. It was a miserable night. Mosquitoes are the scourges of the tropics, much worse than snakes in my opinion. They carry malaria, yellow fever, dengue and God knows what else that's yet to be discovered. The only good I can possibly think of is that they feed bats, the little hijo de putas. So be it for the ecosystem.

The following day we entered the river. It's always much easier going into the boca from the sea rather than going out to the sea from the river. An experienced botero will ride the crest of the wave, no problema. The safest time to take on the boca is when the tide has reached its height and is about to recede. This is called the ebb. Many, many people have drowned going through bocas. I knew two or three personally and I myself have been swamped in a boca and almost sunk. Most tourists are better off not knowing these things.

We had now crossed from the state of Cordoba into the state of Choco. This Pacific State is very sparsely populated and is mostly a thick rainforest. It seems that there are many spots in the world that lay similar claims to geographical or ecological curiosities. For what it's worth, the Choco jungle boasts of holding the record for the highest amount of rainfall. Colombia claims to have the highest number of species of plants and animals per unit area of any country in the world. I am not very good at plant identification, but I know that any rainforest, and I've been in many different ones around the world, all have incredible diversity, the likes of which, cannot even be compared with a temperate forest. One can walk on a rainforest trail for over a hundred meters and never pass the same species of plant.

The animals I do know and recognize. In the Choco there are jaguars, ocelots, peccaries, tapirs, deer, armadillos, numerous species of monkeys, thousands of different birds and even the rare spectacled bear. In some parts of Colombia the rivers have piranhas and electric eels. For me there is no greater pleasure in life than being amongst these animals. To spot animals in the wild reassures me, giving hope that we humans will not destroy the world. Change it; absolutely, positively, no doubt about it, for certain we have done and are still doing that. If only we could walk more softly and practice moderation.

After traveling up the large Rio Atrato for six hours, I realized that Quibdo was not the destination of this boat. Quibdo was many miles away and our botero was only going a few villages up river. We de-boarded at the first village where Gabriel noticed a car. It was a Russian made jeep, a Gaz. We discovered that there was a road from Turbo to Medellin. It wasn't much of a road, but if we could get back to it, we could catch a bus from there.

Ah yes, back on the wonderful bus. I can say one good thing about the Colombian busses; they have interesting, colorful, elaborate and wild paint jobs. They all look like they came from a Grateful Dead concert. It looks like they were put on one of those spin art things from the county fair. Even the lug nuts on the wheels are painted different colors. I've even seen them where each side of the nut was a different color. That's like six different colors on one nut.

So Gabriel went up to the man who owned the Gaz and hired him to take us back to the road towards Medellin. Like the boat, the jeep took two people to navigate, one in the seat and the other standing outside on the running board. The poor guy on the running board had a terrible job. Every time we would come to a big mud puddle he would have to run out and walk all through it to find the hardest ground and best spot to cross. Even when he wasn't in the mud puddle, he would be getting a continual mud bath from the front tires. Within ten minutes of our journey, he looked like one of the mud people from the rock festival. We didn't exactly stay clean ourselves for that matter.

After getting tossed around in this jeep for hours, we made it to the highway, just as night was falling. It was really a tough trip. There were times when we were all outside of the Jeep in the mud, pushing to get us unstuck. I have no idea where our drivers stayed that night, but we were dumped off in a dirty pile by the side of the road. Eventually we were able to flag down a bus and hop on. It didn't matter to me if the bus driver were to kill us all at that point, I fell fast asleep. I woke as the sun was rising. On board the bus, was a radio DJ who was telling jokes and entertaining everyone. His voice was deep and powerful. Only once before had I heard such a deep voice, an undertaker at one of the funeral parlors that Billy Bush and I had visited.

The bus ride to Medellin went along well, no accidents. We were crossing the Andes. This particular range was called the Cordillera Occidental. Many of the vistas were breathtaking. We saw more of the beautiful mountainous countryside, from a road this time rather than a trail or a river. We ate more empanadas and other bus window food. The Colombian people are totally uninhibited. Everyone on the bus was having a big party, especially with the help of the DJ. They were always laughing, singing, and interacting. In the USA bus rides are a sobering experience, quite different than here.

Arriving back in Medellin, at my suggestion, Dina and I stopped in a bookstore, which sold books in English. Even though I was not expecting to hear English, I thought, at least I could read it for a change. It was in this small store that I discovered Billy Burroughs had written a book. It was the story of our trip together in New York.

Eventually Dina, Gabriel and I went our separate ways. With our romance fading, Dina and I slowly drifted apart. Gabriel went back up into the mountains and continued making art. I saw them from time to time, usually when they came to the Club.

La Cajita de Musica was now open and going strong. Mario and Benjamin were quite excited. The club had become an instant success. Mario had set up a fine sound system with large speakers throughout the club. From the States, he had brought down the latest popular music and the local rich kids were all flocking to the club. It was the 'happening' place to be. The restaurant was being pushed out the door and never would have a chance to develop. Mario's original idea was to serve dinners from 5 until 10 and then open the other rooms for music and dancing. As it happened, all the hip young people in Medellin wanted to come for the music, it overwhelmed the dining idea. In a short time the restaurant section closed completely.

There was one other popular Disco Club in town, EL Poco Loco. It became the second choice. One evening Mario, Ben and I discussed the idea of bringing in a live rock band. It sounded like a great idea to me. I offered to return to the States, hunt up a suitable band and bring them down. This was all going to be done at my expense and as such I would have an interest in the club. We worked out an agreement and I became a silent partner.

I returned to Miami and searched for bands. It was difficult to find a group that was free enough or willing to take on such a job. The members had to be young with no commitments, and they had to own all their equipment without any payments due. And of course they had to be naïve enough to jump into this crazy scheme. Their end of the bargain was that they would get the experience of their young lives, all room, board and expenses taken care of, but no guaranteed money. Hopefully as the club made money, they would receive a fair salary. I found just the band: Pann, Carl, Jimmy and Randy.

SEPTEMBER 30, 2020

Watched the debate last night and it was very difficult. I just kept feeling sorry for Joe. He doesn't have it as a debater, and facing the narcissist, lying bully turned him into a not so impressive candidate in my eyes. Many times he was stumbling for words and often he struggled to make his points. I kept thinking that I wish it was Kamala up there and not Joe. Of course this doesn't mean that Joe is not my candidate. I will feel comfortable about his abilities at the helm. It's just that he stinks as a debater. He would often direct his gaze at the camera and attempt to talk directly to the people. Again, this was not the best tactic and I wish I could warn him off from doing this again.

Having working cameras and conducting hundreds of interviews in my life I had learned that when someone looks directly at the camera they are consciously going right into the viewers' living room, and sometimes the person is not invited or welcomed. In this case there would be many viewers who do not want Joe Biden in their living room. In any circumstance this tactic of looking directly at the camera should be done very sparingly and carefully, which our boy Joe did not do. Honestly it was a sorry approach and made him look desperate.

But Trump, as expected, was worse. He continually interrupted and seemed to reject the basic idea of allowing American voters to hear from both candidates. He boasted, lied and was as obnoxious as he always is. The whole debate was a mess. Trump was often reprimanded by the moderator, Chris Wallace. Joe called him a 'clown' on a couple occasions. Trump began railing on Biden's son, calling him a loser and a nobody. I will not watch anymore debates between them, however I will watch Kamala vs. Pence and hopefully will not feel bad at the end.

Recently I find myself dealing with an unfamiliar emotion, if stress can be called an emotion. Along with the many disruptive life conditions that I now have, the mental pressure that I feel when I think of this world being the future of my children and grandchildren is taking a toll on me. Fear has a way of disguising itself in some people, and I think I'm one of those. As everything around me becomes more unstable, I find it difficult to know what to preserve and even more difficult to focus on what could be.

Whatever society may claim, it can control you. Sometimes I just don't feel that I am up to the fight.

In all of my political ramblings, I have deliberately avoided the one issue that recently has become the strongest influence upon our democracy. The issue that many people, journalists in particular, are aware of. The issue that is more powerful than either of our presidential candidates, or the platforms that they promote. This is a platform more powerful than our country itself, a global platform that extends beyond borders. Of course, I am referring to our social media platforms. At the forefront is Facebook. I don't use Facebook, I have no need or use for it, therefore I am hardly an expert, which is why I haven't gotten into writing about it. But I believe the time has come.

There are experts, and I am able to listen to them and read their essays on the subject. Those experts have exposed the crimes that are being committed by these media platforms. The way they target humanity has brought about more divisiveness than even Trump can accomplish. Their purpose is to make money, and they have no concern about the damage that they do. They have almost destroyed our free election by influencing the results. The Russians and the Chinese know this and they are now taking advantage.

All of these similar platforms are responsible, but I shall lump them all together and call them Facebook for now. By storing personal data on all the users, Facebook is able to analyze a person's behavior, their likes and dislikes. They then profile them politically, and use this data to target advertising and worse to spread false information. Sadly, what happens on Facebook, stays on Facebook.

It's impossible to research anything. Nobody can find out what the ads are, how much money is being spent for them, who has been placing them, or even what Nationality they are. In America we don't have sensible election campaign finance laws, but we do have laws that prevent foreign states from interfering. Well, we can forget those laws, Facebook openly disregards them. We have no idea of the full extent of it.

By appealing to extreme groups, and supplying them with biased news feeds, they accomplish two things. First, they stir up emotions, hate and fear, unfortunately all negative emotions. Secondly, they push extremism. It has reached a point that is dangerous. The saddest thing is that Facebook is sowing hate and fear all across the world. The gods of Silicon Valley have the power. 100 years of electoral laws have been destroyed by technology, our laws are broken, our democracy doesn't work anymore.

It is ironic that Facebook set out to connect people and it is now driving them apart. No one really wants this, but as most people sit back and play with their phones, they are letting it happen. If there is any chance to change this, we must take back control of the power that Facebook and all the other tech companies have given themselves.

I'm of the opinion that every day must start with an historical perspective and when I do that, it is very sad. I know that most recent generations have had the thought that they might have been better off in the old days. I would have to be willfully ignorant if I didn't feel like that now. Today I'm finding it very hard to tip my scale in the right direction. As for the fire, there is still a lot of smoke, but we are safe.

Tomorrow would have been my neighbor and close friend, Susan Buck's 77th birthday. I have been helping Stu prepare for a memorial gathering at their house. Many family members and friends will be there. This was on the card that was given to me at the funeral home.

In honor of Susie, "Give what's left of me away to children and old men that want to die. And if you need to cry, cry for your brother walking the street beside you. And when you need me, put your arms around anyone and give them what you need to give me. Look for me in the people I've known or loved. Love doesn't die, people do. So, when all that's left of me is love, give me away. I'll see you at home."

29

October

The memorial for Susan yesterday was a combination of sadness and happiness. There were many people from different places coming together to pay homage to Susan and to give support to Stu and the kids. Stu had a very large tent erected in the driveway with tables underneath for the food and drinks. In the mid afternoon a speaker was brought out and Stu began reading a brief history of he and Susie, a eulogy. At times his voice cracked and tears came, then Willie, then Robbie, and more sadness and tears. The mic was passed around and a number of people spoke about their relationship with Susie and a memory of a special moment, or a special trait that Susie possessed.

Before this began, I was by the road directing people as they parked in the fields. The sky was filled with smoke but I believe it kept the temperature from being unbearable. As is so often the case in today's world, the lesser of two evils. The prediction was for another record breaking heat of 104. I remembered many of Stu and Susie's friends from the old days. People I had partied with, taken trips with, sometimes sporting events, and often up to Lake Tahoe. Once a group of us went to the Mexican Baja together on a fishing, (and partying) trip. Most of Stu's brothers and sisters were there. The one noticeable feature was how time has changed all of us. Some have suffered illnesses, others were walking with

364

difficulty. Stu's brother Steven, who was once a vibrant piano player in a number of bands, now struggled to move about with an oxygen bottle. I could elaborate with more examples, they all lead to the same point. Susan has reached the destination where we will all be going, slightly ahead of us.

My close friend Toni, as I helped her to park, got out of her car and immediately told me her story. Earlier in the week she had called a psychic hoping to get some insight and comfort about her ex husband Marshall, who had died a couple of years ago. The psychic said, "There is someone here who is trying to come through. Someone you know who has just recently died. Do you know someone who has died recently?" It was Susan.

The psychic knew about the problem saying it was something to do with her colon, but that wasn't the actual cause of her death, all true. She then said that the woman wanted Toni to tell her husband and her two boys that she was alright. Toni said she started crying at that point and was totally in shock. Toni is not one to exaggerate or make things up and I'm not lying or putting a slant on this. This is what happened, take it as you like.

I woke up this morning with a text from Abel. Trump and his wife Melania have got Covid. They are now self quarantined in the White House for a minimum of two weeks. I'm not sure how political actions will progress forward. It is now speculation with all the experts from both sides weighing in, giving their opinions. Apparently he has mild symptoms, unlike his buddy Boris Johnson, the Prime minister of England, who had also contracted the virus, and nearly died from it.

Will it now continue to be politics as usual, absolutely not. Strategists have a new bullet to put into their weapons. The question will be where do they aim their gun and when do they shoot it off. Can such an occurrence as this change the election, absolutely so. There are talks of postponement, of conspiracy. I think it might be time to turn off the news.

30

Back to the USA

1973

It is now the early part of 1973. The United States and North Vietnam have just made an agreement to end the war and bring our soldiers home. Times in the United States have changed since I left. Being back in the States was a slight culture shock for me. For the most part, I had some changes that needed to be made in myself. Many people here were still smoking pot, cocaine was beginning to come across our borders, but I was finished with that part of my life. I had done speed with Billy Burroughs, and acid with Timothy Leary. Once I sat out on our lawn and did cocaine with the governor of Antioquia, in Medellin. I was through with drugs. Like John Lennon, and Richard Alpert and so many others, I turned to Eastern religious philosophy to find some answers.

I had enough adventures for a while and so decided to stay close to home. In West Palm Beach I noticed a new building being built with a very impressive metal sculpture of Atlas holding up the world. A new chain of health spas was being developed. It was the beginning of a new wave. There were young people who were just beginning a world of drugs, but others were beginning to become health conscious. With my background training, I stopped in to investigate. The 'European Health Spa' had just opened. The Mormon religion was going into the health business, popping these impressive spas up all over the country.

I talked to the Director of the Spa. He had been imported from Salt Lake City. He was a nice man, not too insistent that all walking, breathing human beings should become Mormons. I appreciated that. I talked to him about massage. The club had no facilities for offering massages. They had a suitable room, but no plans developed along those lines. Nor did the head offices in Salt Lake as I was informed. I made a deal with him. I would become the club's masseur and prepare him a plan to begin an exclusive Mormon Massage School so to speak. In the course of my schooling, I had taken Florida State Board exams and was certified as a professional masseur.

I will not forget the day I received that certification. The test was administered in Miami and spread over two days. I chose to spend the night in Miami and leave my car on the street. When I came to retrieve it, to my surprise, it was sitting on blocks with no tires. Not only did it have no tires, but also it had no brake drums either. It was easier for the nice boys to take off one nut per tire. Bless their little hearts. They must have been working in adverse conditions, being dark and all. And the poor little souls probably spoke very little English, being a long way from home like that. They were probably very homesick for the Mariel prison where they had just been taken from.

Actually, the Mariel prison dumping had not yet taken place, and in truth I am very impressed with what the Cuban people have done for Miami. They are hard working, good people who have established themselves in most honorable fashion and in my opinion, uplifted the Miami area. Maybe a Gringo stole my tires. Have you ever tried to go brake drum shopping on a Sunday afternoon? To whoever stole those tires I have one thing to say, may you rot in hell, and never see your parents again, exactly like the dream I had as a child.

So, I'm thinking, I have got a new career started here. I have been in the States less than a week, and already, I am all fired up about being a Mormon Massage Teacher. I felt as if I would have converted to the religion if that deal had worked out. I knew the

Mormons were almost as rich as the Pope, and I had been so broke for so long, I needed a good in with somebody rich.

I do not mean to be disrespectful, but since I cannot remember the Spa manager's name I shall call him Mr. Mormon. So, Mr. Mormon gives me the room, perfect for a massage room, he provides me with towels and I put in the table and bring my own sheets. I get to keep all the money, and arrange my own hours. It was a great deal for me and helped the club by providing another service for the guests. Within a few weeks I was making more money than anyone was at the club except maybe not Mr. Mormon.

There were some real characters at the club. I will never forget the psychiatrist who was a total lunatic. One day he came into the club and started raising hell with our locker boy. I mean he was yelling and cursing at him like a Marine drill sergeant. The poor locker boy was studying to be a Baptist minister. He was one of the nicest kids you could imagine. The deal was this, the guests were supposed to bring in their own towels and locker boy had been told not to give out any more. Well, when Doctor Psychiatrist was refused a towel, he went ballistic. It is not like locker boy would not have given him one eventually, but he was instructed to deny people at first, preparing them for the new BRING YOUR OWN TOWEL policy.

The direction of the Doc's outrage began at the top of the ladder, with choice words being directed at the European Health Spa organization, extending from Mr. Mormon, and all the way to poor locker boy. It must have been the psyche word of the week that he wound up throwing at locker boy. "You're a hassler, you know that, you're a real hassler, you really like to hassle people don't you, you hassler." Locker boy didn't even flinch, he had the Lord on his side. On this day there was only the one lunatic. I tried to stay out of harm's way on that one.

Then there was the Presbyterian priest who would come in for a massage once a week, every week, same time, right on schedule. His massage was on Saturday afternoon, 3 P.M. Now he was not a particularly strange character, he was very much normal, and a very kind person. For most clients I encouraged silence, but with the priest it was not to be.

We would always talk about philosophy and psychology. When I first met the 'father,' I didn't know he was a priest, and I would freely criticize a lot of the Western religious attitudes during the course of our talks. He would often bring into the conversation many religious principles, and I just rattled on. One day I asked him why he wouldn't be quiet and why we were always getting into these deeper philosophical discussions. At that time he told me that he was a priest and that every day after his massage he would go home immediately to his desk and write the sermon for Sunday's service. I was truly the devil's advocate.

I had to deal with a gay client that was somewhat aggressive. That was a difficult situation for me. I liked the man but I didn't like his manners. His first tactic upon entering the massage room was to lock the door. I would immediately unlock it. His next trick was to place his hands above the table and try to grab 'Swinging Sam' as I walked around. I should have whacked him in the ass a few times, although he might have liked that. I assume that I handled it OK, he never turned me gay, and I never got him pissed off.

The massage service was popular with the clients. On busy days I probably did as many as 14 or 15 half-hour massages. I tried to schedule all my regular clients to receive their massages on the same day, so I had days off and more free time. I had it down to three days a week.

Through the experience I had gained with Carmen and the computer business, I was able to prepare a professional proposal for my Massage School ideas. Mr. Mormon was quite impressed when I presented it to him. He sent the proposal to Salt Lake City immediately. I had researched the subject and had all the money figures worked out. I assumed the School would be established up in Salt Lake and provide Mormon masseurs and masseuses to all the Spas across the country. I waited for word from them, but my idea did not go anywhere. They were not going to buy me, for whatever reason, most likely because I was not a Mormon.

I continued as a masseur for several months. During this time two dramatic things happened in my life. I met the 'juice girl,' Cathy True. Cathy was a very bright University of Florida graduate with a great personality. We fell in love. Why she was a lowly Spa 'juice girl,' I never figured out. Why I was a lowly Spa 'massage boy,' she never found out. The second thing of significant importance is that I began diving again with Artchie. Together these events would change my life and send me into a different direction.

OCTOBER 3, 2020

So Trump is in the hospital now. The world leaders are all sending him wishes for a speedy recovery. There is a list now coming forth of all the other Trump aides and allies who are testing positive. The scenario being reported is as follows: Trump was at the White House Rose Garden last Saturday to announce the nomination of Judge Amy Coney Barrett to the Supreme Court. He attended a rally in Pennsylvania on Saturday night, and another event in Ohio on Monday. He was at a fundraiser and rally on Wednesday in Minnesota, where he did a shorter speech than usual. By Thursday morning Mr Trump would have been aware of the positive test result for Hope Hicks. She is a close confidante to Mr Trump, a presidential adviser and former White House communications director.

Despite having been in close contact with Hope Hicks, he went ahead with a fundraising trip to his golf club in New Jersey. According to public health guidelines he should have isolated himself, after being in close proximity to someone infected with the virus. Others that are now infected are his wife Melania, Kellye Ann Conway, a former presidential adviser who was at the Rose Garden, sitting in the front row without a mask, Senator Mike Lee who was also at the Rose Garden, Senator Thom Tillis from North Carolina, also at the Rose Garden, Bill Stepien, Trump's campaign manager, three journalists who spent the weekend at the

White House or were traveling with Trump. This list will continue to grow. Biden has pulled all his negative ads from the TV. The campaigns are changing, that's for sure. Those with the power to make decisions are swimming in uncharted waters.

One of Trump's allies and someone who also had Covid is Brazilian President Bolsanaro. He immediately contacted Trump with well wishes. This is another leader who is responsible for unimaginable damage to our planet. Under his watch, illegal land clearances, illicit deforestation, and wildcat mining have soared in the Amazon. Very much like Trump, he continues to speak in a defiant tone, railing against the media and socialism. He declared Brazilian sovereignty over the Amazon and denounced what he termed 'radical environmentalism.' His answer to the world's concerns is self praise for promoting an environmental policy that does not exist.

It is beyond any doubt that the number one issue that needs to be addressed by all political leaders is concern for our environment, our planet. First you must see this, then you must initiate action that will help. I'm afraid that people like Trump and Bolsanoro don't even see it.

The problems can only be fixed if we act together as human beings, not as Americans, many of whom think that our economy is the factor that trumps all others (a somber pun), or as Europeans, or Chinese. We must act as earthlings.

It's been well over ten years ago when one evening my friend Brenda and I were babbling on about the dismal condition of the world. Brenda kept saying, "Earthlings first, we gotta be earthlings first." The next afternoon I applied for and bought the domain name "Earthlings First." I never did anything with it and it has probably been canceled. I never paid another fee.

OK, I have checked GoDaddy and found that the name has been taken. I could have gotten "Earthlings-First." However I tried for 30 minutes to sign into my account to no avail. After trying a couple of unaccepted passwords, my attempt to change it failed. The message said that I have been sent a code which I need in order to proceed to the next step. I checked all three of my emails and no message. I then went to the telephone, hoping to get human help. My wait time (due to Covid) was to be 60 minutes.

"Do you want to wait while listening to music, or in silence?" Ha, so anyone who wants to get "Earthlings-First" can go get it with my blessings, and Brenda's I'm sure.

It's 4:15 in the afternoon. I just left the house for the first time today. It's 103 degrees and windy. The smoke has been blowing away from us, clearing the sky. Our gain is most certainly a hazard for people on the other side of this fire in Napa County. So far, nearly 3 million acres have been burned in California, and we still have a lot of the fire season remaining. This is almost double the record of any previous year. This fire is only 6% contained.

OCTOBER 4, 2020

I left off with fire news, finally something good to report. It appears as if within a week, because of a current hurricane breaking up in the Pacific, the west coast could see a rainstorm head in. We shall see.

The hot political topics of the day are, of course, Trump's condition as he is being treated at Walter Reed Memorial Hospital. Conflicting reports continue. His doctors say he is doing well. Mark Meadows, the White House chief of staff has said that his vital signs are alarming. It seems that the next few days are critical. The virus symptoms begin with mild fever, etc. but can worsen after six or seven days. It has also been reported that before his doctors can speak publicly, anything they report must be OK'd first by Trump. The debate fiasco and the releasing of his tax records are also big news this week.

I hadn't even talked about his tax forms. I'll be brief, in the past 10 or 12 years, he has paid little or nothing in Federal taxes. For the last 2 years his tax was $750, and his supposed business and personal debt was a minus $400 million. Either he's a cheat or the world's worst businessman. Many of his business deductions are a ridicule to the fairness of our system. It is so sad, insulting and absolutely shameless and dishonest.

When this all came out to the public, I wondered how he could possibly get away with such a blatant crime. I found with a little research that the IRS operates disgracefully. Of the 1.5% of taxpayers that are audited, the super rich are not even considered. They have teams of tax lawyers that will fight and tie up the IRS in court for years. The IRS therefore doesn't bother and goes for the rest of us.

When Face the Nation went out on the streets to get an average person's opinion, the result was to be expected. A political cross section showed that nobody has changed their position. It is unbelievable to me how polarized we are, and how dangerous America has become. Although Trump often called the virus a hoax and openly ridiculed people that wear masks, his contracting the disease has had no effect on his followers. Of course the term idiot compassion comes to my mind.

My biggest concern now is what affect the election will have on our once stable democracy. For the past four years our great country has been, and is even more today, being torn apart and morally devastated by the divisiveness. We are in peril, without any efforts being made to change things. The only hope that I see is if Biden wins by a landslide and Trump must then transition the presidency peacefully. This is unlikely. I'm afraid the worst is yet to come.

Trump has been setting things up with his continual claim that the Democrats are rigging the election and that mail in ballots will all be fraud. If he loses, he plans to bring the election results to the Supreme Court and have his appointees hand him the presidency. I am afraid that the America I have known all my life is gone. The rest of the world is watching. My passport no longer beams with the pride of a great country. Its power that once allowed me access to every other country in the world, is now being blocked at the international borders.

Of course I am sick at heart over this situation, this loss of freedom. More importantly, I feel the bitterness, and at times must deal with keeping my spirit up. I have continually written about the many solutions I have discovered over the years to handle the negative side of life. I truly believe what I have said, and I know I can and must practice what I preach.

When I look at the positive, the one piercing fact above all else is this. I'm still here on this beautiful planet, unlike Susan. I am healthy, unlike many others that I saw on Thursday. My faculties are intact, unlike Suzanne. Holding such a perspective, I don't dive toward the gloom or drift towards pessimism. Before I sat down at this computer, thirty minutes ago, I was traveling in my timeline, recalling many special moments that I had spent with my parents as a young child. In those days my father especially loved to drive across the country and show us kids the beauty of the diverse continent on which we live.

We would plan each day as we progressed along and looked at the maps. Mom and dad had an overall plan but even for them every day was an adventure and subject to change. This was the way I was shown, I was taught, to live. From Florida to Washington, Maine to California, from Canada to Mexico, we saw it all. It was all real, nothing virtual, no GPS to take control, no cell phones to disturb or distract us. We were indeed the 'sole masters of our fate.'

So fortunate am I to have had such enjoyable experiences. Being able to go back in my memory and spend time again in these places with my parents is a precious gift. They directly gave me the ability to do this, by demonstrating life without fear of the unknown, life without stress, with faith. It became part of my shell. It is "Who I am Now."

OCTOBER 9, 2020

For the past 5 days I have been working at my friend Andrew's house doing a bathroom remodel. Working alone lifting up heavy sheetrock to the ceiling is a task. Still able to do it, even at 74½. I have today off waiting for Andrew to pick the tile needed for the next phase. During the week, craziness from the White House continues. Trump left the hospital saying that his doctors have the cure for Coronavirus. Of course that is another absurd lie. He went back to work and one of his first actions was to call off all negotiations for the stimulus bill. Congress and most of his party are shocked. Whatever his reasoning, the move can not help his hope for re-election.

A vice presidential debate took place a few nights ago between Mike Pence and Kamala Harris. The two candidates did act in a somewhat more civil way, although refusing to stop rambling when the time limit was up. Pence was the worst and on occasion Kamala Harris responded similarly, I believe in an effort to get equal time. However Pence would never stop doing it and hardly ever answered the questions that were given him. I cannot grasp how anyone could possibly not see the valid points that Kamala continually brought up, and still side with Mike Pence and the Republican platform. Unquestionably I approached this debate biased, but any sense of open-mindedness that I have left would not let me be swayed towards Pence.

I continued my practice of trying to look deeper into the person, somewhat filtering their words and searching for the overall truth of their ideas. By this method and combining fact checks, Kamala Harris comes way out on top. Pence isn't as bold in his lies as Trump, however most of the time when he speaks, "The President and I this, the President and I that," it's like evil bats flying out of his mouth, coming from a dark cave. He may believe what he says, but I sure don't. It is so sad that we have come to this divisive state. Without any doubt, Trump has been responsible for much of this.

He refuses to condemn any political violence and actually encourages it at his rallies and public statements. During last week's debates with Biden he said that the violent white supremacist groups should "stand off and stand by." These hate groups are never condemned by him, rather they are given a rallying cry, in terms, a revolutionary call to action. And it is working. Yesterday the FBI arrested 6 men from a hate group who had been plotting to kidnap Michigan governor Gretchen Witmer and take over the State government.

They had been planning this move for almost a year and had been monitored and actually infiltrated by the Feds. Their plan was to take place before the election. They had bombs and weapons and an elaborate plan including 100s of conspirators. Why? Because of the Democrat governor's response to Covid. She and Trump were repeatedly at odds with their technique on how to handle the pandemic. The *New York Times* reported, "Yesterday's arrests are the latest evidence that a small but meaningful number of Americans believe that violence is the only answer to the country's political divisions. We're seeing more and more citizens expressing openness to violence as more and more partisan leaders engage in the kinds of dehumanizing rhetoric that paves the way for taking violent action."

After seeing such a thing as this, I can only hope that the general population would worry. The Feds have caught this group, but what about others that are out there. They want a civil war and believe that This type of violence is the way to get it started. The assassinations of President Lincoln and John F. Kennedy were the acts of a sole individual. Today our country is so filled with a polarized hate for the opposite side, that thanks to social media many individuals like John Wilkes Booth or Lee Harvey Oswald are being joined by others of like mind. Revolutionary groups are being formed, maybe somewhere a small army is in the making.

It was on this day in 1781 that our country's Revolutionary War ended. The former British colony was on its road to freedom. Today's right wing extremists are so far removed from the people that began the war. Their ideas of freedom are so different from the revolutionaries that fought the British and founded our great country.

Trump is inciting this type of behavior by continually calling Biden and other Democrats socialists who plan to take away all of our citizens' freedom. He doesn't understand that we are a social democracy in the United States. Our first social programs began soon after our Civil War to help veterans of the war and their families. We presently have a social security system, medicare, medicaid, welfare, food stamps, unemployment insurance, Pell Grants for college students, government subsidized housing, child and dependent care tax credits, the list goes on. All of these programs have a huge impact on the way we live today. And there has been resistance to the forming of all of them.

Sometimes these programs succeed and accomplish what they intend to do and in other cases they simply don't. The Republican's want to eliminate many of today's social programs, and to withhold funding for any new ones. In defense of their position, there is evidence, studies that show regardless of existing social programs, poverty levels have not changed in 50 years, nor has the average yearly income for lower earners.

Other studies claim regardless of all the money dumped into public schooling, kids are not getting smarter. The question now becomes, should I believe these studies or look for others that imply the opposite to be true. Or, should I believe these studies and begin to compromise my thinking on these issues. The one thing I do know is that as a politician in charge, as someone who has fought to be our leader, you must not ignore the social problems and do nothing. You must try to change the programs that aren't working, if it's broken, fix it.

When I was younger one of my heroes was Che Guevara. He was a Marxist communist who fought a two year revolution with Fidel to take over Cuba. After working in Castro's government, he then moved on, fighting for human rights and equality in Africa and then to Bolivia. As a young medical student he took a motorcycle trip all around South America and saw the poverty, the hunger and the lack of medical care that was prevalent. He also saw the capitalist exploitation of Latin America by the United States. Because he was smart and empathetic, he turned to a globalist fight for the people.

For the leftist movement he was an icon because of his fight for class equality. To those on the right, he was an authoritarian who promoted a violent revolution. The revolution that was being planned in Michigan has a much different agenda than the political ideology that motivated Che. On this day in 1967, Che Guevara was captured by the Bolivian army and soon afterwards shot and killed. He was 39 years old.

OCTOBER 10, 2020

Today I will forget about politics, forget about the pandemic and be thinking about how wonderful life can be. As usual when Phil and I head out to SF Bay on his sailboat, we will be experiencing the contact with the natural world that every sailor knows. We won't be engaged in a competitive race, but we will be in pretty good winds that will require attention and action on our parts. We will also be sitting back on top of the ocean, gliding along, realizing how fortunate we are.

OCTOBER 11, 2020

There is a war going on between Azerbaijan and Armenia. Shelling and fighting has been raging now for the past two weeks and I was completely unaware, unconcerned. This is happening about 7,000 miles away. I haven't noticed a single mention on any news source that I watch or listen to. From countries in the Mideast, people are being drawn in to fight for their homelands, on both sides. Fighters have travelled from Lebanon, which has a large ethnic Armenian population, to join the fight. Turkey is now participating, and is backing its ally Azerbaijan. Hundreds of people are dying each day. And I had no clue until yesterday as I was crossing the Golden Gate Bridge.

Another protest march was taking place on the Bridge, this time much larger than the other one I witnessed for Belarus on Sept. 6. Yesterday, under the same situation, by chance timing, I saw the marchers, waving red, blue and orange flags, carrying signs which I couldn't read because of my driving. I was able to make out condemnations of Turkey on some signs. There must have been a dozen police cars traveling alongside the marchers. Their line extended from well past the middle of the bridge all the way into the San Francisco entry. I wondered how many other protest marches that I have missed, how many causes that people are fighting for around the world that I know nothing about. Can I worry about all of them? Is my ignorance a willful act? Should I be praying every day for World Peace?

I thought my job yesterday was to get out on the water, become one with the ocean and dump out the stress that I'm carrying into the choppy waves. I didn't plan to dangle my feet in the water and wait for the sharks to attack.

As I drove across the bridge I tried to forget about Armenia, Azerbaijan,Turkey and Belarus. I really don't know how much fight I have left in me. Lately it seems I'm simply trying to exist making the unfair choices that I often see in front of me. I was almost able to postpone any negative thoughts about Trump and his colleagues. That was, after Phil and I had our normal discussions on the subject. Phil, I'm afraid, is leaning towards the idea that we are not going to be through with Trump after November 3.

We hashed out all significant insights we had about our present political situation, or perhaps I should say irrelevant insights. And then, played with the wind, watched the dolphins, took in the cool clean air under the grey skies. It was as if the beginning of Winter was pushing its way toward the bridge. A Regatta was taking place, so there were a lot of sailboats out, participating in this yearly event. I believe they were racing to the three bridges in the Bay. A large freighter came in, obviously from China. It was completely filled with shipping containers, unlike what we had been seeing. Another followed later filled with cars, maybe it was from Japan. Perhaps international trade is beginning a slow return to normal.

The last time Phil and I sailed was the warmest day I can remember ever being on the Bay, an unusual, short sleeves day. It was the opposite yesterday. However weather conditions usually do not affect a day sailor, as I have become. As long as a severe storm is not forecast and a possible fight to stay in control of the sails and stay on course, I will opt for going out.

Up to a point, higher winds and rougher seas do not take away the thrill of sailing. Rougher conditions make sailing a challenge and present a different type of gratification. For the same reason that young people like to take roller coaster rides or watch horror films, living on the edge can be exciting. I believe everyone has the desire for adventure. Sometimes that desire turns into a passion.

31

Back to Colombia

Randy played lead guitar. He was a Japanese American, a small guy with long black hair below his waist. He was the bandleader, the smartest of the group, with all the assurance of youth. He had a gentle face, with somber, clever eyes. Jimmy was bass player. He was a well set up type of guy, bigger, very good looking, and easy going. His hair was blond and thick, of medium length. Jimmy walked stately and his mannerisms were almost noble. Carl played drums. He was the most intense of the three, a truly wild man. His hair was black and curly and bushed out all over his head. He was on the chubby side with a dark mustache and rather shifty eyes. Of necessity, the four of us were to become a close-knit group.

So all the arrangements were made, the guys said their goodbyes to family and friends, and we departed excitedly from Miami. They were leaving the United States for the first time, what an adventure it was to be. We were loaded with equipment, including amplifiers, microphones, stands, speakers, a big drum set, etc. Even for a small group there was a lot of equipment. When we arrived in Medellin, everything from the plane's baggage cargo went directly into the 'Aduana,' the customs department. That means that all the equipment, except for the two guitars that were carry-ons, now became property of the Colombian government. I knew that a small import tax might be levied; I was prepared for that. But I had not realized the extent of hassles and bribes that are part of the routine. It would take 10 days before we got the gear.

That evening, Benjamin met us at the airport. Happy as could be, we all packed into his old Volkswagen, and left the airport. Our first stop was 'El Poco Loco.'

This is where Caesar broke into our car and got the valuable guitar. Caesar was a be-bopping, hot shot, an upscale Colombian. Oh yeah, he was a great musician himself, and he was going to be the manager of the group, and he would help us guys, and he was going to take care of us, and "Don't worry, if anything goes wrong with 'La Cajita,' I'll be there."

He took care of the group all right, beginning with the Les Paul guitar. At least this is how we figured it. He was definitely the number one suspect. We tried various ways of threatening him and trapping him into confessing and giving up the guitar. None of it worked and to this day I still believe that our good amigo Caesar is probably plunking away on that 'Les Paul.'

Mario had a couple rooms in the club for the band. During the following week, the boys settled in and with Benjamin's help, began searching for another bass guitar for Jimmy. Mario and I took care of the Aduana, through legal and illegal routes. One of the head officers who had his greasy fingers in our business was gay and a trifle less than honorable. He made it known that he expected a formal introduction to Randy, ASAP. I sensed his interest was somewhat passionate.

We finally got all the equipment to the club by paying a couple thousand dollars in bond and bribes. Benjamin was able to locate a bass guitar for Jimmy, and we were on schedule for opening night. It was a great night, a huge success. The guys killed the crowd. Most of our clientele had never seen a live band of this caliber. Their stage presence was enough to turn half the female population of Medellin into love slaves. That was not a good thing to have happened. No, no, that was a very bad thing that happened. Carl however was not convinced. He thought that this was the best thing that had ever happened in his life. Jimmy was not too far behind him in that line of thinking. Randy on the other hand was much more cool about the whole affair. He often called Carl and Jimmy a couple of prostitutes. And now the fun was to begin.

'Groupies' are not exactly looked upon favorably in Colombian society. Consider the fact that most of the girls that could afford to come to our club were definitely from families of the upper class. Upper class means money. It also means power, and political influence, we are talking like the governor's daughter here. Into this equation we add pot, psychedelic mushrooms, and cocaine. It doesn't take Signor Einstein to figure out the rest of the story. To make matters worse, within a few weeks of our arrival Mario takes this wild notion that Carl is making a pass at sweet little Mary, his wife. Mario and Mary walked around the club like Mr. and Mrs. Stonewall Jackson. They completely ignored me and became very cold and distant. Apparently they were stuck between a rock and hard place. The band was great for business, but they hated Carl with a passion and wanted nothing more than to boot the guys out onto the street.

The street is not exactly where the guys should be. On those occasions when we would venture into town we created quite a stir. When we walked through the Plaza Bolivar in downtown Medellin, people would stop working. Employees would rush out of their shops to look at us. Everywhere, all around us, from every direction there were hundreds of eyes staring at us. It was like walking through the crab fields with Dina and Gabriel. You would think we were The Four Horsemen of the Apocalypse. This should have given me a clue.

Our band did not belong in Colombia. I was oblivious to the blaring signs about me. I should have been tipped off when on the very night of our arrival; Jimmy's guitar was stolen. The writing was all over the wall, but at my young age, I was not able to read so well. On the positive side, we had some great moments together and all got out of Colombia alive. Incidentally this fact should be known as 'The Great Miracle of Medellin.'

The Colombian churches should have put up a statue of us at the airport, and people could come and stare, make novenas and crawl for miles on their knees to come and give thanks and receive the blessing. A National Holiday is the least they could have done, 'The Day of the Escape of the Four Gringos' would have been fitting. This is not the slightest bit of exaggeration. In all my life I have never been so lucky, as the day I set my feet back on U.S. soil.

Having live music at the club was good for business, the club was doing well before, but now it was the talk of Medellin, and even other larger cities began receiving news about La Cajita de Musica. It was absolutely the number one musical news in Colombia. We were like the hottest show on Broadway.

At this point the only things that Randy, Carl and Jimmy had to their names were their tickets back to Miami. All their equipment was tied up with the paper work at Aduana. As far as the government was concerned the equipment belonged to Mario, and could not leave the country unless Mario signed the papers and released the bond. The guys did not feel very secure about this. They were playing and partying all night, but often in the sobering light of daytime they would come to me and plead with me for reassurance that everything in all our lives was just fine.

This was all a very sticky situation. The guys were stuck, Mario and Mary were stuck, that's for sure, and as for me, I was stuck right in the middle. I had a responsibility to the guys for getting them down here and I had an investment in the club, which I hoped not to lose. Meanwhile Benjamin was trying to smooth things over. In a way, he was also stuck.

One lazy afternoon on the band's day off, Benjamin came into my room and asked me to get the band ready to play a set. His brother and their family were coming over from Bogota. Now the little angels of the band happened to be under the influence of magic mushrooms at that given moment. There was no way that they could get it together to play. There were many rock groups of the time that could have played under those conditions, but not my little angels. They were not as conditioned to the lifestyle of the rich and famous. So they didn't play and Benjamin lost 'face' with his family. To lose face for a Latin man is a fate worse than death. You are no longer a 'macho man.' It is worse than being an unmarried non-virgin of the Renaissance Period.

From outside appearances everything at the club looked simply fine. The band was playing five nights a week to a full house. The music was great and well received. The club was doing a good business and should have been making money. But looking at the club from the inside, from behind the scenes, it was a disaster. No one was communicating, everyone involved was angry with each other, and nobody trusted anybody.

La Cajita de Musica drew regular clients that would often show up two or three times a week. In order to thicken the plot, I would like to introduce some of these characters. First, Fabio Prieto, a well dressed, distinguished, middle aged businessman. Sr. Prieto is very handsome; he is of medium build, thick black wavy hair, slightly graying at the temples and sporting a thick salt and pepper mustache. He speaks perfect English, which he much prefers to use over Spanish. Fabio usually dresses in expensive suits of the latest fashion. In his most casual appearance he would be wearing a blazer or sport coat.

He would generally arrive at the club early in the evening with other guests, always upper class Colombians. They would have one or two drinks and leave early, before the crowd of young people began flocking in. During their visit Fabio would often flag Mario or Benjamin over to his table for introductions to the other members of his party. Fabio did business with politicians and the top business leaders of Medellin. He was a promoter, a public relations man. He worked in all forms of the media including television. Fabio saw big things happening with our band. There was no other rock band in Colombia that compared to 'PANN.' My boys were like the 'Beatles' storming the USA. He wanted Jimmy, Carl and Randy all to himself.

The next character to meet is Primo. I never learned his real name, he was called Primo, which means cousin in Spanish. He was a large man, over six feet tall and overweight with a big stomach. Unlike a lot of Latin males, he wore no facial hair, but was the type that needed to shave after every meal to prevent a beard from appearing. He always dressed casually, often with flower shirts and he always wore shaded glasses. Primo looked like a typical mobster, and he was one. He and his party would never arrive at the club before eleven. He had a lot of money and he threw it around like candy. For that reason, everyone loved Primo.

Since Mario and now Benjamin were both at odds with the band and also at odds with me, I found it difficult to squeeze money from the Club. I was struggling to support the four of us. Primo could see the problem and wanted to help us out. Once when I went to his office to change money, he handed me an extra hundred-dollar bill. Amongst other things, he was a moneychanger and moneylender, but I think his main source of income came from contraband goods. He brought televisions, refrigerators and other industrial goods, including automobiles into the country illegally without paying any import taxes.

Primo maintained an office in downtown Medellin. I would go there to change dollars into pesos. He offered an exchange rate considerably higher than the banks. Primo needed dollars to do his business in the States and I needed more pesos to survive.

Meanwhile back at the club. Benjamin has lost face with his family and he is burning inside, plotting revenge. His idea is to get the band busted and steal their equipment. The first part of his plan was not so difficult. The heat was already on the club big time, brought on by the amorous activities of Jimmy and Carl, especially Carl. He had been screwing around with some congressman's daughter; but decided to dump her, choosing variety over loyalty. The young girl started a ball rolling, which would eventually lead to the club's demise.

In Colombia the government's special police force is known as the DAS. This is the US equivalent of the DEA or Russia's KGB. These DAS agents were raiding our club on a regular basis.

In La Cajita de Musica, my job was standing at the door, collecting the cover charge. Many nights I was greeted by the DAS. Six or seven of them would come bursting through the door. They would immediately stop the band. They would turn all the lights on and begin a haphazard search/frisk routine. Usually they would get a few young people with some coke or pot and haul them off in their wagon. My night was soon to come.

The method that the agents used in conducting a search was crazy. They would spread out throughout the dance floor, begin picking people at random with absolutely no structured order. Sometimes they would miss you completely, other times you would get searched three or four times by different agents. During one of these searches, the agents went into all of the rooms, even our private bedrooms that were attached to the club. I had brought large plastic bottles of vitamins with me from the States when I first came to Colombia, thinking that perhaps I would practice physical therapy. During the search, the agents confiscated all the vitamins and claimed that they were barbiturates and amphetamines.

That night Mario saved me from being hauled away. The agents had me right on the ramp, getting ready to walk me into the wagon. God knows what would have happened had I been taken away. Somehow, Mario got me out of that and by the next morning I was out of Medellin and up into the mountains where Mario and Mary owned a small farm, a finca. I hid out in the finca for over a week, while the club's attorneys apparently straightened the matter out. However, there were some important people that wanted La Cajita de Musica shut down. Busting me would be a good place to begin.

Had I the first shred of intelligence in my head, the next flight to Miami would have had my name on it, in giant capital letters. I sat up on Mario's farm, la la la-ing around, having a good old time, digging up potatoes from the garden, cooking sancocho as Dina had taught me, and making big bonfires at night. Occasionally, I'd walk down the road to the nearest bar for a warm cerveza. My favorite brand was Aguila, Colombian beer with a big eagle on the label. Many of the local *borachos*, drunks, would drink *aguardiente*, Colombia's national drink, like scotch in Scotland, or tequila in Mexico.

After a week of being up on the finca, hiding out from the DAS, Mario told me that the heat was off of me. Our lawyers had worked it all out. As I said before, Mario was 'King Bullshit' so I really never knew if that was true, but he promised he had paid off the right people. As the situation appeared, it seemed safe for me to leave the finca and return to the club, which I did.

Soon after returning to the club from the finca, I called the US ambassador and spoke with him about the trouble with the DAS. His advice was to pack up immediately. There would be nothing he could do for me. Even if I was framed, President Nixon was begging for drug busts in Colombia to make his administration look good. Any bust at all of a foreigner was a feather in DAS's cap. I was seriously planning to negotiate some money from Mario and Benjamin if possible, and make my departure from Colombia.

In the good old days, before the club had become 'Dante's Inferno,' Mario, Mary, Benjamin and I would often take journeys around the countryside. One day we were out on a Sunday drive through the Mountains. The mountains of Colombia are magnificent. If one can survive not being killed by bus drivers, it is a great way to spend a day. . (new chapter)

Colombia boasts the highest coastal mountain range in the world. The Sierra Nevada chain coming from North America splits into three ranges as it enters Colombia, becoming the Andes. The rivers and the valleys formed between are spectacular. Many of the mountain slopes in this area are covered with coffee bushes. On the less steep sections cattle ranches are found.

Our destination that day was a Country Club Resort, deep in the mountains. We planned to arrive in the afternoon for lunch. On Sundays all the rich farmers and cattle ranchers would come to eat, drink, dance, socialize and listen to the bands. The resort had tennis courts and other diversions for the family. . (new chapter)

As we were pulling into the parking lot, a man driving an expensive Land Rover was also just arriving. It turns out that he recognized Mario and walked up to our car. "Mario, Mario, como esta?" He and Mario were old friends who had not seen each other in years. The man was to join us at our table.

Now when I first saw him, he looked vaguely familiar to me. "No," I thought, "I couldn't possibly know anybody out here." This man was a rich cattle rancher, a real Colombian cowboy. He was toting a pistola, a six-shooter on his side, just like the real cowboys from the Wild West. So he joins us at our table, puts his pistola up on the table and orders a bottle of aguardiente. He is sitting directly across from me, pouring us aguardiente shots, when suddenly it all came back to me. I started to feel weak, my knees were shaking and I almost gagged on my aguardiente. The more we drank, the more he stared at me. I remained sitting, stiff with fear, waiting to see 'which way the cat would jump.' Finally he said in a rather heavy accent, "You ever leeve in New York?" I gulped. "You ever work in a French restaurant?"

It was indeed, Jorge, my long lost fellow busboy, my working partner from New York, and the one that I had last seen with a black eye the size of a softball. At this point his pistol was looking much like a cannon. I didn't know whether to shit or run for my life.

It turns out that Jorge and I had worked together during my time in NYC. We were busboys at a French Restaurant, a couple blocks north of the Lincoln Center. The restaurant was open for lunch and dinner and during the in-between time it closed for a few hours. As busboys we had jobs to do during that time and Jorge would often skip out, leaving me with a lot more work. I tried talking to him but things never changed.

One night as all the waiters, Jorge and I, 'the family,' as it was called, were sitting for our meal prior to opening, Jorge came and sat next to me. He had again skipped out that day. So I started in on him. "Don't talk to me," he said. I pushed his plate away from him. He said "You want to fight?" I stood up and fought. I let him have it in the face. I knocked him out of his chair and when he hit the ground his eye was already ballooning up. I have never seen such a black eye in all my days. Jorge was brought to the hospital and I was fired.

So now, here we are meeting again in Colombia. I finally 'fessed up. "Yeah, that was me Jorge." He responded, "I'll never forgeet that punch as long as I leeve." Well, I didn't know how much longer I had to live at that moment. "Yeah, uh, er, I'm sorry about that Jorge. I'm a changed man," I said.

So, I'm alive to tell the story. Obviously Jorge did not shoot me. We sort of laughed about it, with the aguardiente and all. I proceeded to get extremely drunk that night. When we arrived back at La Cajita, I went into our bathroom to puke and passed out on the floor. It was the public restroom for the guests. Benjamin had to break the lock to get me out. As long as I breathe, I will never again pass aguardiente across my lips.

As coincidental as it seems, I discovered that Mario had been a waiter at the French restaurant in New York at the time of the 'famous Jorge punch.' This is how they were acquainted with each other. I did not remember Mario from the restaurant at all, and as odd as it seems, we had never discussed our mutual paths in New York.

Meanwhile, back at the club again, Jimmy, Carl and Randy are living their exotic lifestyles and still playing 5 nights a week. I was trying to get as much money to them as possible. It was never enough. Randy was developing a serious relationship with a cute girl, Rosia. Carl and Jimmy were with different girls every night and had moved away from the club into an apartment downtown.

One late afternoon Randy, Carl and I had left the club in a taxi going over to a not so nice barrio, so Carl could buy some pot. For me, I hardly ever smoked pot. It made me dumber than normal, so I wisely gave it up. On the way back from the barrio, lo and behold, another roadblock. This happened to be the day after Primo had given me the hundred-dollar bill. When we saw the roadblock, I told Carl to stuff the pot into his underwear. His idea was to get it out of his possession ASAP. Well, unknown to me, he slipped it under the backseat, where Randy and I were sitting.

In Medellin every time you see a cop, you look at him as if he were a waiter at your table, and figure out how much of a tip you have to give him. I thought we were somewhat safe at this roadblock and maybe I could just give the cops some candy or toy guns. That was not to be the case. They proceeded to find the pot. Man, it was like they had a Royal Flush in their hand.

In Colombia, a little bag of pot was no big deal. I felt that we could legitimately claim that it was not ours. After all, it was not our car. The Medellin cops were playing their hand well. They did the good guy, bad guy cop trick and finally I was off to the side in a private consultation with the sergeant. We were getting down to the nitty gritty, the part where the money changes hands and we go free. I asked him if I could walk over to the gas station and change the hundred-dollar bill. That was a joke, if there ever was one. I don't know what I was thinking. We were relieved of that hundred-dollar bill in quick fashion, relieved of the pot, and promptly sent on our merry way.

Being involved in the club and living in Medellin exposed me to a different side of Colombia. How opposite from the peaceful country I had experienced earlier. In this new Colombia I never knew what in the hell was going on. The only truth I embraced at this time was, 'you had better get them before they get you.' I felt that this slogan should be emblazoned on the Country Flag. I saw the rampant political corruption, and the lawless society that resulted. In Colombia kidnapping seemed to be the national pastime. You could never tell who was the good guy and who was the bad guy. In Medellin, there were more roadblocks than mosquitoes.

I will never forget the serious situation that developed between Benjamin and myself. He never was able to forgive the band for his loss of face. It all came to a head one day as Benjamin began to initiate his devious plan. On this day a worker came to our club to look at a plumbing problem. I didn't realize that we had a problem. I recognized the man from Primo's office. I had seen him there on occasion. I knew he worked for Primo at times and I was pretty certain that he was not a plumber. Through Primo I learned that the man was a 'bad man' that was sent out to do jobs on people.

I discovered the true reason for his presence at the club. It was a plan designed by Benjamin. He was still seeking revenge on us and he was paying this character to hurt me and scare me into leaving. In this way, he could carry out plan two, which was to get the band's equipment. The 'hit man' had come into the club on that day so Benjamin could point me out, like Judas Escariot.

32

The News

Zac's up, he arrived this afternoon for a short visit and to bring up some things to leave in the house. He is planning a trip to Washington in a week. I'm terribly afraid that Zac will be moving to Washington. It makes sense, California has lost a lot of its appeal. I know it, Zac knows it, everyone in California knows it. Zac has sent out resumes for work, not in the field of neuroscience, but in psychotherapy. He wants to help people who have drug problems and addictions.

Originally Zac's plan was to complete schooling for a Masters degree, then a PHD. Covid has changed all that. It must be impossible for him to imagine sitting in front of his computer screen for years to accomplish this goal. Again I say, nobody can predict the future in such an insane world as we find ourselves living in today.

OCTOBER 14, 2020

Voting has begun, Both candidates are still campaigning, and the polls show Biden has the lead. In some states it's a few points but overall it appears he's leading by as much as 13%. Texas and Georgia are reporting extremely long lines. People are waiting as much as 10 hours in the hot sun. I never remember such a scene as this. The news shows long lines of cars at some drop off boxes, and there are reports of problems with voting machines and some illegal drop boxes. Chaos has begun just as expected. Just what Trump planned on.

The Senate is questioning Trump's appointee to the Supreme Court, Amy Coney Barrett. Senators are trying to pin her down on issues such as the Affordable Care Act and abortion rights. Today is day three of the hearings. I have watched some of it, and with an open mind, I see an honest person. I hope I'm right and she rules on cases without throwing her religious beliefs into the equation. I see a smart, family woman, a mother who has adopted two Black children. I'm not going to worry about this one.

My work on the bathroom remodel is coming along fine. I am setting tile and the end is near. Tomorrow is a day off. I will be back on the water with Phil. It looks like it will be sunny and warm. Pulling sails, tacking and jibing, sitting at the helm keeping on course, and for most of the day, sitting back on my red cushion realizing how fortunate I am.

OCTOBER 15, 1997

Yesterday I was in The Blue Hole. Actually since there are other blue holes around the world I should be more specific, this one is known as The Great Blue Hole. I'm back in Belize now shooting a promotional documentary, hired by a few hotels here in Belize City and on San Pedro Caye.

In the center of Lighthouse Reef, which is part of the Barrier Reef, is this giant circular sinkhole 1000 feet across and about 400 feet deep. It is a prime tourist destination for scuba divers throughout the world. In 1971 Jacques Cousteau came here with his ship The Calypso, and studied it, concluding that it was once a cave above sea level and was perhaps affected by a tilting of the land, an earthquake perhaps. As you dive down you can see stalactites. The Discovery Channel also did a two-hour special on this special place. Researchers with submarines have gone down to study the Great Blue Hole.

I was with a group of divers and had a large underwater camera to record the tourist experience of the Blue Hole. I would station myself ahead of the divers as they swam by in a group, and then I would swim as fast as I could to get ahead of them and shoot again from a different angle. I did this about four or five times before I began running out of air. I had to surface, alone, since my strenuous swimming technique and the heavy camera made me use up my air much quicker.

In the Blue Hole, boats of course can not set anchors, so they generally get upwind, cut their motors and drift across the 1000 feet while waiting for their divers. When I surfaced, the boat was far away. I was tired and the camera, now above water, was weighing me down as I swam toward the boat. It had almost drifted to the edge, which is a coral ring, and just as I got within 15 feet from the diving platform, the Captain, who hadn't seen me, started the motor. I was in front of the boat and I could feel the pull of the prop. As he zipped past me I was almost scraped by the boat's side, and I was giving it all I had left to swim away from the motor and the dangerous prop.

Sparing the details about my mini-panic at that stage, I will say that it was a close call for me. I didn't ditch the camera, which I had rented for the shoot. I was wanting to drop the weight belt and the air tank, but I resisted and swam with all the strength I had. I finally made it to the other side of the Blue Hole where the boat was. I got onto that diving platform totally exhausted but alive, and I watched the other divers as they began surfacing.

OCTOBER 17, 1989

Today we were hit by a major earthquake. I was at the Santa Rosa Grill with Abel, we were having a small dinner party to celebrate Stu's birthday. Stu and Susie were sitting in a booth and Abel and I were in the aisle when it hit. It was just after 5 P.M., the TV was playing at the bar and we were waiting for the start of the World Series. It is a special series for us because the Oakland A's are playing the S.F. Giants. When the shaking began, Abel and I naturally started to leave the building. The quake lasted for about 15 seconds. As we passed the bar, a large neon sign broke loose and crashed to the floor. From what I'm hearing tonight on the news, it is the largest quake to ever hit a large U.S. city, 6.9 on the Richter. Thousands of injuries and a number of deaths are being reported. A Large section of the upper portion of the double decker Bay Bridge collapsed and crushed the people in their cars below. San Francisco has uncontrolled fires from broken gas lines. I'm going to bed now, but I'm sure tomorrow's news will reveal a whole lot more about this tragedy.

OCTOBER 21, 2020

One year ago today is when I received the call about Suzanne's accident. I wrote about this in June and at that time, I planned to be her permanent caregiver. That is no longer the case. As things have developed, it is Sally who has assumed that responsibility. Since Suzanne has left the facility at CNS and returned to her home, I have been slowly giving up the decision making, for two reasons. Suzanne is definitely capable of making her own decisions and Sally is doing what she does, she is a professional caregiver, and I have discovered that I'm not.

Since this began a year ago, I stopped everything that I was doing and began devoting myself to what I felt Suzanne needed. I kept getting the message from everyone I knew that I must take care of myself. My whole purpose for months was to do what I could for Suzanne's health, both physically and mentally. I quit working. After she was released from the facility, I continued to worry about Suzanne's recovery and was accepting the responsibility of the therapy results, the insurance issues, the staff at CNS, and the caregivers that were coming to the house. I felt so much pressure being put on me by Suzanne's distant family and friends. On average I have been receiving two or three calls every day, it eventually took its toll.

The switch in my position began last month when I deliberately didn't answer a call. Then, I chose not to listen to the voicemail. It was getting to be too much, I couldn't do it anymore. Last week when Suzanne called her old boyfriend and invited him up from

San Francisco to come and stay at the house with her, I made the decision to back off and get on with the rest of my life.

OCTOBER 24, 2020

The past week has continued as per usual with daily news. The coronavirus is spiking throughout the country as predicted. Colder weather is forcing people indoors and, as in any flu, this weather brings on an upsurge of infections. The only state that is not having significant virus outbreaks is Hawaii. Many experts say the worst is yet to come. Dr. Fauci, now Trump's nemesis , is saying that it might be time to mandate mask wearing. This will be such a divisive move, so many people will refuse such an order.

Field hospitals are being set up in many cities where beds are again filled to capacity. It's not only the U.S. that is experiencing this second wave. Cases are doubling throughout much of Europe. Belgium, the Czech Republic, and Spain are reporting as much as an 800% increase over the spring peaks.

As for the political situation, Trump and Biden had their final debate a couple nights ago. I was driving back from sailing and listened to it on the radio. I don't feel that Biden helped his cause at all. One of the things he said is that he will work to continue on the path of eventually eliminating fossil fuels. Trump jumped on that one and is now running negative ads in Pennsylvania where fracking employs a lot of people. Biden has been trying to change the ideas that came from his statement by saying that he will only reduce government subsidies. It was a political error, the truth will not be accepted when it hurts people's wallets. The polls open in 10 days. Millions of voters have already cast an early ballot. The numbers are breaking all records for early voting. One of the Republican popular opinions now is, "I don't like Trump's personality, but I prefer the Republican platform, so I will vote for Trump." This election is getting scary.

OCTOBER 26, 2020

Last night PG&E, the electric company, shut off power to my area. The purpose is to prevent a fire caused by falling branches or trees onto power lines. We had strong winds coming from the East. Supposedly after the PG&E linemen check all the lines, we will get turned back on sometime tonight around 10 O'Clock.

This morning I woke up feeling I had an edge on all this, since I have a new generator which I bought last year. Well the first time I needed it, it wouldn't start. I now have a lovely blister from pulling that cord and changing the carburetor settings a hundred times. After that plan failed, I went to work on my trusty old Winnebago. After charging both batteries, putting in a new fuel filter, and playing with that carburetor also, I was able to start up the motor home, get the generator running and run a power cord into the house. This has most certainly been a test of my mental state. If I were depressed, I would never have pulled this off. Depression and motivation have a direct relationship. When depression shows up, motivation leaves.

There is a lot of talk today about depression. For many the pandemic lockdown is the giant culprit. Social media with all of its virtual relationships doesn't quite fill the need for us humans. Tweets and posts are often repositories for fantasies. Google searches do not quite compare to a face to face talk with a friend. Hanging out on Facebook is not the same as walking hand in hand in the park with another real human, someone you care about. These normal practices that have been our way of life since birth, have been taken away from us. And the adjustment is not easy. I'm sure there are hundreds of books being written on this subject at this very moment. Psychologists, psychiatrists, spiritual advisors are busy at their keyboards.

The one thing that I believe to be the most helpful in halting depression is to go out and do something altruistically for someone else. It not only takes your mind off of your personal condition but ironically, it is rewarding action, often helping yourself as much or more than the one you are helping.

Data gatherers are now able to analyze everyone's actions in a way that was unknown twenty years ago. In 2009 Google released a tool known as Google trends. Anyone that uses the internet becomes a part of Google trends. Within the supposed privacy that a personal computer or iPhone appears to provide, people are now revealing themselves in a truthful way, and they are being recorded. The sites they search for, the questions they ask, even the words they use, tells a tale about that person. How often a person uses the word happiness or sadness, anxiety, stress, joy, delight, these are all now recorded forever.

But, we must realize, we are not recorded during a walk in the forest. In this walk, whatever thoughts we choose to present, whatever words we use, sentences we speak, become vibrations that will travel several feet ahead of us and then vanish in the atmosphere. We all now have a choice, to live by walking in the forest, or to live in the virtual world. We can live as a bit of data or we can live a private life, but we cannot do both. I am now going to shut off my generator and stop using fossil fuels. Don't tell the people in Pennsylvania.

33

Back to Colombia

I asked for Primo's help and he assured me that he would straighten up the matter and that things would be turned around. I then confronted Benjamin. I informed him that I knew of the plan and that now, he was the one in danger. We worked things out and came to a truce. Such was my life at that time, as ashamed as I am to tell of it.

When first arriving in Colombia, all things were new to me. I was roaming about a strange and interesting country. All my experiences were exciting and fun, as it was a learning adventure. Then I stopped somewhere, I got off the bus, and did I ever stop at the wrong station. As you can see, a life centered around a nightclub was not my forte. Most of my life had been spent outdoors in nature, at least most of the happy times of my life. I never was a night person to begin with. I now found myself keeping late hours, drinking more than I ever had, and worst of all, doing cocaine with the rest of them. The unfortunate consequence of my serious errors, I became a cold, insensitive person, and I was not very good at it.

By this time Fabio Prieto had moved in to get the band. He wanted to be their new manager, put them on TV, and produce a big Rock Concert with them as headliners. I was trying to help the guys and keep them from trouble. Although I did not think Fabio had their interests at heart, I let it go. I gave up on the band. They were on their own.

One dreadful night my departure date was set. It was approximately eight o'clock in the evening and I was in my room napping before I went to work. Benjamin burst into the room waking me. The DAS agents were in the club looking for me. This time I was going with them. My room was towards the back of the club. The agents were inside the club; they were also outside near the front entrance and on the front driveway. I climbed out the back window and got up on the roof. When Benjamin and Mario told them that I was not at the club, the agents said thay planned to wait inside for my return. I could hear them in my room. They were searching the whole club. It was a cold night and drizzling rain. I laid up on the roof on the barrel tiles, motionless, fearing to make any noise. For hours I laid there. My karma was coming to me. In the dawn hours, as the sun was rising, I heard Benjamin calling in a soft voice. I climbed to the edge of the roof. He told me it was almost safe. He told me to climb down and instructed me to meet him out on the main road.

I made it off the roof. Because of lying motionless for so long, it was difficult walking even such a short distance to the road. Benjamin was there waiting in his car, he had one of my suitcases with most of my papers and a few articles of my clothing. He drove directly to the Medellin airport. On the drive, I changed into dry clothes. At one time Benjamin was wanting me dead and now he was, more than likely, saving my life.

My body was aching, my head was bursting apart with pain, and I was terrified. The good news, I was able to get booked on the next flight. Benjamin, who at this time also feared the DAS, assisted me in clearing through customs. For his own safety, as quickly as I cleared customs, we said goodbye and he was gone from my life, forever.

I have never felt worse in my life. Every bone in my body was aching from the strain and the cold rain. I was in total fear. I could not have imagined ever coming out alive from a Colombian prison. An hour before take-off, two men came up to me and demanded I follow them. They were cops. We went into a room and they searched me. They had already gone through my bag, which I had checked in. They began asking me questions about 'La Cajita de Musica.' I acted as if I knew very little about the club. I told them that I was simply a tourist who visited there occasionally, because of the good music. And then they started drilling me about the guys in the band. They wanted to know where they lived, especially Carl. They were after him. These men knew nothing about the DAS agents who were waiting for me. They let me go and I boarded the plane.

We had a scheduled twenty-minute stop in Bogota, where I decided to make one last effort to help the band. I went inside seeking a telephone, with the intention of calling Carl to warn him. In order to reach a public phone I would have needed to clear customs again. Instead, I spotted a young sales girl working behind a food counter, who I thought might help. I then wrote a note with a phone number. The note read, "Carl, you must leave Colombia immediately, do not use the airport, take a bus to Bogota." I spoke to the girl with some explanation, and gave her pesos, asking her to please make this call for me. I then boarded the plane for Miami.

The passenger-loading ramp had been removed, and the plane was about to take off. I felt safe and began to thank God for my unbelievable good luck in escaping, but then I noticed through my window that the passenger ramp was being wheeled back to the plane. Two men in suits came inside, walked down the aisle, directly up to me and said 'Pasaporte.' I handed them my passport. One of them showed me a badge and said, "Come with us, we have a security problem." I walked between the two of them toward the exit door. Before getting off the ramp I was handcuffed. They brought me through the airport and into a back room filled with four or five more men. My suitcase was in the room also. One of the men released the handcuffs and asked me to remove my clothes.

When I did that, he put the handcuffs back in place. I was bent over a desk and checked for anything hidden in my rectum. I was then brought to stand in front of the main man who was sitting at a desk. He was being called 'El Doctor.' I knew that these people were DAS agents and that I was gone. I tried to ask him what I had done and why they had me here. He was staring at me, but would not answer. One of the others began taking my suitcase apart. The Doctor called to him and he brought the bag closer. He was checking it at my feet as everyone in the room looked on. Standing naked, handcuffed I implored for him to answer me. "Why am I here, what have I done?" He spoke to me in poor English. "What is this?" In his hand was the note I had written for Carl, the one I had given to the counter girl. "Oh God, they are not DAS," I thought.

I began to explain that Carl was in a band and that some people were planning to rob them, get their equipment and harm them. At that moment I noticed that one of the men who was searching my bag had a letter in his hand. It was the letter that I had written one night after discovering Benjamin's plot. I said to the Doctor, "Look, this letter will prove it." I had written the letter explaining all about Benjamin's plan. In case something were to happen to me, I thought that maybe someone would find this letter, and that Benjamin would get caught. In the letter I had detailed all I knew about Benjamin's connections with the Mafia. There were things in that letter which I have not written about in this story, yet.

I was trying to save my life in any way that I could. I had to turn on Benjamin in order to do that. They handed me the letter and I began interpreting into Spanish. The Doctor said, "Why didn't you go to the Medellin police?" I replied, "Oh no, the Medellin police are not honest, they are crooked." They all laughed. For the first moment I felt hope.

The mood changed, one man came behind me and took off my handcuffs. The Doctor told me to get dressed. Someone else was putting my suitcase back together. I could hardly believe it; they were letting me go. I was still talking, attempting to make more explanations. They should not have been freeing me, I thought. What about the DAS in Medellin? Didn't they know about that? How could I be so lucky?

The plane had been held up for this entire time. As I walked back up the ramp and re-entered the plane, every eye was on me. It seemed like a long ride back to my freedom. The plane was nearly full, but I was very much alone at that time. Sitting in my seat, I was exhausted and confused. The pain in my body, the lack of sleep, but most of all, the fear that I had experienced this day was taking its toll. Although I do not think I fell asleep, I went into a dream state. I was recalling my entire Colombian experience. The Captain announced we were coming in for a landing.

My last panic, I thought there was no way we could have made it to Miami in this short of time. I thought the plane had turned around and was bringing me back to my doom. I looked out the window and saw the spread of Miami with its millions of lights. From terror to hysteria, I sighed and could only smile, knowing I would never again be on an Avianca Airline. When our plane landed and I set my foot on the ground, I felt that I was the one of the most fortunate men that has ever lived.

Carl and Jimmy were soon to follow, making it out of the country safely. Of course they came out with only their bags. Randy lingered on a little longer, unsuccessfully working to recover the equipment. He and Rosia, his new wife, came back to Miami. He bought new equipment and eventually, started a new band without Carl or Jimmy.

I never saw any of them again. I understand that 'La Cajita de Musica' failed and I heard that Benjamin, Mario and his family returned to the States. The only news I ever received about them was that Benjamin was in a U.S. prison. He had been arrested for cocaine smuggling. Mario had started a very successful seafood business in Miami.

Despite what Timothy Leary says, I believe that nothing in our world happens from chaos, without purpose. Because of such intense experiences like I had in Colombia, I know that there is a force of energy that doesn't exactly control us, but has a sort of regulator on us. It cannot force an action, but it will always be there to help us, or at least it's there to guide us. Anyone can choose to ignore it, or should I say, anyone's ego could choose to ignore it. Our true self, our spirit if you will, our conscience, will not.

"If you never ask for more than you can have, you might be counted a happy man." This is my life. This is my truth.

34

More October

OCTOBER 28, 2020

It is only 6 days until the election, 73 million people have already cast their ballots. That equals the total in the 2016 election. In my uneducated assessment, it says that Biden will win. It says to me that people are eager for change. I hope I'm correct. But the other day I began thinking about an alternative to my opinion. After accepting Amy Barret as a Supreme Court Justice I took on a somewhat different view of what I consider my political adversaries (mostly all Republicans). I saw in Amy not someone who would shift the courts decisions in a way that I feel is wrong, but I saw a good person, someone who adopted two children from Haiti, children that needed a mother and a home. She's like me in that respect.

My feeling now is that if Trump does win, I will do all in my power to look for something good that he might do in the next 4 years. I don't know how I might maintain this attitude since he is so bad. Dealing with that, I am still OK with my new outlook. It has relieved me from the hate, the stress, the disillusionment that I was holding inside. I figure we will survive regardless. Germany survived after several years of Adolph Hitler. World War 2 lasted for five long years, we'll only have four years of another Trump regime.

What I continue to think about is the future of the planet, and that's the hardest part for me. I have grandchildren that will be living here in the year 2080, if things last that long. And for their sakes I am praying for Biden to win, by a giant landslide. It will bring me so much joy and happiness if it goes that way. If Trump is not arrested, as some newscasters are predicting, he will have to be satisfied as a news political analyst. Hopefully his negative divisiveness, his pervasive threat to our democracy will slowly ebb away. His last hooray will have been his attempt at making people distrust our election process.

As things stand today Trump and his band of Republicans are trying to make it harder to vote while the Democrats are trying to make it easier. Trump's lawyers have filed over 300 lawsuits in 44 different states. The Texas Republican governor is only allowing one drop off box per county in his state, that is so incredibly absurd, Harris County where Houston is, has 4.7 million people. In Michigan a conservative judge overruled an order by the Democrat Secretary of State, and now its voters are allowed to carry concealed weapons to the polls.

Lawsuits are trying to restrict and change everything from when the ballots are counted, the time limits on their legality, the accuracy of signature comparisons. Protecting people's voting rights during this pandemic should be the number one priority, and it is just the opposite, very sad.

Meanwhile there is a Senate Commerce Committee hearing today. The CEOs of Facebook, Twitter and Google are all being questioned about their practices regarding the censorship and blocking of information. Mark Zuckerburg, Jack Dorsey and Sundar Pichai respectively, all say the same thing. They want freedom of speech but not the harmful, widespread misinformation that is harmful or promotes violence. In other words, no destructive lies folks. You can't Tweet "Don't wear masks, they don't work," or start a website group with "Let's kill the governor." I watched some of the hearing this morning and the Republicans are all claiming that these giants of the social media business are one-sided and that they delete conservative views while allowing the liberals free reign.

The Democrats are saying that they don't remove enough stuff. One Senator was demanding to know the political leanings of all the employees working for the companies. The lawmakers on this panel are pushing to repeal or rewrite the legal protections that these tech companies now have from accountability. According to all the CEOs, the law known as Section 230 is the only thing protecting free speech.

The virus is going like crazy and may become worse than the initial attack in the Spring. Hospitals all over are beginning to overflow. And it seems that five people in Vice President Pence's main team are all now infected.

As for the crazy climate, we have another hurricane about to hit New Orleans. Temperatures are above normal in most states. Our high today in Healdsburg will be 80. I can never remember late October being this warm.

OCTOBER 29, 2020

The surging virus, the restrictions, the lockdowns, this constitutes the majority of news airtime today. Not only in our country, but all over the world Covid is spiking. France and even Germany, who was doing so well at controlling things are now both reporting dangerous hospitalization threats as they announce new lockdowns. And not only here, but citizens in most countries are tired, fed up and furious with these controls.

A new term, pandemic fatigue, is common. I have often compared this pandemic to World War 2. It is similar in many ways, causing deaths and destruction to so many people's lives. During those times, which very few people alive today can remember, the government had a "war cry," to inspire the population, not so today. People want to socialize again, to reunite with family. The unseen virus is not enough to quell the demoralization that exists in all of us. When restrictions began lifting, we were not prepared for getting locked down the second time. If it's not us or a family member who is in the ICU, it becomes difficult to keep in mind how dangerous this virus is.

Dr. Fauci, considered to be the expert said, "Things could get seriously much worse because we are in a trajectory going in the wrong direction, and I don't see anything that anyone's doing right now that's going to change that. And that's what's really bothering me." The poor guy has been getting threats to he and his family. He also said, "In my wildest dreams, I would not have imagined that something that involves each and every one of us, ourselves, our families, our parents, our children, could not be approached in a uniform way. Instead, this triggered a degree of divisiveness the likes of which I've never seen."

I'm afraid Trump has made our people defy authority. He openly claims that all states run by a Democrat governor are being led off course. He has forever denounced the usefulness of mask wearing, and social distancing, and has insisted that this virus will be gone quickly. Other countries realize this is not true and are much more prepared now as this second wave is battering us.

Our neighbor Canada is an example. Their rate of new cases is far below us, and their citizens are following the guidelines set up by their officials. They have repeatedly urged social distancing, mask-wearing and other forms of caution. Most Canadians look upon their government leaders as heroes, while Trump calls Fauci a disaster.

Asian countries for whatever reason seem to be handling it better. Perhaps because they live in a culture with less of a cowboy-like attitude and more like everyone is a part of the herd. I can recall for many years, seeing Asians in the airport or walking down the street with a mask. I was uncertain of their reasoning and thought maybe they had been living in Beijing and wanted protection from pollution. "But our air is clean, you can take that mask off lady." Now I wonder if they had a cold and were trying to protect the rest of us.

The stock market had its worst day in months yesterday. It has shown a history of rebounding throughout all of this. In my mind it should not be taken as a sign of our economic condition. It's more like a Casino than a true indicator of where we are financially. The "big boys" are either losing money or making it, but it doesn't affect most of us.

OCTOBER 30, 2020

Four days until the election. Both candidates are campaigning in the swing states. It appears as if Biden has a comfortable lead, but some analysts are predicting a very close outcome. Some say Florida is crucial, others say Arizona. There was even one talk about what happens if the electoral votes are tied. Watching the Trump rallies for me is so disheartening. All of those people jammed together with no masks, yelling and screaming, and not realizing that they are sharing their space with an uninvited guest. How can they possibly ignore all of the science, all the medical experts, and all of the undisputed evidence, about the virus. It's one thing to have 'pandemic fatigue,' it's another thing to willfully breathe in an infected person's breath. And that is exactly what happens if you don't stay 6 feet apart, especially without a mask.

Studies about the aerosol transmission of viruses began in 2003 after SARS had infected thousands, killed hundreds, and caused a worldwide scare. The World Health Organization, which Trump has pulled us out of incidentally, organized and conducted research into this area of virus spreading. Since that time it is no longer speculation, rather scientific fact, that exhalations carry the virus into the air and if we are as close as 5 feet to an infected person, our chances of becoming infected are pretty good. As expected, the louder people speak the more aerosol is admitted, and the greater chance of becoming a host for our hungry new Covid enemy.

Recently, new studies have been done on the effect of Trump's rallies and wherever these huge gatherings are taking place, the new cases which show up in that city are often 200 or 300, as much as 700% above the normal rate in the state. That is true in every single rally of the past two months. Today there are 100 thousand cases of infection per day, that's like 1 every second. We have surpassed the peak of March infection rates. My conclusion, it's time to accept the new restrictions that may come, to wear our masks whenever we're in public, and don't yell about it.

OCTOBER 31, 1951

At age five, 1 remember my first Halloween. My mom made me a ghost costume. I can't remember if I went out to trick or treat, but I am rather proud of the fact that I am able to recall the wonderful memory of my mother at that time. Some of my other first memories are chasing the ice truck down the road trying to pick up chunks of ice. This ice delivery system was normal for that period. Like everyone else in those days, we had an icebox, electric refrigerators were on the horizon. I also recall being lifted to the little door outside of our kitchen, crawling through and unlocking the kitchen door. Very similar to a cat door of today, this little alcove was where the 'milkman' delivered milk to most houses in the suburbs.

My sister and I were so fortunate to have had the parents that we had. They loved us without any conditions and guided us in the right direction. I shall suggest that it is acceptable to be directed without your knowledge. We were raised as Christians, Catholics to be more specific. However, it strikes me peculiar that if fate had it for me to be born 10,000 miles to the East, I would then have been learning good Muslim standards. Or had I been born 500 years earlier. I would probably have been learning about 'The Great Spirit.' As life for me was turning out, I was about to be engaged for the next 11 years in trying to believe that God is in heaven and that Jesus wants us all to worship him and the Bible.

I must say that I gave this my best effort, but try as I might, I could not switch from thinking that my mommy was God, to thinking that some new thing was now going to take over. To me it was never really important enough, besides the fact that it did not make a whole lot of sense. I was much more impressed with learning the obvious physical properties about me, not the unseen spiritual mysteries of life.

I felt as if I had just flown out of this great big pumpkin pie, and I wanted to know all about the new things I was seeing, to hell with the spiritual world. There was way too much I did not know about, of that which I could see.

By the way, the Christian 'hell story' they were going to teach me threw me for a loop. One night I remember suffering through a terrible, terrible nightmare. I had gone to hell and would stay there forever and burn and burn and never be able to see my family again. I must have been about six years old. It was super traumatic for me and it took a few days to clear those terrible thoughts from my mind. This is not the type of education a six-year-old should have been given. In a serious vein, I do not think young people should ever be pushed toward a particular religion. As I got older, away from catechism, which stressed that the Catholic religion was the one true religion. I began to see that most of the world's religions believe that they alone hold the key to eternal salvation.

And as I continued growing up and reading about the main prophets who brought forth the accepted spiritual beliefs of our time, the true answer that I was searching for came to me. It's not in the Bible, or the Koran, or the Bhagavad Gita, or the Vedas. It's in our own consciousness, and that's what every prophet was telling us. I don't believe that they wanted to be worshiped, and I never really could do that. It was the followers of Jesus and Buddha and Mohammed who decided to invent a religion around what they interpreted as the sacred teachings of their particular prophet.

The idea that Jesus was God came down by word of mouth for three or four generations before it was actually written down. Was it susceptible to individual interpretation. Of course, it was. Basically it was Moses who is given credit for creating the Old Testament, and Paul, one of Jesus's disciples, takes the majority of the credit for the New Testament. Paul happened to be very smart and a brilliant speaker, a gifted storyteller. Now here's an interesting fact that I found when googling the History of Jesus.

"There is no definitive physical or archaeological evidence of the existence of Jesus. There's nothing conclusive, nor would I expect there to be. Peasants don't normally leave an archaeological trail."

I assume that when a person becomes a Biblical scholar, they are taught otherwise. Again, from Google I found. "The reality is that we don't have archaeological records for virtually anyone who lived in Jesus's time and place." In today's world where so much information is at our fingertips, I would think that other Christians would be Googling this, as I did. For most of today's followers, Faith seems to satisfy them. I'm not interested in pushing my point or debating with anyone. I don't want to win. To me the notion of God is more like a toothbrush, everyone has one, but it is not a good idea to use someone else's. P.S. I do believe that Jesus existed and that he was an enlightened being.

35

November

One more single day to kill before the Big Election. It is being called the most important election of our modern history, and I don't think that's an exaggeration. The percentage of time I have devoted in this book to talking and opining about Trump and the condition of our country is a testimonial to this. I had once planned to finish writing after tomorrow's election, but now I plan to keep up this literary babbling until the Coronavirus comes into check. Hopefully we will have a new leader at that time.

Today is a continuation of all the absurd antics being conducted by Trump and his party. For example, in Texas the Republicans are attempting to throw out more than 120,000 early votes cast in drive-through locations in the state's largest county. This effort has already lost twice in lower courts but today it is set to appear before a Republican appointed judge. Of course the county is heavily Democratic. On Saturday, a Biden campaign bus was surrounded by several cars and pickups on a freeway in Texas, in an attempt to run it off the road. All of these vehicles were displaying flags and banners pro-Trump. The FBI is now investigating. Joe Biden canceled two events in the Austin area. Trump people want violence, Biden people want peace.

There are also extreme, dangerous actions in New York and New Jersey. Trump caravans have blocked traffic on a New Jersey freeway and have created a roadblock on the Mario Cuomo Bridge entering N.Y.C. If Trump can't win legally, his supporters will do all they can illegally. This is almost beyond my imagination for such occurrences in the 'Great U.S.A.' As with the Coronavirus surge, and as Dr.Fauci warned yesterday, 'The worst is yet to come." Anyone looking for a good stock investment tip? It seems that companies selling police equipment such as weapons and body armor are booming, as these sales are now being made to the general public at a 500% increase in their businesses.

My daughter Mia is in a tough spot, her car broke down and she can't afford to get a new one. As a result, she has lost her job. Last week I sent her $5,000. And she now has a lead on a replacement. When I spoke to her yesterday, she asked if I would talk to Sarah, her oldest daughter about Trump. It seems Sarah is being influenced by her father. He and Mia have been divorced for many years now. Sarah believes that Trump is the best choice because of his policies on the economy and education. Without wanting to insert a wedge between her and her father, I tried to make a case on the state of the environment, and a forward look to her future. At the end of our conversation I told her that I don't want to be coming between her and her father, but I told her to at least open your mind to what I'm saying, I kind of, sort of, suggested to her to push a 'Life Cruise Control Button.' Sarah is in high school, she values education, she's a reader and at the top of her class. I mentioned that she should look at a map and see that 99% of areas that support a good University are all supporting Biden. Educated people, educated women are all in the camp of the Democrats.

The Weather news story of the day is definitely the 28th storm of the year, Hurricane Eta. It's a slow moving category 3 hurricane and intensifying by the hour. Expected to slam into the coast of Nicaragua tonight, raising tides by as much as 18 feet above normal and bringing 18-25 inches of rain. Some areas could get as much as 35 inches of life threatening rains, causing river floods and landslides. This is no joke, in 1998 Hurricane Mitch killed over 10,00 people in Nicaragua. Flash flooding will occur in many places. Every Central American country as well as some Caribbean Islands and Southern Mexico will be affected. I know so many of these areas that are now bracing for the impending dangers. Of course I know the Belizean coastline and the ocean towns of Costa Rica, as well as the area of Mexico's Yucatan that will be affected. And I also know the land on either side of Nicaragua.

I spent a lot of time in the Blue Fields of Southern Nicaragua where I made a documentary. It was in a small uncharted river, where I came close to being bitten by a deadly eyelash viper.

With a chain saw I was cutting logs from the river and branches overhead that blocked our boat's passage. At this time Dr. Lopez, who hired me and was in charge, was driving the small aluminum boat. I was standing in the bow about to cut a low hanging branch when he yelled, "Cuidado Tom, culebra." Within a foot from my face I came eye to eye with the solid yellow viper and its long eyelashes. Had Dr. Lopez not seen the culebra and yelled, I'm sure it would have struck me. I seriously doubt if we had any antivenom meds on board the houseboat, but I do know that if a neurotoxic snake hits you close to your brain, you have a good chance of passing over into the ethereal unseen.

On another night I had the pleasure of sleeping in the local Blue Fields jail for not having permits to film, even though I did have them. I was in a dugout and the papers were in the houseboat. On that day I had my tripod taped to the front of the boat and I was shooting rolling footage of the larger San Juan River and the jungle banks. We passed a boat filled with several guys in camouflage uniforms. They stared and passed by but soon turned around and came back to us. It was only myself and a helper who was driving my boat. One of the meanest looking soldier/policeman I have ever seen outside of the movie theaters was the sergeant and leader of the nefarious group that took us in. Approximately 30 hours later, thanks to Dr. Lopez, I was again a free man.

For the undisturbed natural beauty of the Blue Fields I fell in love with that area, but for the unregulated military government, I fell out of love.

On the other side, to the south of Costa Rica is Panama. During my time living in Costa Rica, I was ahead of the curve exploring a coastal area of Panama known as Bocas del Torro. Since my visit to this beautiful, charming, untouched area, it has become discovered. The tourists arrived, as did the inevitable investors. I haven't been back, but I can imagine the area being torn up by high winds and rising tides.

In Bocas del Torro I was taken by the excellent snorkeling on the live coral reefs, far better than Costa Rica, similar to Belize. Once, while snorkeling there I saw a huge patch of a particular type of coral that has suction cups, similar to the tentacles of an octopus. I had never seen such a large patch. It had been fun for me when diving in Belize to put my hand in a small patch and feel the suction. When I saw such a large patch I went down and laid in the patch on my back. As I withdrew from the patch and swam to the surface, I felt the hundreds of little pops letting go, so much fun. Ah, but then the fun ended, I began to feel a little sting, then a lot of sting, then a tremendous amount of sting. I had to leave the water. My whole back turned red. I made it to the cool little hotel room I had rented and my friends helped me to get some ammonia which eventually cured me. A bottle of ammonia works better than pee by the way.

Last night I went to the Safeway store to buy my food, as usual. I could easily live without an 'icebox' er, I mean refrigerator, since I hit the Safeway just about every day. Last night I was talking to one of my regular checkout friends and I said, "yeah thanks to these masks, neither of us have become sick." The dude behind me said, "that's not true." I wasn't quite prepared or willing to get into it, however I couldn't stop myself and replied that 95% of all the scientists agree that they do help and that he should research it. He said, "Oh, I've researched it." I left it at that and walked outside into the darkness. Daylight Saving Time was lifted yesterday.

NOVEMBER 3, 2020

Election Day, it's finally come. I have never felt this way about an election in my life, and I'm sure I'm not alone with this feeling. The numbers show how many people are coming to vote. All previous turnout numbers are being shattered. This election, engulfed in the middle of the pandemic, has become somewhat of a social laboratory. It's a fact that viruses don't care about political parties, but studying the different responses within the different parties uncovers some interesting facts. The virus and the strong divided political feelings have affected so many of us in many different ways. Extreme violent groups have formed, Antifa on the left, The Proud Boys, for example, on the right. They stand for political ideologies, for medical and scientific interpretations, for law and order, for respect of authority and fellow humans, all different, separate realities. It shows how so many have grown up trained to develop one polar view or the other. It may be the creative aspect of our culture that has cultivated such aggressive, and competitive traits. The violent responses, not only to Covid restrictions, but to many of the other political differences are a sad commentary on our species in general.

Ideally, a solution to stop the tension would be to reach a midpoint agreement rather than choosing one view at the expense of the other. To come up with a new idea incorporating both sides would be the best answer and could perhaps arrive at a place even superior to both extremes. I think that's what our Constitution is supposed to create. But today, my particular vote must be for one side or the other, and I am not deciding on even 1/4th of Trump. In California, my vote will not be a game changer, as it would be in several of the swing states, since California is overwhelmingly in support of Joe. "May the best man win," I mean that.

If Biden wins there will be major changes coming regarding the coronavirus and the administration's dealings with the pandemic. Biden has already set up a team of advisors to help with forming a new nationwide response. There will probably be better testing at the national level, he will more than likely encourage states to implement mask mandates, and for sure he will get us back into the World Health Organization, so we might work globally to coordinate our efforts and stop the spread. Hopefully his leadership will restore integrity to our scientific institutions. Universities and pharmaceutical companies as well as the C.D.C. and the F.D.A. can all work together to advance our knowledge, and our treatment.

After today we will no longer be voting against something, which seems to be motivating this election. I'm against Trump, his supporters are against a socialist who will take away guns, destroy our economy, fill the country with illegal immigrants, allow rioters and looters to overtake our cities. etc. etc. Negative ads will no longer be on our TV's and all of the anxiety and stress of the election will be over, finally, and we can look forward to building a positive future. At least that's what should happen, it's to be seen. If Trump loses, will he and his supporters accept it? Walls have been erected surrounding the White House, many large city businesses are boarding up their stores. It's as if a Hurricane is expected. Our country has become something much different in the past four years, and it is so sad to witness.

Tonight I'm going to my friend Toni's house. A small group of us will be eating together and watching the election. I suspect that even with the unprecedented amount of early voting, we still may be receiving an indication as to who will win, perhaps not. Nothing is certain, that is for certain.

NOVEMBER 3, 2020

OMG, WTF.

NOVEMBER 5, 1968

Richard Nixon has just won and will be our next President. It was one of the closest elections in history. Neither he nor Hubert Humphrey had over 50% of the votes. That's because so many racist Southerners cast their votes for the third party candidate, former governor of Alabama, George Wallace. I am living in the South yet I am appalled that George Wallace was even able to run as a candidate. Racism is definitely alive and well and it is such a shame. How can there be so many people in our country that are basically either inherently evil or incredibly stupid? I can only hope now that Richard Nixon will be a good leader and guide us through these topsy turvy times.

NOVEMBER 10, 2020

A lot has happened in the past week. First and foremost, Joe Biden has been elected as our President. Sad to say that Trump has yet to concede. So many Republicans are telling him to admit defeat, even his wife, but scumbag that he is, he refuses. He is still claiming voter fraud and demanding recounts. The experts all say that his approach is ridiculous and has no base. One of his claims is that people have used dead people's identities to cast false votes. This is so absurd, even laughable if it wasn't so sad. News reporters have said nothing like this has ever happened in 100 years.

The vote tabulation in the beginning looked as if Trump was going to win, and that is because the first votes counted were from the poll booths, cast on election day. I was devastated, as were all my friends, except Danny. But then as the ballots from early voting and mail in ballots began coming in, the tide turned and Biden's numbers began to overtake Trump. During the campaign, as Trump was claiming that the election will be a big criminal fraud, he encouraged all his supporters to vote on election day, insisting that there was no need to worry about social distancing since the Coronavirus is also a big overinflated hoax.

And so most early votes went for Trump. However the later votes, something like 87%. in many places went for Biden. There were six states that were late in declaring a winner. Pennsylvania, Nevada, Georgia and Arizona were all counting votes and held the key to victory. From Tuesday until Saturday the count continued, people were glued to the news stations. Biden's numbers kept climbing and Trumpers were going crazy, egged on by their leader.

Threats were flying at the public servants who were counting, there was even an arrest made as heavily armed people came to disrupt and take over an election counting center in Arizona.

Finally on Saturday, Pennsylvania went officially for Biden, giving him the necessary electoral votes to claim victory. Despite the joy of victory, the sadness of defeat is present. I'm feeling a sadness of victory also.

I had avoided any contact with Danny since the election began until Friday night when it was certain that Biden would win. He texted me and I felt I should respond, so I called him and eventually brought up the election. He started in with, "Yeah, and now they're trying to steal the election." I couldn't believe that he had bought into that lie. My emotions took over and I went off. "Are you kidding me, do you actually believe that? How can you be so fucking stupid?" I couldn't control myself and I kept on going. I told him to look at Biden and see, "He's going to work to bring our divided country together again, to repair what the evil Trump has done. His response. "Well, that's not gonna happen." This is why I'm sad, I'm afraid Danny may be right, at least for the present.

Since the early 1900s, our country has been working to become a 'we country.' We were pretty successful at it and it wasn't until the later 1960s that a switch started happening. Although the 60s brought much needed change, we started to become an 'I country.' And now, that individualism has made it ripe for Trump and his followers to destroy us. Teddy Roosevelt once said, "The fundamental rule of our national life is that, on the whole and in the long run, we shall go up or down together." One of Danny's last remarks was, "Enjoy your march to socialism."

Saturday was also the opening day of crab season here for non commercial fishermen. Phil and I went sailing, celebrating the wonderful news and bringing a crab pot to throw into the sea. Of course sailboats are not designed for crab fishing, but we had a plan. We found a 60 foot ledge outside of the Golden Gate Bridge and threw our single crab pot overboard. The plan was to sail around for a couple hours and then pull it up and see. As we were sailing back to the float, we had to pull in the jib (foresail) to slow us up, allowing me to haul in the trap. As I was tying the line to the winch, a strong surge hit us and the mainsail boom came flying across and struck me in the left temple. I was shoved onto a different winch and lacerated the top of my head, I then fell into the floor of the cockpit, bleeding and unconscious for a few seconds. Phil watched the whole thing happen and was horrified. "The first time in 40 years of sailing, I've ever had anything like this happen," he later told me.

I remember the pain of being struck in the face, and then I'm on the floor as Phil is putting towels on my head. Phil is a retired physician so I was in good hands at that point. I went down below and Phil applied a dressing. I couldn't feel the cut, it was my head, my face, my jaw that was in serious pain. As a nurse would ask, "on a scale of 1 to 10, how much pain are you in?" At that moment it was in the high 50s. Have you ever been hit in the side of the head with a baseball bat?

I stayed below, we left our pot and Phil sailed and motored us back to the Marina. I felt a jolt as he got us into our slip single handedly. I went topside at that point and Phil said, "I got it, I got it, don't worry, go back and lie down, keep the pressure on your head." We then went to a Critical Care facility close by on Fulton Street in the Marina District, but it was closed. He wanted to take me in my car to the ER up in Healdsburg and worry about juggling with his wife to get his car back. I insisted on driving and he followed directly behind for the 60 mile drive.

After an hour and a half I was out of the ER, my head wound was sutured, my exam completed by Dr. Woo, and a cat scan showed no internal brain damage or bleeding. I had little sleep Saturday night but last night was much better. The nausea that I had, has gone away, not much of a headache left, but my jaw is the main problem.

Apparently there's a jaw controlling muscle that has its insertion in the upper temple and the swelling and damage keeps me from opening up my mouth without a lot of pain. The mirror and I have become serious enemies, enough said...

If I'm OK by tomorrow, we plan on going back out to pull the trap. The irony is, that I won't be able to open my mouth wide enough to eat any unlucky cabs that might be waiting for us. I'm on soup and mashed potatoes right now. At my age, healing comes at an algorithmic, decelerated rate.

Today the temperature didn't rise above 50 degrees, tonight there will be frost. I heat my humble abode with a wood stove, but I'm not planning to fire that guy up until the rains come. Presently I'm sitting at the keyboard with a sweatshirt and a jacket on. I'll be going directly from here to under a sheet, blanket and a comforter. Like most sailors of yon years, I too shall be sleeping with my clothes on. I'm breaking down in my malady filled life. This morning I set up an account with American gas and sometime soon I hope I will see the guy pull up who will certify the safety of my tank and fill her up. I will turn on the heater that I haven't used for several years.

NOVEMBER 11, 1960

"Great catch TBone. Are you alright? Yeah, I'm fine. OK, lets run the same play, only T. flare out more towards the sideline, I'll run a 19-option, on two." I got on the line, then I stood up, "Where am I, how'd I get here?" Time out was called and eventually 'Beanie' the Park Director, who was watching the game took control and called an ambulance. I was headed to St. Mary's Hospital with another brain concussion.

My first brain concussion, which was much more serious, was a hit and run bicycle accident, this time it was a blow to the head in a football game. I recovered but continued to make regular trips to Jackson Memorial Hospital in Miami for the brain tests. The original concussion had left me in a coma for a few days and I was never completely cleared.

NOVEMBER 11, 2020

Still waiting for the gas man, the temperature hit 28 last night. I still have all my clothes on. I do plan to get into a hot shower soon, but I have to watch the cut on the top of my head. I'm not sure if I can run hot water on it. I talked with Phil this morning and canceled on the idea of going out in the boat. I just can't imagine jumping around on that boat in that ocean. I'm still not recovered, obviously.

The power of a full sail is something that only someone who's been on a sailboat during a jibe or a tack really knows. And I got that power blasted right onto my thick skull. And yes, it was another concussion, added to my list. A brain concussion is simply a blow to the head and brain. What makes it serious is the force of the blow and the impending damage. More serious concussions result in loss of consciousness, and Saturday it did happen to me. I was out for a few seconds lying in the cockpit and I don't fully remember the accident, only the pain I felt in my temple and then waking up on the floor.

When you do get knocked out, you lose memory of that time and often some of the time preceding the accident. Imagine if you were go to sleep some night in your nice comfortable bed, but then when you wake up something's different. You're not in the bed where you should be, you're sitting in your living room. "Where am I, how did I get here?" A crude explanation, but that's the way it is, hopefully it won't happen to you.

It appears as if another huge hurricane is heading toward Nicaragua and Honduras. About this time of year in 1998 I was in Guanaja, part of the Honduras Bay Islands, located about 25 miles off the coast. I was in Honduras intending to promote an idea for a documentary. I was also combining the trip with a plan to help my friend John Terry, an actor, who had bought some land there and was thinking about building something.

The ocean front property that John had bought was being managed by an older couple Bill and Nancy, who had built themselves a small shack. They were long time sailors in their seventies, a very nice couple who had realized at their age, they could no longer be worldwide sailors. They had sadly resolved to become landlubbers and had chosen this great place to do it in.

I was staying in Guanaja at a hotel owned by one of John's new friends. This hotel had agreed to become a sponsor for my project, as well as a diving company and another Hotel in Roatan. I was still working to get more sponsors when Hurricane Mitch started heading towards us. On October 28, Mitch blasted into the Bay Islands and lingered for three days over the Islands before hitting mainland Honduras and killing over 5 thousand people.

Bill and Nancy lost their house and survived by moving into a cave on the Island. I was thinking about doing the same thing, hunkering down with them in the cave for what we thought would be several hours, not three days. I missed out on that adventure by heading back to Costa Rica the day before Mitch hit. Both of my potential sponsors lost their hotels as well as every other hotel owner in all three of the Bay Islands. Roatan, Utilla and Guanaja were basically flattened.

When Bill and Nancy gave up their boat, they thought they had chosen a safe life. They were wrong. Actually their choice is a safer one, they didn't drown and die, or get hit with a boom and knocked out.

Maybe sailing is not ideal for seventy year olders, but I'm not ready for bingo and shuffleboard quite yet. I do promise myself to never try and make a long ocean crossing, even with Dr. Phil as my sailing partner.

John Terry and I have a relationship that extends from our days in North Carolina. We were following similar life paths Both of us had left South Florida looking for another way that might make us whole. Similarly, we came from families of privilege and had no need to struggle up. But we chose to start over, learning about a different connection to the land. In North Carolina we lived in humble Appalachian shacks and began learning how to build a life rather than being handed one. John inspired me and helped me to build the log house.

Moving to North Carolina I felt as if I had left a plastic world based on a Ponzi scheme. It wasn't long after my childhood that Florida began changing. The first shopping malls appeared, fast food restaurants were born, and housing projects began at an unchecked pace. As people moved in, lots of money was to be made. The flat land had no boundaries to stop the growth. It soon became the land where you drive for five hours and you don't know you've been anywhere. In South Florida, where John and I grew up, nobody made anything, except housing tract houses and eventually condos. There was new money flowing in every day and people worked to find their niche in temporarily intercepting the flow, as the money jumped from realtors to car dealers to Publix Market.

After living in North Carolina for a number of years, John eventually moved to Hollywood and became a successful actor. I also moved to California and got on the opposite side of the camera, I was running my own production company. John retired from acting and bought a sailboat. I have also become an avid sailor, that is until I bonked my brain last week. Today My friend John is still the one who calls me when a fire comes close or when news stories require it.

Local news: The virus is surging, there are now 17 states that have more cases than during the first phase. Hospitals all across the nation are in trouble, attempting to handle the mounting number of new cases. There are more people in the hospital now than at any other time during this pandemic. Hospital parking lots have become sites for mobile morgues. In El Paso, Texas, the number of cases more than exceeds the cases in some entire states, El Paso has 10 mobile morgues. It seems that the opening up of restaurants, gyms and theaters, as well as other crowded indoor events have been responsible for the new surge. New lockdown restrictions are inevitable. Despite the gloomy outlook, the search for a vaccine is going forward. Dr. Fauci has predicted that we will have a tested vaccine ready for distribution by April.

Last but not least, for today's report, we have the Trump saga. He still refuses to concede and has filed a handful of new lawsuits. He's been firing many more people in his staff. The guy is beyond belief. Biden continues to do work on the transition, but the one thing that is harmful to our nation is that his team does not have access to all the relevant and essential information within the White House. Not ever in the history of our country has such a thing as this occurred. It is shameful, pitiful and embarrassing.

NOVEMBER 13, 2020

Covid and Trump's irrational behavior are again dominating today's news. There is a saying that man is not a rational being, he's a rationalizing being. What that means is that we try and justify our opinions, to intellectualize them and make them right. A rational being would be one who is wise, logical and impartial. They say hell is the impossibility of reason. It's not only Trump and his fellow politicians, but also the millions of his irrational followers who are now making life in America a hell of a place to be.

NOVEMBER 15, 2020

It has been 8 days since I got whacked on the boat and last night I was finally able to sleep on my left side. Phil went out on Friday with a friend and searched in vain for our crab trap. This fishing from a sailboat idea has really not gone well for us, in any sense. We are both laughing about our boggled attempts to procure food from the sea.

I have been putting in a lot of time working. After finishing the bathroom remodel, I moved to the upstairs apartment and tore out the squeaking floor, replacing it all with new plywood and adding a few more joists. Then, new vinyl and baseboards. I worked Friday night till 7:30, 10 hours on my knees, ugh.

This morning it's lying in bed watching the Sunday morning news, ugh again. It's all about the surging Coronavirus. Hospitals all over the nation are in dire conditions, many states set new records for the number of infections this week. As for the country itself, we now have over 70,000 cases, predicted to hit 100,000 soon, deaths have been reported at 1,000 a day for the past 10 days. In many areas panic buying is now taking place and the markets are again emptying their shelves.

Of course the economy has not improved and for many families, a trip to the food bank means waiting in a line of cars for over a mile. More hospitality businesses are being locked down by their local governments and for many, it may be the final straw. Our administration is not able to provide a stimulus package as different political sides argue as to who should get what and how much. On top of this we have total chaos concerning the presidential election. Biden has won despite any of Trump's continuing claims of fraud. His 30 current lawsuits have either been thrown out or are on their way to be. All states have now certified the vote count. Georgia went for Biden as did Nevada, and Trump won North Carolina. The head of Homeland Security just announced that this election was the most secure in American history.

I can't help but wonder about the Trump supporters who are conducting protest rallies (fights are ensuing and arrests being made), still claiming that the election was rigged and that Trump won. What has made them so blind to the truth? Do they see their opponents as so deeply evil that they have lost all hope, convinced that this outcome will lead to disaster for them? Sadly, the true disaster stares them in their unmasked faces. Their lack of respect for science and their fellow human beings is beyond sad, it is sorrowful. It is a dismal place they are running to, blinded by such anger and being influenced and led by the worst man who has ever held the office of President. The Republican governor of North Dakota has now reversed his policy and is suggesting that citizens wear their masks. North Dakota is one of the states that is being hit very hard by the virus.

In 11 days we celebrate Thanksgiving and it will probably be a not so thankful day for many. New government guidelines are being imposed, most of which ask us to celebrate virtually and not to hold the normal family gathering. Many state officials are saying, "Don't leave home unless you have to." I close this paragraph on an ironically positive note. Since travel is being cut back, gas prices are the lowest they've been in 15 years. That tells me that the government is asking us not to travel while "Big Oil" is saying, "C'mon everybody get in your vehicles, look what I'm doing for you." It had always been standard policy that gas prices shoot up during the holidays.

NOVEMBER 17, 1970

Today Lt. William Calley and 14 of his men go on trial for what is being called the My Lai massacre. This case is a crucial statement for justice in the horrible situation of an unjust war. It was on March 16 in 1968 when he and his company marched into a small village of Viet Nam. They found no Viet Cong, only older men, women and children. On his orders they murdered the entire village. They shot people as they ran from their huts and then rounded up the remaining and killed them all. Could any possible excuse for this action be formed by the attorneys, following orders, insanity? These actions were covered up for almost a year until coming to light. I'm 24 years old, this could have been me in that company of soldiers. What would I have done?

Because this war is totally wrong, immoral and a mistake, such instances such as My Lai makes me OK with the fact that I didn't go. There will always be a part of me that feels a little unpatriotic, since many of my friends chose to fight for their country. I guess history will paint us an objective picture.

NOVEMBER 17, 2020

If the highly acclaimed novelist Jean Paul Sartre were alive today, he would find a world of shock and confusion. Through his popular novels with his promotion of existentialism, Sartre put the word and the philosophy of existentialism on main street in many countries throughout the world. The idea of existentialism is, that although human existence is rather meaningless, people have the right and a certain obligation to form an individuality. It's rather amusing that in the early part of his life he was an advocate of communism. He claimed that by using free will and being socially aware, we can create our own reality and our own meaning for life, since the world has none of its own.

Biden is trying to bring some sort of sense into our country, a meaning for us all to grab onto. Trump, Danny and his other followers are rejecting this plan. Every sentence that Trump utters, every opinion and belief he has, are the culmination of 70 years of lies and a truly disgusting form of living. Yet many people, from an existential approach, are creating their socio-political life by following this man.

It's raining outside, I have a nice fire going in my woodstove. With a screen on the front, the stove has warmed up the house and it's lighting up this grey morning. Myself, as well as every other Northern Californian, are welcoming the beginning of the winter rains. The ski resorts are receiving snow and most importantly wildfires no longer threaten us. It looks as if I will not have a need to fill up the propane tank after all.

Since my life in North Carolina taught me about woodstoves and making fires inside of my house, I have always chosen that cozy intimate way of surviving in the cold. It is extremely more difficult than switching on the wall thermostat, but for as long as I can use my chainsaw, bust and carry in the wood, I shall continue to dirty up my floors a little, and smoke up the house on some occasions.

My woodstove mon, it's the boss. I can control it with the damper, and one of the best parts is I cook on it. The stove extends out of the fireplace about ten inches. It has a steel top where I can easily fit two pots or cast iron frying pans. By controlling the airflow and adjusting the fire and coals inside the stove I can manipulate the heat to high, medium or low. In 1740 one of my life heroes Benjamin Franklin, because of a wood shortage in Pennsylvania, invented the wood stove. I wish that the "Founding Father" of our country was here with me today. He would be impressed with my stove, and most certainly have something to say about our current politics.

Being home on this rainy day has given me the time to read and watch more about our current political situation. Just finished watching another live Senate Committee hearing with Jack Dorsey and Mark Zuckerberg on the witness stand. The heat was hotter than my woodstove. Twitter and Facebook are being accused of bias by supposedly allowing liberal voices to speak out while conservative views are being censored and blocked.

Many people believe that any deleting is free speech restriction and that people should get it all and then make their choices. I see one fault with that logic, it's not legal to yell "Fire" in a crowded theater when there is no fire. The one who made the choice of yelling 'fire' has possibly damaged others safety. That person should be stopped in any way possible. Lies and disinformation should be stopped. The point is, people do not always make a decision based on common safety. All people are not good. Just as any other criminal who commits a crime, laws preventing posted harmful lies are necessary to stop them.

Another strong complaint against Dorsey and Zuckerberg is that they have no accountability for what happens, since they are by law free from lawsuits. Of course both CEOs deny that they should be held accountable for other people's thoughts and posts and claim they are being as fair as they can, taking into account that lies and disinformation must be stopped for the safety of everyone. They have rules to stop the inciting of personal harm or terrorism. Both CEOs explain to various senators that they are a growing, learning organization.

Some tweets and posts are not being flagged and deleted quick enough. There are many people in our crazy country who believe they are exercising their first amendment by threatening to shoot political opponents and politicians. Not OK, they are being arrested by local officials and put in jail to await trial. Herein lies the power of our social media platforms. Both Twitter and Facebook should flash up a page before their sites open up. "Warning, Extremely

Dangerous, the following site can cause serious damage to the user."

So much of today's hearing was centered on issues regarding the election. If anyone looks at the election process with honesty, they must agree that Biden has legally won, either that or they are blindly ignorant of the available facts. And a fact is a fact. To give a little bit of credit to the Republicans, there are a few more each day that are giving in to the truth. Even Marco Rubio, the popular U.S. Senator from Florida is now slightly admitting that the election was fair and that Biden will be our next President. Incidentally he was on the receiving end of a death threat by a Palm Beach County resident woman who wound up in jail. To quote the popular Republican Senator, "A lie can travel halfway around the world while the truth is just getting its pants on."

Here's another fact, a University study has proven that children who are continually using social media suffer health damage including eating and sleep disorders, depression, anxiety, etc. I may have said this earlier, but when this Pandora's Box was opened, a devil monster was inside and it's up to the parents of those affected children not to let that monster leap out. If you decide to have an untamed wild animal as a pet, you need to keep it in the cage or on a very strong chain.

And now for the rainy day report on Coronavirus. We are now averaging 150,000 new cases a day, hospitals and their staff are suffering beyond what was expected, with no end in sight. This morning a nurse in South Dakota was almost in tears as she related how many people were dying on her hospital beds while declaring with their final words that the coronavirus is a hoax and does not exist. Their family members agreed, "Dad must have had pneumonia or the flu." In the words of another one of my life heroes, Gandhi, "There is no happiness like truth, no misery like untruth. Truth is not to be found by anybody who has not got an abundant sense of humility."

Even more crazy than denying the election results, we are dealing with almost half of our population that deny Covid as existing or being a serious condition. I must tell them, with due respect, that your personal freedom will indeed be taken away from you, when you die. Trump's advice will not help you when they start throwing dirt on you. It is so very sad to see the victims on TV who have lost family members. They cry, "Life will never be the same without my mother," or "How will I ever live without my child?"

The pandemic is an issue that should be given top priority government attention, yet Trump is doing nothing. In fact he is adding to the problem by not letting Biden work with the information of our present government medical staff. He's refusing any type of transition, it's almost criminal behavior. He's playing golf and Biden says, "More people will die." There is some positive news, Pfizer has their vaccine almost ready and another company Moderna just received news that their vaccine is approved and is 94.5% effective. Vaccinations could possibly begin by the end of December.

Tonight's news contains, guess what, more virus cases, more insane Trump behavior. He is now withdrawing half of America's troops from Afghanistan and Iraq, 6,000 troops, against the advice of most military experts. Sad to say but as we withdraw, Al Qaeda, Isis and the Taliban advance. They will soon be claiming victory and encourage more terrorists to come aboard. His next action was to call some advisors and explore his idea of conducting a military strike on Iran.

Since Trump sent a drone to bomb and kill one of Iran's top Generals, a war hero, on January 24 of this year, the tension between our two countries is beyond description. It has always been hostile, but since that attack, which was actually a declaration of war, Iran has vowed to never rest until retaliation is completed. The Trump reasons for the assassination was that General Soleimani had killed many American soldiers and was planning more attacks. Regardless, the attack on that General had the same reaction to the people of Iran as sending a drone to the Vatican and bombing the Pope would have on the Christian world.

Today's actions by Trump at this time are proof by most standards that he is absolutely irrational, irresponsible and has the mind of a child. As a lame duck President is he actually wanting to again declare war on the Mideast? We have a little over 8 weeks left until Biden replaces him. I hope we survive.

NOVEMBER 18, 1978

Almost 1000, people committed suicide today in the jungles of Guyana. Followers of a Christian religious cult from California have been living in a huge socialist commune founded by their leader Jim Jones. Today they all drank a poisoned Kool Aid, a third of them were children. Apparently many of his followers were being kept there against their will, and their relatives had got word out to a Congressman in our government. Leo Ryan, a Democrat from California went with a group of journalists to investigate.

Ryan along with four other members of his party were ambushed and killed as they tried to leave. And that night Jones gathered the members of "The People's Temple," as they called themselves, to the deadly suicide meeting. The children were given the poison with a syringe into their mouths and then the adults proceeded to willingly drink the Kool-Aid.

NOVEMBER 18, 2020

Today began with more rain but it is now a sunny afternoon. On this wonderful day I can't stop hearing or thinking about Trump, Trump, Trump. It's so ironic that the word trump means precedence, or help, or leverage. Antonyms are disadvantage, misfortune, weakness. That dumb vile President has even turned our language backwards.

I believe I mentioned about him leasing out public land in the Arctic National Wildlife Refuge to the oil companies. Bids are flying in today and people are pushing to get this done before Biden takes over. There are many other anti-environment laws that are being pushed. It does appear that Trump knows he has lost and is relentlessly trying to do the things he promised during his campaign of 2016.

NOVEMBER 19, 2020

In an hour I'm leaving for the San Francisco Marina to get back on that wild horse that threw me. After 12 days to recover, I'm feeling fine and ready to go pull sails and ride the wind. I'm sure that Phil and I will be laughing about our skills at sailboat fishing. It'll be cool on the Bay, fall weather is definitely upon us. My porch thermometer is reading 45. As long as we don't get wet, which we never do, the cool weather does not bother either of us. It's not like winter fishing in Alaska. On the other hand, it's not like cruising in the Caribbean either. I must say, I miss the warm ocean waters more than I can relate. As soon as this virus is behind us, I will be heading to the warm beaches, that is a for sure bet. Maybe I'll be lying in a hammock between two coconut trees going over this published book, raking in all the royalties.

NOVEMBER 20, 2020

Sailing went smoothly, no accidents this time. The fog was thick surrounding the Golden Gate so there was no attempt to go outside. We sailed in the Bay heading to Angel Island, around Alcatraz and Eastward along the piers of SF. Because of the fog and colder weather there were hardly any other boats out. The winds were calm and it was a beautiful day. The number of boats estimated at all the Marinas in the Bay area is close to 75,000 and we had the Bay to ourselves for most of the afternoon, no cargo ships and only one tanker being guided in by a tugboat. Quite unusual to be so calm and peaceful. As always, I felt fortunate to be in such a position, able to do something that I love. No virile attacks and very little thinking of Trump's antics. But this morning is a different story.

The White House is becoming much like a scene from Saturday Night Live. If only Trump's behavior didn't border on extremely dangerous, it could be laughed about. His lawsuits are failing with every court in the land. The head of his legal team, Rudy Giuliani is denying fraud to the court judges and saying just the opposite to the press. They are succeeding at creating chaos and they may be causing irreparable damage to our system. Some people believe Trump may be attempting to make some sort of deal before he concedes in order to save himself. Others think his actions are simply hateful spite to our country, for not voting him in. Many of the lawyers involved in these lawsuits have quit. They cannot agree to invent unsupported facts, or to cover up and suppress the real evidence.

He is now calling in Republican State Legislators from Michigan and Pennsylvania to meet with him in the White House. Probably as Lindsey Graham attempted to do earlier in the week, he will be asking them to use their power to get votes thrown out. The other day he tweeted, "We would have won Michigan if they just throw out Wayne County." Wayne County is 90% Black. He doesn't have enough mental stability to see the facts and the pointlessness of his actions. It's either that or else he's acting to "burn everything down and poison all the wells" as he ends his pitiful term.

The virus continues snowballing, hospitals and staff are all in critical conditions in most every state. The bright side is that it looks as if vaccines will be ready before the end of December. Of course Trump's conduct will delay the distribution.

I believe it is well past time to again back up to a more pleasant time in my life and talk about something beautiful.

36

Belize

I always longed to return to British Honduras, and now I had a reason. On my trip back, I was quite excited to see many of my old friends. Of course we had all grown from little street kids. One of my closest friends was Alfredo. He was now married with a couple children, and was making his way as a lobster fisherman. He asked if I would stay and help him to catch lobster this year. I had not planned to be back diving so soon after Artchie's death, but fate kept me here in the sea for a while longer.

Alfredo had a big new motorboat and lots of traps; we decided to set some trap lines out by the cayes. The cayes are a chain of some 200 small islands, dotting the Barrier Reef. Most lie just to the West of the reef and as such are protected from any rough seas. The reef here in Belize is the second largest barrier reef in the world. It is over 175 miles long and stretches from Isla Mujeres in Mexico, all the way across the Belizean coast, ending in Spanish Honduras.

On the Southeast coast of Florida there exists a few patches of live coral, but nothing like the Barrier Reef. This coral reef is a marvel in itself. Only in later years have I come to realize how special it was to have been able to live close to this environment and have it's influence as part of my makeup. Of all the diving I did in Belize, I am certain that I went to some spots that no other human had ever seen.

In order to work our trap lines, Alfredo and I set out to build a small shack above the water. Even though we were miles out from the mainland, the bottom was close to the surface. There were patches of coral reef everywhere and a type of grassy vegetation covering the bottom. It was an ideal habitat for lobster. By beating pilings into the bottom from the prow of our boat, we built a rectangular shack with a tin roof. I lived there, just above the water, for eight months, diving and trapping lobster. Once or twice a week Alfredo would come out from Belize City across the deep water, 'the Blue,' to my little shack. Together we would pull traps and he would bring me out needed supplies. With his powerful motorboat he could make that trip in an hour. Alfredo would take our catch back into the market. Belize had a fishing co-op and every fisherman belonged. It was the law of the land. In order to sell your catch, you had to be a co-op member. The co-op was good for the fishermen. Similar to a labor union, it kept the prices up and set up insurance plans for the members, even a bit of a pension program.

At this time, I was in my late twenties. Perhaps it was the age when I wanted to slow down. My life had been zooming by at a very fast pace. I had finished all the schooling I would accomplish, passed through and survived the infamous 60s. I was not into drugs, and fortunately I was not damaged by the terrible war in Vietnam, since I had not served in the military. I was in good shape, a young man with a lot of experiences, ready to stop and reflect on things. My little shack on the water provided me time to do just that. For months it was only the sea and I. I had books to read and paper to write stories. And I had many pets, the creatures of the reef. I gathered starfish, and anemones, conch and whelks. I even caught a small eel and put him into my open aquarium. My aquarium was nothing more than a pile of rocks and old shells that I fashioned into a habitat for these fish and sea plants. I had them placed just in the front of my shack somewhat as an artificial reef. It was easy for me to keep many of these creatures. I knew what they liked and I also kept feeding them. They would come and go, as free animals will do.

My pets were very important to me. I would spend a couple hours every day with them, adding things to their mini world, feeding and simply observing them. When a storm would come in I would worry about them, even though the water would never get really bad. Out in the cayes, the tide would only change the sea about a half-meter. At low tide, the water was one meter deep extending up to a meter and a half at high tide. This is pretty much the same year round, except when late summer comes and the Caribbean coast is subject to hurricanes. I kept a radio in my shack and was always aware of the weather forecast. That year we were spared from hurricane threats. Should the need have arisen I would have relied on Alfredo for boat transportation back to the land. Alfredo was one responsible person. I never worried for my safety.

One of the adjustments that were necessary was living with the limited amount of freshwater at my disposal. The only source was collected from rain. I had a 55-gallon drum that caught all the water from the roof. Fresh water was a luxury. I used it to cook of course and to make drinks. I would brush my teeth with fresh water, but only rarely could I wash the salt from my face, and never would I take a shower with this water. I had only short pants and a few tee shirts that I wore sometimes at night or during a storm when the air would cool down somewhat. All my clothes and bedding were salty. It was not a problem for me.

Over time Alfredo brought out more lumber from town and we added onto the shack. The first phase was a small dock and later we put up an outhouse on the end of the dock. It was simply a bench with a hole and a half piece of plywood that kept it private from the house. The outhouse was to become part of my morning ritual. When Alfredo came out he would also bring reading material for me. He loved to read the small cowboy novels. I had to convince him that they were not my style. I kept magazines on the outhouse bench.

A typical day for me would mean waking as the sun began to break the still and quiet of darkness. Everything woke up with the sun. The schools of baitfish would become jittery and begin jumping at the slightest stir. The birds would leave their evening roost, and go wherever they went to find food during the day. And all the larger fish would become rambunctious and roam the shallows searching for breakfast. Without a doubt it is the most active time on the sea.

I would roll from my cot, click on the radio station from Belize City and go for my daily water ration. I would feel so secure if the barrel were at least half full. My next move would be to start coffee water boiling and get down the flour from my tin. Every morning I would make fresh bread. Most times I would cook it Belizean style, which is fried, rather than baked. When the water boiled I poured it over the coffee grinds through a sock into the next pan. I would then take my cup of coffee, the rifle we kept at the shack, and my binoculars to the outhouse.

With the aid of the binoculars, I could see all of our trap lines and a distant caye that was approximately four miles away. It was nothing more than a mangrove gnarl with a few budding trees. Although quite tiny it provided roosting for hundreds of seabirds. There were gavilans (a small hawk), gaviotas (seagulls), and fragatas (frigates) that slept there. After making sure that our trap lines had not been robbed, I would watch the birds as they slowly flew away from their island.

The fragatas were the most amusing. These birds usually roost on higher ground. Their sharp, thin, angular wings are designed to glide rather than propel. If they had a choice they would perch on cliff tops near the sea's edge. In this way they could fall off the branch and be in flight. They fly very high in the sky, but it's difficult for them to get started from the ground. I could see their hesitancy in taking flight from this low flat terrain. I watched them as they pushed themselves and worked much harder than the other birds to get up. On occasion I would spot one of the rare red-footed boobys. These white-faced birds with their red legs are rather funny looking, and fun to observe. One of the few remaining nesting islands for this species is on Half Moon Caye, which was not too far away from my shack.

After the morning bird departure my eyes would begin to search the open sea. There were always two things that I would be looking for. One was the delfin (dolphin). I would always try and spot them and if close enough, would make an attempt to catch them in the water and swim with them. The next thing I would look for would be a source of food. I would search the water's surface for the large gallo (roosterfish). These black and white striped fish have a tall spiny like dorsal fin that they often keep above the water, much like sharks do. The larger gallos' fins stick up above the water as much as twelve inches, making them easy to spot. This is where the rifle comes in. Very rarely did I succeed, but it was a challenge to try and shoot these gallos. When I did get one, it was a celebration. I had a new meal, different from the reef fish that I could shoot with my spear.

I kept a small boat tied to the dock. It had no motor but I could go places with my long 'push-stick.' On the few occasions when I would hit one of the large gallos, I would quickly run from the outhouse, put up the rifle, grab my mask and jump into the boat. It was important that I reach the fish quickly or another hungry animal would take him. By poling the boat I could make my way a little faster than swimming. Here in the shack, fish is what I ate. I always had flour for bread and rice, but basically it was fish. I would eat octopus when I would catch them and crabs and of course conch and lobster. Usually once a week I would pole over to the 'bird caye' and collect the spiral shaped whelks that were abundant there. That was my 'caye escargot', my snail delight. It was a job polling for a few miles and fighting the mosquitoes that enveloped that caye, but the whelks were worth the trip, anything for diversity. I would often pull a trap and get a lobster to cut up for bait. I knew where I could go and fish for little yellow tail snappers.

As one can imagine there are hundreds of different fish on a reef. Over a long period of time the ability to change the fish on your plate was important. I always ate two meals a day. For my late meal it was something I would shoot or grab from my favorite little patch of reef. But for my first meal I would try and get something different. For as many varieties of fish that exist there are almost as many ways to cook them. Hot pepper spice, lime and coconut were some of my favorite ingredients in preparing fish. I would fry them, bake them, boil them, skewer and roast them, pickle them with vinegar and onions, even grind the little ones up bones and all. I would make stews and soups and fillets and steaks and spreads and kabobs.

Many people believe that so many of the warm water fish are not good to eat and even poisonous, but I believe differently. I ate everything from the sea and never got sick. Some say barracuda are poisonous, not so. I have eaten many barracuda. I learned that they make excellent ceviche, a pickled form of raw fish. When cooking them in steak form, the small to medium sized ones are better tasting. Another popular belief is that the parrotfish, because it eats poisonous coral, is also poisonous. That was not my experience. If I had no other option for food I would shoot a parrotfish. They are a great tasting fish. The reason I would get them only as a last resort is because they are such gentle creatures and never run from the spear. I would almost feel guilty taking them. There is one fish however, the Puffer fish, that has a poisonous liver. They are actually one of the best tasting fish but caution must be taken when cleaning them to avoid cutting the liver and contaminating the meat.

In Belize there is a strict law governing spear fishing. This law permits divers to use a rubber-banded shaft, but not a spear gun like in many other countries. With this type of spear, the fish have a better chance to escape. This type of weapon is also known as a Hawaiian sling. It is an aluminum or fiberglass thin rod with a piece of rubber tubing fastened on one end. In order to shoot the spear you hook the tubing around your hand and pull the shaft down as far as possible. You then grab the shaft about halfway up towards the spear. When you aim and let it go, it propels itself toward your object. It works in direct proportion to your strength, definitely not as efficient a hunting tool as a double-banded gun.

Only twice in my life have I ever hunted things from above the water, and both times I was after reptiles. When Alfredo would come out to the shack, one of the things we would often do is go to the nearby cayes and hunt for cayman. A cayman is a member of the crocodile family. They are quite similar in appearance and behavior; only they do not grow as large as an alligator or crocodile. They seldom exceed two meters in length. Alfredo would hunt the cayman in order to sell the skins.

The method used for hunting these animals is rather unique. You always hunt at night. From a fast boat you speed along the banks of the shoreline and shine a light just where the water touches the land. We would use a headlamp, which works quite well. The crocodiles or cayman lie in the shallow water by the water's edge. When the headlamp hits one of these animals a pair of bright red lights shine back at you like two lasers. These are the eyes of the cayman. They shine red because of a chemical existing in the eye's makeup. This chemical aids the animal's night vision. When you spot these red lasers, there is no mistake, you immediately know you have spotted a cayman, and there is nothing else like it in nature. You can also tell how large the animal is by the distance between the two.

The next step is to bring the boat in slowly while keeping the light on the cayman. The bright light will confuse him and he will not move from his spot. We had the rifle, so in this case Alfredo would bring the boat right up to him and shoot him in the head. We carried a long pole with a spearhead tied to a strong rope. We would then spear him and if the shot was lethal the animal would easily be pulled up from the water and lifted into the boat. If it did not kill him, a fight would ensue that could be very tense and exciting. Since these animals were rather small, we seldom lost the fight and usually a second rifle shot would be sufficient.

After we brought the caymans back to the shack Alfredo skinned them out. I did not like the idea of killing these animals and not eating them. Alfredo did not like the idea of eating them since he felt that they were lowly scavengers, at the bottom of the food chain. He really was obsessed with this idea and it would insult him if I cooked the meat in his presence. I would eat the tails, but only when Alfredo left, usually the morning after the hunt. I found it best to prepare the meat in small cubes, flour, and deep fry it. I would have it for at least three meals. It was a welcomed diversity in my menu. With no refrigeration I could never eat all of the caymans that we caught.

To me, hunting above the water on the land seems wrong. It feels much more violent and I have grown to dislike it in any form. In my world of reality it doesn't seem necessary to kill land animals, and the bads of such actions far outweigh the goods. I guess I am an underwater hunter, harvesting seafood is more like gardening to me. I am sure that if I live long enough, and the ocean habitat changes enough, I will change my feelings about this also. As I mentioned earlier, if I had the power, I would ban any and all commercial harvesting of the sea.

Again I have wandered off track. I was describing a typical day in my life at the shack. Returning back to the dock, if there were no reason for me to jump in the water after fish or dolphin, I would generally spend about an hour on the outhouse bench and then be about the business of making my first meal. Catching my meal, cooking, and eating it would generally last until the sun was close to its peak. It would then be time to lie down and read or write. During that year I wrote a short fiction novel about some sea creatures. The main characters were a young rambunctious dolphin named Alfred, and a wizened old sea turtle named Mamoud. As I wrote, I would live the adventure. Every writing session would bring out new ideas. I never knew where the story was headed when I grabbed the pencil and paper.

Inside the shack I had put up a hammock and would usually spend those 'high noon' hours rocking, reading and writing. I loved those special summer days when afternoon storms would roll in from the horizon and bring booming thundershowers. It was only then that I would have a freshwater shower. With the salt gone from my body and the cool breeze blowing, I always felt so fresh when my clean skin tingled. The water catching drum would fill up, the hot, hazy midday sun would disappear, and I would more often than not, fall into a deep restful sleep.

Each day just before the sunset, I would have my second meal, or at least be almost prepared for it. I kept candles and a lantern, but after a few months I hardly ever used them. I was up and down with the sun. My schedule changed slightly as the full moon approached. With the extra moonlight I was able to stay up longer and do little projects on the dock, such as fixing traps, or playing with my gathered sea treasures. By now I was accumulating what I would call my Museum.

In my Museum I had pieces of black coral, and many ivory-like stingers from stingrays that I had caught. I would polish the coral and clean the ivory stingers, making them into pieces of art. For three weeks I worked on cutting sharks teeth out from the jaw of a large tiger shark. This was much more difficult than I expected. I soaked the tough skin and hacked and chopped with my machete, working those teeth out of the tough hide and cartilage. I cured out some of the more beautiful conch, cowry, and whelk shells. I taught myself how to cut out and make things from turtle shells. I had bills from swordfish, and even a sawfish bill. I had saved a number of cayman skins, only the top parts since the bottoms and sides were useful in the commercial market. I salted these top skins down, and dried them out, but they never turned out to be useful for anything, only for remembering the time.

Most of my afternoons were spent on projects like these; I always had many projects. One thing for sure, of all the months I spent there, I was never bored. I did the same things every day, but there was enough diversion to keep me from being bored. When the lobsters were running, Alfredo would come out every other day to pull traps. When we were not getting much lobster, I would be alone for a week. I had a calendar but not a clock, I could tell time by the sun's position. When the sun was four or five fingers from the horizon, I knew I had better be hunting for my evening meal. That meant poling out to my favorite coral reef and diving for a fish. I was always able to get something from that reef. I would then cook my meal, eat, clean up and go to sleep. If I had a good book, I would light the candle and read.

Sometimes at night if the moon were full, I would take the boat out. There were times when I would fish all night with pole and line. Without realizing the time, I would be shocked to see the dawn approaching. The moon had a big impact on my life. Without electricity, it is definitely a strong factor. The fish all know this. So many things happen in the sea in relation to the moon. The first and foremost of course is the tide. But there are many mating rituals that occur relative to the moon's cycle.

To the East of the reef in the Turneffe Islands, there is a caye called Glory Caye where one such phenomenon occurs. On the full moon in the month of January, Nassau Groupers come by the thousands to mate. I was fortunate enough to witness this. It is a wonderful experience, and very special for me since the Nassau Grouper is one of my favorite fish. Like the Parrotfish, Nassau Groupers are extremely gentle in nature and will become your friend if you let them. They can grow very old and become quite large. I have seen them well over 100 lbs. When they get that big they do not want to be pushed around. If they are in a good lobster hole, I learned to leave the hole alone and forget about any lobster that might be there.

The larger fish always live in deep water, Occasionally they would venture in towards my shack or my favorite diving patch, but not too often. Of the memories that I have from living here on the sea, one involves a huge fish. One day a giant fish had some-how got into these shallows and made it to my shack. I was on the dock in the morning when I noticed a very big dark shadow moving towards me. It was way too large, and moving too slow to be a dolphin. It scared me. The tide was high or he would not have been able to come so close. I went inside and got the rifle. He was heading straight for my shack. When he got near, I could see what he was. I saw his two eyes. They were a full meter apart. His head looked like some prehistoric beast. His skin was dark green and all scarred up. He had barnacles on him. It was a giant hammerhead shark. He almost moved in a mechanical fashion, like a big machine or submarine, I expected to hear humming as he approached.

I have dove with many hammerheads on a number of occasions and never felt frightened, but this one was the 'granddaddy' of them all, and he scared the shit out of me, even though I was above the water. I had never seen a shark so big, not even in books. If I had been in the water when he came up I would have attempted suicide with my 'Hawaiian Sling,' just to get out of my misery. Our dock was about five meters and this shark was almost that long. He swam around the dock and the shack on a slow inspection trip, and decided that he might like to stay for a while. If it was shade he was after he couldn't have been very comfortable under my shack because of all the foundation posts. He stayed around the front of the house swimming in large circles for fifteen minutes or so. Eventually he swam over towards my diving patch, which was a hundred meters away, checked it out and to my delight, continued on his way.

Rather near to the shack was a rock pile that I would often dive on in search of lobster. The water was barely above two meters. One day I had poled my boat over and jumped out into the water, as I always did. But on this day as I looked around I realized that I had jumped directly into the middle of a huge school of barracuda. Before this experience I never realized that barracuda would school up in such large numbers. It was a little frightening to see so many of these mean looking fish. As far as I could see in all directions there were barracudas. They were not very large ones and barracudas are usually not aggressive towards bigger humans like us, but if they chose to be, they could certainly have chewed me up in a few seconds. They have the capability with all those sharp teeth. On that day I was able to dive amongst them without any incident. They ignored me and I just went down and picked up a few lobster like always.

There were three occasions that I recall where I had close encounters with barracudas. The first one was a simple matter of a barracuda attacking a bag of fish that I had on my side. I had been spear fishing and putting the fish into a burlap bag tied to my waist. A big barracuda came streaming by and went for the bloody bag. He didn't get me but it was a strong and sudden shock as he pulled on the bag. The second incident occurred while I was diving in very poor conditions, the sea was quite choppy; the water was dirty with poor visibility. I was diving in a channel that had been cut down, resulting in some very good lobster holes. In order to reach the lobsters, I was sticking my arms deep into these holes getting lobsters out when a very large barracuda came rushing at me. I couldn't see him until he was right on top of me. He would speed in, stop just short of my face, and turn his body to me, scaring me to death. I was able to chase him away, but a few minutes later he would do the same thing. The big ones will look at you and do this thing with their mouth, opening and closing and baring those sharp, malicious teeth. On this day it was a serious warning and I decided to get out of the water.

My final close barracuda encounter is worth noting. I was stalking a medium sized 'cuda' with the intention of shooting him for a meal. This one was large enough that he wasn't easily frightened. I was able to swim head up on him. We were staring each other in the eyes when I launched my spear. When the spear hit him, it stuck and he jolted straight forward, directly at me. I was able to slightly move my head and face in time but the blunt end of the spear shaft struck me in my chest. It was with such force as to rip into my skin and leave a six-inch tear down my chest to my abdomen. I have since discovered that when a 'cuda' is hit, he always darts straight forward.

There were many lessons that I learned here in this simple life, some were obvious lessons about existing on the sea, but some were deeper and more subtle, about living with yourself and co-existing with nature. I mentioned earlier how violent the underwater world is, but I wonder if those that are near the bottom of the food chain even realize that they are victims. Perhaps their consciousness does not register such details as death. I understand what Thoreau meant when he wrote, "Life is frittered away with details, simplify, simplify." For those eight months, life in my shack was simple. In the society of the United States I often lived with a very complex diagram showing me how to act out my life, even at death, we often smother those left behind with such complex funeral and burial rituals. I would much prefer to be swallowed whole by one giant grouper.

37

More November

Another cold morning, almost freezing outside. I have a fire going and fires continue to burn as long as they have wood. An extreme fire of discontent and negative action is all around me and it will continue as long as it has the lies of Trump to fuel it. I cannot believe that yesterday he came on national TV and claimed that he has won the election. People who have been humiliated can become the most dangerous.

His reason for calling in the legislators of Michigan was to try and convince them to not let the electoral delegates cast their votes for Biden. Unconstitutional, this has never been done. To their credit, the legislators all refused, and went home. The delegate voting process takes place in December. This is a sad, absolutely unbelievable attempt by a corrupt authoritarian, dying on the vine. When Trump's actions don't match the mounting evidence, the goal of the others in charge should be to push past them. The Republicans who have any power should all be standing up in defense of right action, that's their duty. Perhaps they are keeping their mouths shut for fear of their political future.

I can only say that they are cowards because surely they can see the truth. There are some who are speaking out, urging Trump to concede and let Biden begin his transition, but their numbers are so small. Republican Senators, Congressmen, Governors, where are you?

All of this dismal stuff, including the pandemic has driven our lives to a new low. More lockdowns and curfews are happening throughout the country. I am so very fortunate to be able to live in a way that I'm not as affected by the condition as many others. There are so many people today who are living in fear, struggling for the bare essentials, food, rent money, medical help for themselves and family. They should be getting help from the leaders of our country. We are all paying for this service. It is much like the poor Black man who is getting beat up or killed by the bad white cop, and paying him to do it.

Yesterday was Biden's 78th birthday. He will become the oldest sitting President in our history. It's ironic, the oldest man needs to change the worst situation. Many ancient and world cultures of today teach great respect for the older souls amongst them. As one of these older souls, I can tell you, there are many lessons that are only learned over time. Reading, googling or studying of course helps along life's journey, but many things need to be learned the hard way, by living it.

An old Native American woman was once asked why she was always so happy. She said that she has two wolves in her heart and they are both hungry, one wolf is angry and evil, the other wolf is filled with love, and that's the only one she feeds. If all of us could be as wise as her, we would only feed the wolf that is filled with love.

On my way soon to Palo Alto to visit St. Julie before she heads back to Hawaii on Thanksgiving Day. We will be wearing our masks

NOVEMBER 22, 1963

No. No. No. I can't believe this has happened. Early this afternoon President Kennedy was shot and killed. I was sitting in the principal's office when the secretary jumped up from her desk, she was yelling out, "The President's been shot." Soon people were scrambling about in the office and then classrooms began emptying out into the halls. I left the couch of the office and joined all the students and teachers who were wandering about. Nobody really knew how to act, what to do. In my 17 years of life I have never known of such a horrible event as this. Although there was never an official closing of the school at that moment, it was obvious, school was over.

I was in the swell of students bunched outside on the rolling lawn of Palm Beach High. As I said everyone was shocked and confused. Somehow the school busses began operating and within a few hours we all worked our way back to our homes. My parents as well as every other family in America are tuned in to the news on TV.

The world is shocked. President Kennedy was such a great leader, taking our country forward. It was just a year ago when he stood up to Khrushchev and the Soviets as they were planning to deliver nuclear-armed missiles to Cuba. For three days the world watched as the Russian ships were heading towards us. Kennedy had set up a naval blockade surrounding the Island and we were facing a possible war. I remember how tense that situation was. From my classroom window we all watched as the convoys of military vehicles were traveling down Hwy 1 towards Key West, which is only 100 miles from Cuba.

The Kennedy family has a house in Palm Beach and I have seen President Kennedy twice since he's taken office. Once my friend Louie Soldo and I were walking home from school and John Kennedy was driving a big black Lincoln convertible across the bridge. I was so excited to see him and I was trying to tell Louie to look at his car. Instead I just yelled it, "Hey President." He looked at us, waved and beeped his horn. And now he's dead.

NOVEMBER 24, 2020

I spent a couple days with Julie in Palo Alto. On Saturday night we had another 'Pop up Dinner,' at the hotel's poolside restaurant. Tables are set up outside and spaced farther apart than normal, in respect of the virus. I guess that these dinners are the cool thing to do these days. Our dinner was billed as a "Hawaiian Style Culinary Crossroads Holiday Dinner." The five courses were: (1.) Ahi Poke, wild caught sashimi grade Hawaiian Big Eye Tuna; (2.) Lobster and Shrimp Jook, Chinese style porridge made with lobster and shrimp stock; (3.) Lumpia 2 Ways, Fillipino style egg roll prepared 2 ways, a.) butterflied shrimp, seasoned ground chicken and julienned vegetables, b.) minced pork belly, diced vegetables with a citrus soy glaze; (4.) Kalua Turkey, Hawaiian style slow cooked smoked turkey with a sweet potato mash and Portuguese sausage stuffing; (5.) Pumpkin Haupia Pie, coconut custard on top of pumpkin, etc. etc. Again a sommelier presented different wines with the different courses.

To me, the meal is all about the presentation. Lanai Tubura puts the dinners on and before each course is presented, he talks about how the different dishes came to Hawaii, as well as throwing in his extensive knowledge of Hawaiian in history. His chef Eric Pascual also speaks about the creation of the dish, and how it is cooked. In this way the customers are getting a show with their meal, and everyone seems to be happy and satisfied at the end.

And now for the most important news event in a long time. This morning the General Service Administration has officially recognized Biden as our next President, the lady in charge has given into the truth. We will stop looking like Trump's Banana Republic. The transition can now begin in a co-operative fashion. Of course our current President, being the child that he is, is still not conceding. Many, many Republicans have finally crossed the line, admitting that the election was fair and Biden won. I watched the news conference this morning where Biden introduced some of the newly appointed members of his Cabinet to anyone wishing to watch. They each took their turn at the podium and I was so impressed. It was emotional to me, tears of joy and relief as these mature adults spoke. Amateur hour will soon come to an end. Qualified, experienced people will begin to lead our government.

I feel as if a giant load has been lifted from my shoulders and our entire country as well, whether the Trumpers understand it or not.

A new Department has been created to deal with nothing but climate change. It will be run by John Kerry. In less than two months, women, people of color and a Latino immigrant will be taking the reigns to bring us back from the wild 4 year ride we have been on. Everyone on the team has such an impressive history, and they all spoke from their hearts expressing gratitude for their nomination and a desire to work relentlessly for the American people.

Since I began writing this book, I can finally see an end to the hopelessness and fear that I have been living with, the insecurity of everyday existence. When Trump took office it was unexpected, the polls all showed Hillary Clinton with a big lead.

In 1983 an English born writer Mary Renault died. She was known for her novels about Ancient Greek History. She wrote about Thesus, Plato, Socrates and Alexander the Great, some of the most brilliant people in our history. A quote from Mrs. Renault describes the condition we are now in. "There is only one kind of shock worse than the totally unexpected: the expected, for which one has refused to prepare." Without question, there will be many difficult challenges facing the Biden team. There will certainly be victories and defeats, but we must be prepared like never before. "A journey of a hundred miles begins with a single step." We are about to take a very big first step.

Hope is no longer as elusive as it has been. My prayer is that after Biden takes over, the partisan warfare will slowly ebb and as a country, we come together and work on issues affecting the common good of all people on our planet. However the figures show that only 31% of Americans believe we will grow more united, 26% think we will become more divided and 35% feel that nothing will change. Regardless, Biden and his team will be re-engaging relationships with our allies and working to "Bring America Back Again," to "Make our World Great Again."

Co-incidentally, great news is coming on battling the pandemic. Jackson Memorial Hospital in Miami will be receiving the Pfizer vaccine in a few weeks and inoculations will begin. There is much talk that many people will refuse to get this vaccine, probably the Republicans, following Trump's idiotic influence. I have never had a flu shot in my life, but I will be the first in line to take the needle for this cause. When I was 9 years old I became part of the polio vaccine trials. It worked.

NOVEMBER 25, 1963

Today John Kennedy was buried at Arlington National Cemetery. The whole country is still mourning this tragedy. They have caught the assassin, Lee Harvey Oswald, a 24 year old warehouse worker. My parents and I were sitting in front of the TV yesterday watching Oswald being transferred from one jail to another when another man came from the crowd and shot him at point blank range. This occurred on live TV, millions watched in disbelief. The shooter's name is Jack Ruby, don't know much yet about him or his reason for doing this, but we do know that now Lee Harvey Oswald is dead. What can possibly happen next?

NOVEMBER 25, 1986

The Attorney General has just announced that we have been selling weapons to Iran in an effort to get our hostages back. This is totally against President Reagan's policy of never negotiating with terrorists. It gets worse, the Attorney General also announced that we were giving the money to the Nicaraguan Contras, who are engaged in a guerilla war against the leftist government. The National Security advisor to Reagan has resigned and a lieutenant colonel in the Marines, Oliver North, has been fired. Can this really be happening, despite our own politics, we have no right to help rebels overthrow the government of another country.

NOVEMBER 25, 2020

I can well remember the war in Nicaragua. In the 1960s and 70s a dictator named Somoza was in charge. His family had ruled over Nicaragua since 1937. He was a bad man, corrupt and power hungry. Because of economic reasons the U.S. was backing him. The rich were exploiting the poor and the country was falling apart, the extreme class division resulted in a peasant uprising and war began, being led by a rebel named Sandina. His soldiers became known as the Sandinistas. They succeeded in overthrowing Somoza in 1979. However that didn't last long. A counter-revolution began with a group of rightists known as the Contras. When I traveled to Costa Rica in those years the war was raging, between the Contras and the Sandinistas.

I have recently written about a bad experience I had in the Bluefields of Nicaragua. There was another time earlier when I was on the San Juan River, back in the 70s. We were shot at from the banks on the Nicaraguan side. Perhaps the shooters, who were probably Contras, were not intending to hit us, but only scare us away. We immediately reversed our course and got as close as we could to the Costa Rican side of the river, making it safely back to a dock close to the village of Barra del Colorado. It could have happened on that day in 1974 that my life ended, shot by bullets that were paid for by Uncle Sam. During my time in Costa Rica I met a number of young Nicaraguan boys who had scars from bullet wounds or shrapnel.

Meanwhile the Biden team is wasting no time. Yesterday Biden's officials had over 20 meetings with their counterparts in the Trump party and Biden is now being included in the President's daily briefing of what is basically considered high-level intelligence. The Dow Jones made a huge jump and of course Trump called a news conference and claimed personal credit. In reality the record hitting figure was prompted by Biden's transition and the announcement of the vaccine being almost ready for distribution.

NOVEMBER 26, 2020 THANKSGIVING DAY

I feel thankful today, to the people of our divided but still great country, for electing Joe Biden. Each morning that I wake up, I feel like I want to put up banners,"Thank You Atlanta, Thank You

Michigan, Minnesota, Wisconsin and all the other states and cities that voted for Biden. We now have multilateralism back, multiculturalism, diplomacy, and most importantly empathy, truth and intelligence.

During the campaign, Trump promised that if Biden was elected, the stock market would crash and we would begin spiraling to self destruction. The opposite has and will happen even more. There will still be heavy battles to fight. The damage to our nation may take more than four years to repair. People that refuse to wear masks will still find themselves with a tube down their throat instead, but the vaccine will begin to lift us out of the pandemic. Businesses that have suffered and collapsed may not return, our world is changed and there will come something different, but I now have renewed hope.

I once went up a lighthouse, I believe it was in the Cayman Islands, and I was shocked by what I saw. I was expecting a super million Watt bulb as the source of light. I found a small gas flame and a giant magnification lens. The light was being shot out for miles over the sea to protect the sailors. It made me realize that, done correctly, it only takes a little to accomplish a lot. I don't even have to be the light, I can be a mirror that reflects it, or a lens that aims it in the right direction. I must focus on this principle. Use what little I have, and direct it on the right path.

Biden and his team can't expect to change the hatred of so many people. They must expect this and regardless, they must direct their work towards the good of all. They will be attacked without question, and they must have their defense prepared. The ingenuity of fools is often underestimated. There is a receptive goal waiting, and my guess is that they are such smart people, they will find it.

I can't even figure out the laws of our land. I have been writing about the inherent faults with our social media lives. After seeing the Senate hearings on free speech versus the flagging and deleting practices, I concluded that our government had some right to stop the dangerous lies that harm our people. I was almost certain that there were laws in place, broad regulations, that enabled our government in the case of an emergency, to legally step in and place restrictions. Obviously I was wrong. Today's news taught me that a new popular site has sprung up, "Parler." There are no restrictions, no deletions on Parler, it is a haven for hate speech and I'm sure that we will be hearing much more about it. You can now yell "FIRE" in a crowded theater.

Reality and truth never go away, even though so many people don't believe in them. A fact is a fact, and that is the reason for my hope. Besides the unjust penalty I must pay for getting old, at this stage, I have almost become the person I always should have been. I'm ignorant like everyone else, but with age, I am getting somewhat of a hold on it. Over the years, the people that I have mostly shared my time with have been gliding along, not so sure of themselves on many things. It's impossible to make up a list of things that we don't know, but realizing such, is a good start for a coherent associative approach to the next day in line.

I've said this before but one of the red flags that always pop up in my face when listening to a politician, is when they expound certainty of the subject. It reminds me of the religious zealots who will vehemently defend their absolute beliefs.

Despite admitting my ignorance, I must have some sense of self confidence enabling me to write this book, but self-importance is not one of my personality traits. I'm not in Biden's cabinet, but I am so happy that those important people have stepped up to battle for me. "Fight for the things you care about. But do it in a way that will lead others to join you." Ruth Bader Ginsburg

For me, it's a turkey dinner at Stu's house with a small group of his family, beginning in one hour.

NOVEMBER 27, 1960

I'm going out tonight to a football game. I just put a glob of vaseline in my hair and have it combed with a DA in the back. I hope to get downstairs and out of the house without my parents seeing it. (Note for those who don't know the term DA: a DA is a hairstyle resembling a duck's ass. Elvis has made it popular.)

NOVEMBER 27, 2020

Life has been going on on our planet for 700 million years as nearly as we can tell. That's about 10 million years for every one of mine. Knowing that, probably contributes to my feeling of being rather unimportant in the general scheme of things. When I say I lack self-importance, I may be inconsiderate of the feelings of Abel, Mia, Zachary, Jay and all of the offsprings following, and also my close friends, who I assume place somewhat of a higher value on me being here. So I guess I am important after all. I will never again feel unimportant.

I'm going to celebrate this new found understanding. I have to fight this culture war that's going on. My technique is to just try and talk sense into Danny and the other side. They're the ones who are fighting, not me. Since I often see myself as mediocre, it's easy to be at my best. If I thought I was a genius I would always have to prove it.

Today's news: An Iranian nuclear scientist was assassinated yesterday in Tehran. The blame is being placed on Israel and the U.S. The dead scientist has been the brains and the passion behind their drive for the bomb, However he will be easily replaced. Besides the destruction of his family and the bold statement that such a murder makes, nothing but a delay has been accomplished. More hate, more division, the "fight for right," those things continue to continue. The Mideast mess, "if you have the bomb, I can have the bomb," actually proves that both sides' actions are insane. Ray Bradbury, the science fiction writer has summed it up, "Insanity is relative, it depends on who has who locked in what cage."

God dried all my clothes that I washed yesterday, just like he does with my dishes every day. So I'm about to trudge out into the cold morning and pick my wardrobe from the clothesline. I can see my mom doing the same many years ago, before the option of a man made dryer was around. She and God were tight. She had three or four lines strung between the palm and avocado trees. Such beautiful memories of my parents, I often keep them both alive in this way.

NOVEMBER 28, 2020

As expected the pandemic is forefront in today's news, The numbers continue surging passing the records set the day before. Hospitals are dangerously crowded. Health workers are stressed to the max, and Trump continues to play golf. This is duplicating history, it is exactly as I read when I was very young, The Roman Emperor Nero fiddled as Rome was burning, and Marie Antoinette is mostly remembered because of her response as she was told during the French Revolution that her people had no bread, she responded, "Let them eat cake."

C'mon Trump, this is your moment to go down in history. However you should be warned, because I'm sure you don't read or know much about history. In 1793, Marie Antoinette was tried for treason, and publicly beheaded, and the hated evil emperor Nero committed suicide.

Due to the ever-present, extremely-pertinent, 'all things considered' factor, I'm having an OK time of it. As I mentioned earlier I am still filled with the joy of our new change, and I remain in good health. Trump continues fighting his ridiculous legal battles, going to court with absolutely no evidence backing up his claims of voter fraud. Every judge arrives at a somewhat chastising response, yet Trump's primary legal team of Rudy Giuliani, Jenna Ellis and Sidney Powell continue spending time and lots of donated money. By the way, to quote Matt Lewis in the Daily Beast, the team wanted to show off their "litmus test of insanity for the Republican Party."

I heard a lady being interviewed and angrily complaining about the NFL actions. "What right do these football players have to receive all these virus tests while our citizens and the health workers must wait for days, even risking the chance to be denied a test." The argument is an emotional one for sure and it has merit but, there's a little more to it. The NFL has a total of approximately

1700 players. (That is the exact number of health care workers who have died of Covid.) Doctors, nurses, and the other health care workers number in the millions. The football teams are easily tested since they almost live together during the season.

Now we must also look at the importance of the two. Without question, health care workers are the more important group. But people want, demand and will pay to get their football. Yesterday was the biggest shopping day of the year. Even with the restrictions, sales broke the previous record. And you know what people bought, games and toys. Sports have become such an important part of so many people's lives. It's almost an addiction to some. By proceeding with the games, many have a break from the loneliness of the lockdown.

A football game is similar to how our world works. The ball is the bag of money that drives our economy. One side has it, the manufacturers, the markets. They kick it out to the other side, the buyers. The other side picks up the ball and runs with it, throws it, trying to get it to their goal anyway they can. They are stopped most of the time. The other side is doing all they can to get that money back. The bag of money goes back to the other side, the favorites, the big guys. They take it and try to advance their purpose, they'll even use trick plays. This scenario goes back and forth for a few hours. Hundreds of thousands of people all over the country are now betting money as to who will win, and how much they will win by (the stock market).

This all began in the center stage, on the 50 yard line, halfway, equal terms, ironically with a flip of a coin. The 50 yard line is like La Mitad del Mundo in Ecuador. The referee can put one foot in the home team's turf and the other in the opponents. Perhaps at the coin flip one of those Captains should grab the coin before it hits the ground, and just start running, yelling about the ridiculousness of it all. If he gets caught the League will hit him where it hurts, in his personal money bag.

If the Captain is Patrick Mahomes, that won't matter, he signed a contract this year for 500 million dollars. These are the things that the lady on TV was yelling about, demanding that they should quit football season. And as for the other guy who's yelling about Hollywood and how much the actors are being paid. I'll tell him this, "You gotta look a little deeper into it, son," and leave it at that.

NOVEMBER 29, 1956

I'm on the way to Lido Pools, today's pretty warm in Palm Beach, not like the summer when I'm at the pools every other day, but warm enough. I'm gonna keep practicing my new dive, the full gainer. I've brought my sweatshirt, it helps when I smack into the water flat on my back. I absolutely consider Lido Pools one of my favorite places. I don't use the handball courts or the solariums that are above the locker rooms, one for men and one for women. But I do use both pools. The bigger one especially, since it has two small diving boards and the three decker high dive. I love going through the tunnel under A1A over to the beach, and jumping in the ocean sometimes.

Since it's winter now there might be some waves and I love to bodysurf. I'll walk out on the pier up to the tackle shop. At night my Grandpa Bill works in the shop. I want to have his job when I get old. I can ride my bike here in about half an hour. I like to cruise up Worth Avenue and look in the expensive shops. (NOTE: Lido pools were built in the 1920s along with the fishing pier. The pools were saltwater and were drained every two days and refilled with ocean water. The pier suffered damage from a hurricane and both the Pier and Pools were demolished before the end of the 60s, making way for condos.)

NOVEMBER 29, 2020

I'm being driven totally insane today by watching the news. I'm similar to one of the Republicans in Georgia, who are now threatening not to vote in the upcoming Senate runoff, because the White House is not doing enough to help Trump overturn his election results. If I keep watching, I will be like one of them or maybe I would turn into one of those people in Japan, who I just found, out have increased their suicide numbers tenfold. Maybe I should turn the news channel to sports, to get my mind off of all this.

Oh no, the Denver Broncos don't have a quarterback for their game today, the starter and his two backups all have Covid issues. Yikes, my team, the Niners, have just been told that they won't be able to play in their stadium for at least three weeks. A new restriction issued yesterday prohibits contact sports in Santa Clara County. Julie's Hotel will need to cancel those limited reservations that she did have for the next few weeks.

As I escape into the memories from my past, none are any more fun than the Lido Pools. I spent many hours and many days swimming and learning to dive there, playing in the ocean. Palm Beach was very different in those days. They had not yet begun to isolate themselves from the lower classes that lived over the bridges in West Palm Beach. At least, that is, if you were white. The beach was wide, extending from a seawall perhaps 30 yards down to the tide-mark. Today there is no beach. The waves smack the seawall, even down a few miles South on A1A where Mar A Lago is. Trump can't change that.

Thinking about the hours I spent on the diving boards of Lido Pools makes me grateful that I lived in that period. Nowhere in our country today will you find public diving boards, not in parks, not in hotels or motel swimming pools. The lawyers have made sure of that. Those diving boards represented a free lifestyle that has disappeared today.

At Lido Pools I practiced on the lower boards, eventually graduating to the higher levels. The expert divers today have learned skill and style. The diver is usually a perfect example of physical development. In competition, a professional diver climbs the ladder to the top, stands for a short while, composed. Preparing, and then slowly walking to the end of the board, he turns and steps back a few paces. For a few more seconds, he thinks about his approach, execution and entry, now it's time. One, two steps, and on his third step his knee comes up, all of his weight then comes down, he and the board are thrust downward, then spring up, shot into the air, freedom. He flies, turns, twists. Leaning forward he begins flipping, either in a tight ball or laid out, while still twisting.

In three and a half seconds, it's done, a 2 ½ somersault with a full twist, beautiful, brilliant. He slices into the water and his performance is then judged, on a scale of 1 to 10. All five judges give him a perfect 10. As he climbs out of the pool, he is approached by the media. "Diving is my Life," he says. True, in more ways than one.

Last night I received a call from Danny, the first time we've talked in nearly three weeks. I was happy to hear from him. He was wanting me to check out a possible electrical job in the Art Gallery where he works, something about running a new circuit for some high wattage heaters.

I just came back from meeting with him and checking out the job. Turns out the job was not for me. It was an impractical way of solving the heating problem and would have required a lot of conduit run overhead in a ceiling that is at least 30 feet high. Danny has certainly not abandoned any of his feelings or political opinions.

Our big difference is not simply the stand we take on issues, but how strongly we are consumed by them. Within a minute the anger was there and sprouting out I can label it indignant anger, but also ignorant anger. If Brenda were suddenly dropped in Tehran and forced to wear a burka, we would have another Danny. He asked when I planned to go and see my kids, remarking that if it's not soon, we will be permanently locked down and I won't be able to ever go.

From there the topic switched to mask wearing. He called them face diapers and complained with a promise that they are never coming off. We walked outside and he spotted the trail of a jetliner, "Here they go again, they're poisoning us. I saw another one earlier this morning." I kept changing the subject trying to keep the discussion light and apolitical, but it was difficult. There is just too much inside of Danny to keep down. He has absolutely no clue that he just might be wrong. I'm proud of myself, I didn't call him a "stupid fucking jerk" this time. I hope never to do that again. The crazy thing is Danny is still my friend and I wish none of this had ever happened. We could then share more happy times, like we did in the past.

I wrote about Georgia Republicans earlier and how they have taken insanity to the next level, well now it's Trump's turn on the couch. I've labeled him as a delusional troubled despicable soul with the maturity of a young child, but wait, there's more. Under orders, his legal team continues filing suits without any credible evidence. They walk into the courtrooms and ramble on, like throwing a bowl of spaghetti at the wall and hoping a couple of noodles might stick. But Trump's out on the golf course instead of helping them fight. After losing in court after higher court, I'm sad to say, but some of these appeals might make it to our nation's Supreme Court, and that is a travesty.

While our country is facing such critical issues as the present surge on top of the already dangerous surging pandemic, and the failing economy, we should be putting every effort towards these concerns. There are now 4 million cases of the virus, 2,500 deaths per day and deaths are expected to rise as much as 4,000 per day. Meanwhile Trump finishes golfing and begins planning a huge rally in Georgia. His erratic behavior has been compared to the Russian technique of putting out a firehose of lies and disinformation in order to confuse and undermine any resistance. Trump, probably without a conscious effort, has become the Master at this, better than his nefarious buddy Putin.

Conservatism vs. liberalism is the immediate and critical force that is driving today's division. The main weapons being used in this war are gun control, government power, abortion, immigration, taxes, health care, climate change, and several others. If all of these issues are looked at with a few things in mind, some clarity might surface. Number one: Everyone should realize old thoughts often blur and conceal new situations. Number two: Science and rapid progress have a way of gathering knowledge too quickly for society to adapt and grow with the new wisdom. Number three:

Change is the only constant in our entire existence. Growth cannot happen without change.

If someone believes these three ideas to be the truth, then compromise might take place. Otherwise any logical approach to a solution will not succeed. In the deepest parts of my soul, I honestly feel that Biden wants a compromise and that "Trumpers" don't. Perhaps in my generation only a slight repair of America can be expected, I will sadly live with it, and hope that I am mistaken.

NOVEMBER 30, 2020

Hurricane season has officially ended, record numbers of tropical storms and hurricanes were set, but I believe the hurricane problem is now being put on hold. Biden was out playing with his German Shepherd over the weekend and somehow hurt his foot. In the ER he discovered he had a hairline bone fracture, and a sprained ankle. I hate to say it, but accidents like this don't happen to young folks while playing with their dog. Today he is announcing more of his picks. The press team will be composed of 7 people, all female. I remember when all hurricanes were given female names. One year it changed and male names appeared, This year hurricanes bear not only the names of both genders, but names such as Alpha, Beta, Gamma, etc. The Greek alphabet is here to help.

Trump achieved his wish in Michigan, the recount tally is complete, and there were some slight errors. He paid 3 million dollars to get the results. Biden gained 87 votes. As for the vaccine, it is getting here. Officials are now shifting their efforts towards storage and distribution. It won't be easy, something like this is a 'first' and will require so much in the way of logistics and coordination. The horizon shines with hope, and soon Trump will no longer be around, or at the least he won't have the ability to turn this glow into an obscure glare. Sorry Mr. President, I'm putting the blame on you for something you haven't even done. You "would if you could." though, wouldn't you? I'll make you a deal, you don't let Giuliani file a lawsuit against me for writing this book, and I won't blame you ever again for any hypothetical situations. Now then, will you get to work and help the people who are about to run out of their unemployment benefits? The economy will collapse if this isn't fixed, like immediately.

There's an insect called a botfly that lives for no more than 12 days, they're like creatures from a horror film, remember "The Alien." Their whole purpose is to mate, reproduce and infect us and other warm blooded mammals with their larvae. When the larvae matures, in approximately 3 months, it pops out of its host's flesh, and begins its cycle. Stranger than one can imagine, once it is free of its host, it can no longer eat, it has no functional mouthparts. So it soon dies, what's the point? If you can figure this one out, you're better than me.

I've lived in the tropics, and I've met many people who bore the scars of the botfly. To the botfly larvae, the human's body serves them as our planet serves us. Their life is only 12 days long, and it seems that they add nothing valuable to the ecology of our planet. They exist for no reason. As humans, we should not be like the botfly. We live here, we learn things, and then we pop out, we have a lot more time alive, we should not do nothing, forget everything, and soon die, Oh my gosh, I may be carrying this a little too far, it's time to quit writing for a while.

It's gotten a little warmer outside since the 30 degrees of this morning. Today the news announced that a discovery has linked vitamin D deficiency to Coronavirus. The "Sunshine Vitamin" boosts our immune system and helps to fight off infections and maybe the Coronavirus as well. So, I'm going to quit thinking about botflies and go outside, get in the sun and do a small job for my neighbor.

38

December

DECEMBER 2, 2020

Assuming that I will live 80 years, that's just about a complete cycle of time for a human. Those that study such things, break our existence down into 20 year periods. The first 20 being childhood, then from 20-40 we enter young adulthood, midlife begins at 40 extending to 60, and after that period, we then become the old people, or elders. Big changes come for us with each step we take. We have different ways of looking at things, dealing with them and recording them to our memory. I believe our emotions are big influences on how we interpret life as we progress.

Today I would not see the Lido Pools in the same way that I remember them from my youth. Even as a young adult I had formed some ideas that do not work today. I honestly thought that in the 60s our generation had made a lasting change. I never thought the hippies way of dressing, wearing their hair, the communes that arose, the campus riots, the obvious turn towards spiritualism, the New Order, that all of this could possibly change. But it only took the next generation, 20 years, to completely shift into an alternate lifestyle. There's a big lesson to be learned here.

I have done a lot of writing, postulating on how bad the times are now, and that they may never get better. I was expressing a lot of fear and worry for the future. As I get close to the end of this book I realize that I was wrong. I'm in the fourth period of my life, like the fourth season of the year, winter. A lot of things have been dying and are dead now as Winter descends, but Spring will come as it does every year. We are simply experiencing the end of the circle, the end of the ring. This cycle that is present in every form of life has not disappeared, it continues. We may not see another "Summer of Love," but something similar will emerge. Churchill said that the farther back you look, the further forward you will see.

History absolutely positively repeats itself. We will come out of this winter-like period that we have been living in since the 60s and 70s. Our Spring has almost arrived and an empathetic human being, our President elect Joe Biden is here to start it off. The vaccine is just around the corner, and we now have competency within our leadership. Our nation is on the way up.

Now for the not so optimistic part, We must work on a global scale to prevent another large scale war. History tells us it will come. Adding 80-100 years to 1945 brings us close to the present, making the time from 2025- 2045 the likely period for the next big war. Of all the powerful nations, it's the United States that has the best chance to prevent this. Is war inevitable? Are we predestined? I hope not.

DECEMBER 3, 2020

Dear Diary, The number of coronavirus cases did not break the record yesterday, probably because of less testing since the holidays, but they are steadily rising. The deaths are now around 270,000, and predicted to rise to 450,000 by February. To coin a new paradoxical term, the 'inconceivably expected' is now happening. Investigations are starting and Ivanka Trump, the President's daughter has been called for a deposition to explain why over a million dollars of campaign funds were channeled to the Trump Hotel. Not legal Giuliani, you better get on it quick.

I have learned that it is possible for a President to grant a pardon for himself and his family for crimes that may, (in this case, will) come up after he leaves office. These Presidential pardons are outright shameless in themselves, but this one is an obvious case where laws have been made by lawyers to protect themselves. However, the dilemma that Trump will discover is he can only pardon himself for federal crimes not any that would be on the state level. This new Trump adventure will probably begin on January 23.

I watched a news conference with Biden and Harris today and again I felt relieved, and hopeful. Joe said he wants Kamala to be the first one in his office in the morning and the last one to leave at night. She is going to be involved in everything. Often a Vice President is assigned to handle one important issue, and is unseen most of the time. The environmentalist Al Gore was one such example. Clinton used him in all matters regarding ecological issues, and that's all I can remember him for. This brings me to the reason why Joe chose Kamala. I believe that besides the fact that she is a woman and besides the fact that she is a person of color, she is also 56 years old and in her midlife, old enough to be knowledgeable and experienced and young enough to take the reigns in 2024. When needed she will be able to jump on the wild horse and ride it. In other words, she can play with her dog and not break her foot.

DECEMBER 4, 2020

Might as well start my day off with a bang. Last night I had an amazingly real dream. I was with a few of my granddaughters and we were driving. Honestly I can never remember a dream that seemed so real. I had to convince them and myself that it was a dream. Finally I realized that everyone was driving on the wrong side of the road. I kept saying "Look this has to be a dream, see how we're on the wrong side of the road." It was so hard for me to accept that this was not real. But deep down I knew that it had to be a dream. Now comes the good part.

We were then all in the ocean swimming around inside a huge net. There were dolphins inside and I was so happy that my granddaughters were going to be able to swim and play with them. They swam close to us and we were all petting and rubbing them. We were trying to free them out of the big net. This went on until I woke up. It was 7:30 and I put on the morning news. Within seconds a video started playing that some jetski riders had shot in Florida. The two guys had spotted a dolphin tangled up in a net and apparently had a good iPhone. They shot some great video and the news station was impressed. Their video of them working to cut the dolphin free went on for almost 5 minutes. I laid there between asleep and awake. It was as if my dream world and my real world had blended together. Somehow the Florida boys were able to shoot underwater footage, and it looked exactly as my dream. The only thing missing were my granddaughters. A wild coincidence, if that's what it was.

Last night I got a text from my son Abel (the father of the girls in my dream) about his 2-year-old son AJ. Anyone that's ever raised a boy can probably relate.

"Since AJ walks around trying to boss us around all the time like he's a mob boss, I gave him a mob name. He's little and solid so I've dubbed him 'Marty the Meatball.'"

I told Abel to tell "Meatball" to back off, cuz "The Old Man" was coming down soon. I'm not quite sure how long it will be before I travel, but I will travel to see my family, as soon as it feels right.

DECEMBER 5, 2003

Nelson Mandela died today, he was 95. An incredible man with an incredible life, gone from this world and heading into the next. He was known, not only in his own country, South Africa, but throughout the world as a freedom fighter, prisoner, civil rights leader, and political leader. He spent 27 years in prison during the prime of his life. He was finally released when he was 71, and 4 years later was elected as President. I never have seen such a thing as this. He has been my hero for a long time. The living saint is now gone.

DECEMBER 5, 2020

I'm having fun this morning. I loaded a new TV news channel onto my ROKU device and I've been watching live news from South Florida. I saw an aerial shot of the Florida Keys bringing back so many fond memories of that time period. I'm watching Florida's newsworthy actions as well as a different take on the National News. I'm basically concluding that people are people. I saw a very bright young guy editorializing on Trump, the virus and the social regulations. He could easily have been on our Bay Area stations and no one would realize he was in Miami, except for the fact that, in closing he said, "It's gonna be cold today, better get on your sweater, Miami, low of 52, high around 65." Dude, it's 30 right now on my porch.

A vote was taken yesterday in Congress for the federal legalization of marijuana, it passed. A handful of democrats voted "nay" and a handful of Republicans voted "yea." However, It won't even make it to the Senate. It's ridiculous in my opinion that considering all the priorities that exist, the marijuana issue is even being pushed at this time. It must be a very personal issue for some people and I do respect that. For example, a black person is 4 times more likely to get arrested for marijuana possession than a white person. I know a whole lot of white people that are probably rolling a joint right now as I write.

One of the reporters in Miami covering this made fun of San Francisco, saying that it was illegal to smoke cigarettes inside restaurants and bars, but legal to smoke pot. Eat your heart out Dade, Broward and Palm Beach County, haha.

Yesterday I took my big ladder and went to Sam's house in Marin, putting up Christmas lights in the front of his house. From there, onward to his in laws' house in San Rafael for more of the same. Sam's father in law, a nice guy, said he didn't feel good getting up on ladders. I told him, "It's the most dangerous tool in the shed." Many people get seriously hurt, I've had my day. It happened in North Carolina.

I was helping a friend and fellow building contractor who put up manufactured homes. It works like this, after the foundation is completed a couple of trailers arrive bringing the prefab home to the site. With a crane waiting, as well as a number of other workers to help, the process begins. On this day, we had the two main structures and the roof all hoisted and set in place. The final stage was putting in two dormers on the roof. As the first one was being lifted up, I saw that there were workers already inside to help and so I thought I might help guide it in by getting on my ladder and working from the outside. This house had a basement so I extended the ladder all the way up almost three stories.

Whoever had rigged these dormers had made a serious mistake by putting the 2x4s flat instead of on edge which is 10 times stronger. Just as the dormer was getting overhead I saw and heard the supporting 2x4s start to crack. As it got directly on top of me it broke completely and started to come down. Impulsively, I took one step down and then jumped, almost 30 feet to the ground. The dormer hit the ladder, sending it flying and then came crashing to the ground missing me by only a couple of feet. I sprained my wrist and broke a few ribs, but it could have been much worse.

Back to San Rafael. I realized that Bob, Sam's father in law, is afraid of ladders because of his age. That makes sense, what doesn't make sense is that I'm only two years younger than Bob. Chronologically that's the fact, physically I don't feel that way. I'm not afraid. Granted, I don't want to jump 30' to the ground, but I don't even jump from the bumper of my truck anymore. I can remember as a teen ager jumping off the roof of our house, no problem, mon.

DECEMBER 6, 1969

Another big concert is happening today in California, pretty cool. It's being organized and put on by the Rolling Stones as they're just finishing up their tour. It's being labeled as the Woodstock of the West Coast. Besides the Stones as headliner, the performers are going to be Santana; the Jefferson Airplane; Crosby, Stills, Nash and Young; and the Grateful Dead. It's up in Northern California at a race car speedway. Predictions are that it will draw 300,000 people. We in the 'sixties' have surely rocked the world and this is such a fitting way to wind up this decade. I won't be going to California, except in spirit that is.

DECEMBER 7, 1969

What a shocking surprise. The Altamont Rock Festival turned into a horrific disaster. The Hell's Angels had been hired to provide security and what I thought was going to become a glorious end to our historical decade has ended up as a violent mess. A stabbing murder occurred just in front of the stage as the Stones were performing. One of the Jefferson Airplane's group had been knocked unconscious by a thug in a fight earlier, and as darkness came on the Grateful Dead canceled and got out of there. There were three other deaths at the concert yesterday. I can hardly believe it. A statement has been announced to the world, "Peace and Love" don't last forever.

DECEMBER 7, 2020

Pearl Harbor Day, I'll call it "Sneak Attack Day," the inhumanity of man at its peak. it just demonstrates the sad reality that we are not civil beings. It's not to say who is to blame, or for what cause we resort to such a measure. As a whole, mankind is a very troubled species. Peace and harmony have never existed. Since the beginning of our recorded history we have never had a period without war. We have only waxed and waned like the moon. December 7, 1941 was a full moon of war, 2,403 Americans killed by the Japanese in one hour. Four years later, another full moon, the Americans killed 225,000 Japanese with 2 nuclear bombs.

Today we are at war with a virus. We will see another record today for the number of coronavirus cases and deaths, 16,000 people will die this week in the U.S. Even though this war is man against virus, in a sense it is pitting man against man. Without any question we in America have politicized this war and we are fighting each other as to our method of treatment. People are dying because of this, and it is very sad and heartbreaking to watch. To wear masks, to social distance, to avoid large gatherings, to stay at home, every one of these techniques are being challenged, ignored and thought of as fake, a way to take away our freedom. For me it is so simple to take the right action. I mentioned it earlier as the "what if" test. What if these measures do work? Isn't it worth the inconvenience? Why so many people can't see this is beyond any sense of rational thinking. Those that are fighting the medical experts, are people who think like Rudy Giuliani. He never wears a mask and yesterday was diagnosed with the virus.

New more serious lockdowns are happening all over. Gavin Newsom said if there comes a time when the state ICU beds get 85% full he will put these serious restrictions and it's happening. Restaurants can only have takeouts, no more outdoor dining, many more business shutdowns.

And for some good news, the vaccines are getting closer. England will begin it's inoculations next week, we won't be long to follow. This might be the beginning of the end. It's been a long strenuous wait, and the end will not come before next summer, to be sure. The vaccines are described as a fire hose directed at a huge forest fire. A lot of people in our world are on fire with the virus.

DECEMBER 8, 2020

Known for his extreme wealth, probably the richest man that had ever lived up to that time was King Croesus of Lydia. He lived and reigned 600 years before the birth of Jesus. One of his famous statements was "Count no man happy till his end is known." I suppose he was saying that you must look at the big picture. That seems to be what people don't have the ability to do. It seems to be a developed trait, since children and most teens don't appear to have this ability. When adulthood comes we should have acquired that knowledge and capability. We won't "know the end," as Croesus says, but we can and should work together to make it a happy ending.

I was once told that in an aquarium by the time a tropical fish swims from one side of the tank to the other, he has forgotten about the first side that he left. That always made me feel better when I looked at an aquarium. I do believe that salt water fish are smarter than the freshwater ones, ha. I am convinced that intelligence has something to do with being able to remember your past and foresee the future to a degree. It's not the responsibility of a guppie to save our planet, it's those of us who live here with the brains to instigate positive change. It comes down to the old "live and learn" idea, a collective life and learning of us who are homo sapiens.

Today the Environment Protection Agency has refused to tighten up laws on industrial soot emissions. Their own medical public health experts have shown that the public health suffers, yet money making wins again.

Also in today's news, Trump's legal team is being accused of lying to the public. They have licenses to practice law but not a license to make false claims and openly lie. 1500 former federal prosecutors and other lawyers have signed a letter to the bar associations wanting an investigation.

In Cobb County Georgia, where Biden won by 14% the Republican election officials have only opened up 5 early voting locations for the Senate runoffs, instead of the 11 they had for the Presidential election.

On a personal note, I just received a call from an acquaintance, Linda. She retired from her own radio show and is now wanting to begin a podcast. She asked me if I would join her. I barely know what a podcast is. I don't participate in social media platforms as I've mentioned, but I agreed to meet her and talk about it.

A dark Covid winter is upon us, Trump never ceases to act insanely, harming all of us. Biden and team are at our doorstep, here to save us. Maybe it's time for me to go online. If so, I will cautiously walk on that line. I don't feel it will help things if I simply fortify the beliefs of like minded people. And knowing as I do that so many people never listen, I wonder if the entertainment value of the move will outweigh the intended helpful change, that may never occur.

DECEMBER 9, 1971

Today the Peace talks that were taking place in Paris have broken down. The North Vietnamese walked out. This is terrible. It's been over a year since the Kent State shootings and all of America is ready for peace. The massacre at Kent State caused so many protests and riots, it has definitely changed things. People are getting disgusted with this war and also Nixon. He promised to end this war and instead has expanded it by invading Cambodia. How and when will this end. Not only us young people but the whole country wants to know.

DECEMBER 9, 1980

Oh no, Somebody shot and killed John Lennon last night in New York. A young crazy assassin shot him 4 times in the back as he was coming to his home late at night. His apartment was on 72nd Street and Central Park West just several blocks from where Billy Michael and I had our place. This has shocked the whole world. What a horrible moment in time.

DECEMBER 9, 2020

V-Day (Vaccination Day) hit England yesterday and the vaccinations continue. It's like a wartime spirit in our Mother Country. Optimism is spreading. It's coming soon to us. There were a couple of negative reactions to the vaccinations yesterday, symptoms like anaphylactic shock occurred in one person. He's fine after a day, but doctors are suggesting that people who have serious allergic reactions to things, better wait before getting the shots.

Watching the Miami news station has made me proud of our state government here in California. A Florida Senator Matt Gaetz recently held a big fundraiser in New Jersey without any precautions and New Jersey's governor was livid. He came on TV chastising the action, his words, "I hope you're watching this Senator Gaetz, we want you out of our state and never come back."

The Governor of "the Sunshine State," Ron DeSantis had his people raid the home of a research scientist, Dr. Rebekah Jones at gunpoint. She has been tracking and reporting on virus infections and deaths. She was fired last week because she wouldn't alter the facts for DeSantis. The cops came in and took her files and her computer. Here's a copy of some of her tweets:

1. "There will be no update today. At 8:30 am this morning, state police came into my house and took all my hardware and tech. They were serving a warrant on my computer after DOH filed a complaint. They pointed a gun in my face. They pointed guns at my kids."

2. "They took my phone and the computer I use every day to post the case numbers in Florida, and school cases for the entire country. They took evidence of corruption at the state level. They claimed it was about a security breach. This was DeSantis. He sent the gestapo."

3. "This is what happens to scientists who do their job honestly. This is what happens to people who speak truth to power. I tell them my husband and my two children are upstairs... and THEN one of them draws his gun. on my children. This is Desantis' Florida."

And yesterday's tweet, "If Desantis thought pointing a gun in my face was a good way to get me to shut up, he's about to learn just how wrong he was. I'll have a new computer tomorrow. And then I'm going to get back to work. If you want to help, my website is still at home."

DeSantis, Gaetz, just two more scumbags who are in Trump's camp. They make all the wrong decisions. I feel sorry for my family that still live in Florida and have their state laws made by people such as these two. Florida, another Republican State, the one that put George W. Bush in power instead of Al Gore.

Meanwhile in Georgia, the Republicans are shutting down more early voting sites all over the state, again attempting to suppress voting. It seems that Republicans everywhere are obsessed with, breaking all the rules, doing anything they can to win, regardless of the effects on social discipline. I just don't expect justice or a fair process from Republicans anymore. They're dying and they know it. The deep rooted belief in American democracy will come through in the long run.

A 19th century abolitionist, Theodore Parker, said, "The arc of the moral universe is long, but it bends towards justice." I hope he was right. The arc is overhead now.

I can remember my very first political action. The year was 1956, I was 10. Dwight Eisenhower, the Army General hero of WW 2 was running for President against Adlai Stevenson, my dad was for Eisenhower. I would sing the slogan song at school. "Oh, whistle while you work, Stevenson is a jerk. Eisenhower's got the power, whistle while you work." My dad and I won. Eisenhower turned out to be a wonderful Republican president.

For today's Republicans who are interested, he built all the Interstate Highway systems, 41,000 miles of new Interstate Freeways that flattened our world, bringing our country closer together, making us safer in emergencies. Like Roosevelt who created Social Security, both of these government acts, were done with collective taxes. It works like this, everyone chips in together for the good of the whole. That's called socialism. Think Fire Department, Police Force, socialism.

Whenever the socialism argument is thrown at the Democrats, I wince. Communism is one thing, socialism is another. Spend some time in Cuba and then Sweden, or even Canada and you will see the difference. Of course nobody would choose to share equally with someone who does not do their equal part. "Yeah sure, these lazy bums are sitting at home collecting unemployment, while I work my ass off every day." This appears to be the underlying issue and it's valid reasoning for sure. But looking at the whole picture can provide the solution.

In the early part of this book I talked about the inherent problem with democratic capitalism versus socialism. I said then that a new system must be developed and that I didn't have the answers. Since I still adhere to this, the larger issue for me becomes, dealing with man's inadequacies. Cure the man first, then the political system that he lives within. Above all, practice empathy, non-violence and patience. I love you Bernie Sanders, although your timing sucks.

DECEMBER 10, 2020

Coronavirus deaths were 3,100 yesterday in our country, another record. Many states are running out of ICU beds and it's getting worse. Trump is still doing his rallies in Georgia, claiming he has won. Hunter Biden, Joe Biden's son is being looked at for some possible tax violations. Meanwhile, I'm going out to get some more firewood.

We have only had the one rain to help with our condition here, usually we have had a number of rainy days by this time in December. Since the first rain I have been having fires in my woodstove most every night. I cooked a big pot of bean soup the other day on the stove, and I think I'll figure something else to make on it this afternoon and this evening.

This is my life as a "lockdowner," watching some news, reading some books and my weekly magazine, and finally cooking. I usually talk with Julie every night. When I sleep I sometimes have dreams worthy of reflecting on. Last night was a "doozie." Up on my hill at my house were gathered a whole team of politicians. I mostly stood outside watching, as they were all running around inside. I even saw Trump. He was walking toward a young guy and he made a very genuine kind greeting. I soon realized that something serious was taking place, I noticed a fire on the hill. I wanted to run down to Stu's house to warn him, but I realized that I better get either my car or truck first. I tried to call Stu but the signals were cut off.

I got back to my driveway and my car and truck were gone, the fire was getting worse. The house was empty and one woman came out. I knew I had to get away quickly, the fire was raging up the hill. I yelled at the woman,"What has happened, what have you done?" She looked at me and said one thing, "Your Book."

I hope my next dream is happier than that one. I'm going to pray to Morpheus, the Greek goddess of dreams to do me right next time. By the way the drug morphine was named after Morpheus.

Since the fire season of last year I have been working to get our house, the one I live in and Julie owns, to pass an inspection for the insurance company. Reasonably, they want clear space between brush, trees and the house. I have already written about this situation. Well today after my series of cleanup and photos, the company agreed to cover the house. Now I'm able to set up the front porch as storage for my firewood. Just in time, since I got home an hour ago with a truckload of wood.

DECEMBER 11, 2020

No new news is the news. Maybe a new station should air in the mornings and call itself the "Daily Olds." There should be an alternative to the new if there really isn't any. Maybe when I turned on that TV this morning the station should have come out with the truth, "Sorry but today's news program has been canceled, because there isn't any new news." More of the old stuff, there's always the option of believing that "No news is good news." I guess when the optimist tells you that, they assume you're expecting the worst. If I dig around, I can probably find something new, OK Joe Biden's heading to Georgia. Morocco recognizes Syria and wins Trump's nod on Western Sahara.

By tomorrow we may find out how the Senate is doing with their new stimulus bill. Perhaps after the weekend we will know whether or not the Supreme Court will agree to hear the case being filed by the State of Texas and signed on by 126 House Republicans, to overturn the results of the election. There are also 17 Republican State Attorney Generals who have signed the petition and are backing this suit. These presumably intelligent lawmakers aren't asking the results to be overturned in Texas where Trump won. That one was obviously not rigged, but they want the states of Pennsylvania, Michigan, Wisconsin, and Georgia overturned. Every one of these states have already ruled on, and found no evidence of any fraud.

I'm going to repeat this, over 100 House Republican elected officials are behind this absurd backing of illegitimate claims. They are either immoral, ignorant, naive, uninformed or oblivious and have sadly displayed to our entire country how foolish our government can act. This is passive violence to coin a new term, sinfully obusive.

LATER THIS AFTERNOON

There is some news today after all. Starting tonight at midnight Gavin Newsom's strict "Stay at Home" order will go into effect. There will be no more outdoor dining, all barber shops, nail salons and gyms shutdown completely. All grocery stores and pharmacies must maintain a 35% capacity limit, retail stores only 20%. All but essential services are basically ordered to close, and people are asked to stay home for the next 3 weeks. I feel for the business owners but it's not going to phase me and my "Modus Operandi."

DECEMBER 11, 1958

Boy oh boy, a jet plane that can carry people has been invented. My dad has a friend that flew yesterday from New York to Miami. This is almost unbelievable for me. The jet had over 150 people in it and made the flight in about 3 hours. They say the jets will be flying all the way across the country in less than 6 hours. This will change the way people live, that's for sure. There have been planes before this that carry passengers but much slower and not as big.

Stewardesses walk up and down the aisles and bring drinks and snacks to the passengers. They are dressed in military uniforms but I don't think they are in the military. Our country and world is changing. My dad can remember when the first cars were being mass produced by Henry Ford, and one day I'll probably be telling the next generation that I remember when jets first began carrying passengers. What's next?

When our family drives from Kankakee to Florida it takes 3 days and two nights. We stay in Motels every night until arriving in Palm Beach late. I always make dad get a motel with a swimming pool so I can use their diving boards and practice.

Dad says when the Interstates get built, we can make that drive in only one day. That's nothing compared to what these new Passenger Jets will be able to do.

DECEMBER 12, 2020

Besides the pandemic surge continuing, yesterday the U.S. Supreme Court denied the case to overturn the election results. The court didn't rule against it, but rather, they denied any basis for even hearing the case. First of all, Texas has no right to interfere with another state's election process. And, as expected every point in their case was totally false, but I wasn't sure how the court would look at it. Every single judge, including the 3 that Trump appointed were critical of the attempt to misuse the court. The Supreme Court's action should finally put an end to this ridiculous Trump mockery of our democracy, but of course he and his fans will never admit defeat. These fans are the same people that are on their deathbeds while dying of Covid and with their final words, deny that it even exists. "I must have lung cancer." I'm not making this up.

As for the 126 Republican Congress members and the 17 state attorneys general who backed this suit, may you all feel ashamed and please resign. There are some sensible Republicans who see this for what it is, a shameful last ditch effort for those public officials to align themselves with Trump, knowing that is what their voters want. By continuing to deny the truth of the election those who have put their names on that lawsuit are helping to inflame Trump's violent supporters and you all deserve a just reprisal.

If only enough Republicans, from the Press Secretary, through the Cabinet and both Houses would stand up, admit to the truth and claim Biden as the legal winner of this election, it might, just might, help. It would be a lot easier for our country to move forward. Trump is now probably wondering why he didn't appoint Jared Kushner, Ivanka and Eric Trump as his Supreme Court nominees.

No stimulus bill yet, it was blocked again in the Senate. Bernie was on TV demanding a compromised bill. He challenged all of them, "How dare any of you Senators think you can go home for Christmas vacation until we get a bill to help our people."

I'm reading a book about a 24 year old boy and his father who are sailing together 17,000 miles from Connecticut around Cape Horn, the Southern tip of South America. This passage is known to every sailor in the world and recognized as the most treacherous, dangerous undertaking that a sailor can attempt. All the ocean from the Atlantic to the Pacific is squeezed into this 300 mile wide passage, creating monstrous waves, wicked currents, and winds near gale force. The "Horn" is spoken of in whispers by the experienced. David and Danielle Hays took this on, in a small 25' boat that they built themselves. At this point in the book, they have just left the Easter Islands and are heading to the "Horn."

Phil's boat that we sail is 32'. Every single additional foot in a sailboat makes a huge difference. Time now to leave this computer, listen to the rain, throw more wood in the stove, and get ready for more of David and Danielle's big adventure.

Finished reading "My Old Man and the Sea," the father and son made it, a very exciting book. There is something special about the motive, the force that drives people to risk everything for such a purpose. It was Kurt Vonnegut who wrote, "We are here for no purpose, unless we can invent one. The human condition in an exploding universe would not have been altered one tenth if, rather than live as I have, I had done nothing but carry a rubber ice cream cone from closet to closet for sixty years." Dan the son, had this thought after passing the "Horn" and continuing the 3,200 mile journey homeward without dad.

DECEMBER 14, 2020

I woke up this morning and had a jaw dropping, heart stopping, gut wrenching, emotion sinking moment. I clicked on the news and a man at a podium announced "On behalf of the great state of Tennessee. I hereby cast 11 electoral votes for Donald J. Trump." It took me a few seconds before I realized that that was OK. Even though it still affects me that even one state is so backwards that it would have voted for him. It didn't mean that Trump had somehow succeeded in overturning this. I continued to wake up and become happy again. Today's the day that Biden becomes the official President.

Next on the news was the Doctor sitting in his chair in NYC and becoming the first American to receive the inoculation for Covid. Things are turning around. This is a historical day. It's the beginning of the end of a most exceptional year. A year like I have never experienced. It will be the first year that I will ever receive a shot for a flu or a virus. It will be the first time I have been so intensely involved in an election. The first time I have ever been ordered to stay at home, and the first time I have continually recorded my life for a solid year.

"Pick a year, any year." Of all my 74, this has been the one that shall stand out above all of them. And in a little over two weeks I will have it all down for the record books. Why, 12 months ago, did I pick this year? I can't answer that but I must admit that I'm not surprised at the coincidence. Things like this just happen, if you don't stand in the way, and you let life happen. Coincidences are a way of letting God remain anonymous.

Like a Santa Cruz surfer who sits happily in the big ocean waiting for the right wave to come along. He has trained himself with the skills to hop onto the wave and ride it in for as long as he can, enjoying every second. He understands that he didn't create that wave, he never could make even the tiniest wave. But he can pick which one he chooses to catch. He can make it his own. It is a one time shot. And with his talent and by his skill he can then create his own artistic path, a thing of beauty,

I had no control over how those 74 years came to me, but it was me who surfed them from January to December of each year. Sometimes I wiped out for sure, and as the years kept coming, I chose the ones that I wanted to "hot dog" on. Just like the surfer, I seemed to get better with more practice at it. I had a bunch of accidents, but I have never felt like giving up, ever, not even close.

DECEMBER 15, 2011

The Iraq war has officially ended. A ceremony was held today in Baghdad and it's official. The crazy war started by Bush 5 days after the 9/11 attack is supposedly over now. Abel, my son, my hero, will not die in Iraq. He has told me that he and his troops, half the time, had no idea what they were doing over there. And he also told me that we have screwed up that country beyond belief. Heroes like Abel and so many others on both sides have sacrificed, many are not alive today. They deserve our lifelong respect and gratitude for what they have given.

DECEMBER 15, 2020

Today like yesterday, and the day before that, I woke up and turned on the news. This time it was Biden giving a wonderful speech as he is now the legal, official, conclusive, definite, valid President. If only those Republicans that believe Trump, would listen to Joe with an open mind and heart, many of our problems would dissolve. I could become friends again with Danny. The Midwest could become friends with the Northeast, the farmers could become friends with the urban dwellers, Texas could become a friend with California. Florida could become a friend with, uh, er, uh. Giuliani could go out to lunch with Bernie. Gavin Newsom's ex-wife could date Donald Trump Jr.

I won't dwell on the negative on this fine sunny cold morning. I received a call last night. My new friend and neighbor Drew wants me to redo his hot tub deck, a perfect, very simple job for the likes of me. I will quit hitting this keyboard, put on my ever-ready blue jeans, and away I go.

Later in the day and so it goes, nothing's as easy as you expect. In the construction world, the rule is that you figure out what the job will cost, double that, add 20% and if you're lucky you'll come close. I never thought that the deck screws would be the older rectangular headed ones, or that the holes would all be gummed up with some sort of deck sealer. What I'm saying is that the small little number 1 opening is varnished over and a drill bit won't seat itself in order to back out the screw. My first attempts wound up in stripping the screws. I have now found a solution, drill out each screw with a tiny bit first. That only triples the time needed for that part of the job.

For the second dilemma, whoever designed this, allowed for 18 inches of overhang with no joist support underneath. 2 ½ sides of the deck are now floppy when you walk on it. That is not an easy fix since the overhanging parts sit right on top of the ground. My brain is presently working on a solution for this one. Good luck brain. Please multitask while I type.

DECEMBER 16, 2009

If you had an extra 310 million bucks what would you do with it? How about doing what James Cameron just did, make a movie. The most expensive production in history was released today, and I went to see it, helping James get his money back. "Avatar," what a name for an amazing movie. In the Hindu world, an Avatar is a descended deity.

The movie is an amazing display of today's ability to use computer generated imagery. Besides that, the colors are amazing. Every scene is breathtaking. The story in itself is so moving, fitting for today's situations. Without a doubt, Avatar has taken the title as my favorite movie of all time. It topped "Star Wars." This must say something about what I like, who I was then, in the summer of 1977, and who I am now.

As a filmmaker, what I derive pleasure from in movies is not the same as the more sophisticated experts in the field. Give me something new, give me an action adventure, forget the dramatic lighting, or the novel music under. I'm more like the average guy watching a film. I don't like when I sit in the theater and expect myself to be analyzing every cut, every camera angle. And I dare say that all the other average movie watching guys like me are going to be rushing to the theaters for Avatar, just like they did for Star Wars.

Cameron has blended spirituality, timely ecological circumstances and environmentalist views into this film. He also shows how imperialism affects its innocent victims. Without a doubt he is comparing the Iraq War and its militaristic approach as a way to take what you want. The number one main character is a U.S. Marine.

Star Wars and Avatar, my two favorites, both war movies, hmmm.

DECEMBER 16,2020

I have the hot tub deck figured out, so moving on, I saw Mayor Pete first thing this morning. Pete Buttigieg is the former mayor of South Bend Indiana and one of the contenders who ran against Joe Biden. He was Julie's favorite. She loved his message, that he wanted to heal all the divisiveness in our country.

Pete was selected yesterday as the next Transportation Secretary in Biden's cabinet. He will be the first openly gay person to hold such a high government post, that is, if he can get a couple Republican senators to go along with his nomination.

He is the youngest Cabinet member chosen, 38 years old. In his speech today he recalled how it was when he was a teenager, a gay guy in the closet. He was so happy to spread the message that in today's world, conditions have changed, for the better.

If Pete had been born 35 years earlier, he would really see the change. When I was a teenager it was almost legal to beat up a gay person. It was called "rolling a queer." not a very far step from "lynching a nigger." This type of language is tough and abusive, but the fact is, the words mean nothing compared to the mentality behind them. Very few people today use either of those words, and it's difficult for me to even put them down in this writing.

Pete, you are here today and soon to be part of our national government as proof that we have moved ahead. May the shock of yesterday's mentality hit us for a moment and make us grateful that such a mentality no longer exists and that our country is where it is. I am sure that you are going to make the office of the Department of Transportation, a division of our government that citizens will now recognize. This Department began when I was 20 years old, it's time to turn it into a household word.

Pete spoke this morning of a 2nd railroad revolution. My dad always told me that when we stopped using the rail as our main means of moving goods across this country, we made a very serious mistake. And my dad always knew what he talked about. He was not overly opinionated, a rare gift for smart people. Like the older television commercial, "When Mel Martens spoke, people listened." I love you Dad. For as long as I live, you remain alive.

Meanwhile Trump continues onward, backwards of course. He is talking about firing another of his Cabinet Members and by the way Barr just walked off the job a couple days ago. Can anyone in their right mind justify a reason for firing a main principal member of your Cabinet when there are only 35 days left in your miserable term.

We are leaving the "Valley of the shadow of death," in 5 weeks Mr. Trump. It would be very considerate if you acknowledge this, step aside in some semblance of normal decency. Please reconsider the big rally that you are planning to hold on November 20, in order to take away from the inauguration. By firing new people, by tweeting more insane lies, by pulling outrageous actions such as this one, you are adding nothing to your legacy. You have been there and done it all, except...

If what some predict is true, you may want to start getting your orange wardrobe together. Perhaps you can be like my acquaintance of old, Pablo Escobar, and begin the design and construction of your own prison. My advice, look for a different attorney, Giuliani may not have all his marbles in order.

DECEMBER 19, 2020

"These are the times that try men's souls,....That the harder the conflict, the more glorious the triumph." Thomas Paine

Thomas Paine was the famous author of "Common Sense," the pamphlet that actually brought the colonists together in order to begin the American Revolution. In December of 1775, the Americans were losing their war with the British and it looked as if soon many more soldiers would drop out of the army and return to their homes. In essence we were about to lose, when on December 19, these famous words were published by Thomas Paine. George Washington read this to his men who had pretty much lost all hope. It inspired them and on Christmas night, the army forged the icy Delaware River and defeated the British. It was a turning point that won the war.

Today these are again the times that try men's souls, and women's. When I watch the news and see all these 60 million people who are defending Trump and supporting his ridiculous actions, it tries my soul. I wish I could forge an icy river and blow them all up with cannons. I know our world would be a better place without them, or at least I think I know that. I'm sure, interspersed within those maddening crowds are some good people, how in heaven's name can they not see what they are doing.

And of course, we have the surging Covid which is not backing down in its battle. Just the opposite, it continues to flood hospitals and wear down all our medical workers. The news people are updating us on the vaccines. Moderna vaccine was approved a couple of days ago and has now had its first recipient in the U.S. The big talk is how many people will take the vaccine, some polls are saying 50%, others as high as 65% Vice President Pence and his wife went on public TV and took the shot. Thank you both, perhaps it will have a beneficial influence and help "Make America Great."

Finally for today's news. It was discovered a few days ago that Russia has hacked into many of our governments computer systems and has probably been doing it since last March. It proposes grave risks to not only our government but private business as well. This is a big deal. Not only have they been reading all communications and emails, but we don't know if they're able to control some of these networks. The security threat is unprecedented and will take years to correct, if at all.. Trump's not responding to this. He's at the golf course. What can he say anyway, Putin's his buddy who probably holds him on a short noose.

I was supposed to be heading out on the blue Pacific today with Phil, but he called earlier, just as I was fumbling out of bed. Rather hesitant about getting out from under the balmy covers, I was resting comfortably after the three days (18 paid hours, to be exact), of being consumed by the deck job. The phone rang, Phil was a little "not right," and that was fine with me. That ocean will still be there after Christmas.

I spoke last night with Linda and I believe tomorrow will be our first recorded Podcast. I'm still not sure how I feel about this. I will suggest that I shall be a visiting guest and not a regular.

As I was writing that last sentence, Linda called. I told her that I did not want to be a partner on her project but only a guest. Tomorrow she will be coming to my house and we will begin. I don't think this will last very long.

DECEMBER 20, 2020

I believe that as you get older you have the unconditional right to be yourself. And in my case it seems to be a little easier to practice. The trick is knowing who you are, I believe that's why I began writing this book in the first place. This morning after a lot of thinking I decided to give Linda a call and back out of the plan to get involved in her project. I don't know what I was thinking when I accepted her offer in the beginning. Perhaps it was my lack of social contact lately. But it's not me.

Earlier in this book I have stated my position and feelings about social media, and with that as a conviction, I just don't want to spend any time adding to the ruckus and fuss of it. Linda "Just wants to bring joy and laughter," as she says. She felt that I could offer opinions on current events. Even if I attempted to be pragmatic, it still becomes as preaching to me. Perhaps my writing of this book is preaching as well, but I do see a difference. I'm sure Linda doesn't view a podcast as a platform for preaching, to her it's entertainment for the public.

With such little knowledge and experience as I have with a podcast, with tweeting, or even with Facebook, Linda might have the better definition, and I respect that. It might just be entertainment, but in my relative world, when I see a podcast I see Trump every day and every night doing his ridiculous tweets. His intention is not to entertain. It's to tell people the way it is, the way he sees it. And he wants them to take his advice and follow his way.

John Steinbeck in his greatest work, "Grapes of Wrath," wrote of a most difficult time in our history. A period of desperation, hardship and misery. He wrote of life during the Great Depression. His work was published in 1939. The 80 year cycle of the 1930s puts us right here in today's world.

One of Steinbeck's characters was Preacher Casy. Old Preacher Casy did not want to preach anymore. He "just din't wanna go do no more preachin,' he just din't wanna go be tellin' everybody anything, no more."

Just like Preacher Casy, "I don't wanna be like no Michael Savage, or no Stephen Colbert." I am not an evangelist, I'm writing this book for myself. It's what I've been doing lately. "I don't wanna do no dern podcasts."

In the future, my grandchildren and great grandchildren will know a little bit more about their grandfather, whose history would otherwise fade into obscurity. And "I for sure, don't wanna be like no Donald Trump, who thinks he should be a tellin' everybody everything."

In reference to Steinbeck's "Grapes of Wrath," I'd like to suggest to those who have never read this book, or to those who feel that there is no hope for the future, please read this work. As sad as it is, it's the way it was at that time. This really happened and although Steinbeck doesn't write through to the recovery, we know that the cycle ended and the point is that the people pulled out of it. They weren't dying from a virus but their lives were hell and they had no help like we have today.

Another recommended fiction novel currently relative, was written in 1946 about the life of people suffering through the Bubonic Plague, written by Albert Camus and simply titled "The Plague." As for some educated insight into our political dilemma, a good one just published is "On Tyranny," by Timothy Snyder.

DECEMBER 21, 1970

Elvis Presley went to the White House today, anonymous and uninvited. At the gate he was recognized and gained permission to enter. Dressed in tight purple pants and an open-collared shirt, he had his usual jeweled chains, a big giant belt buckle and even a purple velvet cape. The "King" got straight to Richard Nixon. His purpose was to offer his support to help fight the war on drugs. Elvis is against the drug culture, against the hippies, against student protests, against the Black Panthers and other factions of liberalism. He thinks that all these people hate America.

A crazy thing that the news reported is that Elvis had a gun on him and it went undetected by any security agents. He presented it as a gift to Nixon, a WW 2 Colt pistol.

DECEMBER 21, 2020

Today is the Winter solstice for us here in the Northern hemisphere. It is that day when the earth's north pole tilts the furthest away from the sun. We will experience the longest night and the shortest day of the year. For much of my life I never paid much attention to this phenomena because I was living close to the equator and not concerned by the earth's tilt. At my latitude in Healdsburg (38°36' N), I am definitely affected. It is still not a severe change, but definitely different than my ancient ancestors had to endure.

According to anthropological studies my roots and all homo sapiens began somewhere in Africa, close to the equator.

Contradicting the creationists theories, we began this ride anywhere from 200 to 300,000 years ago. That's a lot of generations ago, a whole lot of cycles have taken place. Homo Sapiens eventually distinguished themselves from their evolutionary parents, the gorillas and chimps. We did it in a slow progressive fashion. Humanoid groups probably jumped from the trees searching for food, eventually becoming bi-pedal, walking on two limbs.

The science concludes that this evolution was occurring in a number of places at the same time, all in Southern and Eastern Africa. These man-like primates eventually bumped into each other and competed, fought. The homo sapiens won. After 100,000 years or so our great grandparents decided to leave Africa, probably due to climate conditions or food shortages. In due time, as they walked North, they would begin to feel the colder climate and come to experience a day like today, the Winter Solstice.

Today's Winter Solstice news headlines: The vaccinations are proceeding in orderly fashion. In a few cities the number of Covid hospitalizations have leveled off and have even begun a downward trend. Not so in California, especially L.A., which happens to be the second largest city in our country. Ambulances are being sent to other locations, and at best are told to wait an hour or so before they can unload their patients. In one L.A. hospital the gift shop has been turned into an ICU ward.

Because of a Roku device I bought for my TV I have discovered a way to add many different news channels and I can surf around from Seattle to Miami. I get a pretty good take on how things are working, and it's all good. Last week there were approximately 200,000 vaccinations nationwide. As more vaccines are delivered, plenty of people are ready. One poll is showing that on average, only 42% of Republicans are willing to take the shot. In order for this to reach an effective herd immunity, the experts say we will need 75%. There is a long way to go and I believe that many of the Republicans that are now opposing may come around. I'll stay positive on this.

I can remember in the beginning of the pandemic, Danny was saying that the vaccine was going to contain a tracking chip that the government and Bill Gates had created and that this was the real purpose behind the whole Covid plot. By the way Pfizer, the main vaccine supplier at this time, is a German company. They're not exactly close friends with Bill and Melinda.

DECEMBER 22, 2020

Three days until Christmas, I could have included in this book many previous Christmas experiences of my life. All special, memorable days, with family of course. I remember being the child, so excited about opening all my presents. I have special memories of all the wonderful Christmas dinners that my mom made. And then as a young parent I repeated the experience through different eyes, I watched the joy of my kids, Abel and Mia. And then I did it again as an older parent with Zachary.

I can remember many times as a young child on Christmas day I made a special effort to get in the ocean, knowing I was fortunate to be living in the tropics. Oftentimes I would be bringing a speargun, those were "the good old days," ha. Without a doubt Christmas has been the most special holiday event of my life.

When Abel and Mia were young I often drove my family from North Carolina down to Florida and spent the holidays with my mom and dad and my sister and her family. In addition to the big Christmas dinner at my parents, we would always have a huge Christmas Eve gathering at my Aunt and Uncle's house, with the large extended family, including many of my cousins. About a dozen regulars at Auntie Boots and Uncle George's are no longer alive today. "To die is poignantly bitter, but the idea of having to die without living is unbearable." Psychologist Erich Fromm.

In my second parenting life, as Zachary got older I often left California, returning to Abel and Mia and all the grandchildren that had begun mounting up, more young children opening presents. This has been my routine for the past several years, but not this time. This year is right up at the top, one of the strangest Christmas times of my life.

I'm staying here, being compliant with the Covid restrictions. I feel that it would be safe to make the flight without catching the virus. From what I can tell, the Airlines are very health conscious and protected, but I prefer to respect the advice given and stay at home. I cherish all the wonderful memories of my past and so, even if I'm alone this Christmas I won't be sad. What I already possess is far more valuable than anything I would receive.

DECEMBER 23, 2020

Trump is being Santa to many of his criminal buddies and friends. So far he has given pardons to 64 of his cronies and family members. Why a President is given this power is rather ridiculous to begin with. It's like giving the Pope, when he leaves office, the power to pardon people out of hell. Our Constitution supposedly allows presidential pardons only if it's a Federal crime against the United States. That issue has never even been discussed, for as long as I've known this process to go on. So I guess the Pope should be able to raise people up from the eternal fires even if their sins were not against the church. Aha, eternal damnation has a back-door escape route. Oops, I forget, the Pope doesn't have the same power as Donald.

On a more serious note, there have been a couple of new Covid strains discovered, one in England and one in South Africa. They are much more contagious, but don't seem to be more harmful or resistant to the vaccine. England is being locked up by the rest of Europe. The news showed miles of trucks, over 1,500, unable to move supplies. Truck drivers are stuck dead on the road, sleeping in their cabs with no hope of moving, or getting home by Christmas.

DECEMBER 24, 2020

Joe Biden continues appointing more people for his administration. Many of his appointees are experienced old hands from the Obama administration. He hopes to undo a lot of damage done by Trump and his band of rookies. He is very adamant about his planned fight against Covid, saying it will be his number one, two and three priorities. He certainly has just reason for this. The virus killed over 20,000 people last week and this coming week will probably be more.

Another of his main fights will be dealing with climate change and associated environmental issues. In my eyes he has his priorities in the right order. I believe there are now many people being directly affected by climate change and the timing will be right for his actions to succeed.

If somehow the Senatorial runoff race in Georgia is won by the Democrats, it will be the greatest labor saving move for Biden since Adam discovered "love at first sight" in the Garden of Eden. This runoff election should, by all moral rights, be a landslide victory for the Dems, and here's why. Not only does common sense tell us that it's wrong to capitalize on an elected government position for personal gain, but respective decency as well as the law forbids it. What I'm talking about is "insider trading."

Both of the Republican Senators that are running in Georgia have been doing just that, Kelley Loeffler was discovered making stock trades after classified briefings about Coronavirus. With no guilt, she claims it's the American Way. She happens to be one of the wealthiest Senators of them all. As for David Perdue, the other Republican candidate, he didn't even show up for the recent debate for fear of the questions he would have to answer. This guy made as many as 20 trades per day while he was serving his last term. Records show he made 2,596 trades during those 6 years. Any way you look at it, these two had access to so much inside information that the rest of the public did not have.

My guess is that at least one of them will win, if not both of them. Why, because the following three issues are more important to voters in Georgia than anything else, abortion, gun laws, and immigration. It's the veil that covers over all else. To those who will vote for Loeffler and Perdue, abortion equals murder, gun restriction equals keeping from being murdered, and immigration deals with keeping the would be murderers on the other side of the tracks, or fence I should say. If Jesus were like them he would have spent his later years of life handing out condoms, AK-47s and "Speak English" signs.

Besides consuming himself with the pardons, Trump blocked the stimulus bill that Congress finally came up with. He'll probably pick up a lot of good points with this move. He is claiming that the personal check amount agreed upon for qualifying individuals, $600, is disgraceful and wants to increase it to $2,000. That is the figure that Nancy Pelosi wanted to begin with. She can't believe her ears. Neither can I. My conclusions have been confirmed, Trump has finally and forever lost his mind.

Switching to a personal story, yesterday I received what I thought was a Christmas card from my good close friend Freddy from my years in North Carolina. I opened it up and inside was a plain postcard that I had sent to him and Steve, another good friend. My handwriting has not really changed. It was dated **November 25, 1985**.

Dear Steve and Fred, I've made it! Finally! Spent 9 days in Tennessee putting a new motor in the bus. I still had to leave her and carry on with the Datsun. Everything's great here, the future looks quite promising. I've got lots of work with good pay. Now living in Oakland, then north of the Bay to Healdsburg to build a spec house. I'm coming home for Christmas to spend with the family. It's an inspiring change to be here, lots of interesting input. No AIDS yet. See you all soon. I've met a Washington attorney who wants to make a movie. Tom

DECEMBER 25, 2020 CHRISTMAS DAY

Happy Birthday, Jesus. Although no one really knows if this is your birthday, it's OK for us all to assume. This day was chosen because of an idea that you must have been conceived when the Angel Gabriel came to Mary and gave her the good news. That was supposed to have been on the vernal equinox, when the sun is directly over the Equator. Nine months later is December 25.

Let's keep assuming here. If you didn't pop out prematurely or a little late, and if Gabriel really did show up at that exact time, and if it's true that Mary wasn't pregnant until he laid this news on her, then we're right on the money.

Now if any one of these conditions are inaccurate, then Christmas isn't your birthday. But, it doesn't even matter. As the people in Costa Rica seem to inherently realize, Easter is really the big deal here. They celebrate Easter way more than Christmas, as I mentioned in my earlier writing. And it actually is the event that gives all the credibility to the Christian faith.

Easter separates you from all the other leaders/prophets of the present day. None of the others, Buddha, Mohammed, Moses, etc. had risen up from the dead. So, if we have the true scoop on that happening, then that's why you deserve the credit that you are getting from almost half of today's world population.

On today's news there was a feature about the Calvary Church in San Jose. California that is, not Costa Rica. They have now run up their county fines to almost a million bucks by refusing to stop their indoor gatherings. They held another one last night, in your honor, and the news people were there again. The preacher was interviewed saying that you want them to worship you and nothing will stop that from happening. A few of the unmasked worshippers were also stopped by the news people before entering and they voiced identical indignant claims. Their religion comes first, coronavirus spreading comes somewhere behind that.

Jesus, help me out on this one. Rather than get worshipped and celebrated on in church, wouldn't you rather have these people stay home like the rest of us? If you really went into the Jewish Temple that time and yelled at and beat up those money lenders, then that proves you can be a lot more than a timid, non assertive leader amongst men. I realize that you're not with us today in the flesh, and you can't walk into the Calvary Church in San Jose and tell those people to get out, but maybe subconsciously you can enlighten the preacher and some of the others to quit acting like the Trumpsters act, and get with the program, Amen.

Rain is approaching, I have tons of firewood in the dry, on my porch, and in the warm house. It's freezing outside, and I'm feeling just fine. Another Christmas Day, unlike most of the others in my life. I'm alone today, at least physically, however I've been getting phone calls and messages, and for today, that's sufficient to keep up the ole' Holiday Spirit. I can see in my mind's eye, the grandkids ripping open their presents, and my mom hustling around in the kitchen, getting the dinner ready. I really can see the whole picture.

I know that there are many families today all gathered together, and it makes me happy for them. I hope that they realize the great gift of being part of a good family. And I trust that soon the pandemic ends and I will have another familiar Christmas Day. I would love to hug one of my kids and maybe even jump back into the warm ocean where I came from.

DECEMBER 26, 2020

Christmas has passed, time for me to turn to another birth, metaphorically that is, the birth of this book. This book is something that I have created, and fed during its incubation, 12 months in the womb of my computer As it continued to grow I watched my genes (my past) develop and influence the form. In less than a week I will stop the continual information and the emotion that I have been feeding into it. There is so much more that I have left out, but I'm sticking with my plan to keep this as a one year project.

In the preface of this book, I said that I wanted to find out Who I am Now. All along I've known that I'm not a scientist, a scholar or a philosopher. I guess I am now a writer, and a current news reporter, a researcher and an editor, a historian. But most of all I realize that what I am now is what I've been all along. I haven't changed much since I was that young boy exploring anything that crossed my path, getting into a lot of mischief, without doing too much harm to anyone.

I was, I always have been, and I still am, the rebel that doubted his first grade Catholic School teacher. And I'm still the guy who understands how fortunate he was to be born into Mel and Mary

Helen Martens' life. I'm still the man who loves a family more than anything else in this world. I respect others, I listen, and I'm basically regarded as a 'good guy.' I'm proud to say, "That's my legacy."

Now I need to turn my attention to the next phase and that is how to publish this book. I've done a little research. I can be a self publisher, I can pay a local company to help me be a self publisher or I can start sending out manuscripts and hope that a larger, real book publisher might deem my work suitable. That could be a timely and probably frustrating process. It would however, if accepted, put this book out into the public. Honestly, I don't think the public will be looking to read about this depressing year for some time.

Through research, I found pertinent information that I've included in my writing. For the record I often consulted news sources, including *The New York Times, The Washington Post, The New York Post, the Wall Street Journal*, CBS, ABC, NBC, FOX, and CNN televised News, also many news magazines such as The Week and others. I may not have personalized their reports enough to prevent it from being plagiarism, but that seems to be a ridiculous deception in the first place.

I'm not doing this to make money and If I have violated some rule of authorship, then I apologize and will accept my penalty. If I used direct quotes it is only to pass on information that the sources wanted public anyway. Without any selfish motivations, I wasn't that careful at some times when I related current events.

There have been places where I did mention that this idea was written by the *NY Times* or some other publisher, but there have been many times I simply put down news facts or thoughts that agreed with mine and I didn't realize that I should make a note of it in a source section. I never considered my action as being disingenuous, and I hope that this is not looked upon as sneaky or devious. I always feel as if I am sharing some information that another writer would want to be shared.

BTW, Joe Biden has had an issue with this since his days in law school. I guess he and I may have that in common, ha.

If plagiarism has occurred, it would hold less than 1/10th of one percent of the content, so I am more than willing to generously share 2/10ths of 2 percent to all those who feel violated. Call me up, don't bother with the courts.

When it comes to lawsuits, remember the woman who sued McDonalds for giving her a coffee in the drive-through that was so hot she burned herself? She was awarded 1 million dollars. Most people who read that were stupefied. "How utterly ridiculous, getting a little burned and getting a million dollars, how absurd." Here's the rest of the story. The bottom of the styrofoam cup melted when they passed it to her. She got third degree burns and had to have reconstructive surgery. The court after considering, decided that they would take away that particular day's coffee profits from the McDonald's franchises and give the lady the whole coffee enchilada. It was actually over a million bucks. Justice prevailed.

Uh oh, I better make a note and give Julie credit for this. She, being a practicing attorney at the time, and my girlfriend, informed me about that case as it was happening.

Changing the subject, when I was 6 years old I began learning about all the different games that could be played with a ball, and I soon became hooked and obviously almost 70 years later, nothing has changed. One thing that kept me from getting into more trouble in high school was my love of sports. The hours and hours of time I logged in football, basketball, baseball, volleyball, even ping-pong were astronomical. I was athletic enough to make the first string on all of the teams. During the summers I would play in the park leagues when our family was not traveling.

And now back to the present, It's time to go to Stu's house, and escape more reality. One of the few good things about winter is football and Stu's TV is beckoning. I really wonder how they get away with pulling these games off during a pandemic. I mean a football game is like a crowded playground, an indoor high school gathering, and a bar room brawl all rolled into one.

DECEMBER 27, 2020

The time is ticking away quickly for this book to end, and I believe I have left an important part out.

39

Time to Have Kids

I would like to share the experience and the realizations that came upon me about pro-creating, the urge to bear and raise a child. I'm in my late twenties in North Carolina.

One day I had a most sudden shock. It was on a cool autumn day in North Carolina, beginning much as many previous mornings had. I walked out of my little shack to begin what I thought would be a normal day. I was planning to check the garden, cut a little firewood from the property, culling out some of the smaller hardwoods, and continue with one of my building projects. Suddenly a very strange feeling came over me. I was no longer interested in any of my projects. At first I didn't know what was causing this strange state, it was a rather depressing feeling. Then it hit me, as sudden and unexpected as an embolism. I wanted to build a swing set; I wanted to have kids.

I had never thought of this before nor had I ever discussed it with Cathy. Very excitedly, I ran into the house and informed my loving mate of this new discovery. "I want to be a father," I said with seriously heavy emotion. The words knocked her off her stool. She was more shocked than I, so shocked in fact that she began laughing and denying it. She did not want to believe that I was serious.

Cathy was not ready for kids and was quite afraid of the idea, the responsibility. I understood her position and hoped to be patient. Maybe Cathy wanted to hold on to the "get up and go" lifestyle so that we could continue to hit the road whenever we wanted to. We were both quite happy with our present state.

Up until that day, I had never even given the subject a thought. I realized on that day that I did want children, but I was not insistent. I did not want this to become an issue between us, but it was soon to happen. This one very important difference in our life's direction, would soon destroy our relationship. In the months that followed she became very cold, afraid of sexual contact, and feeling as if she was not meeting my needs, that of parenting.

Why did such a desire to have children come upon me so suddenly and why was it so strong? Since it became a serious issue between Cathy and I, I thought about it all the time and made attempts to analyze my feelings. To begin with, the fact that we owned our land made me feel quite stable and secure. And secondly, I was truly in love with Cathy. I wanted to create a child with a mixture of our genes and personalities. I thought a child who was half of each of us would be an incredible kid, and I realized it was a way to get even closer to the person I so loved. But there is another reason, a very illogical explanation for this sudden compulsive urge.

At this time, on this very day, and very near to me physically, and my world with Cathy, a very special child was being born. Born because of a casual sexual encounter, to an unwed mother, and being born without a father's care. Abel was entering this world. In three years he would become my son. His mother would become my wife and together we would have a next child, my daughter Mia.

Of course, there is no way that Cathy nor I should have been affected by an unconnected event, such as Abel's birth. We did not know his mother at that time. Abel should not have had any influence whatsoever on my life. But the fact is that this very important life plan hit me so suddenly, with absolutely no previous thoughts on the subject. Certain thoughts and ideas came to light 3½ years later. And here's where I'm about to go off the chart. What if Abel did come to me on that day.

If all humans are connected by some sort of spiritual light, then of course Abel's birth and his needs could have affected my life at that time. I have explained my idea about a life timeline. Even though we are living as a small dot on the graph which is placed at this exact moment in time. Tomorrow that dot will be a little back in my past. It is still the graph of my life and I should be able to go back to that dot. If I have a soul existing within me, then I should be able to travel in either direction along my graph, my timeline. I'm about to slam shut the door of any science lab, and talk about something that I've never shared before.

Sometimes I'll wake up early but I don't get out of bed. I lay in the darkness under the covers, still half asleep. I lay there and think. This is how to learn meditation. And this is the perfect time to go back in your timeline. I'll go back to a particular special moment and start to gather everything I can remember about that moment. I won't stop until I get it all.

I try to be like Chen Tai Li and include every detail that makes that memory complete. I meditate and wait, silence my mind and let the hidden powers come. If I can't keep still, I'll concentrate on details like what clothes I was wearing and how the weather was, who else was there at that time. Then I try and become the light being that I am and go back to that moment. I promise that this practice becomes easier each time I do it. Usually I'm going back to be with my mom and dad. And the more I go to this gymnasium of time travel the stronger I get at it. If I should ever master this, the next step would be to go forward in time.

As impossible for me to imagine what this would be like, it's just as easy for me to feel and know that the power to do this is here. If it's not in my brain alone, it's in the universal mind, the holy light of God. And I am walking the talk..

Do we live only in the present, or are we living simultaneously in all time? Could the future be known and Abel's needs and my needs and all our needs be worked out in the past? I wanted children, Cathy didn't. To this day she has never had a child. Assuming that Abel's spirit came to me on that day and started to affect my life with Cathy because of the "Bigger Plan," then that's the way it happened. To me this explanation is feasible, I've had other experiences in my life that are no more radical than this, and I choose to accept that Abel came to me on the day of his birth.

Is it possible that I could be reaching into someone's life that I don't know right now? Are there others that I will meet in the future, reaching into my life at this moment? I say yes, it is an absolute possibility! If elephants and whales can pass messages across space and time, then humans must also have this power.

Abel and Mia were soon to become my children and amongst the greatest blessings in my life. Eastern thought says that a child will choose his own parents in order to work out karma and attain spiritual happiness. According to that way of thinking, Abel had chosen me, and later Mia, and even later Zac.

On this side of the world, where I am now living, away from India, I am not following the local religious beliefs. Physically I'm far away from the Hindus, the Janes, the Buddhists and the Sikhs. Those are the ones that believe in reincarnation and would easily accept my ideas.

But as closely as I can figure it, western thought says no spirit, no unborn child has chosen their parents, Our religious teachers tell us that thinking something like this is absolute absurd fiction, ignorant fabrication and sinful at best. In the western world in order to attain happiness one needs nothing but good birth, good luck, good friends, health, wealth, beauty, strength, fame, honor and virtue.

It seems that whatever course we set for ourselves, there will often come a surprise change. Whether we are a scientist in a sophisticated laboratory or a monk in a sealed cave, we shall always be learning more, provided we keep an open mind. Therefore, I must conclude, anything is possible.

So my wife would become Kathy. I met her as 'Sunshine', a nickname leftover from the 'hippie days'. Soon after separating from the other Cathy, with a "C," Kathy and I would fall in love and begin raising kids. (Note: Kathy and I were married by a friend near the creek on my property where I was building the log house. Turns out that his pastor's license wasn't legal and we were never married. I found this out last year from Abel.)

As that period of my life ebbed away, Abel and Mia grew up, moved away from home and began to create their own worlds. And then came Zachary.

I have hardly spoken about Zac in this book, and there is so much to tell. It begins with me wandering into Suzanne's life out here in California. As God would have it, either the Eastern or Western God, and I say that in every aspect of the truth as I know it, Suzanne welcomed me. Zac was almost 3, and one of the cutest kids I had ever seen. Suzanne was a single mother raising Zac on her own. She welcomed my help, I fell in love with him and It all started over again. For the following 16 years Suzanne and I did our best at parenting this very special kid.

He was then off to the University in Santa Cruz. Tuitions, housing and all expenses were paid, thanks to Julie, Uncle Jeff, and Aunt Karen. We are so blessed to have them in our lives. I have mentioned that Zac graduated with honors, and a major in Neuroscience. That says a little about him. Did I mention that he is 6'4", looks like a movie star, does all kinds of physical training, plays incredible guitar, and is one of the sweetest people you could ever hope to meet. There is one blur in this masterpiece. He grew to include drugs in his repertoire.

I accept that nothing is perfect in this world, and this is one of the imperfections that I am currently living with. For now the problem is under control. Zac is in a rehabilitation center in Seattle and every day I pray that he will keep this problem as part of his past. Time will tell. His drug problem began when he was in high school, I had no clue. But now he recognizes the problem and has initiated the solution on his own. That is so important. And that is all I will say about this.

DECEMBER 28, 2020

Tic tic tic, 2020 is about to leave us. The horrible 2020, it is being called. the worst year in the history of our lives. Since the depression of the 1930s, our economy has never been so bad. In America, the land of opportunity, there are now over 23,000 receiving weekly unemployment checks. An untold number of people have lost their businesses, 1 out of 6 privately owned restaurants have closed for good. The Airlines have lost over 10 billion dollars. Schools throughout the country have been like a roller coaster, open then closed, but more often they have been shut down while the kids are suffering. Online education is not the same. Many rural areas are still without internet providers. I have no idea what those children are doing.

As for social contact deprivation, psychologists are worried about long term effects. Without outside contacts, the lockdowns have caused an increase in domestic violence, divorce rates, suicides. It has been an exacting, stressful year, and a lot of the problem will spill into next year. But, as I see it, we will be pulling away from this mess and cycling upward into hope and a future of positive change.

Personally, I haven't suffered nearly as much as many others, and I am grateful for that. All my children and grandchildren have made it through without noticeable damage. I have lost a few friends to the virus, while our country has lost 330,000, and continues to lose more each day.. Presently we are at the highest death rate since the beginning of the pandemic. Vaccinations should begin to slow the infections down, there is definitely a recovery plan in the making.

As for our government, I can't say anything new about Trump's insane behavior that I haven't already said. He continues on Twitter every day with outrageous lies and divisive comments that tear at the heart of our nation's democracy. In time Trump will be gone, just like the virus. We will need a lot of time to heal the damage that he and the virus have done. Hopefully that's a possibility.

DECEMBER 27, 1972 NORTH CAROLINA

After several months of living free and learning the ways of the mountains, I need to seek outside work and leave my little homestead in order to make money. The weather is cold, winter has settled in. The only money I have brought in is a small amount, earned by picking apples at a neighbor's orchard. My savings are gone.

My hope is to work in the area of physical therapy. Last week I went to the local hospital and applied. There were no openings in the physical therapy department, but I was told that the hospital is in need of male nurse's assistants, 'orderlies,' as I know them. I have been accepted for this position and will begin in a week.

MARION GENERAL HOSPITAL

I have grown to love this work and my fellow employees. All the staff, including nurses, lab technicians, doctors, housekeepers, are wonderful people. Many of the hospital workers have become new friends, as well as some of the patients that I have met.

As an orderly, I don't have stature, and of course my salary is well below that of a physical therapist, but it is sufficient for me. There are other advantages as well, I am able to work on the afternoon shift, leaving the mornings free for projects on my new farm. Since my main hobby has now become building, it is an ideal situation.

Most of the families residing in this area of Western North Carolina have come from farming communities. From the time these mountains were first settled, up until the late 1800s, farming was the only way of life. But then changes began to take place, and today the region is basically supported by the textile, timber and furniture industries. As I see it, these people have changed very little from their ancestors. There are still many families who rely solely on farming, and many who subsidize their income with smaller farms. Most everyone I meet, at the very least, has a summer garden. Working with the soil, living with and learning nature's way, this is the key that has made these people so special.

Over time, working in the small town hospital has exposed me to just about every family in the community. I must repeat that the huge majority of people here are beautiful, friendly, kind, and caring people, unlike in any area that I had ever lived before.

One of my patients knew of my plans for building a new home and offered me their family's old 'home place'. They wanted the home removed and in turn offered me the salvage rights to all the building materials.

Their old family house was built in 1920, colonial style, near to my farm in the small town of Old Fort. With two other acquaintances I contracted to tear it down. The huge, rambling structure has many bedrooms, two kitchens, eight fireplaces, oak floors, many eight panel doors, large double hung windows, antique claw foot bathtubs, metal shingle roof, tons of antique brick, and thousands of board feet of framing material. There is much work to be done and plenty of material for the three of us to share.

As conditions turned out, my two associates backed out of the project before the first nail was removed. For nearly a full year, I worked on that house, single handedly. At times it looked like the Empire State Building to me. I would drive my old pickup there in the early morning, and begin tearing things out until about one o'clock in the afternoon. I would then load the pick up full of materials and drive to my friend Clyde's house. Clyde and I would visit while he worked on his projects, then I would bathe in the creek, change into my white clothes by the creek bank and drive to the hospital for work.

Within a couple months of beginning the job, I had to stop and build a large barn on my farm to store the vast quantity of used materials. A year later I had done it, finished, miracles never cease.

DECEMBER 29, 2020

Shortened Christmas break for the Senators, they went back for more sessions in order to vote on the changed stimulus bill that the House passed and Trump wants. It is now up to $2,000. instead of the original $600. We shall see what fate awaits the paupers on the street, that includes yours truly. It is an extremely important and urgent matter for so many families who are struggling not only to pay rent, but to bring food to the table.

THE PESSIMIST

I heard yesterday about a science fiction film, showing earth in the future. At that time earth had inhabitants with super advanced AI (Artificial Intelligence) capabilities. The scientists of the day fed many scenarios into their computers, dealing with earth's problems, and expecting solutions. Every time the AI said, "no solution available, there are too many humans on the planet." The AI took over to solve the problem on its own. It set off the nuclear bombs.

This is about as likely as anything else, depressing, discouraging, of course, but believable. If it's not the nuclear bombs, it will probably be another more deadly virus. Something's gotta solve the pressing population problem and man has proven he will never do it.

THE OPTIMIST

I'm remembering one of my favorite movies of the past. Star Wars, with Han Solo, the wise Obi Wan Kenobi, and the evil Darth Vader. I related to all these characters. Darth Vader represented all the negative aspects of the life I had been living. He was the Vietnam War. He was the switch that was taking place from the spiritual "heaven on earth" hope of the "sixties" to the hopelessness of the materially centered world of the 70s.

As I looked to the other side of time, there was Luke Skywalker and Princess Leia, coming up as the valiant youth. Luke battled to rescue Princess Leia from Darth Vader, Obi Wan was there providing the spiritual leadership and of course, Han Solo, the everyday guy. And in the end, they succeeded, they saved the world. They combined the wisdom of the old with the courageous strength of the youth, and they also had the power of "The Force."

For us to save the world, we must be able to use the experience of the past, but we must also be open to change, like the Democrats. We cannot hold onto some outdated practices that may have worked in a different period. And most importantly, we can not isolate in non co-operation and anger, like many of the Republicans. I hope somewhere we can find "The Source" to help.

DECEMBER 31, 1951

It's dark outside, Kathy's sleeping. I miss mommy. Ada is here watching us. Mommy and daddy went out to a party.

DECEMBER 31, 1961

It's New Years eve tonight. I think my parents are going out, I want to stay up and watch TV when midnight comes. I love our color TV. There is supposed to be a special broadcast in color about New Years.

DECEMBER 31, 1971

I'll be working tonight at Nando's so I guess when midnight hits I'll be inside the restaurant near the piano bar, singing "Auld Lang Syne" with a bunch of drunk, super rich people. Maybe afterwards I'll hit one of the clubs.

DECEMBER 31, 1981

Steve is having a big New Years party at Green Acres. There's supposed to be a great band, I'll see if I can get someone to watch the kids and Sunny and I will probably be heading out there.

DECEMBER 31, 1991

A Costa Rican New Years is just like the ones back in the U.S. Joanne and I are planning to go out for a nice dinner but I doubt that we'll stay up for any celebrating.

DECEMBER 31, 2001

Suzanne and I will probably be watching the ball drop in Times Square on TV and stay home with little Zac tonight. Everything has been going fine, and 2001 has been a good year.

DECEMBER 31, 2010

Gonna go to a small party tonight at Bonnie's house. The mood this year is still subdued because of the 9-11 bombing. Our world will never be the same. I've always liked to watch the Times Square ball release. Seeing a million people gathered together for a big celebration always affects me. But not in New York this year, that's for sure.

DECEMBER 31, 2020

Another New Year's Eve. I guess I'll be on the phone with Abel, Mia, Zac, Suzanne, Brenda and Julie. I'll be texting Jay and many of the other grandkids, my sister and nephew Chris, Sam, Danny, Jackie, and some of the others in my contact list. This is "the Way of the Day," the way I operate, the way we all operate. I'll go down to Stu's again this afternoon, hang out with him and watch a football game. And then I'll come home and probably be fast asleep when the clock ticks twelve.

So the end of the book is coming close. The absolute craziest year of my life is ending. Although I won't continue with my writing about it, I'm sure there will be plenty more of the same for the next few months, and I hope that it will not extend much longer than that. Covid cases are still surging forward, yesterday topped all records in the number of infections and deaths.

The infamous Trump's idiotic presidency will come to a gloomy, and hopefully a somewhat insignificant end in a few weeks. He will have his legacy, to get rid of low flow shower heads, without any other crowning achievements. He worked quite diligently at crushing many of our civil American Institutions, He absolutely destroyed many of the ecological programs that Obama put in place, reversed our position as a world leader, and drove like a mad man down the highway of tyranny, but in the end he lost.

I truly believe the recovery cycle which I have written about is here, alive and well and on its way forward, towards a positive future. The cycle is not just here for Americans but it's a cycle that all humans are involved in, every form of life. The ancient Mayans with their mystical intelligence, believed in and actually devised their incredibly accurate calendars around cycles. The Hopi Indians believed we were in the Fourth Cycle, and would soon begin to move upwards.

By believing in this, I can feel hope for my family and future generations. I can walk out of my door and still happily connect with the fabric of our creation. I can see the beauty of it all. And as soon as we conquer Covid and the lockdowns are gone, I'm getting Zac and heading on a trip to visit every National Park and Nature preserve that I can. Happy New Year's.

JANUARY 5, 2020

Well I've decided to break my promise and continue writing for a while longer, at least as long as it takes for Mia to pour over the book and correct my grammar, syntax, punctuation, etc. I also feel like I'm leaving the story at a very crucial stage. I can't leave this story half finished. Everything current will drive right ahead into the future without my commenting on it, but maybe when this book is read by my great grandchildren, perhaps they will be glad to read the results of this crazy period and they'll be happy to see what their gene contributing forefather had to say about it all.

Starting with today, the Senate runoff race is being wrapped up as Georgia voters go to the polls. This will be extremely critical in shaping the future of our country and the world to a lesser degree. If the Democrats can possibly defeat the two Republican incumbents then things will be so much easier for Biden. Of course, this is my opinion, but we should then be able to progress forward and I, as well as most of my friends will be so happy. This term will then be known as the Filibuster Years.

I saw Kelly Loeffler on TV the other day, one of the Republican candidates and I swear, that woman is disgusting. She is phony, hypocritical, and is either misguided or intentionally evil, just like Trump. She looks like she could be one of Trump's girlfriends.

I could hardly refrain from writing when news came a couple of days ago about Trump calling the Georgia Governor's office.

He got through to Georgia's Secretary of State and his call was recorded and later released to the press. Both Georgia's governor and Secretary of State are Republicans and to their credit, they both acted like decent honorable people.

Trump was attempting to bully them into overturning the election. He kept telling them that it would be easy for them to get the 11,780 votes he needed. Basically he was wanting them to discount some of the precincts or to simply change the results. He was very fortunate that his language wasn't quite enough to get him immediately arrested, but there is possible legal fallout facing his action. Yet many of today's Republicans, those living in his camp, won't even know about this. They will stay tuned to Fox news as will their close friends, and they might hear a distorted version or they won't even hear anything about this call .

Tomorrow Congress meets to certify the election and there will be over 100 House Republicans who will contest the electoral college and refuse the symbolic process of counting the votes. Basically this disenfranchises the will of the people, telling them they should not get their way. It is the final slam of our Democratic process which was once the beacon of the Free World. There are some Republicans that realize this is wrong and will not participate, Kelly Loeffler and her running constituent David Perdue are not amongst them. Those that do stand up should be given a medal by Trump before he leaves, because he will leave. This abhorrent action will not influence Biden's position to move into the White House. I know that Trump will never concede this election and hand over the keys. He'll probably just leave them under the door-mat and run off.

Turning to the World of Sports as an essential accepted diversion from this dismal daily news report, I would like to congratulate Steph Curry. He plays basketball for my local boys, the Golden State Warriors. Last night he accomplished a feat never before done in the NBA, except for maybe Wilt Chamberlain in 1962. Steph scored at least 30 points in both halves of the game, totaling 62 for his career high. Now what makes Steph Curry extra special is that my grandson Michael played on Steph's college alma mater. Here you go Michael, credit coming your way.

Michael was a standout in high school but he is barely six feet tall. His prospects for playing with the 'Big Boys' in college looked bleak. However Michael is not a defeatist and he walked on the court at Davidson College in North Carolina and made the team. His dad Jay and I are especially proud. The last time I visited them in Gainesville the three of us were on the court playing HORSE and 21. Need I say who was the victor. OK Jay here you go. And in second place, we have Jay Brown.

Steph received some screen time during the Sports section of today's news. They talked about him being such a dedicated hard worker, they showed him practicing where he made 175 three-point shots in a row. As a pretty good point guard in high school I am qualified to say that Steph's action there is beyond any physical athletic performance in the history of mankind.

Last night was another crazy dream night. I was working for some medical facility and the boss came to me saying that too many people were refusing to get the vaccine. Next thing you know I was skydiving with a nurse. We were hooked up and she was getting out a syringe to give me the inoculation. Next I was climbing on the top of Mt. Rushmore with a Doctor who was planning to give me the shot when we got on top of George Washington's head.

This sounds amazingly nuts but as I was waking and thinking about the dream, I decided to keep the light off, stay under the covers in my semi awake state and give it more thought. My next vision was getting the shot while I was skin diving, and then I was too awake to get any more dreamlike visions. But when I did wake up completely, I kept thinking about the dream and I realized that the idea could be used in some way to help people overcome their negative thinking about being vaccinated.

If people could self inoculate I'm sure there would be a jillion people on YouTube, and probably some diehard Trumpers who would look for some crazy place to get the Covid fix while making themselves virally famous at the same time. Maybe get the first shot in the Nevada desert, the second shot in the Bikini Atolls, in honor of our nuclear bomb program, or one in the North Pole and shot number 2 in the South Pole. If Madison Avenue execs, Dr. Fauci and the CDC put their heads together, they have my official permission to take over my dream and run with it.

Here's a start:

"Honey Noc" We all know that this term refers to getting pregnant on your honeymoon. But not anymore.

Congratulations to Chris and Patty Westin from Peoria, Illinois, they were married this week. Chris, a democrat wore a solid powder blue tuxedo while Patty, a republican chose a novel all red wedding dress. The couple went straight from their hometown chapel in Peoria to CVS pharmacy in Honolulu, Hawaii and got inoculated on their honeymoon. For their creative "Honeynoc," they receive this week's "Inoculation Award." We are hoping that Chris and Patty enjoy their time in Mahaloland and just maybe this happy couple will be heading back to Peoria next week with a "Double Honeynoc."

We have a number of "Celebnocs" to report this week including Sean Penn, Hale Berry, and Judge Judy. In closing tonight we'd like to remind you, stay healthy and "Be the first on your block to get the noc." And good night from all of us here at Fox News.

JANUARY 6, 2021

Both Democrat Senators won the runoff. I can hardly believe it. Kelly Loefller for sure has lost, but the other race is not official yet. It does appear certain that Jon Ossoff will beat David Perdue when the remaining votes come in.

This confirms what I have read about the swing of the cycle. We have begun to move upward. It's gotta be, and I am so excited today, and so happy to watch and take in the future. It's been a long hard year. Today "I've got Georgia on my mind. Cuz her arms reach out to me, cuz her eyes smile tenderly. Still in peaceful dreams I see, the roads lead back to you."

Thank you Georgia, thank you people of color. I have tears in my eyes. I wanna eat some peanuts and bake a pecan pie. Going sailing tomorrow.

Well, just when everything looked rosy, I received a call from Julie, "Are you watching the news?" The large protest rally that Trump encouraged in front of the Capitol has become violent. People have stormed the building, breaking down doors and are now occupying parts of the building, including the Senate Chamber and Nancy Pelosi's office. Trump is inside the White House and doing nothing to stop it. This is unbelievable. I can't believe what I'm watching.

After taking a few hour break, I'm back at the computer. Order has been restored. So many of our political leaders have taken their stand against this mob action, this violent assault on our Capitol. Some people have called on Pence to invoke the 25th amendment and remove Trump from office. Former Secretary of Defense said, "This is a violent assault on our Capitol, an effort to subjugate American democracy by mob rule," and said it, "was fomented by Mr. Trump. He used the Presidency to destroy trust in our election and to poison our respect for fellow citizens. He has been enabled by pseudo-political leaders whose names will live in infamy as profiles in cowardice."

Quoting Barack Obama, "History will rightly remember today's violence at the Capitol, incited by a sitting president who has continued to baselessly lie about the outcome of a lawful election, as a moment of great dishonor and shame for our nation. But we'd be kidding ourselves if we treated it as a total surprise."

JANUARY 7, 2021

The world has been watching and is responding, it's very disheartening to see. Although this is just the latest in the string of events that Trump has done to destroy the United States' image and position as the leader of Democracy, this is one of the worst. Trump has been telling his people that American Democracy is a fraud, he has now presented to the world, proof of his statement.

This is indeed a dark moment in our history. It will take a long time and a lot of work to restore the integrity and honor of our government and just as importantly, the faith and hope that so many world citizens had in Democracy,

The ruler of Iran said that this has shown what a failure Western Democracy is. Other mideast leaders commented, "This proves that an authoritarian government is what our people need." I think of the poor families around the globe sitting in front of their TV's watching their hopes of a better life distinguish. A small intelligent child who had once dreamed to live in a country like the United States, yesterday sat in his very humble dwelling, and saw his future disappear. The thought of this family and this child breaks my heart.

I know that this is the reason Angela Merkel, the President of Germany was extremely angry yesterday. Even Trump's buddy Boris Johnson, Prime Minister of England, was shocked and disgusted. Every leader around the globe has reacted similarly.

JANUARY 8, 2021

Phil and I went out on the water yesterday and had marathon discussions about the current condition, venting and trying to put our lives in perspective. The water was very calm, the day was cold, very little wind, and there was only one other sailboat in the Bay.

I told Phil about my last talk with Danny. Danny and I talked a couple days ago. He asked me when I was leaving for North Carolina. When I told him I was on hold from all travel plans because of the Covid surge. "It's horrible about what's happening in LA." Danny responded, "Well, if you believe that." I said, "Danny, don't tell me that you deny this, are you saying that all the health officials in all the medical facilities around our country are lying and in on some sort a giant conspiracy?" He just said, "Well that's where we agree to disagree." So sad for me to be so far away from a once close friend.

Phil and I switched positions often from the helm to just lying back on the cushion. I steered us under the Bridge and out of the

Bay, past where we had set the crab pot almost two months ago. The ocean had some rather large surges, caused by the stormy weather. We were under the power of only our jib sail, and I thought of the book I have just read, the father and son crossing the "Horn."

I realized that one of the reasons I love sailing so much is that it reminds me of my previous life on the ocean. Wonderful memories that come back to me, that is when Phil and I aren't talking. That's probably half the time.

After sailing we had our takeout dinner from "Squat and Gobble," sitting in the cockpit rather than going below. Phil is super cautious. From our slip in the Marina we watched as the sun went down. The water was like glass, the clouds were amazing, the orange-red color of the sky matched the color of the salmon I was eating. How about that?

For an hour neither of us wanted to leave. We talked more, it got dark and colder. I finally broke through the ice, "Phil I'm getting too cold, time for me to go."

I am now updated on the situation concerning Wednesday's insurrection at the Capitol. It appears that many Republican politicians are jumping off of the Trump Bandwagon. Some of his Cabinet members have resigned and a number of Senators and Congressmen have reversed their positions and are now denouncing Trump and his actions. It doesn't appear that Pence will be invoking the 25th amendment and removing Trump immediately, but the leaders of the Democrats will apparently begin with another impeachment proceeding.

Many of the protesters have been arrested and many more to come. They didn't consider that the Capitol cameras would identify them. Obviously stupidity is not a crime, but their actions are. A fifth victim has been reported. A policeman, who died in his effort to block the rioters.

Trump finally came on TV and chastised the rioters, after saying on Wednesday afternoon, "We love you all, you are very special." He also just announced that he is not going to attend the inauguration of Biden. This has only been done once before, when

Andrew Johnson stayed away from Grant's inauguration in 1869. The last time the Capitol or White House was breached was in 1814.

There is no way to predict what will happen from day to day. My main concern is what the Trumpers are thinking now, and what they will do next. And what is going to happen with Trump. He will continue to polarize Americans without a doubt, the question is how and to what degree. It appears certain that he has lost any chance to run again in four years as he planned, or ever return to politics in any way. He has cemented his position forever as the worst President in our history.

I'm so sad to say that regardless of what Danny and all those like him believe, the worst pandemic in history continues to surge and infect, killing record numbers of people every day. California is the hotspot of the world. The L.A. hospitals have no room left for more patients, and not enough staff to attend those who are in the beds. The new mutated version of Covid is here and expected to take off, we're in big trouble.

JANUARY 9, 2021

Nancy Pelosi, the Democrat leader wants to impeach. It doesn't seem to me that there is enough time. The conservative Republican Senator from Alaska wants Trump to resign or get taken from office by Pence and the Cabinet. Many are calling for the resignation of that idiot Senator Josh Hawley from Missouri and Ted Cruz from Texas, the ones who started the idea of protesting the electoral vote count. This was based on lies that the election was fraud. They are justly being accused as part of the responsibility for the attack on the Capitol.. Now if you multiply this in your head by 5, you will get an idea of what's going on in Washington.

Wednesday when the Senators were on the floor, literally, hunkered down behind chairs seeking protection from the attackers, one of their phones rang. It was Trump calling. He began telling the Senator how he might be able to get more votes. He was actually talking to the wrong Senator, he had made a mistake and dialed the wrong number.

Trump has no concept of truth, he is without a doubt deranged and probably doesn't even realize when he lies. Yesterday morning, because of his lies, his Twitter account was closed and permanently canceled, "due to the risk of inciting more violence."

This morning I made an effort to watch Fox News. I couldn't stay tuned for long watching those Republicans who are still fighting the truth. The news hosts, the guests, including Republican politicians, all fighting, to convince their viewers that Trump is still good and is the respected leader of the party. They are still fighting the lockdown, bragging about Florida's governor Ron DeSantis and his policies of "Open Freedom for the People." In other words no masks, no social distancing, no business lockdowns. Yesterday there were 283,000 new infections and 4,000 deaths.

When I was a child I always felt that I had special qualities. I was never afraid of anything. I still feel like that, but it's not as relative to crucial issues as it was then. I wonder if everyone else feels like this. And I wonder if my special qualities enable me to see more truth than those who I disagree with.

This past week has felt more like a year to me than a week. Thankfully I broke it up with the sailing trip on Thursday. And today I will be going down to Stu's and watch the football marathon of the NFL playoffs. Football is without a doubt the most important unimportant thing in my life lately.

JANUARY 11, 2021

This morning's news continues with the developing actions by our defenders of justice, the Senators and Congressmen in Washington, to get rid of Trump. The options are: To disgrace Trump and get him to resign, not a chance in hell of that happening. Get Pence to invoke the 25th Amendment, again extremely unlikely even though he and Trump are not talking these days. Or the final option to impeach him for "incitement of insurrection," and that is what Nancy Pelosi will be working on today. By impeaching him it will assure that he can never run again for the Presidency.

There are those that say any of these actions will just throw gas on the fire. Of course they are the Republicans who say that this will not help to bring our country back together, as if their previous actions have ever worked toward that goal. These are people who signed the paper started by Josh Hawley and Ted Cruz to deny the electoral votes. Josh Hawley, the punk Senator from Missouri was actually using this to raise funds. All of those that voted against the electoral vote validation were in essence denying the legitimacy of our election, claiming it to be fraudulent. This is just so sad. I don't need to repeat how much of a lie this is.

As crazy as these Senators are, they appear sane compared to some of their Republican followers, many of whom were at the Capitol wearing their QAnon shirts. These people believe that Hillary Clinton has been leading a group of Satan-worshipping cannibalistic pedophiles that run a global child sex-trafficking ring from a pizza parlor in Washington DC. There are even a couple of Republican Congresswomen, Lauren Boebert from Colorado and Marjorie Taylor Green from Georgia who support QAnon. Last week Marjorie Green was thrown out of the Senate floor for refusing to wear a mask. I'm not making this up. If people can believe this, and they do by the thousands, they will believe anything.

There were others at the insurrection that were waving flags that said "Blue Lives Matter." The Blue Lives Matter movement was started by far right extremist groups after the killing of George Floyd, and in response to the Black Lives Matter movement. It is another way to express white supremacy. What it means is that anyone harming or killing a police officer who is fighting protesters should be sentenced under hate crime statutes. Basically they wanted the Black protesters to get death penalties for battling white cops. How hypocritical and absolutely insane for those Blue Lives Matter people to be rioting against the cops in the Capitol. Ignorance and stupidity, violence and hate, misplaced loyalty, unwarranted accusations, all in abundance last Wednesday.

We saw misguided, deceived people being spiked on by Trump, Rudy Giuliani, Josh Hawley, Ted Cruz, Rick Scott of Florida, and those other Senators who signed on, defiling our democracy. These are basically thousands of misinformed, foolish people calling their actions a revolution. White people seeing their country being taken away from them. There is no other way to look at this. This is what is happening and this is what we must deal with.

Could all of this have begun as a backlash to the social revolution of the sixties? It might be that today's young and middle aged citizens look at all of us baby boomers as a rotten bunch of people that they must put up with for a while longer. Behind this way of thinking lurks the anger and eventually the hate that gives power to Trump and his cronies. Listening to these leaders' lies, tuning into the right wing radio stations and viewing those sites that support them, they get brainwashed. This enables them to swing the lead pipes and bust down the doors.

Soon after the insurrection at the Capitol, these rioters made their way back to their hotel bars, sat with a beer or glass of wine, looking at their phones, proudly bragging and laughing about the whole thing, believing they were in the right and had done nothing wrong. They then hopped on their flight, went home and back to work, posting pictures and videos on Facebook, YouTube and their own personal sites. And then one by one as identifications are being made, they are being arrested by the FBI, from Texas to Tennessee. Some of the charges being filed are seditious conspiracy, trespassing, willful injury of Federal property, unauthorized entry, theft of Federal Property, assault, gun charges, and last but not least curfew violations.

There will be so much more to this story. It's really a shame that the government has to spend time and energy on this when all hands should be dealing with the pandemic and vaccinations. As I see the new surges taking place, I would guess we are not near the end of this pandemic but probably somewhere near the middle of it.

JANUARY 12, 2021

I was hoping when I woke up that I would see a golden sun breaking the horizon over there above the mountain range and that it would soon be shining bright in a gallant blue sky. Well, that ain't happening. Sorta like my dull spirit, the flat grey clouds and cold, damp, foggy air sits on my deck telling me to shut up and stay inside.

I watched the depressing news, thought about Danny, when I told him, this will be over and things will get better. "They'll never stop trying to control us, this is the beginning of the end." This morning's news concentrated on the civil unrest, telling me about all the violent threats that our leaders are receiving over the phone, and how more protests and riots will be taking place during the inauguration. Our local governments are being told by Washington to prepare for demonstrations not only in Washington, but every-where. I pray that they're wrong.

There was a slight mention of a new mutated Covid strain dis-covered in Japan. My expanded knowledge this morning is mak-ing me want to become a crane and stick my head under the sand. Biden must have his moments, like I'm having now. I can only say bless him and Kamala and all the others who are willingly step-ping into this mess of an existence, as our protectorates. In 8 days they will need to bear the major responsibility to fix our problems. And that's just here in the U.S.A. Every other country and every small corner of the world is equally suffering.

Meanwhile Trump has decided to come out of hiding. He's heading to Texas, something to do with him walking around the "Great Wall of America," the wall he half built, and must consider his greatest achievement. Such a sorrowful joke, that he dares to ignore our problems and do something like this. Right to the very end this sorry excuse of a human being continues on with his dis-gusting behavior.

The day has been moving along and I am feeling less disheart-ened, less defeated by circumstances. The sun god has not shown his face but for whatever reason I want to pull my crane head out of the sand and find the good in things. So I'll begin at the top, the core of my unhappiness, and of course it is Trump. I'm going to try and show the few things that some intelligent people believe he has done right in the past four years. Are you listening Danny?

Trump pulled us out of Nato, seems like a bad move, but Trump's reasoning is that we were basically supporting the organization while other countries were paying very little or nothing. He demanded that our European allies pay their 2% that they committed to.

His people brought some peace to Western Asia, by forming an alliance between Israel and the United Arab Emirates, a confederation made up of seven independent emirates, including Abu Dhabi, with the world's wealthiest capital Dubai. Bordering the dangerous mideast, this peace has a possibility of helping the U.S.A.

In the beginning part of his term he worked successfully, by being tough with Xi Jinping, the President of China. and this action began to equalize our trade relationship. He once said, referring to Xi, "We love each other."

Finally, and I'm not sure of this one at all, but perhaps his policy on Iran, helped to weaken their government, which is good for us. Time will tell on this one.

I never thought I'd be writing anything good about Trump, but I've said it, and I guess it shows that there is some good in most everything. Like the Yin Yang symbolizes, even the bad has a little good in it. So now I want to move forward without harboring so much negativity. I bet tomorrow the sun will shine.

JANUARY 13, 2021

The sun is slowly pushing the fog and clouds away this morning, wishing to appear as the gigantic shining Vitamin D ball that it is. I'm poised to jump when it achieves its goal. Away from this screen and keyboard. I'm becoming affected by life's circumstances in a not so good way today. Depression definitely narrows one's perspective, and I shouldn't let this happen

I've got a plan to drive down to Healdsburg, the town where so many tourists used to come, ride their bikes around and spit good wines into buckets. But I won't be doing that, I'll be parking close to the Russian River and blazing a trail to parts unknown.

This countryside is a far cry from the jungles where in my past, I really did blaze trails, machete in one hand, video camera in the other. I don't expect to find a myriad of natural wonders. I won't see any orangutans or howler monkeys, or stumble across any rare flowers or plants. Every step I take along the river will be on somebody's private land. Hopefully they won't mind that I'm there. I won't be breaking down any doors or windows, or carrying a lead pipe ready to smack them in the head. I just want to move these legs back and forth and breathe in some fresh Covid-19 free air, oxygen produced from the trees and flora that these people now own, after paying someone a huge amount of money, or having inherited it all.

Journey completed, hike taken, sun and clean air consumed, good energy from the trees and plants absorbed, slumped calf and thigh muscles roused to action, (slightly opposed to that plan) and eye contact made with similar human participants in the plot to avoid all current broadcasts of the dreadful state of our present condition.

Now back to the news. Of course as soon as I returned, I desperately flipped on the TV to see what I had missed. His excellency Trump has been impeached. New York State has broken every business contract with all Trump businesses, (being denounced and claimed as illegal by Eric Trump) and finally the mass vaccinations planned for our survival have been dismally declared as off to a clumsy, incompetent start. The death tolls have been averaging 3,000 per week and predicted to soon hit 3,500 and possibly 4,000 within a few weeks.

Before executing my plan to hike along the Russian River, I rethought the idea, and decided to search out one of the county's

Parks that offer legal hiking trails. Up to this point I have not been one of the local old folks who walk in the woods with a stick. But I was able to find one such Park nearby and drove directly to the parking lot associated with the 874 acre tract of woods, complete with an entry gate, some porta potties, and a machine where I could stick in my credit card to get the little piece of paper that I was supposed to put on my dash.

Avoiding that part of their plan, I found a spot to park on the road. The woods were exactly like my backyard, no Scarlet Macaws or Toucans in the trees, no orchids or lianas hanging down. Just what I expected, I found. There were no breathtaking, exciting surprises, like stumbling upon a crocodile eating an iguana, which I have done. But there was peace and quiet and an opportunity to think of things differently, from a place in the woods. I felt good driving back home. I probably should do this every day. Maybe I will eventually start paying for parking and even buy me an RMI walking stick. Can't begin tomorrow though because I'm going sailing with Phil. Can't begin this weekend because I'm going down to Palo Alto to be with Julie, who's coming back from Hawaii.

JANUARY 14, 1980

The government released control of gold this week and the prices just soared up to over $800 dollars an ounce. Herb called me today with his latest plan, searching for gold in Costa Rica.

40

Back to Costa Rica

This time we decided to fly to Costa Rica. Our driving trip had been an adventure that we didn't care to repeat. After landing in San Jose, we learned that the best gold fields were in the Southern Pacific Zone, one of the least developed areas of Costa Rica. By bus, we headed to the Osa Peninsula. This region is not easily accessed, since there are a very limited amount of roads. The area we needed to reach was close to a National Park named "Corcovado."

The bus took us to San Isidro, it was the nearest city to Corcovado that offered direct service from San Jose. The trip was long, nearly twelve hours to traverse the highway through the rugged mountains. We passed Mt. Chirripo, which is Central America's highest peak. At this elevation there is often ice and frost in the early mornings. After spending the night in San Isidro, we caught the next bus to the small town of Palmar Norte. From there, a taxi ride on dirt roads through banana plantations, and we made our way to the tiny fishing village of Sierpe. The next leg of the journey was by boat. In any section of North America or Europe, this trip would be offered as an attraction in itself. Traveling through the jungle on the River Sierpe, and through some smaller cuts in the mangrove swamps, we were to see crocodiles, three toed sloths, many troops of monkeys and a wide variety of tropical birds.

The boat then headed out to sea through another one of those dangerous "bocas" that I had grown to respect with a proper amount of justified fear. Fortunately the sea was not so rough on that trip. We arrived further down the coast and within a few days we were able to secure another boat passage around the Osa Peninsula.

At the southern end of the Osa, jutting out into the sea is the virgin rainforest of Corcovado, now a 108,022 acre National Park. Besides its incredible wealth of trees, plants and animal life, we found a large amount of gold panners sifting the park's rivers, hoping to find their fortunes. In a short time I began to see that this practice was harmful to the environment. The sediment from all the activity was settling into and filling up the large lake that was in the jungle's basin.

As we ourselves began prospecting through the rivers, we came upon a few of the larger dredging operations that were totally destructive. By cutting away at the rivers' banks they were able to work huge amounts of soil through their sluice boxes. In the process they turned what was once a clean and pure jungle river into a polluted muddy slough. This was nost what I had hoped to find here. Our plans were not working out.

In the beginning this did not sink in. Herb and I ignored the obvious, or perhaps our dreams kept us from admitting what we were facing. At one point, we acquired a couple of horses to make our way along the coastline. We were carrying some digging tools, a metal detector, and a five-inch dredge.

Our plan was to find a rich spot and set up our small dredge. When we came to the River Tigre we gave up our horses and started walking up the river, into the jungle, camping along the way. The hiking was not easy. Although the area was a declared National Park, there were certainly not any trails. It was not rugged mountain land, but it was far from being flat. We were often walking in the river, climbing over fallen trees and scrambling up muddy banks to go forward. There were times when I was ready to give up, but I knew that there were other families of "panners" ahead of us, that they had made it in and were able to come out on a regular basis for food and supplies. If they were doing this, I should also be able to make the trek in. I figured the farther up river we could make it, the more likely we were to find a rich spot.

Although the Park had jaguars, and of course, all the poisonous snakes you could imagine, the real danger existing in this jungle were the wild boars. They would often travel in packs of 20 to 30 and sometimes the packs were as large as a hundred. The boars are mean, fearless and aggressive. We could never sleep on the ground at night or we would be easy prey for these ruthless wild animals. They can attack, kill, and devour a man completely, down to and including his bones in a matter of minutes.

At the mouth of the Tigre, before heading up, we heard a story of three men that were missing. They were panners, "oreros" in Spanish. They had come from the river the week before and had traded their gold for supplies and a generous amount of guarro, the local spirits of Costa Rica. It is presumed that they fell asleep drunk on the ground that night. All that was found were remnants of their clothes. Fortunately for Herb and I, we never encountered any packs of boars. We heard them at times in the jungle, and came close enough to smell them, which is an odor I will never forget, but we were always cautious and walked slowly and quietly in the opposite direction. We never came upon them face to face. We had been hiking up the Rio Tigre for less than a week when we met Victor.

Victor was an Israeli who had hand dug a mine on a cliff just above the river. He had two Costa Ricans in his employ, who were busy carting earth from the mine by wheelbarrow to the cliff's edge. From there, the earth was poured down a wooden shoot. A rather large pump had been hauled in and was being used to bring water from the river, up the mountainside, to the top of the shoot. The diggings were washed down the shoot and the sluice box at the bottom trapped the placer gold as the muddy wash splashed back into the river. There was nothing easy about this operation. The diesel fuel for the pump was hauled in through the exact route that we had come. Victor had been digging his mine for six months and the returns were becoming less and less. He was ready to abandon everything. Because we showed up one afternoon, he was pushed over the edge.

We were likewise surprised to see another foreigner in the river and were delighted to hear Victor's tale. After spending the night in his camp, Victor turned over the operation to one of his employees and joined forces with us in our prospecting for the "mother load." Victor was by far the most knowledgeable on the subject. He taught us how to analyze the topographic maps from a prospector's view. We had been using the maps only for a directional aid, where Victor could read the contours and make educated guesses where gold might be. It all has to do with the flow of rainwater, and the rivers' turns and bends. Where creeks and rivers turn or slow up is where the gold will be lodged or deposited. By determining how the topography of the land had changed over thousands of years and guessing where the ancient rivers may have run would give us leads.

With Victor leading the way we began an arduous search away from the river and into dry canyons. We would "punch holes," that is to dig a small hole down to the bedrock and wash our samples in a pan, searching for "color."

There was always a little color, or gold flecks in our pans, but never enough to indicate the veins for which we searched. When the color was good, we would punch holes as often as every hundred yards, hoping for a steady increase. We explored through a number of canyons and many logical sights but to no avail. After a couple of weeks we found ourselves back on the Tigre. We continued punching holes, hoping to find a rich pocket, as yet undiscovered.

We came upon another foreigner, actually he was half Costa Rican from his mother's side, but had been born of a British father and raised in England. We had heard of him by other oreros on the river, and he had become somewhat of a goal in our continued trek. We had finally reached "Hampton." I hadn't understood his name from the Spanish translation. The oreros kept telling us of another gringo up river, named "Amtone."

I expected to find a strapping, handsome young man with a pith helmet, an elegant camp and a booming successful operation on this rugged river. Instead, Hampton was a very thin and worn man in his late seventies, sleeping on a makeshift platform under a small piece of plastic stretched between two twigs. He had one pot on a wood fire, in which to cook his rice. Being wet in the river for ten hours a day and pushing large boulders had obviously worn his old body down, but his spirit, his sophistication, and his dignity still shone through. Upon arriving at his section of the river, he immediately cleaned his pot and invited us for tea.

Hampton was an Oxford graduate. His father had been a famous geologist who had come to Costa Rica in the early 30s, working for the government. I could see Hampton was not strong and I worried for his safety. He had only one son in England whom he hadn't been in contact with for many years. I wanted to know what kept him up that river. He admitted to his frailty, he could now only work the river about six hours a day and had long since given up making the trip down to trade his gold for supplies. Once a month, for a small portion of gold, the next closest orero would bring in his supplies.

For a few hours we talked, mostly about his experiences, he was grateful to have company that day. Our visit with Hampton was something I will always remember. Such an intelligent man who had led such a rich life, and here he was, miles up the river in the rainforest jungle, choosing to spend his waning years like this.

As ironic as it seems, I don't think at this point he had much of a choice, perhaps this was his destiny. After our afternoon visit we turned around and headed back down the river. In pensive silence we hiked, struggling down over the boulders, across the slick, algae covered rocks along the bank, and into the river. Each of us knew without discussing the matter that we were leaving the Rio Tigre for good. The time was not far away when I would give up my dreams. Archaeologists from the National Museum of Costa Rica had just recently taken an interest in searching for gold and jade artifacts. This began in the late 1970s and continued through the

80s and 90s They did some horizontal excavations and were beginning to take an interest in protecting and regulating the business of gold exploration and mining.

Our hike back out of the jungle was much quicker than when we had come in. We made the trip in two and a half days, stopping only once to observe one of the large dredging operations. Very close to the river's mouth and back on flat ground the dredging company had managed to cut in a small road, bringing in two large 'dozers and a backhoe. Their sluice box was approximately10 meters long by two meters wide, and had two workers on each side with long steel hooks. Using their hands and with their long hooks, they walked along a tiny ramp and worked the rocks and larger boulders down to the bottom, pushing, shoving, pulling. At times they would get into the box bracing themselves and kick the bigger ones, inching them along. For whatever reason these men chose to work here rather than pick their own spot on the river and work for themselves as oreros.

The claim here was owned by a European company but was being managed by a very friendly, amiable Costa Rican man, Gustavo. His employees worked all day, 12 hours of light, 12 hours of work. After 6 hours, the men took a lunch break. During this time and at the end of the day, Gustavo would pick up the heavy black sand that accumulated in the trough at the bottom of the sluice. In six hours of work the trough contained roughly two five-gallon buckets.

Gustavo brought us into his shack of an office and showed us his final method for extracting the gold. To my surprise, his young 12 year-old son was swirling this rich sand with a pan, no more sophisticated than the pan I was carrying in my backpack, I watched in amazement. The color in this five-gallon bucket was like I had only imagined.

Each pan that the child worked contained a whole bag of gold, larger than what a family of oreros would gather in a month or more. In each six-hour shift the yield was approximately $5,000. Sitting next to the boy sat a large round machine that was not being utilized. It appeared to be a type of cyclotron, a machine intended to spin out the gold. Through centrifugal force these machines could separate the gold from the other material. However, the final stage of this operation was being done in typical Costa Rican style.

During the beginning years of the gold explorations, the Costa Rican government was ignoring the obvious environmental damage being done. By requiring permits for claims and high taxes on these large operations they hoped to pay off the interest on their high foreign debt. The government owned institution, Banco Central, had set up a branch in the small town of Jimenez to buy the gold from all the oreros. But this was soon to change. With pressure from archaeologists and the National Museum, in January of 1986, the government declared an end to gold mining. In February and March of that year the Park Service and National Guard of Costa Rica marched into the Park and up the Rio Tigre removing all the oreros. I often wondered what became of Hampton.

Although we left the area and took a break by returning to San Jose, we had not given up our ideas completely. I purchased a couple books and began reading about the history of the area and about "treasure hunters." This led me directly to the subject of grave robbing. My initial feelings were a little negative, but the excitement of the subject kept me reading, longing for more information. I obtusely recorded all the things that I read, without really forming an opinion. After all, all of the gold, jade, and intricate ceramic sculptures in San Jose museums had been found in gravesites

We had made friends in San Jose and were staying with Bianca the wild gringa and her boyfriend Guillermo, who as I was to discover, was a serious manic-depressive. Bianca was a serious alcoholic. Her morning showerhead poured out guarro instead of water. She once told me at two in the morning, as I was begging for sleep, "Tom, you're almost fun."

Bianca was receiving an alimony check from her ex-husband, an attorney in the states and Guillermo was a budding artist working the open market and occasional street fairs, selling his beadwork and hippie paraphernalia. With this income they survived, living to party. Bianca and Guillermo were big-time into archaeological artifacts.

Herb was usually off during the daytime meeting the more conservative crowds. One of whom was a man named Balfour. Now Balfour was one of the Costa Rican upper class, coming from a prominent and wealthy family. One evening we were invited to his huge cattle ranch where he showed me his private collection of artifacts. A few years prior, Balfour was a huacero who had as many as twenty people hired to do his digging. He was proud to show us some of his pieces but he also adamantly issued a warning, "Every time I was to uncover a rich grave, ill fortune would fall upon me."

I tempered his advice with the opposite message I was receiving and came up with a theory of my own, that is, I would not form an opinion. Although I think I was more susceptible to Balfour's influence. I really wasn't interested in searching for graves, but I did want to try another area for gold. After all, this is what we had come down for and there were still a couple months of winter left in the states. Since Herb and I were of like mind we set out again, this time for the opposite side of the Osa Peninsula, away from Corcovado. Victor was still with us. The three of us made our way back to the Osa for another attempt.

We hired horses again, took our topo maps and headed into the countryside. We found mostly cultivated land. The jungle had been stripped away, making room for cattle ranches and subsistence farming. The region had not been completely clear-cut, there were patches of trees, and stretches of second growth jungle, which kept the area habitable for wildlife, but it was certainly not the rain forest that it had once been. We continued our course of following the rivers and punching holes when one day we came upon a huge, perfectly round stone ball.

I knew about these balls, I had seen some that had been removed from the wild, but for the first time I came upon one undisturbed. In the entire world, these balls are only found here in this region of Costa Rica. They range in diameter from two feet up to three meters and often are only a few centimeters or 1/8th of an inch from being perfect spheres. Their origin is unknown, speculated to have been carved by those from ancient cultures, yet with such accuracy as is unexplained. Similar to the great pyramids, the secret to this engineering feat has been lost with the passage of time. We can only guess. Those educated in the field propose that they were made as a tribute to the gods, or that they were carved and placed as identifiable trade route markers, or finally that they were possibly monuments to mark off "sacred burial grounds."

I was rubbing this remarkable stone ball, and sitting on top of it, and standing up on it, and trying to get some mystical message zapped into my brain from it, when I heard Victor yelling from the distance. He had found another one approximately 50 meters away. And then we found another, and another. There were four in all. Being much more observant than before, we noticed some unnatural looking mounds of earth overgrown with vegetation.

Inside of these four balls we had discovered some *huacas*, some graves. I was like a small child in a candy store. All the time spent on trying to decide the moral implications about grave robbing had been indeed time wasted. The excitement of that moment is impossible to relate. My heart was racing and adrenaline was pumping. Had I been in the middle of a city or in someone's backyard the feeling would not have been the same, perhaps I might have been a little more sedate, but we were miles and miles from civilization. This was nature, and this feeling was natural.

Herb was walking around with the metal detector and called to us. The discrepancy meter was indicating that there was something unnatural below. I ran over to him with a shovel in hand and began tearing at the clay earth. Victor joined us and slowed me down. Here again, Victor was more experienced in these things and led us to a methodical dig. If it were in fact a grave, we first needed to layer the earth off in stages, and then locate the two ends. Within a foot of the surface we came upon a bed of stones. They were not fieldstones, but rounded creek or river stones that had been specifically carried to this area of the jungle. And the stones were lying in three criss-crossing layers, just as one of my books had described. We had found an ancient Indian grave, of this I was sure.

We dug under Victor's direction, taking turns since the digging was difficult. The earth here was highly compacted, red clay. We eventually located two ends approximately a meter and a half apart, final assurance that we had found a grave. This was it. This was the moment that I had dreamed of all my life. Every time I dove underwater I had secretly hoped that I would come upon a sunken pirate treasure chest filled with gold and jewels. And now I had found it. It wasn't under the sea, and it wouldn't be Spanish doubloons or pieces-of-eight, but I knew there had to be something there. I thought it might be a little gold frog, but even if it was a pot, I would be happy, or maybe a ceramic flute or a cup, or a statue. I had wavered back and forth about this for months but at that moment there was no question of what to do. I became who I am, an Indiana Jones sorta guy.

I did it. We dug up the grave that day, disappointingly finding nothing much of value. The hard ground yielded to our prying shovels and picks. We found only remnants of shell beads that had probably once been a necklace. We continued to dig and explore that ancient graveyard, finding many potsherds and a very fine specimen of a stone hatchet, pieces that would remain with me for years.

Nighttime was fast approaching and we had to get back to the beach where the light of the moon would guide us to our overnight camp. The following day we left, securing boat passage back to Sierpe and eventually the bustling, congested world of San José.

My feelings would soon change about grave robbing. I would never again have an interest in doing this. Perhaps as Balfour had experienced, had I continued as a huacero, I may have found that disturbing people's graves would lead to bad luck, bad karma. Life's experiences often changed my feelings about many things; experimenting with drugs, making lots of money, diving for fish and lobsters, or searching for truth through others. Many of my learning paths would affect change. So what does this prove, that the only constant in life is change itself.

JANUARY 14, 2021

It is suspected now that some Republican politicians had supported the insurrection by conducting private tours of the Capitol a week before the riots, when all tourist tours had been suspended, There are many independent investigations going on. The FBI, the local and state police, Congress and the Senate are all conducting their own research. The FBI has now over 170 cases under arrest and investigation. More arrests are being made every day.

But what I realize is that the majority of those at the gathering on that day, did not rush up the stairs and break into the building. They participated in a rally for the person they thought should lead our country, then they went back to their hotel. They have grievances and want solutions. Now if responsible politicians don't answer them they will, and did turn to an irresponsible one, Trump. It's sad that in four years of his term they never saw what kind of person he really is, how incompetent, incapable and without any doubt, unqualified to be at the helm.

I often criticize and blame the Republicans as a group, when I should not be doing that. There are so many good people who belong to their party for valid reasons. They look at their problems and see the Republican platform as the right party to help them. They have that right just as I have the right to choose the Democrat Party.

Back to the ones that did march up those Capitol stairs. They are bad people, no doubt. But the other side has bad people also. The group that is called Antifa are violent, though often exaggerated and blamed for actions that they have nothing to do with. They were being falsely accused of the assault last week. Many people saw Antifa on that day but they saw them in their mind only, wanting to eliminate blame from the far right. Human nature in action.

When Nelson Mandela assumed power in South Africa, he didn't expect or exact any revenge for all those officials before him who were guilty of horrible assaults on their people. The Apartheid government was racist, white supremacist, and purely evil, but Mandela forgave them and never pursued criminal charges.

After WW2 the opposite occurred. The Nuremberg Trials conducted by the Allied forces demanded justice on all the guilty Nazis. With unprecedented efforts, prosecutors searched the world over to find the guilty ones and bring them to prison or the death chamber.

My comparison is rather lopsided, but the point is we now need to make a decision that will work best for our country's future. It's up to our elected officials to work this one out, good luck.

The virus is stampeding along. Just since 2021 began we have recorded 40,000 deaths and have been adding 200,000 cases daily. The hospitals and health care workers can see no end. Biden must get the vaccination program in hyper-action as his number one priority. I say forget about the idiot Trump, let him smolder, forget the past and create a new positive future. Nancy Pelosi, I'm talking to you, probably not in the same words that Mandela would use.

The sun is really out today, and I will soon be heading to the SF Marina. As my dad often said, "It's good for what ails ya." Love ya dad. Love ya mom. Nancy, call me and you can come with Phil and I, it'll do you a lot of good. I guarantee it. Ask Mitch if he wants to come, we'll make room. I'll make sure that the boom doesn't whack you in the head.

JANUARY 16, 2021

While Phil and I ate our takeout dinner in the cockpit last night, talking about how much longer "Squat and Gobble" will be able to stay open, Biden was delivering a speech to the people about his plan for fixing the economy. Although I missed the speech I understand his main focus was on the pandemic.

I believe it was Winston Churchill that said, "Never let a good crisis go to waste." Just such an action, a response to our last somewhat comparable financial crisis happened 12 years ago. It was then that the Republicans handed over the White House to Barack Obama, a Democrat for those who don't know. At that time our economy was in terrible shape, a period they were calling the Great Depression, a crisis. Well Barack fixed it and also worked diligently to bring healthcare to millions of uninsured people.

Biden's got it worse. There are so many today that have no money and no job. Of course this is due to the other crisis, Covid-19. Unlike Trump, Biden understands this crisis, it's not a hoax, it's real. And he will put all energy forward. He will fix it, my question is how long will it take.

As I left the house yesterday morning heading to San Francisco, the two books I had ordered were in the mailbox. I'm very excited. Hopefully I will gain some helpful info and mood changing facts. The books are, "The Plague, and "An American Plague." I've started in chronological order with An American Plague, about the yellow fever epidemic of 1793. When I pick it back up I'll be on page 40.

"The Plague," is actually a rather famous book, written by Albert Camus who received the Nobel Prize in literature. His novel deals with the Bubonic Plague which actually first appeared in the 16th century but reappeared in 1921 and then again in the 1940s, the period that he sets his novel.

The way I see things both of these serious plagues were dealt with and overcome with far less medical knowledge than we have at our disposal. I hope I will get more hope by reading, struggling through those crises, like I did with "Grapes of Wrath."

More news is coming to light every day about the insurrection. It was well planned, supported by some ex military people and politicians. Their goal was to 'capture and assassinate' elected officials, including Pence. My previous idea (yesterday), of letting this 'smolder' has changed. These guilty people need to be 'burned.' We need to prosecute. We can't be Mandela like and forgive these horrible people. They must be brought to justice and pay for what they did and intended to do.

I have been summoned away from writing next about the pandemic or reading about the plagues. It's time for some 'hands on' stuff. I need to work on the carburetor on Robbie's (Stu's son) quad. I know the problem because I've looked at it. I will need to completely pull the carburetor and replace some parts. And then it will be off to Palo Alto to spend the weekend with Julie, she returned from Hawaii last night. We will be watching football, the playoffs are down to 8 teams.

JANUARY 18, 2021

It's sunny and blue this morning. As a former Egyptian sun worshipper (past life), I walked onto my deck and thanked "Ra". Actually I'm not able to go back that far to When Ra created the world and stood at the spiritual tiller, directing them and giving all those Egyptians something to worship. I'm stuck here some 7,000 years later. I can't say that I worship anything. I like and love things while forming tons of opinions on most everything that crosses my path. I must be careful how I narrate these opinionated stories because they will likely become who I am. The stories we tell turn into the lives we live.

Now the saying goes, everyone's entitled to their own opinion but not their own facts. I'm subtly trying to reach the Trumpsters out there. Before you leave your home on Wednesday, Inauguration Day, please remember to walk gently and go in peace to that State Capitol building. Remember this one, "Live by the sword, die by the sword." Even if you do intend violence, you're lucky that your fighting ground will not become a recurrence of Tiananmen Square, or Kent State. And that's because you have been given a wonderful country to call your home. Don't screw it up. Try this bullshit in Iraq or Syria, or Russia or China. There you will receive Justice.

I didn't leave last night for Julie's but I'll be turning off the morning news and heading down in an hour. Her hotel is empty, her restaurant is closed, even the outdoor dining at Poolside has been shut down. Julie's Hotel, Dinah's, is a small representation of the whole picture of our economy. Of the 160 former employees at Dinah's there are very few remaining on the payroll. Biden's team has so much to work on.

JANUARY 19, 2021

As always Julie and I had a good time this weekend. We watched football, walked in the Wetlands again, talked politics, and laughed a lot, despite it all. Her Hotel has become the recipient of a big government check that will allow it to keep operating and all of her employees will have a job. Their families will have food.

I wonder what Danny would have to say about that. Today is the "Free Food Day" line in Healdsburg. I wonder if Danny will be parked in line this morning. If so, I'm sure he'll be in his old Toyota pickup with no back window, not his newer model, leather seated Volvo. I haven't spoken to Danny since the insurrection and honestly I have no desire to.

Sadly I now see my former friend as a misguided soul. Someone who may very well be sitting in the charity line this morning while cursing our new leaders as a bunch of socialists. He sees our country as a country that has now taken the wrong turn. Despite all the evidence proving that our election was fair, to people like Danny, the truth is irrelevant. They will do anything to preserve their all-consuming, emotional Trump vision of America the Great. And I'm afraid they won't be going away anytime soon. Therein lies our problem.

Several years back when Danny and I took a trip to Florida together, we ate at the Miami Cuban restaurants, we rode bikes around Key West. One night as the sun was setting, we stopped at a bar on Duval Street. It was Karaoke night, and Danny got up on stage. I had my small video camera ready and suddenly we both realized, there were only men in this bar. As Danny began his song it was rather flat, no one was paying heed to my buddy Danny. I walked up to the bar and I lied to a few guys sitting there. I told them we were making an important video and asked if they would help. On that note we had "Danny and the Gay Backups," engaged in their Premier Key West performance.

We slept in tents along the way, we went to an Art Festival on Miami Beach, and on that same trip I also noticed that Danny was not an experienced snorkeler. After we were out on our paid snorkeling trip in Marathon, I had to kind of stick with him on the surface and get him back to the boat. These memories along with happier, similar ones are the ones I choose to remember now.

I don't see Danny as a person who hates Hispanics or Gays, and I can't see him carrying Confederate flags to the White House or defending 'White America' over the multi racial coalition that brought Biden to power. Why he chooses to align himself with such a right wing conspiracy believing bunch of idiots does not make sense to me. As Danny said in our last two conversations, "We agree to disagree." I guess I must leave it at that. I take comfort in the fact that 90% of my other friends see the world as I do.

Last night and this morning have been super windy. I am so glad that we took down the huge Pine trees that were just behind the house. Yesterday the temperature in Healdsburg hit 80 degrees, a record for this time of year, global warming saying 'hello' again to Trump in his next to last day of office.

The warmer day reminds me of living back in the tropics. However I am 2,668.56 miles north of the equator. I can still close my eyes and be back on the docks in Belize City or at a market eating eggs, rice and beans on a small stool in a shack in Nicaragua. I find myself desperately longing for the next trip South.

It's almost noon now, it's sunny and the wind is still fiercely whipping through the tops of the trees. I walked on a packed beach yesterday, Martin Luther King Day, along with many others taking advantage of the warm day. I need to walk again today. For me walking the beach is so much better than downtown Healdsburg, or the local Park trails. The problem I have is the beach is not right outside my door, it's hardly a hop, skip, or jump away. It's 37 miles to those sandy shores. That's like an hour and three gallons of gas in my Four Runner.

Even though I'm not living in the small house on the lobster diving beach in Costa Rica, I realize that I'm very fortunate to be where I am, so I must adjust and find the perfect spot for my walk. To be continued.........

I walked along the Russian River. I took "Plague" with me, sat by the river and began to read. I finished "The Plague" at Julie's Hotel. It was the story of the yellow fever epidemic that began in 1793 in Philadelphia which at that time was still America's capital. Quite the difference in dealing with a viral plague when the medical authorities had no idea what a virus or even bacteria was. The expert of the time Dr. Rush's form of treatment was to induce vomiting and bleed the patients. Thousands died as the virus spread in Philadelphia and began occurring throughout the country. The disease was being spread by mosquito bites and nobody had a clue at that time. It wasn't until 1900 that this came to light, and in 1937 a vaccine was invented. I will soon find out if the Bubonic Plague (the subject of 'Plague'} is spread by rats, which so far is being implied in my river reading.

Switching the subject to Trump and myself, since it's his last day in office, and by decision my second to last day of writing this book. Trump has been using his final time pardoning over 100 more of those convicted criminals, who he likes. And I will soon decide how to end my journal, my diary, my memoirs, my newscasts, my new friend, The Book.

It certainly has been a good friend, helping me through these troubling times. And when tomorrow ends and my book is finished I will probably begin with the next one. Writing is my newly found mind gymnasium and psychotherapist rolled into one. Until I'm freed again, I will continue to express myself in this way. I am looking forward to the time when I don't want to write or I don't have the time to write.

JANUARY 20, 1957

It seems that when I was young, I was always getting banged up, much more than the other kids. One year in junior high, we opened up the basketball season with me as a starting guard. I had broken my thumb during practice a couple weeks prior, so I was wearing a hand cast on my left hand. During the summer of that year while riding my bike, a car hit me. I can't remember any of that, because I received a good brain concussion that gave me amnesia. I did recover OK, I think. But anyway, I was allowed to play on the team, according to doctor's orders, only if I would agree to wear a boxer's helmet.

I must have been quite a sight for the fans. Here I was, starting out front, the playmaker on the team, bringing the ball down with a big white cast and a big black boxer's helmet that was much too large for my small head. Boxer's helmets were not made for little kids. I can remember that there would be people showing up for those games that had never come to any of our games before. They just came to see me. The word got out. I was a fast little player who was always stealing the ball from everybody. I felt like I could run around most of them and between their legs if I had wanted to. I would easily steal the ball from them and take off down to the other end of the court, generally missing the lay-up. On most games I would be our high scorer, usually getting a grand total of about six or seven points.

JANUARY 20, 2021

If I were to label today as special or extraordinary or exceptional, I would fall far short of expressing the true importance of what has taken place. This day Joe and Kamala have been sworn in and Trump and Pence have been sworn out, with a lot of swearing I should add. To witness this transfer of leadership has been the most amazing gift that I/we have received in a long, long time. Our country in an instant has taken a quantum leap forward. Praise the Lord, praise God, praise Allah, praise everyone who has helped to accomplish this. Every campaign worker, every Georgian voter, all the younger citizens that saw the truth and came to the polls. Together we made it happen.

And whether or not the other side fails to listen to Joe and continues to harbor anger and refuses to make the effort for uniting, it won't stop Joe, Kamala and their team. Regardless of their efforts to undermine our new administration, we are still on our way to healing our country. I don't expect miracles but I feel like we have entered into a whole new world, and we have the best engineer we could ever hope for, now driving this train. The path is not going to be easy that's for sure but they can do it. A giant load has been lifted off our country, and the entire world actually. The burden of having incompetent leadership is gone.

After the inauguration ceremony, Biden immediately went to work, undoing the grave mistakes of Trump. Reversing the insane moves he made will take time. Working to acquire and distribute vaccines is of utmost priority and the job will now be addressed.

This is so funny, but I feel like my work is now over also. I don't feel the need to get up, turn on the news and vent. I still have many notes on my phone that I never got to in my writing, but today it's not important for me, like it was yesterday. I have reached the end of this book.

I turned off the TV at 10 AM and I drove down to San Rafael. I met a very bright young man, Nathan. His wife is a cancer survivor and with a low immune system, she is deeply sheltered in place. They have two young children. Nate is a Republican, unlike Danny he has not supported Trump. I had a short but inspiring talk with him and he made me feel more hope for our country's future. I bought Nate's 15' fishing boat, and my new life is about to begin.

After totally finishing the book and being 'beyond bliss' related to this amazing day of days, I find a need to insert this paragraph. Stu called me just as I had returned from San Rafael. I had already called this book 'a wrap.' He said "Let's go get some crab, the market's got it." We drove to the Healdsburg yuppie market, 'Big John's'. I had forgotten my mask, so Stu went in and got two big crabs. He gave me his mask and I went in and got a bottle of local Chardonnay.

Now I have quit alcohol as part of my social lubricant, but because I never have gone through the world with both hands tied behind my back, and because the last time I had crab with Stu I noticed that it was lacking something without the wine. I boldly paraded in, up to the vast selection of wines and picked a "La Crema" Chardonnay I had made a video for "La Crema" back in the day. I thought I could repay them $21.95.

Paragraph 3. As Stu and I cracked, crushed and consumed our Dungeness crab dinner, I was quietly reliving my days of lobster diving as Stu got filled up with crab and left me with half a crab and half a bottle of wine. I sat at the table alone and was able to go back to the time that Judy, the conspiracy theorist ex-girlfriend from college days, and I were in Key Largo. We were staying at a motel owned by an older couple. It so happened that as I was snorkeling off our beach I caught a bunch of crabs that we cooked and ate.

The owners of this Bay Motel were ready to give it all up and their midwestern children wanted no part of it. They offered Judy and I a great deal to take over the property and buy it with their personal loan. It became a dream of ours which I have never forgotten.

Had I decided to accept the offer and take over the ownership of the Florida Bay Motel, my life would probably have been much different. Judy and I would probably have been married and stayed in Key Largo for quite a while. Throughout our lives, we seem to be regularly confronted with important decisions. When a 'fork in the road' appears, I sincerely hope that such important decisive moves are made not only from educated guesswork, but rather from a more serious spiritual influence.

If there has been any question to my position regarding God, I would like to make it clear. I believe in the existence of a higher power, and I do hope that I am right about it. Atheism is not my bag.

And now, back to the closing of the book.

What has been living in my mind for the past 74 years has shaped my realities and created my present view of the world. It has been a pleasure and so much fun to write about the story of my life. By writing, I navigated into the past and I concentrated much more on the present than I would have otherwise. And yet each day has been spontaneous. I never changed that part of who I am. There was no outline, I had no model to follow. To be honest, every day I was shooting for the Pulitzer Prize, not for my writing style but for finding the truth of the moment.

There have been many times when I wished that I could take the knowledge that I have today and go back into the past. Well I have been able to do just that. By writing this book, I have re-lived all those events of my past and experienced them again through the eyes and mind of a much wiser man.

Through all my life experiences, the most profound truth I have discovered is the very simple idea that we should search and find who we truly are. There have been many stages of my life when I wondered if everything happens for a reason. If I do good, will good come back to me? I believe I now have the answer to those questions. I call it my spiritual belief.

I will always continue to search and find who I am now.

My life has given me an amazing family. My sons Abel, Zack and Jay have given me more than I could ever have hoped for. And of course I was able to live with the love of a father for his daughter.

I would like to thank my loving daughter Mia for asking me to write this book. I should also like to encourage others to do the same. All of our lives are special. If we can record them now, they will not remain hidden in our grave. No one ever knows for sure what the future will bring, but we all have our past. Beside the present, it is the richest treasure we can ever find. We're all going to die, and when that happens, there's a story written about every one of us, it's called an obituary.

We have the option to do better.

Acknowledgments

Thanks to everyone who has taught and guided me throughout my life, especially my parents. Thanks to all of my great friends who shared with me and made life such a joy. Finally, thanks to Waights Taylor Jr. for his guidance and assistance in publishing my story.

About the Author

Tom Martens has lived in different locations throughout his life, presently he resides in Sonoma County, California. He appears settled on the outskirts of the small town of Healdsburg.

In Tom's words; "I've certainly opened up my past and beliefs throughout this book, and no need to continue with that part. Without the ability to see into the future, I can assume that conditions for me will continue along the same paths that I have been walking. Many of us will leave deep trails, hard to miss, and hopefully those trails are colorful and filled with joy and love."

Made in the USA
Middletown, DE
05 September 2021